**The French Army in Politics
1945-1962**

A Publication of the Mershon Center for Education in National Security

John Steward Ambler

The French Army in Politics
1945-1962

Ohio State University Press

To My Wife, Joyce

Preface

In April of 1961 Frenchmen had cause to wonder if Paris, the most civilized of earthly cities, had not been transformed into a Latin American capital where the rumbling of tanks in early morning substitutes for popular or parliamentary vote as the normal procedure for changing governmental leadership. The obedient French Army (and its tradition of obedience had once been solid) had three years earlier contributed mightily to the demise of the Fourth Republic and was now feeding an open rebellion against General Charles de Gaulle, a political chief of the army's own choosing. It is easy enough for the Western observer to dismiss the *pronunciamiento* in Latin America—and more recently in Egypt, Turkey, Iraq, Pakistan, Burma, Thailand, South Korea, and South Vietnam—as nothing more than evidence that the social prerequisites of democracy are not present in these underdeveloped lands, or that civilian government has proven inadequate to handle the tensions of modernization. Praetorianism in France, however, strikes closer to home and must be traced to different causes, causes which may be of great interest to Western democracies generally.

The central focus for analysis here will be the problem of *civilian control* over the French military establishment. More specifically, French military politics will be examined primarily from the standpoint of threats to the civilian political regime, rather than from the broader vantage point of general military influences on public policy. Of course, the two are often intertwined. Within the French military establishment greatest attention will be given to the army officer corps, which, by reason of numbers and involvement in recent colonial wars, played a preponderant role in French military adventures in politics from 1945 to 1962.

The selection of the problem of civilian control is not made with the assumption that other problems, especially the *effectiveness* of national security, might not on occasion deserve clear priority over civilian control. The question of primary concern here will be *why* armies obey or disobey civilian governments, rather than that of whether and when they *ought* to obey. In the United States, at present, the problem of integrating political and military considerations into a unified defense policy is probably a more immediately useful approach to the study of civil-military relations than is that of civilian control, despite recent renewed warnings of an American "warfare" or "garrison" state.[1] Yet as Clausewitz, the most eminent of military mentors, has shown, military science provides the tools but not the political ends toward which they shall be used.[2] If civilian politicians do not determine policy goals and limits, the soldier must choose between inaction on the one hand and assumption of the policy-maker's role on the other. As the present study will demonstrate, the soldier left without civilian leadership is prone to choose the latter alternative and in so doing to expropriate for the "military" domain all but the original "political" decision to wage war. Hence, the problem of civilian control remains a fundamental one, despite the overlapping and intermingling of political and military questions in an age of total war, cold war, and revolutionary war.

In civil-military relations, as in social phenomena generally, causality is multiple and complex. All patterns of civil-military relations can be understood only in the context of the entire political system within which they exist. The professional military community itself (its traditions and values, the "military mold" and the "military mind") must be understood, but so too must the political universe in which it moves; i.e., the extent, nature, and strength of the society's political consensus, the contending political forces (their values and styles of operation), the position of military institutions within the government, and the stability of the system. Within this political universe, civil-military relations will be influenced by the links established between the military community and civilian political forces (the social origins of officers, as well as ideological and political ties between military and civilian groups) and by the primary *function* assigned to the military. Though armies always perform more than a single function, at any given moment one function tends to predominate; e.g., national defense, maintenance of domestic order, or training for citizenship.[3]

Unless one insists doggedly upon the uniqueness of political phenomena (as the writer does not), it should appear obvious that a case study of civil-military relations in contemporary France must draw inspiration from broader theories of civil-military relations. An analysis of French experiences will help to test and refine theories developed elsewhere. Two such theories will be of particular interest here. The first looks to military professionalism as the key safeguard of civilian control.[4] The second assigns pre-eminence to the strength and stability of civilian governmental authority and to the political consensus which underlies it.[5] Though neither of these theories is adequate to unlock all of the secrets of French civilian control in strength and weakness, both will provide valuable clues.

The reader may well be disconcerted at times by the frequent resort to such imprecisions as "few," "many," and "most," in the discussion of political attitudes of military officers. The greater precision which systematic survey data would allow is now impossible because of the lack of such data for past periods and the inaccessibility of officers to the survey researcher in recent years. Through the use of written materials (supplemented by interviews in the case of present attitudes), however, the climate of officer opinion at various times can be described in accurate, though crude, terms.

The original research for this study was conducted in France in 1961–62 with the assistance of a research-training fellowship from the Social Science Research Council. I am also indebted to the Mershon Committee on Education in National Security, which supported final revisions of the manuscript. Among those numerous persons who accorded me interviews and facilitated my research in Paris, special mention should be made of Professor Jean Touchard, secretary-general of the Fondation Nationale des Sciences Politique and M. Joël le Theule, deputy from Sarthe and *rapporteur* of the National Assembly's National Defense Committee.

I have profited enormously from the careful advice of Professors Leslie Lipson, Eric Bellquist, and Richard Herr, all of the University of California (Berkeley), and Edgar S. Furniss, Jr., director of the Social Science Program of the Mershon Center for Education in National Security at Ohio State University, all of whom read the entire manuscript. They have saved me from numerous errors of fact and judgment; for those that may remain, of course, I am alone responsible.

I am grateful for the permission granted me to quote extensively from Jean Lartéguy's novel *The Centurions* by the original French publisher, Les Presses de la Cité, and the publishers of the English edition translated by Xan Fielding, E. P. Dutton & Co., Inc., which gave special permission to substitute my own translations for Mr. Fielding's.

1. Such warnings are given, for example, by Harold Lasswell, *National Security and Individual Freedom* (New York: McGraw-Hill, 1950); Lasswell, "The Garrison-State Hypothesis Today," in Samuel P. Huntington (ed.), *Changing Patterns of Military Politics* (New York: Free Press of Glencoe, 1962); by C. Wright Mills, *The Power Elite* (New York: Oxford University Press, 1959), chap. 9; and by Fred J. Cook, *The Warfare State* (New York: Macmillan, 1962). Writers who have stressed integration in policy-making more than civilian control include W. T. R. Fox, "Representativeness and Efficiency: Dual Problem of Civil-Military Relations," *Political Science Quarterly,* LXXVI, No. 3 (September, 1961), 354–66; M. Howard, Introduction, in M. Howard (ed.), *Soldiers and Governments* (Bloomington, Ind.: Indiana University Press, 1959), p. 22; and Walter Millis, in Millis, Harvey Mansfield, and Harold Stein, *Arms and the State* (New York: Twentieth Century Fund, 1958), especially pp. 139–44.

2. Karl von Clausewitz, *On War,* trans. O. J. Matthijs Jolles (New York: The Modern Library, 1943), p. 16.

3. See David Rapoport, "A Comparative Theory of Military and Political Types," in Huntington (ed.), *Changing Patterns of Military Politics,* pp. 71–101.

4. Samuel P. Huntington, *The Soldier and the State: The Theory and Politics of Civil-Military Relations* (Cambridge, Mass.: Harvard University Press, 1957).

5. David Rapoport, "Praetorianism: Governmnet without Consensus" (Unpublished Ph.D. dissertation, University of California [Berkeley], 1960); Rapoport, *Changing Patterns of Military Politics,* pp. 71–101; and S. E. Finer, *The Man on Horseback: The Role of the Military in Politics* (New York: Praeger, 1962).

Contents

Part I

The "Great Mute" and the Beginnings
Of Its Demise   1815-1945

Chapter 1

The Parameters of Discipline

Is there really anything ·strikingly new in the recent rebellious activities of a segment of the French Army? Can General Raoul Salan be explained as simply the most recent product of a strongly political army which produced Napoleon, McMahon, Boulanger, and Pétain? I would suggest that he cannot be so explained. In fact, Napoleon and Pétain are separated by over a century of rather consistent civilian control of the French Army, a century in which that army was frequently described, in both military and civilian circles, as the "Great Mute" which lived by the maxim that "the army does not engage in politics." The label and the formula are too pat, of course, for military men at times spoke out and played politics as well. Nevertheless, the story of French civil-military relations from 1815 to 1939 is largely one of civilian control over an obedient military establishment. The secrets of that pattern of civilian control merit investigation, even though they may have limited applicability in the present day, when political and military questions are more closely interwoven. An examination of the evolution of French civil-military relations will provide opportunities for one valuable type of comparative analysis—that involving different historical periods within the setting of a single society.

The present chapter will simply examine the nature and limitations of civilian control in the period from 1815–1939, leaving the primary task of interpretation to the following chapter.

French civil-military relations in this period will be categorized under four general headings: unquestioning obedience to civil authority as this is defined by the civilian political system; jealous defense of military prerogatives in specified realms; enthusiastic and preferential obedience (by at least part of the army) to one of two or more competing governmental institutions; and outright rejection of constituted civil authority.

In keeping with the central concern here, these categories are intended to focus in summary fashion upon military threats to the civilian political system—or the absence of such threats. They are not intended to encompass the entire breadth of French civil-military relations, nor is the following discussion concerned with all of the many direct and indirect influences which military men may have exerted on public policy.

Unquestioning Obedience

France in the nineteenth century enjoyed neither the constitutional stability nor the geographical invulnerability which favored civilian control over diminutive land forces in the United States and Great Britain. Yet, despite the necessity of a sizable standing army, despite a rapid turnover in nineteenth-century French monarchs, emperors, and presidents, never from 1815 to 1939 did the French Army engage in a military coup—the *pronunciamiento* so common in Spain at this time. Overcoming the undisciplined and even mutinous ways of the Napoleonic officer and soldier,[1] the French Army from 1815 onward tended to become a politically neutral instrument in the hands of the government of the day. After some reshuffling in the officer ranks and an initial flurry of military plots against the Restoration Monarchy from 1820 to 1822,[2] a French Army with two decades of experience in battling against traditional European monarchies marched off unflinchingly to Spain in 1823 to re-establish the absolute monarchy of Ferdinand VII.[3]

Both the revolution of 1830 and that of 1848 were political, rather than military, in inspiration and execution. With few exceptions troops stationed in Paris in July, 1830, fought the insurgents until withdrawn.[4] Again in 1848 the army remained loyal to the regime against the Paris mobs. Alexis de Tocqueville, a personal observer of the 1848 revolution, relates how General Marie-Alphonse Bedeau, one of the officers in command of troops in Paris, adhered scrupulously, though unimaginatively, to the letter of the orders he had been issued. He had been ordered not to fight. Even when the armed mobs invaded the Chamber, Bedeau, confused and hesitant to disregard orders, did nothing to stop them.[5] Once the July Monarchy had fallen, no one in the army, not even the Duc d'Aumale, Louis Philippe's son and commander of the African army, thought seriously of attempting to restore it by force. General François du Barail, a young officer in the African army at the time, recalls in his memoirs that the army would have defended the monarchy gladly as long as the king remained on the throne. "But from the moment that the regular government had disappeared," he writes, "from the moment that France had given in to the uprising, the Prince could not have raised a regiment, and did not even think of doing so." [6]

Within the army disgruntled noncommissioned officers in a number of units seized upon the revolutionary situation, both in 1830 and again, to a lesser degree, in 1848, to oust officers whose offenses were as often personal as political.[7] The progression of the concept of an apolitical army is evidenced by the fact that only a handful of officers felt obliged to resign upon the fall from power of Louis Philippe, whereas eighteen years previous almost two thousand had requested retirement after the collapse of the Bourbon monarchy.[8]

Circumstances laid out for the army a more active political role in 1851 and, in more limited fashion, in 1870, as will be seen shortly. In the first two decades of the Third Republic, however, unquestioning obedience generally prevailed, even in the face of a form of government which would not have been the choice of the majority of officers.[9] The transition into republicanism was facilitated for professional officers by the universal respect then enjoyed by the army, which though defeated in 1870, was still the nation's only hope for revenge, and through the choice of Marshal MacMahon as President of the Republic. Throughout his tenure MacMahon felt himself to be as much the protector of the army as of the nation. He virtually ordered military officers to assume political posts on occasion. He considered the Ministry of War to be his own special province.[10] He retained several corps commanders beyond the legal three-year limit.[11] He dissolved parliament in search of a more sympathetic majority in the *seize mai* crisis of 1877. When the marshal's star faded in the wake of that crisis, however, and when the army lost its protector with his resignation in 1879, military officers made no attempt to prevent the accession of genuine republicans to seats of power in the young republic. To be sure, there were a few militantly antirepublican officers who talked of the use of force—notably General Ducrot, who was heard to say that the Chamber of Deputies was in a state of anarchy and that he hoped to dismiss it with his army corps.[12] There is even some evidence to indicate that a military coup was considered briefly by the minority government led by General de Rochebouët in early December, 1877.[13] In its behavior, however, the army adhered strictly to the demands of legality in the face of republican electoral victories.

If the spirit of obedience to the government of the day finally prevailed in the 1870's, the same was even more obviously true of the 1880's, when the Boulanger crisis presented the army with a golden opportunity to do away with the republic simply by joining with the numerous civilian admirers of the man on horseback. Boulangism, however, though led by a military hero, was in no sense a military movement: its appeal was not to the army, but to the crowd and to the lingering glamour of "la gloire militaire." As the result of his conduct as minister of war, Boulanger had won considerable popularity among the army's rank and file, though aristocratic officers on the general staff tended to be skeptical, if not hostile, toward him.[14] The army made no move to aid his revolutionary cause in those crisis years which ended with his flight to Belgium in 1889.[15]

A last period which deserves consideration under the heading "unquestioning obedience" is that of the 1920's and 1930's. To be sure, General Maxime Weygand, both as chief of the general staff from 1930–31 and as vice-president of the Conseil Supérieur de Guerre from 1931–35, clashed repeatedly with his civilian superiors over such questions as disarmament, appropriations for new military equipment, and officer and enlisted strengths.[16] The social and political conflicts of the 1930's, moreover, attracted a few officers into the anticommunist organizations of the extreme Right.[17] Nevertheless, there was a general agreement among most military and political leaders, including Marshal Pétain, Generals Debeney and Gamelin, and Premiers Daladier and Blum, in support of the fundamental principles of French military policy, i.e., the primacy of defense and reliance on a short-term conscript army.[18] In the elaboration of those policies it was the government, rather than the general staff, which took the lead. Military leaders most often followed behind almost passively (too passively for some),[19] even when the nation-in-arms concept (as outlined in 1910 by socialist leader Jean Jaurès) came near fulfilment in the law of 1928, which set the professional core of the army at 106,000 men and reduced compulsory military service to twelve months.[20] There were no protest resignations and, Weygand apart, few open clashes between government and military leaders. If one looks back from the fall of France in 1940, the gravest errors of French military leadership in the interwar years in fact appears to be its passiveness, its lack of imagination, and its *failure* to challenge civilian political leaders more sharply on such matters as modernization of equipment and strengthening of the professional contingent.

Defense of Military Prerogatives

If the French Army behaved on most occasions as a faithful servant of the state in the period from 1815 to 1939, that faithfulness always assumed the sacredness of military autonomy in certain privileged domains. At base the Dreyfus Affair involved an outside "invasion" into one of those realms—military self-regulation within a closed military community.

In the fall of 1894 a Jewish officer, Captain Alfred Dreyfus, was arrested, tried, convicted, and imprisoned on Devil's Island on the charge of transmitting military secrets to the German Embassy.[21] Evidence gradually appeared casting serious doubt on Dreyfus' guilt, despite the efforts of one Captain Henry, a counterespionage officer, to reaffirm that guilt by forging a series of documents. As the affair developed into a violent political issue in 1897–98, the case was finally brought up for review. In 1898, despite the overwhelming evidence now attesting to Dreyfus' innocence, a second court-martial again found him guilty, though "with extenuating circumstances."

Among the Dreyfusards, many like Urbain Gohier, in his book *L'Armée contre la nation*, were convinced that the army was intent upon overthrowing the republic. Already, Gohier warned in the late 1890's:

> There is only one power in France: military power. In fact, military dictatorship is already in existence. It is still collective, thanks to the anarchy which reigns in military headquarters, thanks to the mutual hatred among military chiefs. But the first fist which presents itself will have only to seize it.[22]

Yet Gohier's evidence (e.g., secret use of funds without adequate reporting to parliament) tends simply to indicate the jealousy of military officers over government attempts to "interfere" with the administration of the army.[23]

In fact, the evidence available tends to indicate that there was no military conspiracy to overthrow the republic during the Dreyfus Affair.[24] The funeral for President of the Republic Félix Faure in 1899 was the occasion for a dramatic proof of the army's nonconspiratorial state of mind. Paul Déroulède, leader of the extreme nationalist Ligue de la Patrie Française, planned a coup for that occasion and wrongly assumed that the army would be with him. In fact, he probably had not secured the support of a single general.[25] Déroulède had expected to find General Pellieux at the head of parade troops; instead, as a result of a change of plans, he found General Gaudéreque Roget. Déroulède appealed to the general to march his troops on the Elysée. Roget did no more than to lead them back to their barracks where Déroulède was arrested.[26]

Though the interpretation of the Dreyfus Affair as a military conspiracy is woefully lacking in factual support, it is nonetheless true that military officers in this period were guilty of a number of acts of disobedience and bad faith in their relations with the civilian government. General Auguste Mercier, the minister of war in 1894, for example, ordered the arrest of Dreyfus, and then publicly announced his guilt before the court-martial had taken place, despite a prior promise to the foreign minister and the minister of justice to delay action on the case until weightier evidence was available.[27] Once Mercier and other military leaders had publicly announced Dreyfus' guilt, their reputations and authority were placed on the balance, and every effort toward obstruction was made whenever revision of the case was considered by the government.[28] In the face of fierce attacks on the army in the press and in the Chamber, it was easy enough for the military man, always hostile to civilian "interference" in military matters, to view the whole affair as simply an attempt to discredit the army.[29]

Until the Dreyfus Affair the post of minister of war had been filled since 1870, with only two exceptions, by military officers on active duty. Military officers serving as ministers of war were hardly agents of civil government imposing civilian control on the military establishment: "their function was then exactly comparable to that of an ambassador delegated by the military and charged with representing it before civil authorities."[30] Promotions of military personnel had long been left to military commissions, a procedure which in fact virtually removed control from the civilian government.[31] The army tended to be an isolated community, hostile to the bourgeois values of civilian society, sensitive to criticism of military affairs in the press, and insistent on autonomy in military matters. In fighting for self-regulation military officers did not believe themselves to be seeking political power; on the contrary, what they sought (along with their British counterparts) [32] was the isolation of the army from what were felt to be the corrupting and divisive effects of politics.

The campaign to make French officers on active duty ineligible for election to the legislature, for example, was largely led by military officers who feared a breakdown of discipline in the army.[33] Self-regulation, however, was another matter. When military autonomy was threatened by civilian attacks on military justice, the bulk of the officer corps was willing to sacrifice Dreyfus in an attempt to seal off the walls of the military community.[34]

By refusing to the end to admit its error in the Dreyfus case, by being thrown thereby into league with militant antirepublicans of the Right, the army subsequently lost a great measure of the autonomy which it had enjoyed for so many years. In the service of republican forces demanding that the army be wrested from the hands of clericals and antirepublicans, Minister of War General Louis André (that rare species, a republican and anticlerical general) enlisted the secret aid of police and Freemasons in his purge of antirepublican officers from key positions, especially from the general staff.[35] André's goal was not simply to eliminate antirepublicanism from the officer corps, not solely to reassert the army's professional duty to serve any legally constituted government; rather, he sought a positive republican commitment from officers and men, i.e., a republican "politicization" of the officer corps.[36] Though André was eventually forced to resign when his investigatory tactics were revealed, he left the officer corps divided, in a state of turmoil, and embroiled in the conflicts of civilian politics.[37]

The army fared better in another of its privileged spheres of action—the colonies. The rigorous civilian control imposed upon the army in the *métropole* never extended fully to *la France d'outre-mer*. The extension of the French Empire in the nineteenth century was partially the result of uncontrolled initiative on the part of colonial military commanders. French West Africa, largely the creation of General Faidherbe, and the French Congo as well, owed most of their expansion to independent military forays into the hinterland.[38] Military officers were also responsible for the *faits accomplis* which led to a French protectorate in Tahiti in 1842 and, to a lesser extent, to French occupation of Tonkin in Indochina in the 1880's.[39]

In Algeria in 1830, in Cochin China in 1859, in Tunisia in 1881, and in Madagascar in 1895, however, colonial expansion resulted from decisions taken in Paris. Nevertheless, military commanders in each case were given far more freedom of action than was ever the case in the peacetime army at home. From 1830 until 1870, with the exception of the short period from 1858–60, the army had a strong hand in the administration of Algeria.[40] General Bugeaud in particular, despite his spotty success, left behind an important legend as a military colonizer and governor-general in Algeria from 1841 to 1847. The famous Bureaux Arabes turned many officers into civil administrators with extensive local powers. The Bureaux survived in southern Algeria and were later revived under other names in Morocco and Tunisia, despite their suppression in northern Algeria after 1870.[41] The fame of General Gallieni is largely dependent upon his powerful civil-military role in Madagascar from 1896–1905, as that of Marshal Lyautey is linked to his combined duties in Morocco after 1912. Both men were known for their independence. In 1897 Gallieni summarily abolished the monarchy in Madagascar and deported the Queen, all without consulting the Paris government, which later accepted the *fait accompli*.[42] Following in the same tradition, Lyautey took it upon himself to expedite part of his troops across the Moroccan border from western Algeria in 1904 at a time when France was attempting to woo independent Morocco into its sphere of influence. The Combès government in Paris reacted angrily, ordering Lyautey to withdraw. He replied that he was committed to protect the population in the area and would resign before deserting them.[43] As Lyautey himself often emphasized, colonial service both allowed and encouraged a disdain for those qualities of unquestioning obedience and careful attention to regulations so typical of the French garrison officer.[44]

A final example of privileged military domains is drawn from World War I, particularly from the period of "military dictatorship" under Marshal Joseph Joffre from 1914 to 1916.[45] When war broke out with the hated conqueror of 1870, a French *union sacrée*, joining socialists, Catholic conservatives, and all between, rallied staunchly to the support of the army. Acting on the general though mistaken belief that war was still an affair solely for armies on battlefields rather than for entire mobilized nations pitted against each other, and on the expectation of a brief struggle on the model of the Franco-Prussian War, the National Assembly adjourned *sine die* and politicians generally yielded the field to the generals.[46] Initially, parliamentarians heeded the words of Deputy André Hess, spoken in the Chamber of Deputies in June of 1914:

> . . . When the cannon speaks, it is better that politicians fall silent. The outcome of the war depends on rapidity of movement and decision, and that rapidity is to be found in a single man rather than in the deliberations of a cabinet.[47]

Joffre was quite ready to be that man. As the first two wartime ministers of war, Adolphe Messimy and Alexandre Millerand, focused their efforts on protecting him from his critics within the government and parliament, rather than on controlling his action, the commander in chief withheld from the government information regarding current military operations and attempted (successfully for a time) to keep parliamentary investigating committees out of his jealously guarded "Zone of the Armies."[48] On one occasion in 1916 Joffre went so far as to force President of the Republic Raymond Poincaré to postpone a trip to the front. Poincaré characterized this action as proof of

> the encroachment of the military power upon the civil, of a power which wishes to avoid all supervision and which creates a government apart from the real government, the authority of which it does not wish to accept.[49]

Once Joffre had assumed extensive powers, partially through the express intentions of the politicians and partially through their inaction, he considered the conduct of the war to be his own domain, not to be interfered with by non-professionals. The "dictatorship" exercised by this carefully chosen "republican" general was always intended to be temporary and restricted in character.

It came to an end sooner than Joffre had anticipated as a result of the unforeseen prolongation of the war, his clashes with General Sarrail (who had strong political friends), the inadequacy of defenses at Verdun, and finally, the failure of the Somme offensive. Parliament turned on the Victor of the Marne in 1916, and when his protection by the minister of war weakened, he was forced up and out via the "technical adviser" route.[50]

Thereafter, military leaders played a more subordinate role, first under a temporary parliamentary ascendancy in 1917 and then, following the disastrous Chemin des Dames offensive and a flurry of sit-down strikes in war-weary army units,[51] under the powerful leadership of Premier Georges Clemenceau. Cutting deeply into such questions as defensive policy, which under Joffre had been jealously guarded military terrain, Clemenceau imposed his general authority over conduct of the war.[52] In 1918 and again at Versailles in 1919, the Tiger clashed repeatedly with Allied Commander Ferdinand Foch—on one occasion, at an inter-Allied conference in 1918, cutting short his protests against abandonment of the Allied general reserve with, "Keep silent! It is I who represent France."[53] At Versailles Foch raged as Clemenceau, confronted with adamant allies, abandoned his hopes for the separation of the Rhineland provinces from Germany. For a time in the spring of 1919 the French commander in Mainz, General Charles Mangin, gave behind-the-scenes support to a Rhineland separationist movement, only to be reprimanded and instructed in a government note of June 3 to cease all intervention in political matters.[54]

At war's end it was Clemenceau, the civilian, who was the First of Frenchmen—not Joffre, or Pétain, or Foch. The early unpreparedness of democratic institutions for prolonged war led to an extension of the powers of Joffre and the high command, who thereafter were reluctant to give them up. Yet never were democratic institutions in danger from the military leadership, nor was the civilian government prevented from reasserting fuller control over the army after 1917. The key problem (one which was never fully solved) was that of tracing jurisdictional lines between political and military realms in the midst of a total war. Since World War I produced serious clashes between military commanders and civil authority in Great Britain, as well as in France, it would appear that the unexpected advent of total war and the weakness of civil authorities, more than the breakdown of military discipline, best account for Joffre's independence.[55]

Preferential Obedience

In none of the instances described thus far was the army as an institution required to make an evaluation of the legitimacy of the existing government. Though the areas of military independence were not always clear, those officers who eventually submitted to civilian control in the Dreyfus era or in World War I might well have done so simply out of a sense of professional duty, rather than out of any personal sympathy for the republic. The few cases following forced military leaders into explicit political choices.

The coup of December 2, 1851, in which Louis Napoleon did away with the Second Republic, sometimes has been mistakenly classed as a military revolt in the style of Napoleon Bonaparte's 18th of Brumaire. In fact, though military personnel helped to carry out the 1851 coup, they acted on orders from the President of the Republic and Commander in Chief, Louis Napoleon.[56] The primary issue was not whether a civilian government or the army would control the French state; rather, it was whether the legislative or executive branch of the republican government would prevail over its rival. Caught in that struggle, the army was forced to decide to which of the contesting branches it owed its loyalty. Undoubtedly, the bulk of the officer corps had little respect for the republic.[57] Yet some of the most notable military figures of the day, including Lamoricière, Le Flo, Changarnier, Bedeau, and Cavaignac (a genuine republican) were members of the Chamber.

Looking forward to the forcible elimination of his legislative rival, Louis Napoleon set out well before the coup to recruit officers to his cause and place them in key positions.[58] Banquets were held at the Elysée for thousands of commissioned and noncommissioned officers. General Nicholas Changarnier was removed as commander of the army of Paris and replaced with General Bernard-Pierre Magnan, who understood what was expected of him.[59] Forced to seek support below the top echelons of the military hierarchy, the President found his key man in Armand Saint-Arnaud, promoted him to major general and then, in October, 1851, appointed him minister of war. Even Colonel Charles Espinasse, the commander of the regiment guarding the Palais Bourbon on December 2, 1851, was one of the President's picked men.[60]

When the moment came in the early morning of December 2, republican generals were routed out of bed and arrested along with leading legislators, and the troops were formally reminded that "a passive obedience to the Chief of the Government is the rigorous duty of the Army from the general to the soldier." [61] Once Louis Napoleon had assured himself of the loyalty of key commanders at the top, military discipline guaranteed the obedience of those military troops sent to clear out the inevitable barricades raised in defense of the republic. Though the coup could not have been successful without the co-operation of a group of ambitious officers of Bonapartist persuasion, the army neither initiated the operation, nor, in all probability, would it have followed any but its legal commander in chief in such a move.[62]

A similar kind of situation might have developed in the early years of the Third Republic, since a sharp rivalry developed between President MacMahon and an increasingly republican Chamber. Yet this time, as indicated above, both President and army remained within the bounds of legality.

Rejection of Civil Authority

From the history of French civil-military relations in the period 1815 to 1939, there emerges only a single incident in which a prominent military commander clearly and completely rejected the authority of the civilian government. In 1870, as a French Army suffering from unimaginative and ineffective leadership was being routed by an efficient Prussian military machine, the empire collapsed and gave way to yet another republic. Marshal Achille Bazaine, trapped with his troops at Metz, refused to recognize the new government of national defense. Referring scornfully to republicans as "a handful of adventurers seeking to climb on the misfortunes of their country," he announced to his troops that the army's duty was to serve the country "with the same devotion in defense of its soil against the foreigner and of social order against evil passions." [63]

In a fashion which became familiar again after 1940, Bazaine felt it his right—indeed, his duty—to determine the legitimacy of the government in power. His example was not imitated in 1870. After the final German victory he was court-martialed, found guilty of abandoning the battle and of treating with the enemy, and sent to prison, where he served only eight months of a life sentence before escaping to Spain. [64] The French Army as a whole, revived by a startling defeat, returned to its role as servant of the state. Not until 1940 (a tale to be told later) did a French military leader again clearly reject the ultimate authority of his government.

The picture which emerges from French military behavior in these years is clearly not one of a coup d'etat army. If the army's record of *apolitisme* was not altogether as pure as some recent scholars have suggested, [65] it was nevertheless impressively clean in view of the variety of regimes which officers were called upon to serve. With relatively rare exceptions the French Army from 1815 to 1939 was, in Dennis Brogan's characterization, "a faithful, even a docile servant of the state." [66]

---

1. "Few armies have pushed insubordination to such a point. Collective demonstrations, individual rebellions, mutinies were everyday affairs." Georges Lefèbvre, *Napoléon* (Paris: Félix Alcan, 1935), p. 192. See *also* ibid., pp. 126–28, 150, 159.

2. Pierre Chalmin, *L'Officier français de 1814 à 1870* (Paris: Librairie Marcel Rivière, 1957), pp. 232–34 (hereinafter cited as *Officier français*); Raoul Girardet, *La Société militaire dans la France contemporaine (1815–1939)* (Paris: Plon, 1953), pp. 126–27 (hereinafter cited as *Société militaire*).

3. Girardet, *Société militaire*, p. 127.

4. Guy Chapman, "France," in Howard (ed.), *Soldiers and Governments*, p. 55; and Girardet, *Société militaire*, p. 129.

5. *The Recollections of Alexis de Tocqueville* (New York: Macmillan, 1896), pp. 52–53.

6. General François Charles du Barail, *Mes souvenirs* (Paris: Plon, 1897), I, 333. All translations are mine unless otherwise indicated in the notes.

7. Chalmin, *Officier français*, pp. 237–46, 257–63; Chalmin, "La Crise morale de l'Armée Français," in J. Bouillon *et al., L'Armée de la Seconde République* (La Roche-sur-Yon: Imprimerie Centrale de l'Ouest, 1955), pp. 46–51; and Boniface de Castellane, *Journal du Maréchal de Castellane* (Paris: Plon 1895–97), II, 366–67, 373–74; IV, 49–50.

8. Girardet, *Société militaire*, pp. 129, 132.

9. See below, Chapter 2.

10. J. S. de Sacy, *Le Maréchal de MacMahon* (Paris: Les Editions Internationale, 1960), pp. 352, 366 (hereinafter cited as *MacMahon*).

11. D. W. Brogan, *France under the Republic* (New York: Harper, 1940), p. 143.

12. He was the only corps commander to be dismissed immediately after the *seize mai* crisis (De Sacy, *MacMahon*, p. 379). See also Gabriel Hanotaux, *Histoire de la France contemporaine* (Paris: Ancienne Librairie Furne, Société d'éditions contemporaine, 1908), III, 617; and Du Barail, *Mes souvenirs,* III, 550–51.

13. See François Bédarida, "L'Armée et la République: Les Opinions politiques des officiers français en 1876–1878," *Revue historique*, 88th Year, No. 232 (July–September, 1964), pp. 138–39, 139 n. 1, citing a parliamentary investigating committee's report that was presented by H. Brisson and printed in L. Gambetta, *Discours et plaidoyers politiques*, VII, 398–435. See also Fresnette Pisani-Ferry, *Le Coup d'état manqué du 16 mai 1877* (Paris: Laffont, 1965), pp. 286–308.

14. Paul-Marie de la Gorce, *The French Army: A Military-Political History* (New York: Braziller, 1963), pp. 18–19 (hereinafter cited as *French Army*).

15. Chapman, *Soldiers and Governments*, pp. 59–60; Girardet, *Société militaire*, p. 254; and Jean Jaurès, *L'Armée nouvelle*, Vol. IV of *Oeuvres de Jean Jaurès* (Paris: Les Éditions Reider, 1932), 293. Andrien Dansette, in *Le Boulangisme* (Paris: Fayard, 1946), can summarize the appeals of Boulangism without once mentioning the army (pp. 365–71).

16. Philip Bankwitz, "Weygand, A Biographical Study" (Unpublished Ph.D. dissertation, Harvard University, 1952), p. 471–598 (hereinafter cited as "Weygand").

17. See below, pp. 35–38.

18. Richard Challener, "The Third Republic and the Generals: The Grave-diggers Revisited," in H. L. Coles (ed.), *Total War and Cold War* (Columbus, O.: Ohio State University Press, 1962), p. 93; Challener, *The French Theory of the Nation in Arms, 1866–1939* (New York: Columbia University Press, 1955), pp. 215–18, 252–56 (hereinafter cited as *Nation in Arms*); and Charles de Gaulle, *Mémoires de guerre* (Livre de Poche ed.; Paris: Plon, 1954), I, 21–24, (hereinafter cited as *Mémoires*).

19. [Captain Lucien Souchon], *Feue l'Armée Française* (Paris: Fayard, 1929), p. 197.

20. Jaurès made his case in his book, *L'Armée nouvelle*, written in 1910. The story of the 1928 law is told in Challener, *Nation in Arms*, chap. 4.

21. The *affaire* is described in detail in Joseph Reinach, *Histoire de l'Affaire Dreyfus* (7 vols.; Paris: Fasquelle, 1901–11). A recent work which devotes considerable attention to the civil-military relations aspect of the *affaire* is

Guy Chapman, *The Dreyfus Case; A Reassessment* (London: Rupert-Hart-Davis, 1955).

22. Gohier, *L'Armée contre la nation* (24th ed.; Paris: Editions de la Revue Blanche, 1899), p. 155. See also *ibid.*, pp. xiv, xxvii-xxviii, 138.

23. *Ibid.*, pp. 142-55.

24. "There is nowhere in the Dreyfus Affair a trace of conspiracy, nowhere a vestige of action against the State, no hint of *pronunciamiento*," writes Chapman, *The Dreyfus Case*, p. 62. That statement is perhaps too forceful, however, as Chapman's own evidence suggests. See, for example, *ibid.*, p. 357.

25. Déroulède later said that General Pellieux had been involved in plans for the coup. These charges were made after Pellieux' death; without supporting evidence it is difficult to judge the extent of his involvement. See Chapman, *The Dreyfus Case*, p. 357.

26. *Ibid.*, p. 283.

27. *Ibid.*, pp. 68–70.

28. *Ibid.*, p. 43.

29. *Ibid.*, p. 299; and Bankwitz, "Weygand," pp. 54–60.

30. Girardet, *Société militaire*, p. 256.

31. *Ibid.*, p. 256. See also C. Mangin, L.-F.-M. Franchet d'Espérey, and G. Hanotaux, *Histoire militaire et navale*, in G. Hanotaux (ed.), *Histoire de la nation française* (Paris: Plon, 1927), VIII, 438.

32. Robert Blake, "Great Britain," in Michael Howard (ed.), *Soldiers and Governments*, p. 28.

33. Roland d'Ornano, *Gouvernement et haut-commandement en régime parlementaire français, 1814–1914* (Aix-en-Provence: La Pensée Universitaire, 1958), pp. 114–22 (hereinafter cited as *Haut-commandement*).

34. Girardet, *Société militaire*, p. 257.

35. Chapman, *The Dreyfus Case*, p. 336.

36. "Let anyone note these two dates: 1900-1904. Let him remember that under my ministry four annual contingents, after receiving their education, have returned to political life. Then let him ask himself what influence these classes may have had upon the elections of 1906 which were so admirably republican" (Challener, *Nation in Arms*, p. 54, quoting from Louis André, *Cinq ans de ministère* [Paris, 1907], p. 108).

37. Charles de Gaulle, *France and Her Army*, trans. F. L. Dash (London: Hutchinson, 1945), pp. 82–85, stresses the destructive effect of the Dreyfus Affair on army discipline and morale.

38. Stephen H. Roberts, *History of French Colonial Policy (1870–1925)* (London: P. S. King & Son, 1929), II, 302–7, 341–44.

39. Henri Blet, *La Colonisation française* (Paris: Arthaud, 1946–50), II, 104, 195–215.

40. Roberts, *History of French Colonial Policy*, II, 179–83; and Blet, *La Colonisation française*, II, 111–59, 182–91.

41. Roberts, *History of French Colonial Policy*, II, 179–81; Jacques Weygand, "L'Officier des affaires indigènes," *Revue militaire d'information* (hereinafter cited as *RMI*), No. 269 (March 25, 1956), pp. 63–66; and General M. Boucherie, "Les Bureaux arabes: Leur rôle dans la conquête de l'Algérie," *Revue de défense nationale* (hereinafter cited as *RDN*), July, 1957, pp. 1052–66.

42. Blet, *La Colonisation française*, III, 186.

43. André Maurois, *Lyautey* (Paris: Plon, 1932), pp. 88–91. In March of 1963, Lyautey's reply to Paris in 1904 was quoted by defense attorney Tixier-Vignancourt in the case of Lieutenant Colonel Bastien-Thiry, who was on trial for an assassination attempt on De Gaulle (*Le Monde* [hereinafter cited as *LM*], March 6, 1963). For other examples of Lyautey's occasional indiscipline, see Vincent Monteil, *Les Officiers* (Paris: Seuil, 1959), pp. 67–68.

44. L. H. Lyautey, *Lettres du Tonkin et de Madagascar* (2d ed.; Paris: Colin, 1921), pp. 80, 84–86, 101–3, 117–118, 648, 652–53.

45. Much of the following discussion of World War I is based on Jere C. King, *Generals and Politicians* (Berkeley and Los Angeles: University of California Press, 1951), *passim* (hereinafter cited as *Generals*). This is the best study available on French civil-military relations in World War I.

46. King, *Generals*, pp. 15, 20–21, and chap. 3; Challener, *Nation in Arms*, pp. 92–93.

47. D'Ornano, *Haut-commandement*, p. 147, quoting from *Journal officiel, Chambre*, June 23, 1911, p. 2515, col. 1. But for an objection by General Goiran to this argument, see D'Ornano, p. 148.

48. King, *Generals*, pp. 23–24, 32 (quoting from Gallieni, *Mémoires*, p. 172), 36–66; D'Ornano, *Haut-commandement*, p. 193; and Alfred Vagts, *A History of Militarism* (New York: Meridian, 1959), pp. 240–41.

49. King, *Generals*, p. 129, quoting from Emile Herbillon, *Souvenirs d'un officier de liaison pendant la guerre mondiale* (Paris, 1930), I, 310–11.

50. King, *Generals*, pp. 70, 87–88, 91–94, 108, 115, 117–18.

51. Over half of the army expressed unrest in some degree during the 1917 mutinies. They were simply peaceful refusals to wage war, however, rather than attempts to overthrow the high command or the government. Though Commander in Chief Philippe Pétain placed the blame on pacifist and socialist agitation at a time when the *union sacrée* was breaking down, it seems most likely that heavy losses and war-weariness were the more serious culprits. Pétain's skilful blend of sterner summary judgment powers, frequent rotation, longer furloughs, and carefully planned small-scale offensives succeeded in rebuilding morale and restoring discipline, which had remained largely unshaken in the officer corps. See Richard M. Watt, *Dare Call It Treason* (New York: Simon & Schuster, 1963), especially chaps. 11–14; King, *Generals*, pp. 172–77; and Arno J. Mayer, *Political Origins of the New Diplomacy* (New Haven, Conn.: Yale University Press, 1959), pp. 171–73.

52. King, *Generals*, pp. 195–201.

53. Quoted in Edward Mead Earle (ed.), *Makers of Modern Strategy* (Princeton, N.J.: Princeton University Press, 1944), pp. 303–4 n.

54. De la Gorce, *The French Army*, pp. 160–66.

55. British civil-military relations in World War I are discussed in Blake, *Soldiers and Governments*, pp. 39–48.

56. In 1799, of course, certain members of the Directorate called on Napoleon to rid them of the legislative bodies. Yet, unlike 1851, a military commander—Napoleon—was offered a strong share of political power and used his troops to win it.

57. See below, Chapter 2.

58. H. Guillemin, *Le Coup du 2 décembre* (8th edition: Paris: Gallimard, 1951), pp. 281, 288–89; and E. Ténot, *Paris in December, 1851* (New York: Hurd and Houghton, 1870), pp. 35, 85, 131–33.

59. C. E. de Maupas, *The Story of the Coup d'Etat*, trans. Albert D.

Vandam (New York: Appleton, 1884), p. 236 (originally titled *Mémoire sur le Second Empire*).

60. For details on this incident, see *ibid.*, pp. 153, 166, 192–203, 236.

61. *Ibid.*, p. 257.

62. Girardet, *Société militaire*, p. 139; and, for a concurring opinion by the socialist foe of professional armies, Jean Jaurès, *L'Armée nouvelle*, p. 290. Girardet overstates the point, however, when he continues: "All that the army did on this occasion was to bend docilely to the orders of its direct chief, the President of the Republic, chief of the executive branch and master of the armed forces according to the provisions of the Constitution of 1849 itself" (*Société militaire*, p. 139). Two corrections are needed here: (1) the army reaction is more accurately described as enthusiastic than as docile; (2) a good deal of cultivation and manipulation of military commanders reinforced (if it did not sometimes create) the loyalty of key commanders to the President.

63. Quoted in Philip Guedalla, *The Two Marshals* (New York: Reynal and Hitchcock, 1943), pp. 182, 186.

64. *Ibid.*, pp. 199–230. Bazaine became something of a scapegoat for the pitiful showing of the French Army.

65. Especially Girardet, *Société militaire;* and D'Ornano, *Haut-commandement.*

66. Brogan, *France under the Republic,* p. 700.

Chapter 2

Foundations of Civilian Control

As France entered a long and vain search for a new and stable constitutional consensus in the wake of the Revolution, her army, after 1815, remained virtually immune to the temptations of political power. What were the primary forces and circumstances which account for the surprising loyalty of that army to a variety of regimes from 1815 to 1939?

Two important fields of inquiry—the social origins and political attitudes of military officers—come immediately to mind and demand exploration, even though both eventually will be set aside as of secondary importance in the pre-1939 period. Might it be that the loyalty of the officer corps in these years resulted simply from the recruitment of both military officers and political leaders from the same dominant social classes? The relative harmony of British civil-military relations in the nineteenth century apparently owed something to such social ties.[1] In France, however, the officer corps, even before the Revolution, was characterized by the *diversity* of social strata from which it recruited. French officers never formed a military caste comparable to the Prussian *Junkertum:* even after several attempts in the eighteenth century to restrict officer recruitment to the nobility, on the eve of the Revolution officers of commoner origins still made up one-fourth of the officer corps.[2] The Revolution and the First Empire greatly expanded the social base of officer recruitment and promotion; and the Restoration government, perhaps three-fourths of whose officers were imperial army veterans, failed to undo that democratization, despite the retirement of the *demi-soldes* and the return of the *émigrés*.[3]

Henceforth until 1870 the majority of French officers were recruited *from the ranks*. By 1869 officers up from the ranks, mostly of rather modest social origin, made up 60 per cent of the total officer corps.[4] If the wealthy and the noble-born were predominant in the highest grades, "rankers" were to be found there, too. In 1869, 3 of the army's 8 marshals, 11 of its 87 major generals, 27 of its 163 brigadier generals, and 76 of its 366 colonels were up from the ranks.[5] Even among those elite officers graduated from the Saint-Cyr military academy, commoners far outnumbered sons of noble families after 1815. The proportion of nobles among those graduates, gauged by the number of noble-type names—names containing the partitive *de* (not all of which are legitimate)[6]—dropped from well over half at the beginning of the Restoration to 39 out of 148 in 1833, and 65 out of 301 in 1843.[7]

Encouraged by a general rise in the prestige of a military career, the "enlightened" classes flowed into the officer corps in greater numbers under the Second Empire and especially in the two decades of zealous Germanophobia following the defeat of 1870–71. The proportion of noble-type names among Saint-Cyr graduates rose to 89 out of 284 in 1868 and 102 out of 365 in 1878, though that proportion dropped off somewhat after 1883.[8] By 1898 a quarter of all brigadier generals and major generals came from aristocratic families.[9] Moreover, Saint-Cyr and the Ecole Polytechnique, open almost exclusively to the fairly wealthy by virtue of the prior education and expense they required, contributed half of all new officers after 1870, in contrast to approximately one-third around mid-century.[10] The new attraction of a military career for the wealthy middle classes is explicable in terms of burgeoning military prestige; however, the influx of sons of noble families was partly determined by their exclusion from careers in diplomacy and civil administration after 1879. The army became something of a refuge for aristocrats, conservatives, and clericals.[11]

The number of candidates and graduates at Saint-Cyr fell off sharply in the first decade of the twentieth century, picked up on the eve of World War I, then dropped again in the trough of army prestige from 1919 until the military revival of the 1930's. As a result of numerous wartime commissions and declining recruitment from the *grandes écoles*, the percentage of officers with Saint-Cyr or Polytechnique diplomas dropped to 36 per cent in 1938 from the 52 per cent level of 1913.[12] At the same time the percentage of general officers with noble-type names was dropping from 25 per cent in 1898 to 7 per cent in 1939.[13]

Data concerning recruitment origins and proportions of aristo-cratic-sounding names, of course, cannot compensate for the ab-sence of exact statistical evidence regarding the class origins of commoner officers. Judging from the best work available on the subject, however, we may assume that the officer corps throughout this period drew heavily on the landed, the civil service, and the liberal-professional segments of the middle class, particularly for its military academy cadets.[14] Among those recruited directly or indirectly from the ranks, many undoubtedly issued from the petty bourgeoisie and some (especially among those recruited directly, without examinations) from rural and artisan backgrounds.[15] In periods of high military prestige (the last four decades of the nineteenth century, 1910–20, and the 1930's), youth of "good family" poured into the officer corps; while in years when the army com-manded little respect (1815–51, 1900–10, and 1920–30), there was a ". . . shift of the center of gravity of the military community toward the middle and even the lower bourgeoisie." [16]

Given the essentially middle-class roots of the officer corps in this period, it is not surprising that officers responded obediently to orders to put down popular revolts during the June Days of 1848 and the Paris Commune of 1871. On those occasions the offi-cer's attachment to order and hierarchy was complemented by his class bias.[17] Yet in view of the *variety* of regimes served by officers in the nineteenth century and the *diversity* of the officers' social backgrounds, class bias is inadequate to explain military sub-servience to civilian authority in this period, except insofar as internal social diversity tended to neutralize the officer corps as a political force. Significantly enough, the influx of wealthy and aristocratic elements into the officer corps after 1870 coincided with the *decline* of the political power of those same elements in French society. In the last three decades of the nineteenth century, with its classification commissions favoring the conservative outlook in promotions, the army deepened its conservative and aristocratic character at the very time when the republic was becoming more republican and equalitarian. Yet no threat of military insurrection resulted, despite opportunities provided by Boulanger in the 1880's and by the national political schism of the 1890's over the Dreyfus Affair. In fact, as Professor Girardet has argued, the professional military community developed into an *order*, distinct in outlook from the surrounding civilian society and hostile to many of the dominant values of a wealth-oriented bourgeoisie.[18]

If the social origins of military officers are inadequate to explain the general subordination of the French Army to civilian control from 1815 to 1939, to what extent is that explanation to be found in the political attitudes of the officer corps? A brief examination of this question will take us into the difficult and little explored problem of the French military mind.[19] Investigation of military attitudes toward politics is hampered by restrictions placed upon military personnel throughout the Third Republic: denial of the right to vote, to run for election to the chamber (after 1875) or the senate (after 1884), to make speeches or write articles without the approval of the minister of war, to belong to political parties, to distribute election literature, to serve on election committees, or to organize professional associations for political action.[20] Even when soldiers were allowed to vote—in the Second, Fourth, and Fifth republics (and in plebiscites during the empires)—the choices of officers as a group are impossible to calculate from election results. Legal restrictions on political activity by military personnel were strongly seconded before 1939 by an apolitical military tradition which frowned upon officers who violated the political silence of the "Great Mute."[21] Hence, the political views of professional officers on active duty are nowhere clearly recorded, nor can it be assumed that veterans organizations and politically active retired officers are always representative of officers' views.[22]

To complicate further the problem of determining the political sentiments of the French officer corps, available evidence indicates that a diversity of political and religious views is to be found among officers in the nineteenth and early twentieth centuries. Among those thirty-four officers elected to the senate in 1876 (before the enactment of the *senate* ineligibility law of 1884), there were representatives of virtually all political persuasions, including four Legitimists (Bourbon monarchists), two Orleanists, four Bonapartists, five conservatives, six conservative republicans, seven classed as "left-center," and three as "left." [23] Even in the period from 1880 to 1900, when a comparatively homogeneous officer corps was generally assumed to be ultra-conservative, there were a number of notable (if exceptional) republican officers, among them Iung, Pédoya, André, and Sarrail.[24] There were even some—like young Maurice Gamelin, later to be chief of the general staff—who believed Dreyfus to be innocent.[25]

Yet despite the diversity of officer opinion and the paucity of evidence available, it is possible—and necessary—to venture a few general characterizations of the predominant tone of military attitudes toward politics in these years.

On a priori grounds, at least three factors might be expected to influence military attitudes: (1) the social origins of officers, which, as seen above, were diverse but rooted primarily in the conservative middle class; (2) the lingering remnants of that feudal and aristocratic tradition of military honor, which, in its insistence on fidelity, sacrifice, and service, would tend to clash with such bourgeois values as security, wealth, and comfort; and (3) the professionalization and isolation of the French military community in the nineteenth century (a subject to be discussed in a later section of the present chapter). Concerning these three factors, military honor took on strong political meaning only after 1940,[26] and middle-class ties are inadequate to explain the peculiar stamp of the "military mind," which leaves us with professional military values as the most promising point of departure.

The functional requisites of military professionalism are best described in general terms by Samuel P. Huntington,[27] who, in his book *The Soldier and the State*, suggests that the role of the professional officer encourages him to adopt certain attitudes and values, among which are the following ones. First, in consonance with his professional training and responsibility, the officer tends to emphasize the role of force in human affairs. He tends to view international politics in military terms; yet, being cautious and fearful of losing all, he rarely feels ready for war. Second, the professional officer tends to emphasize the group over the individual, for in institutionalized warfare the *esprit de corps* of the military unit counts for more than isolated individual heroism. Skeptical of individualism, the officer honors self-sacrifice, service, tradition, and unity. Third, conjoined to a necessarily hierarchical, disciplined institution, the officer tends to value hierarchy and discipline over debate, challenges to leadership, and democratic politics generally. Fourth, the *raison d'être* of the military establishment being the defense of the nation-state, the officer tends to harbor strong nationalist sentiments. Fifth, loyalty and obedience are necessary to the functional effectiveness of the military establishment; the safeguarding of those essential qualities imposes a professional role of political neutrality upon the officer.

To what extent were these the values held by French officers in the period under consideration? Though much more investigation remains to be done on this subject, it is probably safe to say that all five of the attitudes described were held by the majority of French officers from at least mid-century onward.

For military officers, who by virtue of professional duty and self-interest were inclined to think in terms of threats to national defense, pacifism was a natural and long-standing menace. One of the major irritants in interwar civil-military relations, particularly when General Weygand served as vice-president of the Conseil Supérieur de Guerre and potential wartime commander in chief, was the high priority of international disarmament on the calendar of Radical Socialist ministers. Weygand, who had no faith in such utopian schemes and did all in his power to squelch French disarmament offers, explained in his memoirs that "charged with the defense of these [French] forces, I did my job. I defended them." [28] Very likely, General Weygand and the majority of his fellow officers would have agreed completely, on this occasion, with that young colonel who so often chided the high command, Charles de Gaulle:

> Without force, in fact [wrote De Gaulle in 1932], could one con-
> ceive of life? . . . Recourse of thought, instrument of action, con-
> dition for movement, that midwife is necessary for giving birth
> to progress. Sh·eld of lords, rampart of crowns, battering ram of
> revolutions, it is responsible, in turn, for order and liberty. Cradle
> of cities, scepter of empires, gravedigger of decadence, force gives
> laws to peoples and rules their destiny.[29]

True to the Huntington model, French officers, though ever insistent on the need for greater military capacity, rarely were eager for war, except perhaps in limited colonial engagements. General Joffre urged caution on the government in the 1911 crisis with Germany,[30] and the general staff opposed French military action (at least without full mobilization) when Hitler moved into the Rhineland in 1936.[31]

At the heart of typical French-officer attitudes toward politics, one finds a pervasive mistrust of republican individualism and of government by debate. From the mid-nineteenth century onward, it appears that the majority of French officers were antirepublican, at least until the republic gained general acceptance after the 1870's as "that government which divided Frenchmen least." Thereafter until 1939, though a vague republican framework was frequently taken as given, military opinion continued to be antiparliamentary in tone.

Though the fact is sometimes forgotten, in 1815 the army was despised and feared by most conservatives, but cherished by republicans as their best hope for restoration of a republic.[32] The Restoration monarchs had at their service an officer corps which, though obedient, contained an important liberal (if not republican) element.[33] Officer opinion tended to veer to the Right, however, especially after the provisional republican government established in February, 1848, proceeded to humiliate the army by purging the high command and disarming troops stationed in Paris.[34] Antirepublicanism gained strength among officers when the army suffered a thousand casualties in putting down the popu-

lar uprising of the June Days of 1848, and when socialists in-
filtrated and propagandized the enlisted ranks prior to the legislative elections of 1849.[35] In conservative civilian circles the army
won new esteem as a defender of the establish social order,
while among liberals Victor Hugo lamented after the December,
1851, coup: "We had other dreams for you, oh our unfortunate
soldiers."[36]

By 1851 republicanism was linked with social disorder in the
minds of many officers.[37] Reflecting on the coup of 1851, General
François Charles du Barail later recalled, "I had no political
opinions whatsoever"; quite simply he continued, " . . . I nour-
ished against Republican institutions that instinctive antipathy
which is deep in the soul of every soldier. . . . "[38] Antirepublicanism was becoming so widespread among officers that for Du
Barail at least, it was simply a military, rather than a political,
opinion. Already the dissenter, the republican officer sensed the
unpopularity of his views. One lieutenant called in an enlisted
man accused of republican propagandizing during the Second
Republic. First he warned him, "Henceforth you will be watched.
. . . " Then he confided: "I am a republican too, but the only
fortune I have is my epaulet. I am obliged to keep my opinions
to myself."[39]

Realizing the potential cleavage between the soldier's pro-
pensity toward action, unity, hierarchy, and discipline, and the
parliamentarian's love of individualism and freedom of expression, Louis Napoleon reserved two *loges* in the Palais Bourbon
for officers in 1851, hoping to deepen their disgust for government
by argument. An officer leaving an assembly session is said to
have remarked, "there were only outcries, vociferations, interrup-
tions, to the detriment of the solutions for which the country was
waiting on economic and social questions."[40] Though General
Cavaignac was apparently a greater favorite among officers than
Louis Napoleon in the presidential election of December, 1948,[41]
it is not surprising that the officer corps responded favorably to a
Second Empire which promised a strong and stable executive
plus higher status for the nation's army.

With the advent of the Third Republic, no one pretended that army officers had been converted to republicanism, despite the revival among republicans of those warlike Jacobin qualities of the Revolution.[42] Three types of evidence tend to support the thesis that antirepublicanism was widespread among French military officers in the last three decades of the nineteenth century. First, there are the political careers of those officers who were elected to the National Assembly after either retirement or resignation from military service. In the main, these officer-deputies felt most at home on the political Right, where civilian colleagues shared their doubts concerning the wisdom of popular rule.[43] Their outlook, though "traditionalist" and somewhat authoritarian, tended however to be less hostile toward social reform than that of business representatives.[44] Of course the officer-deputy was not fully representative of the officer corps, for he was almost invariably an academy graduate and issued generally from a wealthy or noble family.[45]

A second and somewhat more reliable indication of the political sentiments hidden behind the army's generally faithful exterior in the last quarter of the nineteenth century is to be found in the remarks of those relatively rare republican officers who attained the rank of general. Looking back on those years, General Pédoya wrote in 1908: "One dared not declare oneself a republican unless one wished to be banished and left in the lurch, even by direct associates." [46] In 1892 a kindred soul, General Iung, recalled the not untypical general officer who told him in the early years of the Third Republic:

I want no *red donkeys* in my regiments. In any case, I rate them in such a manner as to insure that they will never succeed.[47]

Reminiscing on the 1870's, Iung remarks:

Only one who has lived through those dismal hours can have any idea of the furious tenacity with which certain military circles hound down by every means the unfortunate officer suspected of the least sympathy for the new government. A whole book could be written, a book of poignant timeliness, on the existence of a republican officer, of a *red donkey*, under the Republic.[48]

Even in 1891, Iung notes:

> . . . In special circles, principally in certain military circles, one is accused of politicking if one has the effrontery to declare oneself a defender of the republican state.[49]

Still another noted republican officer, General Sarrail, entered Saint-Cyr a liberal and non-believer. Upon his arrival he was greeted by the school commandant with the query, "Have you been brought up as one of us?" [50]

A third source of evidence is to be found in the recently un-covered private files on officer attitudes prepared in 1876 and 1878 for Léon Gambetta, the prominent republican leader in the early years of the Third Republic.[51] Apparently at Gambetta's request, two anonymous memoranda were drawn up reporting on the professional qualifications and political attitudes of some 700 army officers. From his perusal of the first of these memoranda, which reports on unit commanders, including 187 of the 234 general officers then serving as commanders of units at the brigade level or above, the French historian François Bédarida counts a total of 131 generals, or 70 per cent of those listed, who are labeled "conservatives," "reactionaries," "Bonapartists," or "royalists." [52] Of the remainder, 13 per cent are rated "neutral or indifferent," 8 per cent "unknown," and only 9 per cent "republican." [53] Among the 72 colonels, all of whom were unit commanders, only 6 republicans were found.[54]

The picture of nearly universal antirepublicanism which emerges from the first memorandum is seriously disturbed by the second, which reports on staff officers and military school instructors, the great majority of whom were in the grades of major and below. According to Bédarida's statistical summary, covering 311 of the 411 officers mentioned in the second memorandum (retired officers and a few others are eliminated from his compilations), 32 per cent were rated as hostile to the republic, 63 per cent as republican or liberal, and 5 per cent as unknown.[55] If Gambetta's anonymous informers reported accurately,[56] there were a surprising number of republican and liberal officers in staff and teaching positions in 1878. Even 7 of the 18 generals in the total of 311 were rated as "republicans" or "liberals."[57] Interestingly enough, however, friends of the republic were less numerous among captains (77 of 132 or 58 per cent) and lieutenants and second lieutenants (24 of 43, or 56 per cent) than among majors (37 of 51, or 72.5 per cent).[58] Perhaps the recruitment of officers from increasingly conservative backgrounds after 1870 was beginning to have its effect. More important, it must be borne in mind that those officers in command of , troops were overwhelmingly antirepublican, especially at the higher levels. Whereas 5 of the 11 colonels in the staff and instructor group were listed as liberals or republicans, only 6 out of 71 colonels in the unit-commander group were so rated.[59] Apparently the difference between the two samples is one based on function as well as rank, with the combat officer far less sympathetic to the republic than his colleagues in teaching and staff positions. Unfortunately, the contrast cannot be pursued very far since the first memorandum gives us no information on combat officers below the rank of colonel.

Surveying the configuration of political attitudes among military officers in the early Third Republic, it seems clear that general officers were overwhelmingly hostile to republicanism. Below the grade of general, the "red donkey" was a relatively rare species in the infantry and especially in the cavalry, but more common among staff officers, military instructors, and officers in the technical arms, particularly among graduates of the Ecole Polytechnique.[60] Political attitudes were related not only to rank and arm of service, but also to social origin, as the second Gambetta memorandum indicates. Of the 62 officers with noble-type names in the staff and instructor group, only 4 were listed as republicans, whereas among former recipients of state scholarships in the same group, republicans outnumbered antirepublicans 53 to 7.[61]

Even after the republic had finally taken root in France, the official military elite and many of their subordinates would have concurred with the judgment of Lieutenant Colonel Ardant du Picq, expressed during the Second Empire, that " . . . whoever speaks of democratic society speaks of a society antipathetic to all that which makes up the military spirit." [62] The same theme recurs in the work by General Gaston de Gallifet and Eugène Lamy, *L'Armée et la démocratie* (published in 1885) [63] and again, in oft-quoted form, in the memoirs of General du Barail published in 1897:

> . . . For whoever wishes to reflect a bit, the republican spirit and the military spirit are two contradictory and incompatible states of mind. The army is a sort of hierarchical pyramid, capped by an absolute chief, who is joined to the masses who form the base through the tiered elites by the bonds of passive obedience, submission, and respect. The Republic is the sovereignty of public opinion, the absolute equality of all. It is free examination of all acts of authority. It is the crushing of the elite by numbers. It is the inversion of the pyramid. By its motto alone the Republic is the negation of the Army, for liberty, equality and fraternity mean indiscipline, lack of obedience and the negation of hierarchical principles.[64]

Disgusted and angered by the ideological battles which periodically split the French nation, officers probably tended to believe, as did Colonel de Gaulle, that "in military honor there is a breakwater which does not yield to confusions of opinion." [65]

Tension between French military values and French parliamentary democracy continued even after conservative officers like Lyautey (in 1897) and Weygand (in 1930) asserted their acceptance of the republic as a permanent fixture.[66] In a letter dated February 26, 1897, Lyautey spoke of " . . . the vice of our institutions, of this omnicompetent, *incompetent, unstable* and *irresponsible* parliamentarism." [67] A month earlier Lyautey had spelled out his complaint against assembly government in these terms:

> It is a challenge to good sense, this regime where almost the entire executive has passed into the hands of a parliamentarism issuing from universal suffrage. People who don't know the first word of governmental affairs and who last only three years. And that being the only effective government, at the mercy of which are, Ministers, Bureaux, established corps of public servants, professionals of all categories!—no fixed, stable element independent of popular caprice.[68]

Officers like Weygand continued through the interwar period to bemoan the instability, the inconsistency, and essential weakness of French parliamentary democracy in the face of external and internal enemies.[69] Moreover, military leaders often felt themselves muzzled by politicians who opposed all increments in defense spending. On his final retirement visit in 1935 to the President of the Republic, General Weygand remarked that " . . . our political system made it impossible for the responsible military chief to make himself heard. . . . "[70]

The eloquent Colonel Charles de Gaulle grasped an important cause of these tensions between soldiers and politicians in his lectures (published in book form as *The Edge of the Sword*):

> The politician and the soldier therefore bring to their common enterprise very different characters, procedures and concerns. The former achieves his goal by covert means; the latter goes directly to it. The one, who sees dimly from afar, judges realities to be complex and applies himself to grasp them by ruse and calculation; the other, who sees clearly but from close up, finds them to be simple and believes that one dominates them if only one is resolved to do so. Faced with an immediate fact, the first thinks of what people will say, while the second consults principles.
>
> From this dissimilarity results some lack of understanding. The soldier often considers the politician to be unreliable, inconsistent, eager for popularity.[71]

The future political giant of contemporary France perhaps gives short shrift to the politician and exaggerates the power of principles over the officer's conduct. He is quite correct, however, in pointing out the officer's penchant for direct action in situations which he takes to be less complex than does the politician. Yet though officers like Weygand preferred direct, authoritarian solutions, they rarely had a clear conception of the kind of political system which they would prefer in place of French assembly government.

The army's republican wing seems to have grown slightly after 1900. Prompted in some cases by sincere belief, in others by ambition, a minority group of officers responded to the intermittent appeals of post-Dreyfus governments for a "republicanized" officer corps. A few of the more famous among them were General Louis André, who as minister of war built up extensive files on supposedly clerical and antirepublican officers, General Maurice Sarrail, the darling of the Left in the 1910's and 1920's, and General Maurice Gamelin, whose appointment in 1930 as deputy chief of the general staff under General Maxime Weygand was Premier André Tardieu's condition for the prospective appointment of Gamelin's conservative chief.[72] Unquestionably political contacts, especially with Radical Socialists, played a part in a number of appointments from 1900 to 1939, particularly at higher levels.[73] Yet their frequency must not be exaggerated. In the four years from 1931 to 1935 General Weygand reports that the minister of war appointed only three officers to the grade of general whose names did not appear on the usual list of eligibles.[74] To be sure, Weygand put up strong resistance to political promotions.

Closely related to the widespread mistrust of democratic politics among officers was a deep attachment to social and political *order*, and an aversion to those on the Left whom General Trochu labeled under the Second Empire as "the eternal enemies of order." [75] Among the primary reasons for the unpopularity of the Second Republic among officers was that it was born of popular revolt and that it bred more of the same. For General Saint-Arnaud, Louis Napoleon's key man, the republic signified "disorganization, disorder, anarchy." [76] Disillusionment was common even among those officers who initially rallied to the republic. General Cavaignac, the republican general who was given full powers to smash the June Days riots of 1848, once faced a disorderly crowd in Oran and was prompted to remark, "This is not how I understand the Republic." [77] General Bosquet as well, another of the early army "ralliés," by June of 1848 was regretting the corruption of republicanism into "disorder." [78]

Educated to respect authority and to accept rigid discipline, the officer was often disturbed by the raucous character of French democratic politics. Writing in 1929, Major Lucien Souchon argued that military men must have confidence in themselves and in their mission: "It is for love of organized power that one embraces a career of arms at twenty years of age. Military faith cannot put up with social, political and moral instability, that is to say with the reign of the parties." [79] Undoubtedly Souchon was far more extreme than the majority of his fellow officers when he foresaw the day when "certain military friends of order and authority" might have to "bring the parties to their senses." [80] The repugnance for disorder which he evidences, however, was a sentiment widely shared in the officer corps.

In the interwar period, and particularly in the 1930's, the army's tradition of abstention from political activity was seriously tested by the appearance of a new type of enemy—international communism—who shocked, not only the officer's respect for order, but also his deep-seated nationalist sentiments. In the decade of the 1930's, as the Third Republic watched its authority eroded away by depression, political scandal, government immobility, and violent social conflict,[81] "right-thinking" conservatives frequently came to fear communism more than Hitler Germany.[82] Though the evidence is still spotty, it would appear that the army was affected by these conditions and by the conviction in conservative circles that French parliamentary democracy was incapable of halting the red wave.[83] Apparently the equally vehement anticommunist and antirepublican diatribes of *L'Action française* reached the eyes of a large number of officer readers in these years.[84] The staunch nationalism, the authoritarianism, and the militant anticommunism of Charles Maurras and his Action Française, if not his monarchist leanings, were probably appealing to a large number of officers.

In 1920 communism was already a familiar foe to those hundreds of French officers who had been involved in Allied military interventions against the Bolsheviks in Siberia, Odessa, the Crimea, and Poland from 1918 to 1920. Then, with the creation of the French Communist Party in 1920, the French extreme Left came for the first time to represent a hostile foreign power as well as a violent revolutionary movement. Military leaders felt the sting of communist agitation during the punitive French occupation of the Ruhr in 1923, when the French Communist Party and the communist youth movement led a campaign of protest to the occupation and extended their propaganda and agitation into the very ranks of the French occupying army.[85] Until 1935, when Hitler could no longer be ignored, the Communist Party (with frequent support from the socialists) was a dedicated antimilitarist force.

It is probably safe to say that most army officers shared the fears of the bourgeoisie in general when the Communists rose from ten to seventy-two parliamentary seats in the 1936 elections, when a popular-front government was formed in that same year, and when Maurice Thorez announced to a communist meeting at the Palais des Sports: "The Communist Party will soon be in power. I tell you, comrades, soon." [86] Throughout the 1930's extremists of the Left and of the Right fed upon the threat each presented to the other. How directly was the army allied with emerging movements of the radical Right? Veterans groups, and especially the Croix de Feu (led by Colonel de la Rocque), were an active and militant antirepublican force. Yet, as René Rémond has suggested, veterans organizations probably tend to attract those men who have the greatest difficulty in finding a satisfying place in civilian society. They are not necessarily typical of enlisted men and officers on active duty, nor of all veterans.[87]

Let us look first at some of the most illustrious military leaders of the day, all of whom were retired, though some still sat on the Army Council. Following the violent antigovernment riots of February 6, 1934, Marshal Lyautey threatened to lead a march on the Chamber of Deputies unless the Daladier government resigned (which it did).[88] Marshal Franchet d'Espérey, reaching senility at eighty years of age, was one of two living marshals of France after Lyautey's death in 1934. In the 1930's he was a leader in the Action Française and an active supporter of the Cagoule, a Right-wing conspiratorial network of confused monarchist and fascist leanings, led by Eugène Deloncle.[89] The other living marshal, Philippe Pétain, was more discreet, though he kept informed of the clandestine activities of the Right wing. His public statement on the eve of the 1936 election clearly revealed his Rightist sympathies,[90] and he was aware that members of his staff were organizing underground anticommunist networks within the army.[91] Nonetheless, he refrained from involving himself personally.[92] Another venerable and conservative officer, General de Castelnau, leader of the ultra-nationalistic "Catholic National Federation," apparently viewed fascism as no threat in August, 1936, when he said of the Spanish Civil War: " . . . There are no longer, as formerly, two factions struggling for the prestige and the advantages of political power; today it is war between Muscovite barbarism and Western civilization." [93] After General Weygand's retirement in 1935, that devout Catholic officer revealed in a series of speeches and articles his alarm at the social fragmentation and moral decay of French society, which he attributed primarily to the subversive efforts of Masons, foreign agents, and above all, communists.[94] A more active conspiratorial role was played by General Duseigneur, an air force officer who retired in 1936. His activities with the Cagoule landed him in prison following the Cagoulard assassination of two antifascist Italian journalists in 1937.[95] The officers mentioned so far were all in retirement.[96] What of those on active duty?

The Cagoule was primarily a civilian organization, though it had drawn Marshal Franchet d'Espérey, General Duseigneur, and a few other officers into its net. Another underground network, this one also violently anticommunist though less revolutionary in objectives than the Cagoule, was created within the army itself by a member of Pétain's staff, Major Georges Loustaunau-Lacau. A former classmate of Charles de Gaulle at the Ecole Supérieure de Guerre, Loustaunau-Lacau was determined to mobilize the army against the communist threat, which he felt the Third Republic was too weak and too pacifistic to handle. The major created the secret "Corvignolles" network among active and reserve officers for the purpose of purging communist influence within the army and bolstering military morale.[97] The extent of the Corvignolles network is extremely difficult to determine. Loustaunau-Lacau claimed to have met with considerable success in his efforts to place or recruit agents in each military unit.[98] He claimed in the Pétain trial that "the great chiefs of the army were fully aware of our action: General Georges even told me of his satisfaction with it one day." [99] Loustaunau-Lacau denied having "worked with" the Cagoule, though he admitted having met with General Duseigneur in 1936, on the suggestion of Pétain, and with Deloncle in 1937, the latter meeting having been arranged by Marshal Franchet d'Espérey.[100] On the urging of Franchet d'Espérey, the major then received from Deloncle the names of officers who had been recruited into the Cagoule, as well as information regarding communist activities within military garrisons.[101]

The presence of clandestine anticommunist activities within the army did not go altogether unnoticed by the government. After General Duseigneur's arrest in 1937 all members of the Army Council were asked whether they were in contact with the Cagoule. The uniformly negative replies were not altogether frank.[102] Major Loustaunau-Lacau himself was released from active duty in 1938, after a reserve officer within his network informed on him.[103] He was reactivated in 1939 after the outbreak of the war, was wounded in combat, and spent much of the war in German military and police prisons.

Undoubtedly, the currents of antiparliamentarism and anticommunism within the officer corps were strengthened during the 1930's; yet one must beware of exaggerating the "politicization" of the army before 1939. Most probably the Cagoule and the Corvignolles never reached more than a small minority of officers. The army as an institution obeyed the popular-front government of Léon Blum in 1936, just as it had obeyed all legally constituted governments for over a century. The army was in no mood for a military coup, even though the Cagoule apparently attempted to inspire one in November, 1937.[104] In fact, the underlying strains of antiparliamentarism and anticommunism within the army posed a serious threat to civilian control only in 1940, when the Third Republic was crumbling under defeat, and again after 1946, when the Indochinese war began.

Still, we are left without a solid explanation of the French Army's subordination to civilian control before 1939. Such typical French military attitudes as antipacifism, antiparliamentarism, and

anticommunism hardly suffice to explain civilian control under the
Third Republic, even though the officer's respect for order gives
some clue to his reluctance to join with revolutionaries of any
color. For a first substantial glimpse into the foundations of civilian
control before 1939, we must turn to the last of those attitudes
which Huntington found to be typical of professional officers: fear
of embroiling the army in the vicissitudes of politics.

As the Italian student of political affairs, Gaetano Mosca, noted
over seventy years ago, the nineteenth century saw the emergence
of a new kind of relationship between military officers and civil
authority.[105] In what Mosca regarded as "a most fortunate exception," military officers in Europe tended to become an obedient,
"bureaucratized nobility, combining the orderliness and conscien-
tiousness of the civil service employee with the chivalrous spirit
and the high sense of honor that were traditional in the well-
born." [106] Formerly, under the Old Regime, French officers had
customarily obeyed the king and his ministers because their class
interests or their personal careers were wedded to the monarchy;
now, in the nineteenth century, they were willing to serve any
government, be it Bourbon, Orleanist, Bonapartist, or republican.[107]

The army officer in France after 1815 gradually came to conceive of his role as requiring unquestioning obedience to civil
authority.[108] He tended to value obedience even more than the
older warlike qualities of courage and initiative, though these
latter values were preserved in the colonial service. In 1835 the
eloquent soldier-poet, Alfred de Vigny, reflected the changing
values of the home-garrison army in his tribute to the military
estate, *Military Grandeur and Servitude:*

> Military grandeur, or the beauty of military life, seems to me to
> be of two parts: there is that of command and that of obedience.
> The first, completely external, active, brilliant, proud, egotistical,
> capricious, will be rarer and less desired with each passing day, as
> civilization becomes more peaceful. The second, completely inter-
> nal, passive, obscure, modest, devoted, persevering, will be each
> day more honored; for today, as the conquering spirit withers, the

only greatness which a noble character can bring into the military profession appears to me to be less in the glory of fighting than in the honor of suffering in silence and of accomplishing with steadfastness duties which are often odious.[109]

Duty, obedience, and abnegation became pre-eminent ideals in the French officer corps after 1815. One of the more famous military leaders of the nineteenth century, Marshal Victor de Castellane, voiced a widely accepted truth when he warned: "A soldier must not even believe in the possibility of acting in a manner other than that which is prescribed for him."[110]

High military regard for obedience permeated not only the internal hierarchy of the army in this period but extended upward to include most relations between generals, on the one hand, and the minister of war and the commander in chief (representing civilian government), on the other. At the beginning of the twentieth century Major Ebener, a military instructor at Saint-Cyr, verbalized that military ethic of obedience when he taught: "The loyalty and devotion of the army to the legal government of the country must be absolute. I defy a military man to find another formula which will permit him as surely to safeguard his honor."[111]

Closely related to the military ethic of obedience to civil authority was the emergence in the early nineteenth century of modern military professionalism. Samuel Huntington traces the roots of that professionalism to four major conditions: [112] first, the development of urbanism, industrialism, and technology, which produced a more complex and highly specialized war machine; second, the growth of the nation-state, which created a permanent need for a national army and offered adequate resources to sustain a professional officer corps; third, the rise of democratic ideas and parties, which encouraged the open recruitment of officers on the basis of merit and created a balance between democratic and aristocratic parties and values which favored the compromise solution of a politically neutral officer corps which no group would control; and fourth, the existence of a single source of legitimate civil authority over the military forces.

As the nineteenth century progressed, all but the last of these conditions were present in France. For reasons to be considered below, continuing uncertainty over the legitimacy of changing political regimes had only a slight deterrent effect on the professionalization of the French Army. To Huntington's discussion of the nation-state needs be added a further factor: the Revolution and the Napoleonic Era endowed France with a vigorous nationalism which allowed French officers to fasten their loyalties upon permanent service to the nation, whether temporarily organized as a monarchy, a republic, or an empire.

Only after 1815 did French officers begin to take on most of the characteristics of a modern professional corps. Military service became a full-time career for most officers, whereas under the Old Regime, aristocratic officers (who were nobles first and officers second) [113] customarily returned to their manors or to the court for several months out of the year during peacetime.[114] The Saint-Cyr military academy, founded by Napoleon, produced a trained military elite who had more claim to expertise than had most of their Old Regime predecessors, though France lagged far behind Prussia in this respect until after 1870. Under Ministers of War Laurent Gouvion-Saint-Cyr (during the Restoration) and Nicolas Soult (under Louis-Philippe), officer promotions were regularized and grades rendered permanent, thus lessening the officer's vulnerability to political pressures.[115] The army discovered a new unity and discipline which had been lacking both under the Old Regime, when each officer recruited his own men and considered his unit as personal property,[116] and under Napoleon, when "collective demonstrations, individual rebellions, mutinies were everyday affairs." [117] At last French officers came to view obedience to the government as a professional duty, rather than simply a personal fealty due the person of the commander in chief.

Once the officer became a professional, a technician in the employ of the state, he was more easily persuaded that his art should be at the service of statesmen, whose responsibility it was to determine the ends toward which that art would be used. Karl von Clausewitz, who participated in the Prussian Army reforms which produced the first modern professional officer corps after 1809, defined the limited professional role of the soldier for many succeeding generations of officers who studied him:

> Now if we reflect that war has its origins in a political object [he writes], we see that this first motive, which called it into existence, remains the first and highest consideration to be regarded in its conduct. . . .
>
> The political design is the object, while war is the means, and the means can never be thought of apart from the object.[118]

From this point it is only a short and natural step to a professional military code which accepts ultimate civilian control as a consequence of professionalism, which "exalts obedience as the highest virtue of military men."[119]

Once stated, the "professionalism equals obedience to civilian government" equation must be qualified to indicate its necessary limitations and supporting conditions. First, it should be obvious that no officer corps is motivated solely by professional values. Members of the military establishment have other corporate interests, including status, income, and power. It was partly through his attention to interests of this nature that Louis Napoleon was able to woo a number of key officers into his camp in 1851.[120] Even when acting as professionals, moreover, military officers may clash with their civilian superiors. One cause of conflict (as in World War I) is the difficulty of tracing a clear and obvious line between the political and military realms; another is serious disagreement regarding the demands of national security. Acting as professionals, military men will value obedience so long as it is necessary to the maintenance of military unity and effectiveness. Yet if a civilian government, in military eyes, is guilty of endangering the security—even the very existence—of the nation-state, professional military men may feel obliged, qua professionals and in order to preserve their unity, to disobey rather than to obey.[121]

There were seemingly good reasons for fearing a clash between the French government and its army in those formative years from 1815 to 1851, when civilian and military values were so strongly opposed. Stendahl's Julien Sorel of *The Red and the Black*, electing against a military career, was fully aware that military values were no longer in style.[122] Yet the army accepted its plight of relative social isolation; indeed, it often came to look upon that isolation as a condition necessary for the maintenance of unity and discipline.[123] It did so—and the point deserves emphasis—because in this period there were no serious threats to national security, no crises which might have thrown into relief the standing tension between civilian and military values. From the end of the Napoleonic Era in 1815 to the Franco-Prussian War in 1870, there were no protracted wars and none involving the defense of vital national interests. The Algerian conquest in 1830 (and its consolidation thereafter) required no wartime sacrifices on the part of the metropolitan population. The Second Empire saw a flurry of military activity accompanied by a rise in military prestige after a long forty-year eclipse; yet the Crimean War, the Italian campaign, and the Mexican expedition were all relatively limited in length and in the extent to which they involved the whole nation.[124] It was only in 1870 and in 1914 that war captured the attention of the nation as a whole; in both cases the army was temporarily retrieved from its isolation.

When antimilitarist civilian values clashed with those held by most military men, civilian control was assured (as it often was in the United States before World War II) simply by isolating the military community from political power.[125] To be sure, France's continental location forbade a solution like that found in the United States, where the army was reduced almost out of existence (to a mere 25,000 men) after the Civil War. Strength limitations on the French Army rose from 240,000 in 1818 to 400,000 in 1824.[126] Nevertheless, the absence of serious security threats in the mid-nineteenth century, coupled with the relative isolation of the military community, tended in effect to limit severely the political power of the military within France proper.

In this setting of relative security it appears that social isolation served to intensify military concern with army discipline and unity: in its isolation, imposed by an initially unsympathetic society, the army turned inward for inspiration. "If a soldier is to do his duty well, he must not have too many contacts with the bourgeois," one general insisted toward the end of the century.[127] Such contacts were systematically discouraged. Units were moved every two years, and the majority of officers remained unmarried. Few notations on an officer's record were as disastrous for a career as the one, "frequents civilian circles." [128]

Given this intense concern with unity and discipline within the military order, officers found an additional reason for obeying the government currently in power—the diversity of social origins and political opinions within the officer corps. As a professional, the officer knew that military effectiveness depended upon safe-guarding army unity. Since political action of any type would risk a split within the army, the safest course for officers intent on preserving army unity in the face of changing political regimes was that of strict abstention from politics and faithful obedience to the government of the day. As governments rose and fell in the nineteenth century, the officers who served them in turn were encouraged to look beyond the sovereign of the day as a focus of their loyalty to the abstract notion of the state, whoever might be at its helm.[129] Then, when France turned again to a republic after 1870, when conscription extended finally to the entire popu-lation, it became increasingly clear that army unity could be preserved only if officers kept "aloof" from all politics.[130] Many officers undoubtedly shared the sentiments of the captain who, on discovery that one of his sergeants was a socialist candidate in the 1849 parliamentary elections, asked:

> Why in the devil do you draw attention to yourself? . . . Do you believe I have no opinions? I never talk about them. That allows me to serve all governments. I am not the soldier of Pierre or of Paul; I am the soldier of France.[131]

In a mid-century setting of a professional army living in com-parative isolation, the spirit of discipline tended to permeate the enlisted as well as the officer ranks. The law of 1818 provided for selection by lottery (with the possibility of paid replacement) of those rather few unlucky youths who would be required to serve seven years. Substitution was abolished in 1872; but it was not until 1905 that all young men, without special exemption, were required to serve a full term of service, then set at two years. Throughout the nineteenth century the enlisted ranks were filled largely with men of humble origins, who served long terms, even as conscripts.[132] Yet with the exception of temporary disorder in some regiments in 1830 and 1848, military discipline generally held firm among enlisted men, even when regular troops were thrown against popular Parisian uprisings in June of 1848 and May of 1871, and against striking workers in 1910–11.[133] As opposed to the rebellious behavior of the national guard, which played a key role against the government in the insurrections of 1830, 1848, and 1871 (after which it was definitively disbanded),[134] the regular army could be counted upon to obey the government in civil disturbances as well as in foreign wars. There was good reason why political leaders of the Left, from Rousseau to Jaurès and beyond, who were hostile to the existing political and social order, developed a strong fear of professional troops, as opposed to the militia and reserves of the "nation-in-arms." [135]

Supported by a long period of only briefly interrupted peace from 1815 to 1870, by an inhibiting diversity of social origin and political attitudes among officers, and by a formative period of enforced introversion from 1815 to 1851, the French military community developed a strong tradition of professional obedience to civil authority. That tradition lived on to help guarantee civilian control even when some of the original conditions which produced it ceased to exist.

Despite a developing professional military tradition of political neutrality, the temptations for military intervention offered by a relatively unstable political situation and a weak constitutional consensus might have proven too great in the period from 1815 to 1939 had it not been for the safety valve of colonial service. From the time of the Algiers expedition in 1830 until World War II, French military officers whose thirst for action and power was unslaked by home-garrison duty could usually find both in the colonies. The extensive political, as well as military, powers of the colonial officer, as well as his independence from tight civilian control, have already been described.[136] Ambitious and daring officers who might otherwise have turned their energies loose in political adventures in France itself were able to find exciting substitute satisfactions in the colonial army. Soon after that great colonial officer, the future Marshal Lyautey, arrived in Indochina for his first colonial assignment in 1894, his letters began to sparkle with excitement over the officer's life in the colonies:

> What a shame I did not come here ten years earlier! [he wrote to his sister in December, 1894] What careers there are to be established and led here! Here there is not one of these little lieutenants, post and reconnaissance commanders, who does not develop more initiative, will, endurance and personality in six months than does an officer in France in his entire career.[137]

Here in the colonies, free from the *métropole's* "deadly administration, the iron-bound hierarchy . . . which watches, ready to cut short all vigour, all spontaneity,"[138] the officer was free to throw away the book of regulations (as Gallieni literally did for Lyautey)[139] and realize his full potential for action and responsibility. For the lieutenant as for the general, adventure, independence, power, and even glory were much more abundant in the colonies than in the peacetime home-garrison army. Without this colonial outlet for military energies and ambition, it is likely that the army would have been more of a threat at home.

Those foundations of civilian control so far discussed—notably professional political neutrality supported by the absence of serious security threats in the formative years and by the colonial outlet for restive military spirits—still do not account fully for the comparative docility of a sizeable standing army in the face of unstable political regimes. One persuasive theory of civil-military relations holds that the single most powerful factor which has always tended to draw armies into politics has been political instability stemming from the absence of consensus and authority within a given society.[140] If there is any power in this theory (and I believe there to be), how did the French Army avoid the praetorian path in the nineteenth century? It did so partly because French society was more stable than the parade of constitutions would indicate. Shifts in political power took place among the various segments of the bourgeoisie. The growing urban working class, to be sure, was aware of its alienation from political power after 1848. Yet the bulk of French society, bourgeois and peasant, accepted the authority of each succeeding regime. There was no consensus rivaling that which allowed peaceful and constitutional change in British society in the same period; yet in comparison with Spain, France appeared rather orderly.

Spain, in fact, offers a revealing contrast to French military discipline in the nineteenth century, though unfortunately no thorough studies have been made of Spanish civil-military relations in this period. It is clear, however, that Spanish military officers time and time again entered the political fray in support of civilian political antagonists. The Spanish Army became a political arbiter—though sometimes divided within its own house.[141] The Spanish *pronunciamiento* was closely related to the breakdown of authority after the Napoleonic Wars, when Spanish politics was plagued by the active counterrevolutionary movement which produced the bitter seven-year Carlist war of the 1830's. In France, on the contrary, the bourgeoisie easily dominated aristocrats of the Old Regime, and the French avoided the political chaos which Spain reaped from her civil war.[142] Moreover, the French bourgeoisie, though divided, was neither so quarrelsome nor so ready to call for regular army intervention against other bourgeois factions as was the Spanish middle class.[143] Most probably the French Army would have been drawn more deeply into politics in the nineteenth century, as was its Spanish counterpart, if political instability had been as profoundly rooted in France as it was in Spain.

Again, during most of the Third Republic's seventy-year life, French political institutions enjoyed at least a *faute de mieux* kind of support from most segments of the middle class and the peasantry on the premise that the republic was less likely to disturb their preferred styles of life than any probable alternative regime. Yet that tenuous "stalemate consensus," as one writer has baptized it,[144] emerged shaken from the Dreyfus era—only to be battered even more seriously in the 1930's by depression and vicious political warfare over domestic communism. Two years before Hitler's march into Poland, one of the Third Republic's more moderate military critics, former Chief of Staff General Debeney, warned his compatriots that the nation was fast losing its capacity for another *union sacrée* as a result of the antipatriotic preachings of many state school teachers, of the progressive enfeeblement of the executive at the hands of quarrelsome party politicians, and of the eclipse of public respect for the general interest.[145] Though Debeney refrained from marking out the nation's political institutions as the primary culprit, many officers undoubtedly did just that. It is hardly reasonable to expect military officers to maintain undimmed respect for the government of the day when the civilian population is fast losing faith in it. The new collapse of France's tenuous republican consensus in the dying decade of the Third Republic was clearly a factor—along with the trauma of sudden defeat—in attracting the majority of Frenchmen, civilian and military, to Marshal Pétain's authoritarian government in the summer of 1940.

In summary, it would appear that the social and political diversity of the officer corps tended to inhibit united political action, and its predominantly middle-class attachments and its respect for order made it a natural ally of any government preserving order, particularly against a proletarian uprising. However, neither the social origins nor the political attitudes of military officers afford adequate explanation of effective civilian control over the French Army in the period from 1815 to 1939. Of far greater importance was the officer's strong professional commitment to political neutrality and to military subordination to the government of the day. Developed in a mid-century period, when security threats were few and inconsequential and when the military community lived in semi-isolation from civilian society, the military tradition of obedience to civil authority provided a means of preserving army unity amid changing political regimes, despite the diversity of social origins and political attitudes within the officer corps. When the officer corps developed greater social and political homogeneity (in the last three decades of the nineteenth century), the influx of shorter-term conscripts into the enlisted ranks furnished another restraint against potential praetorian inclinations. The professional military tradition of political neutrality was further supported by a modicum of social consensus which, until the 1930's, lent greater stability to French society than surface political turbulence would indicate. Finally, the faithfulness of the army within France was strengthened by the colonial outlet for ambitious and restive officers, who could find in Indochina, Madagascar, or Africa the independence, power, and status which were often denied them at home.

1. Blake, *Soldiers and Governments*, p. 27.

2. E. G. Léonard, *L'Armée et ses problèmes au XVIIIe siècle* (Paris: Plon, 1958), pp. 165–75, 286.

3. The estimate of three-fourths, for 1824, is by François Kuntz, *L'Officier français dans la nation* (Paris: Charles-Lavauzelle et Cie., 1960), p. 39.

4. Chalmin, *Officier français*, Annexe No. 2; and Raoul Girardet, P. M. Bouju, and J.—P. H. Thomas, *La Crise militaire française, 1945–1962* (Cahiers de la Fondation Nationale des Sciences Politique No. 123 [Paris: Colin, 1964]), p. 19 (hereinafter cited as *Crise militaire*).

5. Chalmin, *Officier français*, Table, Annexe No. 2, p. 370.

6. Sociologist Jesse Pitts, writing in 1963, states that less than half of French aristocratic-sounding names are legitimate. See Pitts, "Continuity and Change in Bourgeois France," in Stanley Hoffmann (ed.), *In Search of France* (Cambridge, Mass.: Harvard University Press, 1963), p. 236.

7. Girardet, *Société militaire*, pp. 79, 84. Figures given by Chalmin (*Officier français*, p. 160) are similar, though not identical.

8. Girardet, *Société militaire*, p. 186.

9. Chapman, *Soldiers and Governments*, p. 60.

10. Girardet, *Société militaire*, p. 187.

11. [L. H. G. Lyautey], "Le Rôle social de l'officier," *Revue des deux mondes*, March 15, 1891, p. 447; Mattei Dogan, "Les Officiers dans la carrière politique," *Revue française de sociologie*, II, No. 2 (April–June, 1961), p. 91; and Girardet, *Société militaire*, p. 199. It should be noted, however, that Girardet's Saint-Cyr figures show a *decline* in the proportion of graduates from aristocratic families from 1879 to 1883, and a "rather noticeable" decline thereafter (*ibid.*, p. 186). The "refuge" notion must not be overstressed; yet it is undeniable that a man like Lyautey himself, a conservative and a clerical, could have made such a brilliant career in public life only in the army.

12. Girardet *et al.*, *Crise militaire*, p. 19. Moreover, the 1938 officer corps included 24.3 per cent up directly from the ranks, a category which had been reduced to only 4 per cent in 1913, as the result of heavy use of officer-candidate schools established in the 1870's and 1880's at Versailles, Saumur, and Saint-Maixent (*ibid*).

13. Chapman, *Soldiers and Governments*, pp. 71–72, n. 18.

14. Chalmin, *Officier français*, pp. 39–40, 89–228, 232, 268.

15. Girardet, *Société militaire*, pp. 188–89, 276, 318–19; and Chalmin, *Officier français*, p. 146.

16. Girardet, *Société militaire*, p. 276, describing the period from 1900 to 1910.

17. See below, p. 44.

18. Girardet, *Société militaire*, p. 87; Chalmin, *Officier français*, p. 52; and Kuntz, *L'Officier français dans la nation*, p. 155.

19. A beginning has been made in the study of political attitudes of military officers by Girardet, *Société militaire*, and, for the period from 1815–70, by Chalmin, *Officier français*. See also Jean-Paul Charnay, *Société militaire et suffrage politique en France depuis 1789* (Paris: S.E.V.P.E.N., 1964) *passim* (hereinafter cited as *Suffrage politique*).

20. Charnay, *Suffrage politique*, pp. 257–58; and Michel Sénéchal, *Droits politiques et liberté d'expression des officiers des forces militaires* (Paris: Librairie Générale de Droit et de Jurisprudence, 1964).

21. See below, pp. 39–42, 44.

22. On this latter point see p. 36 below.

23. Charnay, *Suffrage politique,* p. 108 n. 3. For evidence of political diversity among officers in the period from 1815–70, see Chalmin, *Officier français*, pp. 231–68.

24. See below, pp. 29–31.

25. General Gamelin, *Servir* (Paris: Plon, 1946–47), II, xxvii.

26. See Chapter 10 below.

27. Huntington, *The Soldier and the State*, pp. 59–79.

28. M. Weygand, *Mémoires* (Paris: Flammarion, 1957), II, 388. See also *ibid.*, pp. 389–93, 511; and Bankwitz, "Weygand", pp. 506–7, 533–40.

29. Charles de Gaulle, *Le Fil de l'épée* (Paris: Union Générale d'Editions, 1962), pp. 10–11 (written in the early 1930's).

30. De la Gorce, *French Army*, pp. 77–78.

31. Gamelin, *Servir*, II, 200–217; and Challener, *Nation in Arms*, pp. 264–65.

32. Girardet, *Société militaire*, pp. 7–24; and Joseph Monteilhet, *Les Institutions militaires de la France (1814–1932)* (Paris: Alcan, 1932), p. 12 (hereinafter cited as *Institutions militaires*).

33. Chalmin, *Officier français*, pp. 232–35.

34. Girardet, *Société militaire*, p. 134.

35. Charnay, *Suffrage politique*, pp. 105–6, 156–57, 163.

36. Quoted by Girardet, *Société militaire*, p. 38. See also *ibid.*, pp. 28–33.

37. See below, pp. 34–35.

38. Du Barail, *Mes souvenirs*, I, 437–38. See also Chalmin, *Officier français*, pp. 264–65, who testifies to the currency of this antirepublican bias among officers in 1851.

39. Sébastien Commissaire, *Mémoires et souvenirs* (Lyons: Meton, 1888), I, 140.

40. Chalmin, *Officier français*, pp. 264–65. With regard to antiparliamentarism among soldiers, see the comments of Montesquieu, *Esprit des lois*, Vol. I of *Oeuvres complètes de Montesquieu* (Paris, 1816), XI, vi, 305.

41. Charnay, *Suffrage politique*, pp. 154–55, 183 n. 1.

42. Brogan, *France under the Republic*, chap. 3; Girardet, *Société militaire*, pp. 40, 167–71; Franchet d'Espérey, *Histoire de la nation française*, III, 437–54.

43. Dogan, *Revue française de sociologie*, pp. 88–89.

44. *Ibid.*

45. *Ibid.*, pp. 91–92.

46. De la Gorce, *French Army*, 51, quoting from Pédoya, *L'Armée évolue* (Paris, 1908).

47. General Iung, *La République et l'armée* (Paris: Bibliothèque-Charpentier, 1892), pp. 140–41.

48. *Ibid.*, p. 262. See also *ibid.*, pp. 33–34, 113–14, 207–8.

49. *Ibid.*, p. 40.

50. Quoted in Paul Coblentz, *The Silence of Sarrail*, trans. Arthur Chambers (London: Hutchinson, n.d.), p. 27.

51. Bédarida, *Revue historique*, pp. 119–64.

52. *Ibid.*, table, pp. 142–43.

53. *Ibid.*

54. *Ibid.*

55. *Ibid.*, table, p. 147.

56. Bédarida bases his faith in the objectivity and accuracy of the *fiches* on two arguments. First, republican officers are by no means always rated high in professional competence, and antirepublican officers are not infrequently described as excellent military men. Second, in those cases where transfers led to the inclusion of the same officers in both samples, ratings are usually similar (*ibid.*, p. 125).

57. *Ibid.*, table, p. 147.

58. *Ibid.*

59. *Ibid.*, pp. 144, 147.

60. Regarding the liberalism of technical officers, see Charnay, *Suffrage politique*, pp. 190–91; Dogan, *Revue française de sociologie*, p. 97; Bédarida, *Revue historique*. pp. 147–48; and below, Chapter 10.

61. Bédarida, *Revue historique*, pp. 151–52.

62. Charnay, *Suffrage militaire*, p. 12, quoting from Du Picq, *Etudes sur le combat* (Paris, 1902).

63. Published anonymously in Paris by Calmann-Levy. See *ibid.*, pp. 125–28, 131, as cited by Bédarida, *Revue historique*, p. 162.

64. Du Barail, *Mes souvenirs*, I, 32–33.

65. De Gaulle, *The Army of the Future* (London: Hutchinson, 1940), p. 35.

66. In a letter dated January 29, 1897, Lyautey regretted the growing "lassitude de nos institutions (je ne parle pas de la forme constitutionelle que presque personne ne met certes en cause et qui ne court aucun peril)" (Lyautey, *Lettres du Tonkin et de Madagascar*, p. 481). In order to quell the furor on the Left against his appointment as Chef de l'Etat–Major Général in 1930, Weygand addressed a statement to the chamber, asserting: ". . . I am a republican. I cannot conceive of any other regime existing in France. . . . " (Bankwitz, "Weygand," p. 478, quoting from *Annales de la Chambre*, 2ème séance du 21 janvier 1930, p. 57).

67. Lyautey, *Lettres du Tonkin et de Madagascar*, p. 496.

68. *Ibid.*, p. 479.

69. Bankwitz, "Weygand." pp. 610–11; and [Souchon], *Feue l'armée française*, pp. 196–97. For a more moderate reformist military view (still hostile to the corruption and incoherence of the "régime des partis"), see General H. Mordacq, *Faut-il changer le régime?* (Paris: Michel, 1935).

70. Weygand, *Mémoires*, II, 433. For a similar view, deploring especially

the ingratitude of the nation toward the army in the 1920's, see Lieutenant Colonel Reboul, "Le Malaise de l'armée," *Revue des deux mondes*, March 15, 1925, pp. 391–94.

71. De Gaulle, *Le Fil de l'épée*, pp. 10–11. See also Robert Cantoni, "Réflexions sur le métier militaire," *RMI*, No. 235 (February, 1962), pp. 23–25.

72. With regard to André see above, Chapter 1, n. 36. With respect to Sarrail, see King, *Generals and Politicians*, pp. 70, 87–88. The Gamelin appointment is discussed in Gamelin, *Servir*, II, xxii–xxvii; and in Weygand, *Mémoires*, II, 340–45.

73. See the attacks on political interference in appointments in Reboul, *Revue des deux mondes*, p. 391; and in Weygand, *Mémoires*, II, 372–73, 393.

74. Weygand, *Mémoires*, II, 372.

75. Quoted in Girardet, *Société militaire*, p. 134.

76. Quoted in *ibid.*, p. 135.

77. *Ibid.*

78. Chalmin, *Officier français*, p. 264.

79. [Souchon], *Feue l'armée française*, p. 197.

80. *Ibid.*

81. See, for example, Alexander Werth, *The Twilight of France, 1933–40* (New York: Harper, 1942); and Stanley Hoffman, "Paradoxes of the French Political Community," in Hoffman (ed.), *In Search of France* (Cambridge, Mass.: Harvard University Press, 1963), pp. 21–32.

82. Charles A. Micaud, *The French Right and Nazi Germany, 1933–1939* (Durham, N. C.: Duke University Press, 1943), pp. 222–32.

83. De la Gorce, *French Army*, chaps, 10 and 11; J.-R. Tournoux, *L'Histoire secrète* (Paris: Plon, 1962), pp. 21–36, 75–77, 93–96, and *passim*.

84. Eugen Weber, *Action Française* (Stanford, Calif.: Stanford University Press, 1962), p. 193.

85. De la Gorce, *French Army*, pp. 209–12.

86. Quoted by Tournoux, *Histoire secrète*, p. 23.

87. René Rémond, "Les anciens combattants et la politique," *Revue française de science politique*, V, No. 2 (April–June, 1955), 267–90, particularly 288–90.

88. Brogan, *France under the Republic*, p. 660; and Werth, *Twilight of France*, p. 19.

89. See the testimony of Commandant Georges Loustaunau-Lacau in *Le Procès du Maréchal Pétain: Compte rendu sténographique* (Paris: Michel; 1945), I, 353–54 (hereinafter cited as *Procès Pétain*). See also Tournoux, *Histoire secrète*, pp. 30–36, 307–9; and Weber, *Action Française*, p. 416.

90. Werth, *Twilight of France*, p. 84.

91. Testimony of Commandant Loustaunau-Lacau in *Procès Pétain*, I, 252–55.

92. Tournoux, *Histoire secrète*, pp. 29–30.

93. De la Gorce, *The French Army*, p. 241, quoting from *L'Echo de Paris*, August 26, 1936. See also Weber, *Action Française*, pp. 153–55.

94. Bankwitz, "Weygand," pp. 610–11.

95. Werth, *The Twilight of France*, p. 343; Tournoux, *Histoire secrète*, pp. 75–77; and De la Gorce, *French Army*, pp. 247–50.

96. Other officers—most of whom were also retired—who have been cited as active in organizations of the antirepublican Right in the 1930's include: General Paul Lavigne-Delville (Weber, *Action Française*, p. 383; Tournoux, *Histoire secrète*, pp. 44–47), Colonel Charles des Isnards (Weber, *Action Française*, p. 155), and, of course, Colonel de la Rocque.

97. Testimony of Loustaunau-Lacau in *Procès Pétain*, I, 350–55 (July 30, 1945). See also De la Gorce, *French Army*, pp. 242–47; and Tournoux, *Histoire secrète*, pp. 25–29.

98. See the statements of Loustaunau-Lacau quoted by De la Gorce, *French Army*, p. 246.

99. Testimony of Loustaunau-Lacau in *Procès Pétain*, I, 352.

100. *Ibid.*, pp. 353–54.

101. *Ibid.*, pp. 353–54, 358.

102. De la Gorce, *French Army*, p. 250.

103. *Ibid.*, p. 248; and Loustaunau-Lacau, *Procès Pétain*, I, 350.

104. Tournoux, *Histoire secrète*, pp. 92–103.

105. Mosca, *The Ruling Class*, trans. H. D. Kahn (New York: McGraw-Hill, 1939), pp. 228–29.

106. *Ibid.*, p. 232. Of course, the French officer corps, as opposed to the Prussian one, was not composed primarily of nobles.

107. To put the matter in the terminology of Samuel Huntington, the older relationship was one of "subjective civilian control," the newer one of "objective civilian control."

108. Girardet, *Société militaire*, takes as his major thesis the dominating role of "l'obéissance passive" and "l'apolitisme" in the French Army from 1815–1939. His argument is convincing, though he tends to exaggerate the purity of those ideals and to neglect instances in which they were temporarily disregarded. The same thesis is argued (but grossly exaggerated) in D'Ornano, *Haut-commandement*.

109. De Vigny, in A. Bouvet (ed.), *Servitude et grandeur militaires*, (Paris: Colin, 1960), p. 174 (written in 1835). Vigny spent ten years as an officer from 1815 to 1825. Girardet, in *Société militaire*, p. 100, attests to the scope and importance of the same transformation of values described by Vigny.

110. Girardet, *Société militaire*, p. 101, quoting from De Castellane, *Journal, 1804–1862* (Paris, 1895).

111. As quoted by Girardet, *Société militaire*, p. 324. On the same theme see also General Debeney (army chief of staff in the 1920's), *La Guerre et les hommes* (Paris: Plon, 1937), pp. 144–45.

112. Huntington, *The Soldier and the State*, pp. 32–46.

113. See Alexis de Tocqueville, *Democracy in America* (New York: Vintage, 1945), II, chap. 22, 281.

114. Léonard, *L'Armée et ses problèmes au XVIIIᵉ siècle*, p. 11.

115. General M. Weygand, *Histoire de l'armée française* (Paris: Flammarion, 1938), p. 263; and De Gaulle, *France and Her Army*, pp. 62–63.

116. Léonard, *L'Armée et ses problèmes au XVIIIᵉ siècle*, pp. 2, 203–4, 240–50; and Léon Mention, *L'Armée de l'ancien régime* (Paris, 1900), p. 8.

117. Lefèbvre, *Napoléon*, p. 192. See also above, Chapter 1, n. 1.

118. *On War*, p. 16.

119. Huntington, *The Soldier and the State*, p. 79.

120. Captain Hippolyte de Mauduit prefaced his book on the coup of December second with the epigram, "Qui sait soigner l'armée la retrouve au besoin" (Guillemin, *Le Coup du 2 décembre*, p. 280, quoting from *La Révolution militaire du 2 décembre*).

121. On this point see Finer, *The Man on Horseback*, p. 25.

122. Non-fictional explorations of the same theme are to be found in Girardet, *Société militaire*, pp. 12–20; and De Vigny, *Servitude et grandeur militaire*, p. 49.

123. Girardet, *Société militaire*, pp. 87–93.

124. The Crimean War did indeed produce 95,000 French casualties— 75,000 of them from disease. It also required a level of industrial support which was a preview of wars to come (Charles H. Pouthas, in G. Lefèbvre, C. H. Pouthas, and M. Baumont, *Histoire de la France* [Paris: Hachette, 1950], II, 298). Yet its physical remoteness from France, its relative success, and its brevity in comparison with recent overseas campaigns—all prevented any dramatic clash between the army and the civilian population and government for which it was fighting. Moreover, the revival of military prestige tempered the enforced isolation of the military community.

125. Huntington, *The Soldier and the State*, pp. 97, 143, 189–90.

126. American army figures are from Walter Millis, *Arms and Men* (Mentor Book ed.; New York: New American Library, 1958), p. 119. French Army figures are from Montheilhet, *Institutions militaires*, pp. 6–7.

127. Girardet, *Société militaire*, p. 89, quoting from General de la Motte–Rouge, *Souvenirs et campagnes* (1889).

128. Girardet, *Société militaire*, pp. 255, 88–90.

129. *Ibid.*, pp. 119–21.

130. General Debeney, *La Guerre et les hommes*, pp. 144–45.

131. Commissaire, *Mémoires et souvenirs*, I, 212–13.

132. "Go through the ranks of the Army and count your soldiers. You will not find among them the sons of the bourgeoisie. It would seem that the sons of the bourgeoisie fought against ancient privileges only in order to expropriate them" (General Subervie, as quoted by Monteilhet, *Institutions militaire*, pp. 24–25). See also Challener, *Nation in Arms*, pp. 38–41.

133. Charnay, *Suffrage politique*, pp. 183–94; Girardet *Société militaire*, p. 128–29, 131; Pouthas *et al.*, *Histoire de la France*, II, 265–66, 274; Kuntz, *L'Officier français dans la nation*, p. 84.

134. Monteilhet, *Institutions militaires*, pp. 67–106.

135. J. J. Rousseau, *Considérations sur le gouvernement de Pologne*, in *Oeuvres complètes de J. J. Rousseau* (Paris: 1911), V, chap. 13, 282; Jaurès, *L'Armée nouvelle*, pp. 43, 50, and *passim.*; Monteilhet, *Institutions militaires*, p. xiv and *passim.*; Challener, *Nation in Arms*.

136. See above, Chapter 1.

137. Lyautey, *Lettres du Tonkin et de Madagascar*, p. 84.

138. *Ibid.*, p. 101.

139. *Ibid.*, pp. 122–23.

140. Rapoport, "Praetorianism: Government without Consensus"; and Finer, *The Man on Horseback*.

141. The role of the army in Spanish politics in the nineteenth and

twentieth centuries is discussed by A. R. M. Carr, "Spain: Rule by Generals," in Howard (ed.), *Soldiers and Governments*, pp. 135–48. See also Carlton J. H. Hayes, *A Political and Social History of Modern Europe* (New York: Macmillan, 1920), II, 378–80.

142. Carr, *Soldiers and Governments*, pp. 135, 138–39.

143. The December coup of 1851 is an exception to this general rule, though formal discipline was maintained on that occasion.

144. Hoffmann, *In Search of France*.

145. Debeney, *La Guerre et les hommes*, pp. 363–78. Former Premier Albert Sarraut struck a similar note in his testimony of February 10, 1948, before the Commission d'Enquête sur les Evénements Survenus en France de 1933 à 1945. Recalling the state of French opinion in March, 1936, he stated: "Enfin, il faut bien en convenir, à coté de ces raisons de 'glissement morale,' l'approche des élections législatives, ouvrant un furieux combat entre les droites et les gauches, absorbait l'attention de tous, et détournait du péril extérieur la vigilance des pensées. Chacun songeait à ses chances, ou à ses revanches de politique intérieure . . . " (quoted in Edouard Bonnefous, *Histoire politique de la Troisième République* [Paris: Presses Universitaires de France, 1962], V, 456).

Chapter 3

Disgrace through Discipline, 1939-1945

World War II was the beginning of the end for the French military tradition of unquestioning obedience to civilian authority. The rapid and humiliating defeat of 1940 produced a series of events which badly eroded the foundations of military discipline. The commander in chief, General Maxime Weygand, first refused to continue the war in North Africa and contributed mightily to the fall of the Reynaud government, which favored that policy. General de Gaulle then rejected the authority of the new Pétain government and appealed to the army and nation to follow him. As Vichy was drawn ever more tightly into the Axis net, many French military officers were forced into an agonizing choice between traditional military discipline, on the one hand, and the Gaullist crusade, on the other. The final liberation of France and the purges of "collaborators" which followed seemed to prove that unquestioning obedience to the government of the day was no longer the surest formula for safeguarding a military man's honor.

With the exception of General Weygand's clashes with economy-minded ministers, there was little in the comparatively peaceful nature of official French civil-military relations in the 1930's which foreshadowed the crisis of June, 1940. Such fundamental principles of military policy as the primacy of defense and reliance on a short-term conscript army found general support both in the general staff and among political leaders. With the outbreak of war, however, tensions mounted as the weakness of the French military machine gradually became apparent. Even at the highest levels the army evidenced the debilitating effects of such common peacetime military maladies as formalism, lack of imagination, promotion by strict seniority, and factionalism.[1]

The problem of command articulation, which the long-delayed act of 1938 governing the "Organization of the Nation in Time of War" had supposedly solved, now came to the fore. In an attempt to avoid the tensions which had developed between government and high command in World War I, the National Assembly had given responsibility for "operations" to the high command and clearly reserved general conduct of the war to the government and, ultimately, to the National Assembly.[2] Yet fear of concentrated military authority, added to navy and air force pressures, had forestalled the completion of Paul Reynaud's plan for a tight centralization of defense organization under a Ministry of Defense and a chief of staff of national defense.[3] The titles were adopted, but not the accompanying centralized powers which Reynaud advocated. One unfortunate result was serious confusion in the spring of 1940 concerning the respective powers of the chief of staff of national defense, General Maurice-Gustave Gamelin, and General Claudel Georges, commander in chief of armies of the northeast:[4] a bitter rivalry quite naturally developed between Gamelin and Georges.[5]

French conduct of the war was thrown into further disarray by the entanglement of political and military rivalries. All went smoothly between Gamelin and the government so long as Daladier was Premier, for the two men were close associates and in full agreement on the primacy of defense. But when Paul Reynaud replaced Daladier as Premier in March, 1940, during the Norwegian campaign, tension mounted rapidly. Reynaud had no confidence in Gamelin; yet he dared not replace him because of the government's dependence on the support of the Radical Socialist party, which was led by Daladier, Gamelin's defender.[6] Reynaud attempted to intervene over the conduct of the campaign in Norway, only to meet a firm protest from Gamelin that this was an encroachment on his powers over "operations."[7] The law of 1938 had not settled the old and ticklish problem of distinguishing between "policy" and "strategy," especially at a time when civil-military relations were characterized by mutual distrust.

French defeat in the Netherlands enabled Reynaud to remove Gamelin as well as Daladier, who had been kept on as minister of national defense for political reasons. However, in replacing Gamelin with General Maxime Weygand on May 19, 1940, Reynaud unknowingly enthroned a much more dangerous rival than Gamelin had ever been. Only the day before Reynaud had invited Marshal Philippe Pétain to join the government as vice-president of the cabinet. Thus, the two men who were to contribute most to the fall of the government were brought into the fold by the Premier himself.

Weygand, a militant Catholic, was obsessed by a hatred for Free Masonry, a fear of communism, and scorn for politicians and partisan politics. His experiences as chief of staff under Foch in World War I, and again as army chief of staff in the 1930's in the face of an economy-minded parliament, had instilled in him an abiding distrust for the French political game and those who played it.[8] The election of 1936 and the popular front government which issued from it only reinforced his conviction that the republic offered little defense against the dread communist menace. Weygand's known contempt for politicians had earlier led to suspicions in parliamentary circles that he was a Fascist. Such reports ignored the Christian aspect of Weygand's thought and mistook his authoritarianism for totalitarianism; yet the general hardly conformed to the "apolitical" label which he preferred to wear. On June 28, 1940, after defeat and armistice had forced the republic to its knees, Weygand sent a memorandum to Pétain which reveals the extent of the commander in chief's antipathy toward the republic:

> The old order of things, that is to say a political regime of Masonic, capitalist and international compromises, has led us to our present straits. France wants no more of it.[9]

Weygand proposed a new order, led by a small group of disinterested and untainted men under Pétain, built on the ideals of "God, Country, Family," and capable of curing the nation of materialism

and social conflict. With these lines, which he himself characterized as portraying "the guiding ideas" of "my line of conduct," [10]
Weygand revealed his ideological affinity with those authoritarian
elements of the French Right which had never accepted either the
French Revolution or the French Republic.

Marshal Pétain fully shared Weygand's antipathy toward the old
order, though the two men were known before June, 1940, to be
bitter enemies.[11] Pétain had never plotted against the republic, nor
had he participated personally in the activities of Right-wing organizations during the interwar period, as had Marshal Franchet
d'Esperey, though he had kept well informed regarding their activities.[12] "Too proud for intrigue," as De Gaulle had described him,[13]
the marshal was nevertheless ambitious and eager to exercise power
despite his eighty-four years.

On May 10, 1940, the Germans launched a blitzkrieg offensive
which broke through the French front in Belgium and again near
Sedan in France; within six weeks the battle of France was concluded. The German advance came with such bewildering rapidity
that Weygand soon became convinced that defeat was inevitable
and an armistice was the only hope of French salvation from
anarchy and communism. Reynaud, though lacking in both political support and personal forcefulness, was determined to carry
on the war—from North Africa, if necessary. A bitter struggle
between Reynaud and his commander in chief, a struggle which
had been building since soon after Weygand's assumption of command, now broke into the open during a series of critical and
dramatic cabinet meetings between June 12 and June 16. With
Pétain's support, Weygand reported that only an armistice could
save the army from complete disintegration and the nation from
anarchy.[14] On June 13 both Weygand and Pétain announced flatly
that they would not leave France if the government decided to
remove to North Africa. When the commander in chief was informed by a cabinet member that removal of the government across
the Mediterranean was a political question beyond the competence
of the military, he retorted angrily: "I have had enough of these
fire-eaters who want to fight and still high-tail it out of the country.

As for me, I will not leave the soil of France even if they put my feet in irons." [15] Two days later Weygand went a step further. When Premier Reynaud suggested that the army in the *métropole* might capitulate while the government moved to North Africa to carry on the battle, the general bluntly replied, "I will refuse to obey an order of that nature." [16] Not only did Weygand refuse to take the army to North Africa; he now refused to allow the government to leave France without calling for an armistice. And this he did in the name of the honor of the army. The very concept which had for so long suggested unquestioning obedience to civilian authority was now twisted to justify open rejection of that authority.

The harried Premier dared not replace his insubordinate but politically powerful military chief, fearing the fall of the government would ensue. He finally surrendered to the capitulators during the stormy cabinet meeting of June 16, when he resigned upon losing majority support in his cabinet to the prestigious Pétain and the military chiefs. President of the Republic Albert Lebrun delayed briefly, then, on Reynaud's advice, appointed Pétain as Prime Minister. The marshal's list of ministers, which was ready in advance, included Weygand as minister of national defense, General Colson as minister of war, and Admiral Darlan as minister of the navy. [17] The following day Pétain announced to the nation that the government had addressed a request to the enemy for armistice negotiations. [18] The armistice and the abdication of parliament to Pétain followed shortly.

Throughout those critical days when German panzer divisions were driving south through France with little opposition, Reynaud fought a losing political battle with Weygand and Pétain largely because of the government's tepid support in the National Assembly and the tremendous prestige of the two military men in a time of national peril. Pétain's appointment as vice president of the cabinet on May 18, 1940, had been greeted by virtually unanimous praise in the press from Left to Right. The presence of the military hero in the government produced some sense of security among politicians as well as among the population at large. The president of the senate in the spring of 1940, Jules Jeanneney (who strongly opposed the armistice), later recalled that in June, 1940:

> It was incontestable that at that moment all eyes were turned toward Marshal Pétain. He was like a life-buoy toward which all hands reach out. His was certainly the only name around which union and concord could be achieved in our country.[19]

Despite rumors of a threatened military coup in June, 1940, it was political strength—not threat of violence—which tipped the balance toward Weygand and Pétain. Reynaud later argued that Pétain and Weygand were prepared to resort to a military coup if legal methods had proven insufficient for the overthrow of the government; Reynaud's evidence, however, is indirect and unconvincing.[20] The prosecution in the Pétain trial eventually withdrew its initial charge that the marshal had "plotted" the overthrow of the republic, while retaining the charges that he had not silenced antirepublican conspirators who shouted his name and later drew a number of them into the Vichy government.[21] In the case of Weygand as well, investigations for the high court of justice found no evidence of a plan for a military coup in 1940.[22] The thought that the army might prevent continuation of the war by a coup never seems to have entered the mind of the last President of the Third Republic, Albert Lebrun, who in his memoirs blamed the armistice rather on the lack of boldness of the Reynaud cabinet.[23] There is little reason to believe that Weygand would not have accepted an order for his replacement had Reynaud's political position been strong enough to allow the Premier to issue one.[24] However, he probably would have refused to resign if Reynaud had asked him to do so rather than ordering his replacement outright.[25] If Reynaud had enjoyed the support of a strong parliamentary majority, or failing that, had he been capable of matching his conviction with the forcefulness of a Clemenceau or a Churchill, the military chiefs would have been no match for him, and Weygand would not have appeared so utterly irreplaceable in June of 1940.[26] The handmaiden of praetorianism—governmental weakness—was on hand to tempt military leaders into the game of politics.

Violence, even if it had been intended, was quite unnecessary, for French political society was badly divided and demoralized from the bitter social and political struggles of the 1930's and from the irresistible force of the German military offensive. The historian

Marc Bloch, who was called to active duty on the outbreak of the war and later killed in the resistance, left this picture of the state of morale among his fellow reserve officers:

> They received orders from a political system which seemed to them to be corrupted to the very marrow. They were defending a country which they judged in advance to be incapable of resistance. The soldiers whom they commanded issued from the masses which they believed to be degenerate.[27]

Another *union sacrée* was out of the question in 1939. The Molotov-Ribbentrop pact had aligned the Communist Party against the war effort, and much of the extreme Right, despite its professed Germanophobia, was only too eager to see the collapse of the republic. Even among democratic parties partisan rivalries continued to hamstring governmental leadership.[28]

The sharp contrast between the British and French reaction to extreme national peril in World War II throws into relief the close relationship between civilian control of the military, on the one hand, and the solidarity of the political system and firm governmental leadership, on the other. Especially after Churchill's accession to the office of the Prime Minister, there were no serious tensions between soldiers and statesmen in Great Britain during World War II.[29] Britain, of course, did not suffer invasion and defeat within the homeland itself, as did France. Nevertheless, tensions in French civil-military relations appeared before German soldiers ever set foot on French soil. The behavior of Weygand and Pétain in June, 1940, would have been unthinkable on the part of military chiefs in Churchill's Britain, even if the British Isles had been overrun by the enemy.

The infirmities of the French political system provided the background for the victory of civilian and military advocates of surrender in June and July of 1940. But the more immediate cause was the powerful psychological shock experienced by the army and the nation as a whole as a result of the totally unexpected style and speed of the German blitzkrieg offense. Its paralytic and demoralizing effects were seen in military headquarters as well as on the front, where the panic produced by Stuka dive-bombing attacks was out of all proportion to the casualties they inflicted.[30] Surprise, more than defeat itself, took a terrible toll on political and military command centers as General de Gaulle describes them in May, 1940:

> The collapse of the whole system of doctrine and organization to which our chiefs had attached themselves deprives them of their resilience. . . . In the midst of a prostrated and stupefied nation, behind an army without faith or hope, the government machine turned in an irremediable confusion.[31]

It is not surprising that in this situation Weygand, never a revolutionary strategist, could not envisage continuation of the war from Africa. Nor, when one recalls that the National Assembly on July 10, 1940, completed the burial of the Third Republic by a vote of 569 to 80, is it so very surprising that Weygand renounced a long tradition of military obedience to civil authority by refusing to continue a war which he was convinced was over? [32]

De Gaulle once described the French as " . . . a people whose genius, whether in eclipse or in glory, has always found its faithful reflection in the mirror of its army." [33] The army and its leaders in 1940 were indeed a "reflection," if not a passive or even totally accurate one, of a defeated and demoralized nation. But unlike the faithful mirror, Pétain and Weygand actively *led* the nation into capitulation and political metamorphosis.[34] The trauma of sudden defeat served not only to paralyze the army's will to continue resistance: it also activated and exaggerated the latent antiparliamentarism which had long been part and parcel of the average officer's mental equipment. In the past, officers had often been hostile to republicanism without questioning their duty to serve the republic; now, however, a defeated army looked eagerly to "Marianne" (the Third Republic) and her politicians for a scapegoat.[35] Within two weeks after assuming the post of commander in chief, Weygand was convinced that the government had blundered in taking an unprepared nation into war and had now called him to military leadership simply to slough off onto him the blame for defeat. Weygand conveniently forgot that only the previous summer he had described the French Army as having "a greater value than at any moment of its history." [36]

The key role of military leaders in June of 1940 owes a great deal to the particular personalities—Weygand and Pétain—who happened to occupy important posts. Although the military mold clearly favored antipathy toward republican politics and politicians, the officer corps was by no means a monolith with regard to political attitudes. Moreover, the tradition of unquestioning obedience to civilian authority was still quite alive, as officer behavior in the next few years was to demonstrate. General military hostility to the *régime des partis* provides the background for the behavior of Pétain and Weygand in June, 1940, but not its full explanation, for most officers at the time likely would not so easily have defied the legal government of the day.[37]

Despite the gravity of Weygand's indiscipline, the French military tradition of subservience to civilian authority suffered more in the years to follow from General Charles de Gaulle's famous appeal from London. Pétain's political victory over Reynaud had spared Weygand from acting on his threat to disobey an order to surrender the army if the government should remove to North Africa. De Gaulle, on the contrary, as under secretary of state for national defense after June 5 and as a firm supporter of Reynaud, found himself on the losing side in the struggle for control of the French government. On the morning of June 17 the recent brigadier, perhaps in danger of arrest, left Bordeaux by plane for London in the company of General Edward Spears, Churchill's personal representative to the French Ministry of War. The following day, June 18, before a BBC microphone, De Gaulle launched an appeal to French soldiers and technicians to join him in England to keep alive "the flame of French resistance."[38]

The historic radio appeal of June 18 was more than a simple call for volunteers for a French expeditionary corps. It was the first step in De Gaulle's campaign to turn the French Army and nation against their new government leaders and the armistice policy.[39] On June 19 De Gaulle appealed by radio to the governors of France's colonies to reject the armistice then under negotiation.[40] He then refused to comply with a direct order from General Weygand, now minister of national defense, instructing him to return to France.[41] By mid-July De Gaulle was publicly accusing Pétain of treason;[42] the Pétain government, in return, was quick to brand De Gaulle as a mutineer and, on August 2, 1940, to condemn him to death *in absentia*.

"Le Grand Charles" owes his dominant position in contemporary French history to that fateful decision to reject the authority of the Pétain government in June of 1940. Praiseworthy as that decision was from the standpoint of Hitler's foes, an example was thereby set of a soldier who decides for himself where the interests of his country lie and revolts against constituted authorities if they see those interests differently from himself. Despite the climate of demoralization and fear that prevailed in France in the last weeks of the Third Republic, it is clear that Pétain enjoyed wide support in the National Assembly, as well as in the nation as a whole.[43] Moreover, the government's armistice policy was not so obviously treasonable as Gaullists have pretended in view of the alternative of a harsh German occupation. A recent writer on the subject of stategic surrender argues that "when concluded, the French armistice represented a successful bargain for both sides." [44] The bargain could be viewed as "successful," of course, only by those who believed that British defeat was imminent and that the United States would not enter the war. Such a view of reality in June of 1940, though wrong, could not fairly be described as treasonable. If De Gaulle acted correctly in terms of the long-range interests of Frenchmen, he nevertheless dealt a heavy blow to the old— and useful—French military tradition of subservience to civilian authority.

Faced with the contradictory appeals of Pétain and De Gaulle in the summer of 1940, the vast majority of officers unhesitatingly accepted the authority of the marshal and his government. In the three summer months following the appeal of June 18, the Gaullist movement attracted only three generals (all from the colonies), one admiral, and three colonels, plus a scattering of junior officers.[45] Even among those French troops located in Great Britain at the time of the armistice, De Gaulle succeeded in recruiting less than a quarter of the enlisted men and an even smaller proportion of the officers, giving him a total of only seven thousand men by the end of July, 1940.[46] The Free French Army which was gradually assembled grew primarily through occupying French Equatorial Africa (with British help), then North Africa (with American help), where "armistice army" units were absorbed intact. In the summer of 1940, however, the Pétain government managed to assert its authority over all civil and military colonial governors with the exception of General Catroux (governor general in Indochina), General Legentilhomme (commander of French troops in French Somaliland), and M. Eboué (governor general of Tchad). Both Catroux and Legentilhomme were easily replaced, though Tchad rallied to De Gaulle, giving him a toehold in French Equatorial Africa. When the Free French, with British help, tried to win over French West Africa in September, 1940, they were held off by French guns still in the loyal service of the marshal.[47]

Three factors help to account for De Gaulle's limited success. First, the Pétain government had the advantage of apparent legality and hence profited from the power of military discipline and the officer's desire to be "covered." After all, had not the marshal's leadership been accepted by public opinion and by the majority of politicians? "We executed the orders of a Blum because he was President of the Council," the tragic officer hero of Jacques Weygand's *Le Serment* is made to say; "by what right would we refuse to rally to the one who is best among us when he is the one who exercises power?" [48] In the next few years De Gaulle was time and time again to be frustrated in his hopes by the "stupid sterility" of French military discipline, despite a continuing hatred of the Germans within the army.[49]

Second, military discipline was supported by an Anglophobia which thrived in the navy and had lately appeared as well in the army, where Great Britain was resented for failing to throw all of her military strength into the battle of France, and, later, for supposedly coveting French colonies.[50] Convinced (as were most Frenchmen) that Germany had won the war, the majority of French officers saw little reason for deserting their native land in order to wage a delaying action in favor of the British and their empire.[51] Navy Chief of Staff Admiral Darlan and his senior officers were known to be intensely anti-British, a sentiment which was strengthened by the British attack on the French fleet at Mers-el-Kébir on July 3, 1940. In the wake of that attack, undertaken in the fear that the French fleet might fall into German hands, Darlan was prepared to open hostilities against Great Britain.[52]

Officers found another good reason for obeying the Pétain government in the congeniality of the values which it represented. A discredited French Republic suffered repeated calumnies and disgrace at the hands of the armistice government, even to the replacement of its once cherished motto. Predictably enough, "work, family, country" rang more true to the military ear than "liberty, equality, fraternity" had ever done. The political philosophy of the Vichy government, bearing the stamp of the marshal himself, was comfortably compatible with the dominant values of professional military officers. With a soldier's taste for discipline, authority, and hierarchy and a disdain for ambiguity and disorder, the marshal laid out the job of French education under the new order:

> The French school of tomorrow will teach respect not only for the human person, but also for family, society and country. It will no longer make any claims of neutrality. Life is not neutral: it consists of vigorously taking sides. There is no neutrality possible between the true and the false, between good and evil, between health and sickness, between order and disorder, between France and anti-France.[53]

Pétain again spoke as a soldier when he lashed out at "blind and egoistic capitalism" and vowed to free his country from "the most despicable tutelage: that of money." [54] The same values which Marshal Lyautey had proposed that army officers inculcate in French youth in 1891—discipline, respect, sacrifice, patriotism, social solidarity—now reappeared in the statements of the venerable marshal, who defined the new regime as "national in foreign policy, hierarchical in domestic policy, coordinated and controlled in its economy, and above all social in its spirit." [55]

Many military officers fully agreed with Pétain's view that France in defeat had revealed moral weaknesses attributable to the anarchy of the *"régime des partis,"* and, more particularly, to its educational system.[56] In the summer of 1940 the Vichy government created the Chantiers de la Jeunesse, an organization designed largely to effect the desired patriotic and moral transformation in French youth, who were required to serve for terms of six, then eight months. When French military forces in the *métropole* were cut to the one-hundred-thousand-man maximum set by the armistice terms, a number of those officers released from active duty were assigned to the Chantiers under the command of General de la Porte du Theil.[57] A massive veterans organization, the Légion des Combattants, was also originally formed, in lieu of a single political party, to develop and maintain a high sense of patriotism among veterans. The Légion, however, soon became the tool of collaborationist elements and a recruiting ground for the pro-nazi Service d'Ordre Légionnaire and its offspring, the infamous Milice.[58]

The full extent of the ties between the Vichy regime and the armed forces—and especially the navy—is seen in the vast number of officers recruited for political and administrative posts. Army and air force officers were only slightly more in evidence than under the republic, though military officers now permanently recaptured the Ministry of War, which had been almost exclusively a civilian domain since 1918.[59] General Weygand served as minister of defense only until September, 1940; then he was delegate general of the Vichy government in French Africa until German protests against his fierce anti-German attitude forced the cautious Pétain to remove him from public office in late 1941.[60] Other army and air force officers were used almost exclusively in the administration of their branch of service. Generals Colson, Huntziger, and Bridoux served successively in the Ministry of War, while Generals Vuillemin, Bergeret, and Jennekeyn performed similar functions in the Air Ministry.[61]

With the help of Admiral Darlan, the opportunistic, ambitious, and fiercely Anglophobe vice-president of the cabinet after February, 1941, the government and administration were flooded with admirals. Admiral Esteva served as resident general in Tunisia, Admirals Abrial, Decoux (General Catroux's authoritarian successor), and Robert were governors general in Algeria, Indochina, and Martinique, respectively; Admiral Auphan directed the merchant marine; Admiral Fernet served as secretary general of the presidency of the cabinet; and Admiral Platon headed the Ministry of

Colonies. Moreover, admirals served as prefect of police in Paris, head of a new police school, and prefects of some seven departments.[62] The influx of naval officers into important posts was so overwhelming that a Catholic cardinal was prompted to remark, "I wonder if after my death they will find still another unplaced admiral to replace me." [63] Spurred on by their near unanimous antipathy toward the British (especially after the British attacks on French naval vessels at Mers-el-Kébir and then at Dakar), Darlan and his naval colleagues at times brought France dangerously close to active military collaboration with the Germans.[64]

Along with greater access to public office, military officers who had long felt themselves unjustly criticized, mistrusted, and denied their due respect,[65] now enjoyed a privileged place in official French society. With the chamber and the parties dissolved and the marshal in power, the infuriating voices of antimilitarism were finally silenced. A flurry of parades and military ceremonies helped officers to forget their recent humiliation in battle.[66] For those numerous armistice army officers who later recalled these years as "the most fervent period of my life," [67] obedience to civil authority was no longer simply a passive, professional duty, as it had been under the Third Republic: the officer's subservience to governmental control now took on a more positive, political character.[68]

Contrary to the universal expectation in Vichy in July, 1940, the British did not collapse, and the French armistice policy soon began to lose the aura of self-evident wisdom which had previously surrounded it. The Vichy regime, fearing the ultimate effects of De Gaulle's appeals from London, decreed in Constitutional Act Number Eight of August 14, 1941, that all military personnel would henceforth be required to swear an oath pledging loyalty to the person of the chief of state.[69] The military oath of allegiance had been abandoned since 1870; its revival now had the effect of intensifying the *crise de conscience* undergone by many officers who were forced to choose between traditional discipline and renewed resistance against the occupying power. Yet the majority of armistice army officers had no need of an oath to insure their obedience to the congenial Pétain regime. Most felt as did the major in Jacques Weygand's narrative:

> It isn't just any leader who is making us take an oath of allegiance;
> it's the Marshal. . . . If there is anyone to whom we can swear
> allegiance with our eyes closed, he is certainly the one.[70]

Many of those officers who, for whatever reason, adhered rigidly
to the military dictum of unquestioning obedience found themselves
purged from the officer ranks following the liberation.[71] The typical
Gaullist response to the problem of disobedience was to point out
that the Vichy government was not a free agent and therefore was
devoid of authority over the armed forces. But at least until after
November, 1942, such a judgment was too deeply political to be
reached comfortably by most professional soldiers, especially in
the face of political-military leaders like Pétain and Darlan, who
insisted that to obey was still to serve France.

Vichy complemented the oath with vigorous punitive measures
against those who joined De Gaulle. A law of July 23, 1940, had
proclaimed the death penalty for all military personnel who left
French territory between May 10 and June 30, 1940. General
Catroux, General Legentilhomme, and Colonel de Larminat, along
with De Gaulle himself, were condemned to death *in absentia* at
the hands of military tribunals. Other sentences followed.[72]

The early war years were fraught with disappointments for
the proud creator and leader of "La France Combattante." Condemned by his peers in France,[73] accused of attempting to split the
army, incapable of persuading military commanders in French West
Africa and Syria to renounce their loyalty to Vichy, General de
Gaulle was forced to live out a soldier's nightmare in denouncing
discipline among Vichy's loyal troops and appealing to the British to
join him in attacking his own compatriots and fellow soldiers. The
first serious military encounter between the troops of De Gaulle and
those of Pétain took place in late summer of 1940 in Gabon, where
the Free "French"—mostly Foreign Legionnaires and Africans—
subdued Vichy forces and occupied Libreville with a total loss of
twenty men killed.[74]

Following the unsuccessful Free French and British attack on
Dakar in September, 1940, there were no major fratricidal battles
until the tragic Syrian campaign, which left an indelible mark on

the French military conscience. Vichy sparked an Allied attack on the French Syrian protectorate when German planes were allowed to use Syrian air bases. De Gaulle had long favored an attack on Syria, and the British now rallied to his point of view. To the surprise of General Catroux, commander of the 6,000 Free French troops joined to four or five times that number of British and Australian troops, General Dentz and his officers, as well as most of the 40,000 Vichy troops in their command, considered De Gaulle a rebel and remained loyal to Pétain and to the Vichy government. Obeying orders from Vichy, Dentz put up stiff military resistance to the Allied invasion. Despite his animosity toward the Germans, he finally recommended resort to German air support as the only hope of holding Syria, though hesitation at Vichy and the signing of an armistice on July 14, 1941, kept German aircraft out of the battle. When the fighting ceased, over a thousand Vichy soldiers and eight hundred Gaullist soldiers had been killed.[75] The continuing sense of discipline and loyalty to Pétain was evidenced by the choices of the officers and men of the Vichy troops: only 5,668 out of a total of 37,736 joined De Gaulle.[76]

Following the liberation of France, General Dentz was tried and condemned for his role in the fratricidal Syrian conflict. To Dentz's simple—and truthful—defense of "I obeyed orders," the public prosecutor replied: "At the grade you hold and in the functions you fulfill, one is judge of the orders he receives." [77] The French Army did not soon forget the lesson.

At the time the Syrian campaign did not seriously shake the traditional discipline of the Vichy army, for the great majority of officers and men returned to France in unbroken units, still convinced that a soldier's duty was to obey his superiors and his government. Such an escape was more difficult, though still not impossible, in the confusion of November, 1942, when the American invasion of North Africa and the subsequent German occupation of the Vichy zone critically undermined the authority of Marshal Pétain.

Weygand's successor as commander of French troops in North Africa and French West Africa, General Alphonse Juin, continued to prepare patiently for an eventual resumption of hostilities against

Germany. Yet when the Allies landed along the North African coast in the night of November 7–8, 1942, it so happened that Admiral Darlan, second in authority only to the marshal in the Vichy government, was visiting his son in Algiers and hence took direct command of French forces. All but a small minority of those forces remained loyal to Pétain in the face of the Allied invasion, forcing the American commanders to deal with Darlan.

The Allies had hoped that French troops would rally to their cause without resistance. Contacts had been made with a non-Gaullist clandestine resistance organization in North Africa led by a civilian "group of five," which had attracted the participation of such important military figures as General Mast, commander of the Algiers Division, General Béthouart, commander of the Casablanca Division, and General Giraud, a famous escapee from a German prison.[78] Yet the "five" had been given only partial and delayed information regarding American invasion plans. General Mast and his resistance group were able to gain control of Algiers for a few hours on November 7, 1942, but they moved too soon and were overpowered by loyal mobile guards before the arrival of American troops.[79] In Morocco, General Béthouart arrested General Noguès, resident general in Morocco; but again the move came too soon, for loyal Vichy troops arrived at Rabat and freed Noguès in time for him to order armed resistance to American landings. In Algiers, Darlan ordered a local cease-fire soon after the arrival of American troops. However, despite pressure from the American diplomatic representative, Robert Murphy, and from General Juin, for two days he left standing the order for resistance elsewhere in North Africa.[80] As a result, over five hundred Americans and almost seven hundred French soldiers were killed, most of them in the fighting in Morocco.[81]

The Allies had refused Free French participation in the landings on advice from the "five" that their presence would impede an arrangement between French troops and the Allies.[82] In fact, however, the presence of Darlan in North Africa and the loyalty of French troops to Pétain prevented any such agreement until after much blood had already been shed. General Giraud, who in the plan of the "five" was to take command of the French African army, belatedly arrived in Algiers on November 9. To his chagrin, the army made no move to rally to his leadership.[83]

These first few days following the Allied invasion were days of terrible confusion within the French African army. Pétain's immediate and public response to a request from President Roosevelt for French co-operation in North Africa was direct enough: "We have been attacked; we will defend ourselves. That is the order I am giving."[84] Yet the marshal's cable of November 8 to Darlan indicated that the admiral was free to act as he saw fit.[85] For the next several days Vichy continued to emit belligerent orders, largely from fear of German reprisals against the *métropole*, while apparently reaffirming Darlan's free hand in a series of secret coded cables.[86] The effect on the army was one of confusion, especially when on November 11, in the wake of an armistice accord between Darlan and General Mark Clark, Vichy transferred authority over North Africa from Darlan to General Noguès and, by cabinet vote, ordered French forces to fight "to the limit of their strength."[87] Pétain was now weaker and more ineffective than ever, while Laval gained the upper hand at Vichy. Nevertheless, German occupation of the Vichy zone after November 11, as well as the secret cables, eventually allowed Darlan to regain control over the African army. Vichy continued to condemn the November 10 armistice and the new commander in chief of the African army, General Giraud, who was described as having "forfeited his honor and betrayed his duty as an officer."[88]

Confusion was particularly marked in the bewildered French military command in Tunisia, headed by Resident Minister Admiral Esteva, General Barré, and Admiral Derrien. Conflicting and rapidly changing orders from Vichy and from Admiral Darlan and General Juin in Algiers left the Tunisian commanders at a loss to know whether duty required them to fight the Americans, the Germans, neither, or both.[89] Confronted with final orders from the collaborationist minister of war in Vichy, General Bridoux, to allow German troops to land, and with contradictory and uncertain orders from Algiers, Admiral Esteva (who had opposed the armistice in

June, 1940) and Admiral Derrien dared not take responsibility for opening fire on the Germans. By November 13 German troops had arrived in force to take command of Tunis and the adjoining port of Bizerte. On that date, when firm orders finally arrived from General Juin to open fire on the Germans, it was too late for all but General Barré and his troops, who had fled Tunis on earlier orders from General Juin.[90]

Military commanders stationed in French West Africa in November, 1942, were equally fearful of breaking with formal discipline. They finally rallied to Darlan with their one hundred thousand troops only on November 22, after having been assured by Algiers emissary General Jean Bergeret that the secret cables from the Vichy government had indeed vested the admiral with full powers.[91]

Nothing in the training or past experience of the French officer prepared him to decide at what point duty and honor ceased to require unquestioning obedience to orders from above. It is not surprising that Admirals Esteva and Derrien in Tunis were unwilling to disregard clear orders from Vichy on November 11, 1942, even though they were aware that the Germans had broken the armistice agreements by occupying the Vichy zone. The two admirals paid for their decision (or indecision) with lifetime prison sentences.[92] Again, as in the case of General Dentz in the Syrian campaign, future generations of military officers were unwittingly taught that in some circumstances (but which ones?) obedience may dishonor the obeyer.

In Algiers, Darlan was extremely careful to present himself as the continuing embodiment of legality and loyalty to the marshal. He explained on November 15 and again by radio on November 20 that the marshal was no longer free, hence, the oath of allegiance to him was no longer binding. "Our patriotic duty remains the same: liberate the *Métropole* and the Empire and, I will add, liberate the Marshal, living incarnation of imperial France." [93] Curiously enough, Darlan's argument, with the exception of his reference to the marshal, had a distinctly Gaullist ring to it. For over two years De Gaulle had been arguing that the soldier owes obedience only to a free and independent government. Now, however, after German occupation of all of France on November 11 and the arrest of

General Weygand on November 12 (despite French government protests), the "government in chains" argument was more obviously true.

One can catch a more vivid glimpse of the impact of these November days on the unity and discipline of the French African army through the eyes of Jules Roy, an air force officer stationed in Algeria at the time. Roy, like his fellow officers, was still there because he had pledged his loyalty to the marshal, "who had spared my country from total occupation and had obtained the maintenance of the army in which I remained." [94] Was not discipline the first of military virtues and disobedience a certain road to chaos?[95] Then the Americans landed in North Africa. Roy's unit was the object of rapidly changing orders: first to attack roads leading from the coast in order to halt an American advance; then to allow Axis planes to land; and finally, at dawn, to maintain "absolute neutrality." Meanwhile, Vichy continued to call by radio for resistance against the American invaders:

> Each of us was suspended on the word of his commander and separated from the rest of the army. . . . All the generals who insulted and threatened each other on the radio and on the telephone disconcerted me. The generals had broken relations with each other because each suspected the other was not free. . . . We had lost confidence in our chiefs and in ourselves.[96]

In the presence of such a confusion of goals and authority, Roy found that his *discipline du caporal* was inadequate. "I needed to know and to watch over my personal reasons for fighting. In that, the professional soldier that I was felt he was wrong." [97]

Along with the majority of his fellow officers in the African army, Roy avoided the moral agony of actual disobedience by simply following orders from superiors. This was the predominant pattern all the way up to Darlan, who finally absolved all from their oath to "the old one." The conflict between discipline and honor was thereby dulled, but not resolved. As in the Syrian campaign, enduring lessons were learned in North Africa in November, 1942. Nearly two decades later, in the trial of officers involved in the April, 1961, "Paris plot" to overthrow the Fifth Republic, General Boyer de la Tour, a defense witness for Colonel Vaudrey, testified (with some exaggeration) that the traditional concordance of military discipline and honor had been irreparably broken during World War II:

> In 1942, at the time of the American landings in North Africa, I had organized a clandestine group of Moroccan troops. I received the order to march against the Americans. I refused. If the landings had not succeeded, I would have been a rebel.[98]

But of course the landings did succeed, and in the aftermath of war the French nation tended to judge its officers according to the *earliness* of their hour of rebellion.

Throughout the armistice army, in France as well as in Africa, officers demonstrated a rather consistent reluctance to disobey their superiors, despite the confusion and tensions of those November days. Armed resistance was universally considered to be futile among senior officers in the *métropole*, though plans were laid for preserving the armistice army in case of German occupation of the Vichy zone.[99] On November 9 the order went out to all army units to retreat to designated points in case of German advances across the Vichy border.[100] The next day, however, orders for displacement were annulled, leaving French units sitting peacefully within their garrisons when the Germans swarmed into the Vichy zone on the eleventh. With one exception, all armistice army commanders complied with orders received: only General de Lattre de Tassigny, commander of the Montpellier Division, vainly attempted to lead his troops to a predetermined mountainous retreat. He was betrayed by a subordinate, captured, and imprisoned, though he later escaped and joined De Gaulle in time to become the illustrious commander of the First Free French Army.[101] Plans to keep the armistice army away from the Germans collapsed in the face of Pétain's hesitation and weakness, Bridoux's determined collaborationist policy, and the army's continuing loyalty to the weak old man who was still "The Marshal." From the dissolution of the armistice army by German order on November 27, 1942, until June, 1944, France was left without a French Army on French soil.

The navy followed suit, though here the ties of military discipline were strongly seconded by the fierce Anglophobia of the Toulon fleet commander, Admiral Count Jean de Laborde. Laborde and Admiral Marquis, maritime prefect of Toulon, rejected Admiral

Darlan's appeals of November 10 and 11 for the fleet to sail for West Africa.[102] In response to German demands Laborde and Marquis asked their officers to pledge in writing never to fight against the Axis and to resist an Allied attack. Even though the Germans had recently snuffed out the last vestiges of French independence apart from French control of the fleet, all but one officer signed the pledge. In the early morning of November 27, 1942, in accordance with standing orders, the French fleet at Toulon—the pride of the helpless Darlan—was sunk by its crew when German troops moved into the port.[103]

Discipline was perhaps more seriously shaken in the African army; yet here, too, there were numerous proofs of a lingering faith in unquestioning obedience. The behavior of Admirals Derrien and Esteva in Tunisia is one example. Continued military obedience to Darlan is another.[104] After the worst of the confusion had passed —temporarily at least—Darlan remained the political and military chief of French North Africa. General Noguès yielded the powers transferred to him by Vichy back to Darlan on learning of the secret cables and discovering that the admiral was not a prisoner of the Americans. Even General Giraud, who quickly discovered the loyalty of the army to Darlan, now accepted the post of military commander in chief under the admiral. Those officers who had attempted to facilitate the American landings of November 8 were subjected to rough treatment: General Béthouart and Colonel Magnan were arrested and almost shot on order of General Noguès; General Mast and Colonel Baril fled to the French Levant. Though later officially pardoned for their *manquement à la discipline,* they continued to be treated with some disdain by their colleagues and with the exception of General de Montsabert, who was placed in charge of a small group of civilian volunteers, were shunted off into liaison rather than command assignments.[105] Indeed, the African army had not ceased to fear and reproach acts of military indiscipline.

Confusion in the leadership of the African army was not at an end. First, on December 24, 1942, came the assassination of Admiral Darlan at the hands of a young monarchist.[106] Within a matter of hours General Giraud was designated as the new high commissioner by the Empire Council, composed of Generals Bergeret, Noguès,

Giraud, and Governor General Boisson from Dakar. With Darlan removed from the scene, Giraud could now replace him without disrupting army unity and discipline. The end of the power struggle was not yet in sight, however, for eventually Giraud was forced to deal with De Gaulle, who won an increasingly strong loyalty from French resistance groups in the *métropole*. The intricacies of the struggle between Giraud and De Gaulle need not concern us here. Suffice it to say that Giraud was sorely outmatched in both political interest and acumen. While De Gaulle viewed his role as one of broad political leadership over the entire French nation, Giraud is reported once to have told General Mark Clark, "I am not a politician. I am a soldier. All I want is the post of commander in chief." [107] Outmaneuvered at every turn, Giraud found himself successively: a copresident with De Gaulle of the Comité Français de la Libération Nationale (June, 1943), commander in chief of French armed forces with limited powers as a member of the government (late July, 1943), and a theoretical commander in chief without membership in the government (November, 1943). Finally, in April, 1944, Giraud suffered the retraction of even his theoretical powers as commander in chief and, in preference to the classic inspector general's post reserved for displaced commanders, opted for retirement.[108]

It is not surprising that continuing confusion and rivalry in Algiers had a corrosive effect on the morale and discipline of the African army, which was now preparing to play an active role in the North African campaign. Colonel Jules Roy was one of those unit commanders who waited impatiently for the arrival of new weapons needed to prepare his ill-equipped troops for combat. His impressions of Algiers in the spring of 1943 are revealing:

> When I rushed to Algiers to discover how long it would be before we would have our weapons, I returned crushed. Generals and politicians were fighting among themselves and attempted their own little revolutions within government and military headquarters. Odds and ends of armies shut themselves up within dissident bastions and tried to enlist supporters. Their recruiting sergeants set up their platforms on the street corners. They did not say that they were better equipped than us, nor that they worked more than us. They simply boasted about their pay, their uniforms, or the prestige of their leaders.[109]

With Giraud, De Gaulle—and Pétain—all claiming to represent governmental legitimacy, the tradition of military obedience to civil government quite naturally gave way to a new style of feudal loyalty to a powerful patron. The old formula was no longer relevant.

The rapid ascendancy realized by De Gaulle, the brigadier general, over Giraud, his four-starred rival, united in the summer of 1943 the political and military command of the African army with that of Free French troops, which had been battling against the Axis armies in North Africa ever since January of 1941. Unity of command, however, did not cushion the tradition of military obedience from further erosive blows when army and nation again finally met amidst an atmosphere of hostility, rivalry, and purge.

The French troops which fought with their British and American allies across Tunisia, up through Italy, and then up through the south of France, were often denied the hero's welcome which they merited. The regular army, especially in the eyes of the internal-resistance forces, was the army of defeat, the army of Vichy and the armistice. The early exploits of the Free French did not redeem the African army; and it was the African army—not the Gaullists of 1940 and 1941—who made up the bulk of liberating French forces. Moreover, Free French forces were too few to spare Frenchmen the humiliation of owing their liberation to foreign troops. Even Gaullists of the earliest hour met reserve and apprehension on the part of the internal resistance, particularly in the case of communist resistance elements which had entered the fray only when Russia—not France—was in jeopardy.

The Gaullist provisional government, as well as the regular army, was occasionally the object of abuse at the hands of the internal resistance. The most serious clash was occasioned by the Vercors disaster in July, 1944, when several hundred guerrillas of the Forces Françaises de l'Intérieur (F.F.I.) were killed in a mountainous area southwest of Grenoble. At the height of the battle, which had been launched prematurely, though with the accord of London, the leaders of the Vercors resistance radioed messages to Algiers and London stating that if aid were not sent immediately (it was not), leaders of the provisional government would be considered "criminals and cowards." [110] In Algiers one of the two communist members of De Gaulle's government, Fernand Grenier, commissioner for air, accused the government in a press conference of failing to support the Vercors guerrillas, many of whom were members of the communist-led Franc Tireurs et Partisans (F.T.P.).[111] The Vercors disaster demonstrated and reinforced the justified mutual suspicion of the Gaullist and communist camps.[112]

Mutual distrust characterized, not only relations between Gaullists and communists, but also those generally between regular army troops and the F.F.I. Professional officers tended to underestimate the military value of amateurs and guerrillas, though one of the three branches of the F.F.I., the Organisation de la Résistance de l'Armée, was composed primarily of regular officers and enlisted men from the armistice army after its dissolution in November, 1942.[113] The guerrillas, in return, had little sympathy or respect for professional soldiering.[114] General de Lattre de Tassigny, commander of the First Free French Army (which fought its way north from the Mediterranean), was one of the first to realize that an *amalgame* of regulars and irregulars was essential to national unity as well as to military efficiency.[115] De Lattre exercised masterly skill in synthesizing some 137,000 irregulars from the F.F.I. with his own 250,000 regulars within the First Army. Yet the *amalgame* did not succeed in reuniting army and nation. As this army fought its way into Alsace in the fall of 1944, De Lattre noted a serious decline in the morale of his troops. He analyzed the morale problem perceptively in a report to De Gaulle:

> From one end of the hierarchy to the other, the general impression is that the Nation is ignoring and abandoning them. Some go so far as to imagine that the regular army, coming from overseas, is being deliberately sacrificed. The profound cause of the malaise resides in the non-participation of the nation in the war.[116]

Already, even before the hated *boches* had been defeated, the French Army became acquainted with its new and embittering role of servant to an ungrateful and disinterested nation. Even De Gaulle's recurring battles with his allies for the purpose of salvaging the pride of Frenchmen in their nation and their army failed to save French military men from social isolation and degradation.[117]

Just as the last year of war revealed a new and enduring estrangement of army and nation, so it was in that period that a final serious blow was struck against the military tradition of unquestioning obedience. Liberation was the occasion for a massive *règlement des comptes* as communist partisans took control in many areas. There were undoubtedly some regular armistice army officers among the estimated thirty to forty thousand victims of summary executions.[118] More significant for the future of the army, however, were the sanctions taken against all military officers who had not joined the resistance by the time of the Normandy invasion on June 6, 1944. In the fall of 1944 all such officers who could not present proof of acts of resistance outside the *maquis* were placed on inactive status. By the end of 1947 almost three thousand army officers had been purged or "separated" from the active roles for collaboration or failure to join the resistance.[119] Among them were at least a few like the Captain Champcourt of Jacques Weygand's narrative, who felt honor bound by his oath of allegiance to the marshal.[120] Moreover, the attitude of officers during the occupation was likely a factor in selecting others of the more than twelve thousand army officers separated from active duty in the three years following liberation. The often capricious nature of the purges and separations produced widespread protests and resentment, not only among the victims, but also among their friends and fellow officers who remained on active duty.[121]

Officers drawn deeply into politics in the years from 1958 to 1962 frequently explained that their experiences in World War II had proven the inadequacy of unquestioning obedience as a trustworthy safeguard of military honor and had demonstrated the necessity of reflection and political choice in the exercise of military duty. "Since the Second World War no one in the navy still believes in unquestioning obedience," I was told by one navy commander. Indeed, had not the new legitimacy identified military duty and honor with rebellion of the earliest hour against the old Pétainist legitimacy? Are we to conclude then that the primary causes of postwar civil-military clashes are to be found in the collapse of military discipline in World War II? I should think not, though those World War II experiences undoubtedly lowered military resistance to a praetorian urge produced primarily by other factors. Military discipline was hardly in ruins in 1945, despite the frequent confusion of the war years. Throughout the war, most French officers had simply followed orders from their superiors at each turning. The core of the postwar French Army was the 120,000-man armistice army of Africa, which provided the great majority of important commanders during the liberation and after.[122] Looking back over the conflicting backgrounds of the regular army and internal resistance contingents in his First Free French Army, General de Lattre de Tassigny later recalled that in 1944-45 there was "nothing . . . more representative of traditional military virtues" than the regulars who made up two-thirds of his troops.[123] Had there been no lengthy and frustrating colonial wars after 1945, civilian control could have been restored over a disciplined military establishment.

Yet if World War II experiences did not force the French Army into its postwar political adventures, they undoubtedly played a supporting role. In an institution as attuned to tradition as the army, precedents are important. And the lesson of World War II seemed clear: De Gaulle the rebel had emerged a national hero, while discipline-bound officers of the armistice army often found themselves the objects of purge and disgrace. Apparently there were times when military men were obliged to decide who represented the true interests of the nation. Once the military tradition of unquestioning subordination to governmental authority was crippled, there could be no certainty—in Algeria or after—that the nation's military arms would not be turned against herself.

1. A striking description of these weaknesses within the regular army in 1939–40 is found in Marc Bloch, *L'étrange défaite* (Paris: Colin, 1957), pp. 114–30, 137–38 (written in 1940).

2. Chapman, *Soldiers and Governments*, p. 71 n. 17.

3. See Reynaud's *Le Problème militaire français* (Paris: Flammarion, 1937), pp. 89–91 (reprinted in 1945). Reynaud also was one of the few politicians who took up De Gaulle's plea for new special mechanized units.

4. Gamelin remarks quite accurately in his memoirs that General Weygand, his replacement, was invested with an authority which he had been denied (Gamelin, *Servir*, Vol. I, Introduction).

5. General Sir Edward Spears, Churchill's personal representative to the

French Ministry of War in 1940, reports that Gamelin attempted to under-mine Georges' position as a rival by withdrawing some of his valuable staff members (Spears, *Assignment to Catastrophe* [New York: Wyn, 1954–55], I, 50).

6. Challener, in *Total War and Cold War*, pp. 95–100.

7. Chapman, *Soldiers and Governments*, p. 71 n. 18.

8. Bankwitz, "Weygand," especially pp. 304, 376–77, 435–36, 457–58, 462–66, 610–11, and chap. 14. See also Bankwitz, "Maxime Weygand and the Fall of France: A Study in Civil-Military Relations," *Journal of Modern History*, XXX, No. 3 (September, 1959), 225–29.

9. Weygand, *Mémoires* (Paris: Flammarion, 1950), III, 298.

10. *Ibid.*

11. On June 6, 1940, in conversation with General Spears, Pétain blamed defeat on schoolmasters and politicians, not generals. "The country has been rotted by politics," Spears quotes him as saying. "The people can no longer discern the face of France through the veil politicians have thrown over it" (Spears, *Assignment to Catastrophe*, II, 84–85). In regard to the enmity between Pétain and Weygand, Spears mentions that in one of his conversations with Pétain the marshal once referred to Weygand as a Jesuit (*ibid.*, p. 200).

12. See above, Chapter 2.

13. De Gaulle, *Mémoires*, I, 78–79.

14. Robert Aron, *Histoire de Vichy* (Paris: Fayard, 1954), pp. 16–17 (hereinafter cited as *Vichy*); *Procès Pétain*, I, 220–22 (Weygand's report to the cabinet on June 12, on false information from an aide, that Paris had been taken over by the communists); Weygand, *Mémoires*, III, 216; and Bankwitz, "Weygand," pp. 755–56.

15. Quoted by Aron, *Vichy*, p. 23. See also Weygand, *Mémoires*, III, 217–18.

16. Aron, *Vichy*, p. 44; and Weygand, *Mémoires*, III, 227. The critical events of June 15 are described by Aron on pp. 39–45. See also Bankwitz, *Journal of Modern History*, pp. 237–39; Spears, *Assignment to Catastrophe*, II, 244–75, Reynaud, *La France a sauvé l'Europe*, II, 334–42; and Albert Lebrun (then President of the Republic), *Témoignage* (Paris: Plon, 1945), pp. 80–82.

17. Aron, *Vichy*, pp. 49–51.

18. *Ibid.*, pp. 59–61.

19. Jeanneney, *Procès Pétain*, I, 191.

20. See Reynaud's testimony in *Procès Pétain*, I, 74–83, and especially his memoirs, *La France a sauvé l'Europe*, II, 446–52. In the revised version of his memoirs, now entitled *Au coeur de la melée* (Paris: Flammarion, 1951), Reynaud appears less certain of the "military plot" thesis (pp. 914–56).

21. The original accusation is found in *Procès Pétain*, I, 23–31 (see especially pp. 24–26). In the prosecutor general's final statement in the Pétain trial, see *ibid.*, II, 900–910.

22. Bankwitz, *Journal of Modern History*, pp. 235–36 and notes; and *New York Times* (hereinafter cited as NYT), May 7, 1948. See also Bank-witz, "Weygand," pp. 752–64. Bankwitz concludes that there was no plan for a military coup in 1940, either in June or in July.

23. Albert Lebrun, *Témoignage*, pp. 72–87, 113–16; and Lebrun's testimony in *Procès Pétain*, I, 151–58.

24. Weygand later argued that this was the course which Reynaud should have followed if convinced that the commander in chief's demands were unacceptable (Weygand, *Mémoires*, III, 234–35; and testimony in *Procès Pétain*, I, 399–400).

25. Bankwitz, *Journal of Modern History*, p. 238.

26. On June 11, with Reynaud's accord, General de Gaulle, then under secretary of state for national defense, approached General Huntzinger and found him willing to accept appointment as commander in chief and to carry on the war from North Africa (De Gaulle, *Mémoires* I, 69). A stronger government could have effected the change in military chiefs and made it stick.

27. Bloch, *L'étrange défaite*, pp. 211–12.

28. De Gaulle, *Mémoires*, I, 35–37 (on the investiture of Reynaud); and Bloch, *L'étrange défaite*, pp. 176–212.

29. Norman Gibbs, "Winston Churchill and the British War Cabinet," in Coles (ed.), *Total War and Cold War*, pp. 27–42.

30. Bloch, *L'étrange défaite*, p. 85. For a graphic fictional account of the rapid demoralization and disintegration of French defenses told by Major Jacques Weygand, son of the commander in chief, see *Le Serment* (Paris: Flammarion, 1960), pp. 46, 77–78.

31. De Gaulle, *Mémoires*, I, 47, 64–65. For a strikingly similar description, see Bloch, *L'étrange défaite*, p. 144. The "defeat by bewilderment" thesis is defended by John C. Cairns, "Along the Road Back to France 1940," *American Historical Review*, LXIV, No. 3 (April, 1959), 583–603.

32. Aron, *Vichy*, pp. 140–55, describes the National Assembly vote. Fear played a part in that vote, but so also did parliamentary confidence in Pétain, belief that Germany had won the war, and the feeling that such a rapid defeat had disproven the validity of the *régime des partis*. Weygand's belief that total German victory was imminent was told to De Gaulle (De Gaulle, *Mémoires*, I, 59) and to Reynaud (Reynaud, *La France a sauvé l'Europe*, II, 340), among others.

33. De Gaulle, *France and Her Army*, p. 104.

34. De Gaulle himself actively led a growing portion of the army and nation in an attempt to undo the decision of 1940.

35. One French officer wrote in his diary: "Naturally, the idea of a dictatorship in France, for the moment at least, is in the minds of both officers and men. Literally I have never met a single one of my *poilus* who has not expressed his disgust for the parliamentary regime and has not insisted on the Deputies and their policy as being solely responsible for the disaster" (*A French Officer's Diary*, August 23, 1939–October 1, 1940 [London: Cambridge University Press, 1942], p. 97). See also Spears, *Assignment to Catastrophe*, II, 64; Bankwitz, *Journal of Modern History*, p. 240; Bloch, *L'étrange défaite*, pp. 212–14; and J. Weygand, *Le Serment*, p. 46.

36. Quoted by General Victor Bourret in his violent indictment of the high command, *La Tragédie de l'Armée Française* (Paris: La Table Ronde, 1947), pp. 44–45. Though underlying social and political factors were unquestionably significant, the French defeat of 1940 was primarily a defeat of the French Army. An outmoded military doctrine and an incompetent military command were more to blame for defeat than were governmental leaders, as the Riom trials of 1941–42 tended to indicate. See Maurice Ribet, *Le Procès de Riom* (Paris: Flammarion, 1945); and Challener, *The French Theory of the Nation in Arms*, chap. 7.

37. Even the future vice president of the Vichy council, Admiral Darlan, then chief of staff of the navy, refrained from threatening to disobey a government order, though he made known his opposition to continuation of the war from North Afrca.

38. The text of the June 18 appeal is found in De Gaulle, *Mémoires*, I, 331–32.

39. De Gaulle was quite aware of the revolutionary step he was taking on June 18: "A mesure que s'envolaient les mots irrévocables, je sentais en moi-même se terminer une vie, celle que j'avais menée dans le cadre d'une France solide et d'une indivisible armée. A quarante-neuf ans, j'entrais dans l'aventure, comme un homme que le destin jetait hors de toutes les séries" (*ibid.*, p. 90).

40. De Gaulle, *Mémoires*, I, 91, 332–35.

41. The text of De Gaulle's reply is found in volume I of his memoirs, pages 332–33.

42. Aron, *Vichy*, p. 281.

43. Jeanneney, *Procès Pétain*, I, 191; Aron, *Vichy*, pp. 143, 162–63; Alfred Cobban, "Vichy France," in Arnold and Veronica M. Toynbee (eds.), *Hitler's Europe*, "Survey of International Affairs, 1939–1946" [London: Oxford University Press, 1954], pp. 350–51; Bloch, *L'étrange défaite*, pp. 50–51; and Spears, *Assignment to Catastrophe*, I, 200.

44. Paul Kecskemeti, *Stragetic Surrender* (Stanford, Calif.: Stanford University Press, 1958), p. 69. The author, writing for the Rand Corporation, raised considerable congressional controversy over this work.

45. Generals Legentilhomme from Djibouti, Catroux from Indochina, and Petit from South America; Admiral Muselier (a bitter rival of Darlan); and Colonels de Larminat, Fontaine, and Angenot (Robert O. Paxton, "Army Officers in Vichy France" [Unpublished Ph.D. dissertation, Harvard University, 1963], p. 1 and notes 1–3).

46. De Gaulle, *Mémoires*, I, 94–100; and Paxton, "Army Officers in Vichy France," p. 1.

47. De Gaulle, *Mémoires*, I, 136.

48. J. Weygand, *Le Serment*, p. 80.

49. De Gaulle, *Mémoires*, I, 48, 116–17, 136; and Paxton, "Army Officers in Vichy France," pp. 154–79 (regarding anti-German sentiments in the officer corps).

50. Paxton, "Army Officers in Vichy France," pp. 193–223; Bloch, *L'étrange défaite*, pp. 99–108; Cobban, *Hitler's Europe*, pp. 376–77.

51. In his careful study of the armistice army, Paxton emphasizes the narrow nationalism which came to characterize French military attitudes from 1940 to 1942 ("Army Officers in Vichy France," chap. 2 ["The Officers View the War"] and chap. 3 ["The Officers View the Participants"]).

52. Aron *Vichy*, pp. 102–12.

53. From a message to the nation entitled "L'Education nationale," published in *Revue des deux mondes*, August 15, 1940, pp. 249–53. The quotation is found on p. 250.

54. From Pétain's messages labeled "Paroles aux Français," as quoted by Aron, *Vichy*. pp. 210–11. For the traditional army view, see above pp. 24, 39–40.

55. [Lyautey], *Revue des deux mondes*, pp. 443–59, especially p. 457. The quotation from Pétain is found in Aron, *Vichy*, p. 213. Since long before the fall of France, Pétain had been fascinated by the notion of moral renewal through sacrifice (*ibid.*, p. 34). For example, he told General Spears on

June 12, 1940, "We must pay now, and pay dearly for the anarchy we have indulged in for so long" (Spears, *Assignment to Catastrophe*, II, 174).

56. The armistice army's ventures into education are explored in some depth by Paxton, "Army Officers in Vichy France," pp. 455–511.

57. Robert Hervet, *Les Chantiers de la jeunesse* (Paris: Editions France-Empire, 1962); and Paxton, "Army Officers in Vichy France," pp. 480–95.

58. Aron, *Vichy*, p. 421.

59. During the interwar years only six of forty-two governments called military officers to the post of minister of war. Many of the army's friends in the chamber were also lost as officer-deputies declined from over forty in 1919 to ten in 1936 (Dogan, *Revue française de sociologie*, pp. 88–90).

60. Robert Aron, citing an unnamed witness, claims that Weygand told the cabinet meeting of June 3, 1941, "Je ferai tirer sur les allemands contre les ordres de mon gouvernement, s'il le faut, afin qu'ils ne pénètrent pas en Afrique . . ." (*Vichy*, p. 437). See also *ibid.*, pp. 165, 253–54, 282, 438–42, 459–62.

61. Of these, General Bridoux was the only strong collaborationist. A protégé of Ambassador Abetz, he actively favored military collaboration with the Germans and continued to work with the Germans near the end of the war after Pétain and even Laval had refused to exercise any governmental functions (Aron, *Vichy*, pp. 500, 623, 655, 714–15; and Paxton, "Army Officers in Vichy France," pp. 133–42).

62. *Ibid.*, pp. 174–75; and Cobban, *Hitler's Europe*, pp. 376–77. For a more detailed discussion of officers in government see Paxton, "Army Officers in Vichy France," pp. 393–97.

63. Aron, *Vichy*, p. 175, quoting Cardinal Liénart.

64. In May, 1941, Darlan is reported to have told Hitler that "la France est toute disposée à aider l'Allemagne à gagner la guerre" (*ibid.*, p. 432). He agreed to allow Germany to use air bases and transportation facilities in Syria; he approved a German submarine base in Dakar and the German right of passage in Tunisia. Admiral Auphan, however, was a more moderate voice, especially in the wake of the Mers-el-Kébir attack (*ibid.*, pp. 111–13, 320, 428, 432-34).

65. For example, see Reboul, *Revue des deux mondes*, pp. 378–97.

66. Paxton, "Army Officers in Vichy France," pp. 442–45.

67. This sentiment was expressed by several officers to Paxton, *ibid.*, p. 366.

68. [A senior officer], "l'Armée de l'armistice," *Revue des deux mondes*, February 1, 1941, pp. 357–58, and *passim*.

69. "Je jure fidélité à la personne du Chef de l'Etat de lui obéir en tout ce qu'il me commandera pour le bien du service et le succès des armes de la France" (J. Weygand, *Le Serment*, pp. 18–19).

70. *Ibid.*, p. 23. Regarding Pétain's popularity among officers, see Paxton, "Army Officers in Vichy France," pp. 369–77.

71. See below, this chapter.

72. Aron, *Vichy*, pp. 224–35.

73. Paxton, "Army Officers in Vichy France," pp. 230–53.

74. De Gaulle, *Mémoires*, I, 146–48.

75. Aron, *Vichy*, p. 447.

76. S. O. Playfair, *The Mediterranean and Middle East*, (United Kingdom Series, "History of the Second World War" [London: Her Majesty's Stationery

Office, 1956], II, 221). De Gaulle again claimed lack of British co-operation (De Gaulle, *Mémoires*, I, 214, 219). The Syrian campaign is described by Aron (in *Vichy*, pp. 443-47) and by De Gaulle (*Mémoires*, I, 193–219), who provides rich details regarding his interminable clashes with the British, this time over who was to administer Syria. Quite without British agreement, De Gaulle simply ordered General Catroux to "prendre immédiatement en main l'autorité sur toute l'étendue du territoire de la Syrie et du Liban, quelque opposition qu'il puisse rencontrer de la part de qui ce soit" (*ibid.*, p. 209).

77. Quoted by Maître Isorni, defense attorney for General Pierre-Marie Bigot in Cottaz (ed.), *Les Procès du putsch d'avril et du complot de Paris* (Paris: Nouvelles Editions Latines, 1962), p. 24 (hereinafter cited as *Procès du putsch*).

78. Other members included Colonel Lorber, commander of the Bône sub-division, and Lieutenant Colonel Jousse, who had participated in an earlier unsuccessful plot against the representatives of Vichy in North Africa (Aron, *Vichy*, pp. 539–43). A fuller discussion of French military reactions to the Allied landings is found in Paxton, "Army Officers in Vichy France," pp. 511–77.

79. Cobban, *Hitler's Europe*, p. 400; and Aron, *Vichy*, p. 547.

80. *Ibid.*, p. 548.

81. George F. Howe, *Northwest Africa: Seizing the Initiative in the West* ("U.S. Army in World War II. The Mediterranean Theater of Operations" [Washington: Department of the Army, 1957], pp. 173, 228.

82. The Allied decision drew strong protest from De Gaulle, who argued that to deal with Darlan was to renounce "le caractère morale de cette guerre" (*Mémoires*, I, 64–65).

83. Representing the typical state of mind among officers in North Africa, the Blida air base commander, Colonel Montrelay, told Giraud upon his arrival, "J'exécuterai vos ordres, mon Général, mais je vous demande de me les faire venir par la voie hiérarchique" (Aron, *Vichy*, p. 556). See also Mark W. Clark, *Calculated Risk* (New York: Harper, 1950), pp. 105, 108, 116.

84. Aron, *Vichy*, p. 549.

85. *Ibid.*; and Madame Chamine, *La Querelle des généraux* (Paris: Editions Albin Michel, 1952), p. 112 (hereinafter cited as *La Querelle*).

86. The question of the secret cables has been embroiled in political controversy. De Gaulle implies in his memoirs that the story of the secret investiture was a fabrication to allow Darlan to legitimize his authority (*Mémoires*, II, 60). Since all copies were supposedly destroyed, their existence cannot be proven conclusively. Yet in view of the testimony of a number of the persons said to have been involved (including General Juin, Admirals Auphan and Noguès, and Pétain's physician, Dr. Ménétral), it seems probable that they were sent. See Paxton, "Army Officers in Vichy France," p. 566 n.; Aron, *Vichy*, p. 560; and Chamine (whose obvious sympathy for Pétain probably led her to exaggerate the marshal's role in the affair), *La Querelle*, pp. 119, 160.

87. Aron, *Vichy*, p. 567.

88. Chamine, *La Querelle*, p. 159.

89. The story of the Tunisian command from November 8 to November 19 is told in detail by Chamine, *La Querelle*, pp. 173–247. Regarding changing orders from Algiers, see also Clark, *Calculated Risk*, pp. 116–18.

90. Chamine, *La Querelle*, pp. 223–31, 234; and Paxton, "Army Officers in Vichy France," pp. 572–74.

91. Bergeret, *Procès Pétain*, II, pp. 718–19; Aron, *Vichy*, pp. 577–78; and Chamine, *La Querelle*, pp. 274–81.

92. Chamine, *La Querelle*, p. 245 n.

93. Quoted by Chamine, *La Querelle*, p. 547. See also *ibid.*, pp. 347–48.

94. *Le Métier des armes* (Paris: Julliard, 1948), p. 41.

95. *Ibid.*, pp. 54–57.

96. *Ibid.*, pp. 74, 79, 80.

97. *Ibid.*, p. 61.

98. Quoted in *Procès du putsch*, p. 224.

99. Paxton, "Army Officers in Vichy France," pp. 577–84.

100. Aron, in *Vichy*, pp. 554, 557, and 564, asserts that this initiative, plus the actual displacement of army headquarters, was the work of General Verneau, army chief of staff, whose orders were then severely countermanded by Bridoux. After careful investigation, however, Paxton concludes that Bridoux had a hand in issuing the initial orders, and Verneau participated in the counterorders of November 10 ("Army Officers in Vichy France," pp. 583–85).

101. De Lattre's attempt at resistance, his capture, and his escape are described by his biographer, General Sir Guy Salisbury-Jones, *So Full a Glory* (New York: Praeger, 1955), pp. 103–21.

102. Chamine, *La Querelle*, pp. 118, 284–85; and Aron, *Vichy*, p. 579.

103. Aron, *Vichy*, pp. 582–83.

104. Chamine, *La Querelle*, pp. 123, 124, 127, 132–33, 136, 139.

105. De Gaulle, *Mémoires*, II, 80; and Chamine, *La Querelle*, pp. 350 n. 1, 550–51.

106. A detailed account of the assassination and surrounding intrigues is found in *ibid.*, pp. 435–532.

107. *Ibid.*, p. 123.

108. De Gaulle, *Mémoires*, II, 87–182, especially pp. 124, 163, 178–81, 206–7.

109. Roy, *Le Métier des armes*, p. 216.

110. Robert Aron, *Histoire de la libération de la France* (Paris: Fayard, 1959), p. 282 (hereinafter cited as *Libération*). The Vercors battle and its ramifications are described on pp. 282–318.

111. On an ultimatum from De Gaulle, Grenier retracted his attack in order to remain in the government; in September, 1944, he was replaced (Aron *Libération*, pp. 284–85).

112. Even within the F.F.I., the Franc Tireurs were often feared by non-Communists. For example, in late August, 1944, when the Germans withdrew from Bordeaux, Colonel Druilhe and Colonel Adeline, both regular army officers now in command of F.F.I. units, rushed their troops into the city to take control before nearby F.T.P. units arrived. There were suspicions at the time that the F.T.P. was under orders to establish the "République des Soviets du sud de la France" (*ibid.*, pp. 593–94).

113. *Ibid.*, pp. 310–11, 252–53).

114. F.F.I. units lost one-third of their personnel when on August 23, 1944, the provisional government required an enlistment for the duration of the war from each man (*ibid.*, p. 664).

115. J. de Lattre de Tassigny, *Histoire de la Première Armée Française* (Paris: Plon, 1949), chap. 7 (entitled "l'Amalgame"), esp. p. 183.

116. Cited by De Gaulle, *Mémoires*, III, 165.

117. Among other matters those battles concerned the Free French demand for recognition as the legal French government, an ordered tactical retreat from liberated Strasbourg, and the creation of a French zone of occupation in Germany. In the last two instances De Gaulle simply ordered his troops to disregard orders from Allied headquarters. See Aron, *Libération*, pp. 62–73; Forrest C. Pogue, "Political Problems of a Coalition Government," in Coles (ed.), *Total War and Cold War*, pp. 113–14, 122–23; and De Gaulle, *Mémoires*, III, 168–75.

118. The estimate is by Aron, *Libération*, pp. 655, 724.

119. According to official figures provided by the army secretary of state in response to a parliamentary written question from M. Serre, Deputy from Oran in May, 1949, a total of 658 army officers were purged and 12,679 were separated between 1945 and 1948. Of those listed as "separated," it was explained that 2,299 were released "as a result of the work of the purge commissions." The secretaries of state for air and for the navy replied to identical questions, indicating that in the same years 28 air officers and 50 navy officers were purged, and 892 air officers and 808 navy officers were separated. No information was given on the number of separations resulting from reports of the purge commissions (*Journal officiel, Débats parlementaires, Assemblée Nationale*, May 19, 1949, pp. 2704–5 [hereinafter cited as *J.O., Déb., A.N.*]).

120. J. Weygand, *Le Serment*, pp. 233–34. On the whole, however, J. Weygand exaggerates the importance of the oath and neglects other factors which inhibited resistance activity among officers.

121. "Malaise dans l'Armée: L'Intégration et l'épuration des cadres officiers," *Etudes*, No. 249 (April-May-June, 1946), pp. 77–85; Commandant Jean Prost, "Le Recrutement des officiers" (thesis, Ecole Supérieure de Guerre, 72nd promotion, 1960), p. 8; Jean Planchais, *Le Malaise de l'armée* (Paris: Plon, 1958), p. 19; and Paxton, "Army Officers in Vichy France," pp. 611–12, 619–20.

122. Paxton, "Army Officers in Vichy France," pp. 5–7.

123. De Lattre de Tassigny, *Histoire de la Première Armée Française*, p. 180.

Part II

The Army and the Nation: Isolation and Estrangement

Chapter 4

Reluctant Mercenaries

The years following 1945 in France might be described as the "postwar" period by a French civilian, but hardly by a French soldier. If France as a nation escaped from war in 1945, her army did not, or at least did only briefly until the outbreak of the Indochinese war in 1946. From that time forward until 1962, with the exception of a four-month respite in 1954, the French Army was continuously at war. A French Army which wanted desperately to be national in character found itself left like an army of mercenaries to fight wars which attracted neither the active support nor the continued interest of Frenchmen at home.

Bitterness and anger smoldered within the army until May, 1958, when military support for a revolt led by civilians in Algiers finally destroyed the Fourth Republic. Only nineteen months later, in the Week of the Barricades, the new De Gaulle republic was itself threatened by a civilian revolt in Algiers. Again, as in 1958, the revolt won some military support, especially among paratroop and psychological-action officers. But in the face of a strong and popular President of the republic, the officer corps was now hesitant and divided, and De Gaulle regained control in Algiers. In April, 1961, a new revolt was launched, this time led entirely by professional officers. Again, however, De Gaulle was too strong, the officer corps hesitant; and in contrast to their attitude of May, 1958, the large body of conscripts in Algeria developed a consciousness of their power and rejected the authority of the mutineers. The putsch failed, but the Secret Army Organization lived on as a threat to the Fifth Republic and as a fomenter of sedition in the officer ranks.

After 1945 the French Army was drawn deep into politics: henceforth our attention will be directed to an examination of the multiple and interrelated factors in the period from 1945 to 1962 which contributed to that politicization. The events of May, 1958, January, 1960, and April, 1961, are described in Chapter IX.

Since 1815 the normal life of the career officer in France had been one of semi-isolation from civilian society, a separateness viewed from the military side with an ambivalent mixture of pride and resentment. In the years from 1940 to 1944 that isolation of the military community was deepened as a result of a new wave of antimilitarism in the civilian population which was inspired by the armistice army's humiliating defeat in 1940, its pretentious claims to elite status and national leadership from 1940 to 1942, and, for those officers stationed in the *métropole*, its docile submission when the Germans swarmed into the Vichy zone in November, 1942.[1] Even though the armistice army of Africa fought valiantly in the second battle of France, the professional officer's share of the victor's glory was limited severely by the popularity of the internal resistance and the spectacle of the *napthalinards*—those armistice army officers who took their uniforms out of mothballs just in time to appear at the hour of liberation.

Yet if the French Army's hour of glory was restrained and brief in 1944, career soldiers soon discovered that defense of the imperial frontiers was an even more thankless task than defense of the homeland. The professional soldier won little fame in defending French Indochina against a determined revolutionary enemy; rather, he soon heard from the mouths of French Communist Party spokesmen, and from non-communists as well, that he was engaged in a "dirty war," a "shameful war," a "war which dares not speak its name." [2]

The French Communist Party emerged from World War II having dimmed the French voter's memory of the Molotov–Ribbentrop pact with a brilliant communist resistance effort. The party now controlled over a quarter of the French electorate and, until 1947, participated in the tripartite government coalition.

Even beyond the Party's electorate the "peace" theme of communist propaganda after 1945 struck resoundingly against the war-weariness of a population which had lost faith in its army and saw no more useful function for it.[3] In the face of a communist-led revolutionary movement in Indochina, it is not surprising that French political opinion was seriously divided. The Vichy years had weakened and discredited the nationalistic Right, leaving the defense of the French Empire to socialists and Popular Republicans (the new French Christian Democratic party). The Communist Party drew, in its "pacifist" and "anticolonialist" wake, a small group of *Progressistes* (fellow-travelers), who, as antinationalists without the excuse of dógma, became the blackest of all villains in French military literature.[4] Moreover, though in the early years of the Indochinese war the majority of Frenchmen clearly favored French retention of the colony, non-communist opinion regarding the war was marked from the beginning by hesitation, indifference, and a goodly tinge of guilt.[5] Throughout the postwar world, colonialism was being stripped of its defenses. And the French, so we are told by numerous military writers, are plagued, not only by a declining patriotic spirit, but also by an immobilizing susceptibility to guilt.[6]

The army was not completely without defenders, however, especially as the traditionally nationalist Right slowly regained its strength. Again, as in the Dreyfus Affair, the profound cleavages within French political society provided the army, willing or unwilling, with eager civilian defenders from among the enemies of the government. Serious political conflict regarding the goals and conduct of war often has a pernicious effect on civilian control of military forces. Even in the United States, where political cleavages are not so deep as in France, government control over American military forces was weakened during the Korean War as a result of the antiadministration political support eagerly proffered to General Douglas MacArthur by the conservative wing of the Republican party.[7] Conservative Republicans, like French ultra-nationalists during the Indochinese and Algerian wars, cried out against the "sellout" of national interests, "softness" on communism, and the presence of communists and fellow-travelers in government circles. Like their American counterparts, French officers did not all, by any means, accept permanent alliance with the political Right. Nevertheless, in 1958, 1960, and to a lesser degree in 1961, civilian discord clearly encouraged the entry of factions of the French Army into the political arena.

Condemned to fighting and losing unpopular wars, the French officer watched with mounting resentment as his prestige dropped from an already depressed level in 1945 to a position of social neglect and scorn unknown to his rank since the Bourbon restoration. Already in 1946 officers were regretting the "deep trench" which separated them from civilian society.[8] The material signs of the officer's declining prestige were obvious. In 1947 and 1948 a government commission dealt military morale a double blow: first, in bringing officers within a general salary plan for civil servants; and secondly, by assigning pay-index numbers somewhat below their earlier comparative standing to military cadre. Officers were generally incensed at being considered ordinary *fonctionnaires*. To the officer who conceived of the requirements of his profession—physical courage in particular—as antithetical to the government-clerk mentality, the new legal pay status of military cadre was simply another galling reminder that, like the republics of the ancient world when in decline, the French nation preferred a mercenary army to a truly national military force.[9]

In the words of René Pleven, minister of national defense in 1954, the pay scales set in 1947 and 1948 were "very unfavorable to the cadre of the Army." [10] It was the stated intention of the Lainé Commission of 1947 to downgrade military pay with respect to formerly comparable salaries in the judiciary and the state schools.[11] In a recent study of the French officer corps, Girardet, Thomas, and Bougu have taken the years 1890–1960 and traced the comparative salaries of seven officer grades from second lieutenant to brigadier general and twenty-one civil service ranks from elementary teacher to dean of a university faculty. While the rank order of brigadier general never dropped below third in the list of 28, the position of colonel fell from third place in 1945 to ninth in 1950 to thirteenth in 1960, that of lieutenant colonel from seventh in 1945 to fourteenth in 1950 to fifteenth in 1956 and 1960, and that of major from eleventh in 1945 to twelfth in 1950 to fourteenth in 1956 and 1960. Lesser comparative drops were experienced by lieutenants (from twentieth in 1945 to twenty-third in 1950) and second lieutenants (from twenty-fourth in 1945 to a tie for bottom place in 1950 and thereafter).[12] To take a few of the more striking comparisons, a newly promoted lieutenant colonel earned a base pay of 185,000 francs in 1945, as opposed to the 165,000 franc annual salary of a beginning university professor outside Paris. By 1950 the professor, with a salary of 759,000 inflated francs, had passed by the lieutenant colonel, who now earned 620,000 francs per year; in 1960 the professor had widened his lead—18,338 New Francs to 13,666 New Francs.[13] Similarly, a major at the top pay step within his grade earned 168,000 francs per year in 1945, as opposed to the 150,000 francs to which a beginning principal collector of customs was entitled. By 1950 their annual salaries were identical at 651,000 francs; by 1960 the customs collector had jumped to 18,338 New Francs, leaving far behind the major with his 14,834 New Francs.[14]

While the military officer was partially compensated by a wide variety of allowances, this type of fringe remuneration was also awarded generously to civilian civil servants after 1945 in preference to more permanent and more politically delicate revisions of base-pay scales.[15] Even when military allowances compensated for the officer's low base pay (as in the case of officers on overseas combat duty), he typically advanced in grade and pay more slowly than his civilian civil service counterparts and was forced to retire much earlier.[16]

In comparison with his counterparts in foreign armies, the French officer was even more impoverished. Another government commission in 1953 studied relative pay in various armies and discovered that the 95,000 francs per month, including allowances, then paid to a French major was only a third of the equivalent of 280,000 francs per month received by an American major, and well below the equivalent of 120,000 francs due a British major.[17] Two French captains remarked in 1959 that they were no better paid than British second lieutenants.[18] After 1948 the base pay indexes of military officers remained unchanged, though slight increases in allowances (notably, the bonuses established in 1954 for holders of military citations and military school diplomas)

provided limited relief, especially in the higher grades.[19] Nevertheless, the embittered correspondent whose letter burned the pages of
the *Message des forces armées* was undoubtedly not alone in
dismissing such measures as "tips" thrown to pacify an officer corps
caught in the throes of pauperization.[20]

War bonuses were partial compensation in monetary matters,
inasmuch as a captain's pay in Indochina could be as much as
tripled by special combat allowances. The officer's *malaise* was
not thereby alleviated, however: he was all the more struck on
his return for a tour of duty in the *métropole* by the meagerness of
his base pay. Moreover, war bonuses were cut in Algeria to a
maximum of 50 per cent of base pay,[21] a move which provoked
one officer to remark that the government's "psychological error"
in this matter had caused "profound disappointment" among officers in Algeria.[22] "Military service," that officer noted in his
Journal de marche, "is tending to become simply ordinary servitude, scarcely superior in a moral sense (since it is not in a
material sense) to that of a prefecture clerk." [23] The officer's pay in
Algeria remained sufficiently higher than his base pay so that he
not infrequently found in the prospect of returning to relative
poverty in the *métropole* yet another reason for clinging desperately to the cause of French Algeria. In 1960, when military
allowances often amounted to 100 per cent or more of an officer's
base pay in Algeria and only 35 to 50 per cent in the *métropole*,[24]
one second lieutenant opined that four-fifths of the army *malaise*
would be solved if salaries at home were raised to the equivalent
of those across the Mediterranean.[25] He was wrong, but not entirely.

Added to the officer's financial problems, and partly a function
of them, were the grave consequences of an acute national housing
shortage. In the spring of 1959 a mixed civilian and military
"military sociology committee" at the Ecole Supérieure de Guerre
conducted a survey which reached 700 officers, among them a
sample of 235 married officers who each had at least 13 years of
service.[26] Within this latter group the average family had moved
5 times in the 13-year period from 1946 to 1959, and a fourth of
the families had moved 7 or more times.[27] Moreover, the average
married officer in this sample spent almost 4 years of the 13 separated from his family.[28] Government controls which held rent on

permanent housing at relatively low rates offered little protection to the highly mobile officer corps. The private and volatile military review, *Message des forces armées*, conducted a questionnaire survey in 1956 concerning the "crisis of the army," addressing its inquiry to members of a Saint-Cyr military academy class which graduated during World War II.[29] The 76 respondents, the editors report, were even more disturbed by housing problems than by mediocre pay.

Even when the officer returned for a brief tour of duty in the *métropole*, he sometimes could not find or afford housing that would allow him to live with his family. The Ministry of National Defense estimated in 1956 that sixty-two thousand professional commissioned and noncommissioned officers in the three military services were in substandard housing—mostly in hotel rooms and units with poor sanitary facilities.[30] The government "Moderate Rent Housing" plan, under which some military personnel were included, placed officers into housing far inferior to that enjoyed by their former lycée friends who had chosen civilian careers.[31] Many shared the plight of Major Robert Lagrange, who, when assigned to Paris, was forced to live in a hotel room while his wife and children remained in Brittany with his parents-in-law.[32] The extent of the problem and its effect on morale is seen in the frequent attention given to it in *Message* and in the official *Revue militaire d'information*, which printed numerous reassuring reports of plans for military housing construction.[33]

Were material factors, particularly low pay and an acute housing problem, of fundamental importance, then, in creating the famous *malaise* of the French Army? I should think not, though they were undoubtedly significant, as they had been in the twenties,[34] as evidence of the degradation of the military estate. The Saint-Cyriens who responded to the questionnaire sent out by *Message* in 1956 shared a feeling that the officer had been materially and morally *déclassé*; yet their primary concern was with the "moral climate" associated with the salary and housing problems.[35] For at least a few, however, material factors were undoubtedly crucial, as in the case of the angry unnamed officer stationed in a "large city in the *métropole*" who unleashed his bitterness (as did many of his colleagues) in the pages of the *Message des forces armées*.[36]

He chided former contributors and correspondents for attributing the *trouble moral* in the army exclusively to such factors as successive defeats, the indifference of the nation, and unwise leadership:

> As for me, I have no false shame in denouncing our mediocre material condition as the essential cause of the profound crisis which the army is undergoing. Of course, there are other causes of that crisis; if, however, the betterment of the standard of living of military cadre is not a sufficient condition for resolving it, it is incontestably a necessary condition.
>
> Gentlemen, you desire a faithful and obedient army? Pay it.[37]

The editors of *Message* hastened to add in defense of military honor that, though declining material rewards were regrettable and worthy of attention, " . . . For us, faithfulness and obedience cannot be purchased. They must be merited." [38] The great majority of the leaders of military revolt in the late 1950's and early 60's would undoubtedly have shared this editorial view. In fact, one could expect most paratroop officers (so often in the vanguard of French military revolt in recent years) to denounce the materialist, bourgeois, desk-officer mentality of the correspondent, who was sheltered from war in a city of the *métropole*.[39] His irritation at being unable to entertain properly and at being forced to man a vacuum cleaner (in order to lighten the burden of his maidless wife) could only heighten the combat officer's contempt for certain noncombatant colleagues. Those officers who were most concerned about pay per se, and not as a symbol of abandonment by the nation, likely would have shied from the risks of military revolt.

Material impoverishment was only one of many signs of the neglect and scorn which were now the officer's lot. Uniforms became increasingly rare in French cities, as most officers preferred to promenade in more respectable civilian attire. Even at the prestigious Ecole de Guerre in Paris, similar to the American War College, officers frequently changed into civilian clothes before returning home at night, perhaps through a communist working-class district where a uniform might draw comments. One day in the early years of the Algerian war a French major in uniform prepared to board a bus in Paris. "Come on, lieutenant, all aboard," the conductor called to him, only to draw the rebuke from a lady passenger, "But don't you see, he's a foreigner." [40] And indeed, the major and his colleagues often felt themselves to be foreigners, or worse, when they returned to the *métropole*. Another important sign of declining military prestige was the startling drop in the number of applicants to Saint-Cyr. The wealthier classes generally were now discouraging their sons from a military career. [41]

The decline in military prestige was particularly galling to those very capable men who entered the officer corps just prior to World War II, when applicants to Saint-Cyr were particularly numerous. After fifteen to twenty years of service, most of these men found themselves still blocked in the grades of captain, major, and lieutenant colonel, understandably resentful at seeing their former lycée comrades of similar or lesser ability now far above them in status and in salary. [42] The problem of blockage was probably less serious than after World War I, and as a result of numerous casualties among lieutenants, it was nonexistent in the lower grades. By the mid-1950's, however, a discouraging "hump" had developed in the middle grades, retarding or blocking ready access to positions of high status and responsibility. [43] From 1948 to 1955 the average age of all colonels rose from forty-seven years and seven months to fifty years and seven months, and that of all captains from thirty-two years to thirty-four years and eight months. [44] It is not surprising that military disobedience and revolt in the years 1958 to 1961 drew much of their impetus from able officers in the middle grades. [45]

The social and psychological isolation of the army from French civilian society was deepened by physical isolation occasioned by colonial wars. The above-mentioned survey conducted in 1959 by the "military sociology committee" of the Ecole de Guerre found that among those 395 married and unmarried officers in the sample with at least 13-years service, 72 per cent had spent less than 6 of the previous 13 years in the *métropole*. [46] In 1958, the year of the *treize mai* crisis which overthrew the Fourth Republic, the average army officer in the middle grades had spent at least one 30-month tour of duty in Indochina, 2 to 4 years in Algeria, and frequently one additional tour of duty in Germany.[47] Such radical *nomadisme*, now the lot of almost the entire officer corps rather than simply the semi-specialized "colonial officers" of the pre-1939 period, inevitably disturbed the officer's family life; more important, however, it encouraged the military community to attach itself deeply to colonial lands at the very moment when empires were crumbling, to fashion a system of military values that rejected the search for security and comfort which dominated a rapidly evolving homeland.[48] Indochina in particular left many officers with the *mal jaune*—attachment to the oriental colony and bitterness at its loss.[49] Officers returning home after long colonial tours often felt themselves strangers in their own country.

A paratroop officer turned novelist re-creates that vivid reaction. Jean Larteguy, now a journalist and writer of three best selling military novels, follows a group of French officers returning to France after their release from Vietminh prison camps:

> They were all there, pressed one against the other, leaning against the rail. The paradise of which they had dreamed so much in the camps was slowly approaching and already they no longer wanted it.
>
> They dreamed of another lost paradise, Indochina; it was about that paradise that all of them were thinking. They were not suffering sons who were returning home to have their wounds cleansed, but strangers. Bitterness mounted within them.[50]

Isolation from the *métropole* sometimes deepened the officer's attachment to the colonies, but also it often led to estrangement and embitterment with regard to French civilian society, especially in the case of younger combat officers, who bore the brunt of the colonial wars.

The army could have borne loss of status more gracefully had it not felt that in Indochina, and again in Algeria, the country whose flag it bore had abandoned, and worse, betrayed the cause for which the army was fighting. The "abandonment" theme, so common in French military literature,[51] is not without a factual base. Following the advice of "leathernose" Colonel (then Deputy)

Robert Thomazo, we shall look first to Indochina in an attempt to understand "the motive and the revolt of certain centurions."[52]

Some insight into French civilian disinterest in Indochina can be gained through examination of national-opinion polls conducted by the Institut Français d'Opinion Publique, though changes in question format during the time period make it difficult to trace opinion trends with confidence. In February, 1947, when the Indochinese war was still young, an Institut national poll found that a small majority of those respondents who offered an opinion favored the use of force to put down the Vietminh rebellion.[53] But two months later 55 per cent of all respondents favored negotiations (which the government also hoped for at that time), as against 29 per cent who favored continued use of force.[54] The most striking feature of those responses was the party cleavage they revealed: nine-tenths of communist and two-thirds of socialist respondents opposed continuation of the war. Radicals and Popular Republicans were "very divided," while the Right was the war-party stronghold.[55] Opinion was still badly divided in April, 1951, with 51 per cent favoring reinforcement of French troops and 41 per cent preferring withdrawal of all troops.[56] By May, 1953, 65 per cent of respondents in a national sample who offered an opinion favored an end to fighting in Indochina, either by negotiation (46 per cent) or by withdrawal (19 per cent).[57] Yet French forces there continued an increasingly violent war for more than a year.

The same pattern of wavering public support for colonial war is evident in polls conducted by the same institute during the Algerian war. In polls taken between April, 1956, and January, 1958, about half of those persons expressing an opinion felt that the cause was hopeless and that France would be out of Algeria within five to ten years.[58] As for preferences in conduct of Algerian policy, by January, 1958, 56 per cent of all respondents favored negotiations with the rebels (a solution which was unacceptable to the army), while only 26 per cent opposed such negotiations.[59]

Opinion polls do not reveal the intensity of feeling, which was remarkably low on the subject of colonial wars. Except during the battle of Dien Bien Phu in 1954 and during the years 1955 and 1956, when reservists and draftees were first thrown into the

Algerian war, only the extreme Right and the extreme Left generated much excitement over Indochina and Algeria. Officers like Captain Bernard Moynet were annoyed on returning home on leave to find films being shown everywhere on the exploits of American and Russian troops in World War II, but none regarding the French Army in Indochina or Algeria.[60] Nor did the press contribute materially to developing public support for French forces in the colonies, though journalistic attacks on army brutality were common, as will be shown shortly.

More tangible evidence of "abandonment" was also abundant. The government decided in 1948 that military citations earned in Indochina would no longer appear in the *Journal officiel.* In 1951 it was officially announced that blood donated to the Office d'Hygiène Sociale would not be used for the wounded in Indochina. It was only in July, 1952, after six years of war, that a law was passed finally entitling veterans of Indochina to veterans' benefits. Those veterans waited another eighteen months before the law became effective. In 1953 only fifty to a hundred deputies appeared on the floor during important parliamentary debates on Indochina.[61] Early in 1958 several federations of civil servants protested against a government suggestion that government employees might be attached or assigned outside France proper. An officer-editorialist for *Message* barked back threateningly:

> Let us say it clearly: If the Nation were to disinterest itself in the Algerian War as it disinterested itself in the Indochinese War, the Army could not alone support the weight of the struggle without grave risk for our institutions themselves.[62]

At the time of writing the editorialist and the angry young officers for whom he spoke were only two months away from the crisis of May 13.

If there had been any doubt in the minds of French officers in Indochina about the unpopularity of the war effort, it was definitely erased by the government's staunch refusal, on firm political grounds, to send conscripts into the battle. Any government which might have dared to do so likely would have been swept aside by a solid Left and a split Center in the National Assembly. French officers in the field, though professional soldiers, were embittered at the realization that, like mercenaries, they were being called upon to fight a war that was not national in character. A *Message* editorialist wrote in 1955:

> It is too simple to pay at the rate of an average civil servant people whom one flatters so that they will let themselves be killed, while on the home front the country goes off on a week-end jaunt between two good beet sales and with the blessing of deputies who call themselves "national." [63]

Hope was rekindled among military officers in 1955 and 1956 as the government decided to recall conscripted reservists and to extend the length of military service as necessary beyond the normal eighteen months. The largest groups (fifty thousand in May, 1956) were recalled by the Socialist-led government of Guy Mollet.[64] What greater proof could one ask of national support for the army in Algeria? Even *Message* rejoiced and complimented conscripts for their performance in Algeria.[65] Ministers of national defense General Pierre Billotte in 1955, then Maurice Bourgès-Maunoury in 1956, insisted on the importance of the army's task in Algeria and of the need for "an unshakable will" against the rebels.[66]

Yet military euphoria, such as it was, was short-lived. The *rappelés* protested, violently in some cases, against their recall to active duty. There were demonstrations—near riots—and some mistreatment of officers occurred in Paris and Rouen and aboard a few trains carrying reservists.[67] In military circles these incidents were often blamed on "communist militants," as was the later indiscipline of conscripts against the April putsch of 1961. Yet at least one eyewitness, a unit commander, reports that poor military organization and the reservists' distaste for military life were more important than politics.[68] For certain French military "defenders of Western civilization" the communist bogeyman and his dupes were responsible for all manifestations of antimilitarism and anticolonialism.[69]

Reservists and conscripts soon accepted military discipline and carried out their assigned tasks, but usually without great enthusiasm. There were indeed numerous tales of dramatic conversions of skeptics and even communists to the cause of French Algeria.[70] Yet conscripts, like the French population generally, lost enthusiasm over the war as it dragged on. *Message* editorialists returned with heightened anguish to their attack on public apathy in regard to the war.[71] Conscripts did not oppose the May 13 movement in 1958 (nor did the country as a whole); but they played an instrumental role in defeating the attempted April putsch of 1961. One anti-putsch conscript leader at that time described the attitude of his fellows in these terms:

> The soldiers don't have the feeling of being at home here and of defending a French territory as they would have done if the battle had taken place on metropolitan soil. . . . I have never heard a conscript from the *métropole* say "Algeria is France." For these men, Algeria is a foreign theater of operations.[72]

A questionnaire survey of recently returned Algerian veterans conducted by *La Vie catholique* in late 1960 revealed that 359 out of 607 respondents felt themselves "in a foreign country" in Algeria.[73] In the main, the army failed to convert French youth temporarily in uniform.[74]

An army-youth committee formed in 1953 by Minister of Defense René Pleven to improve relations between French youth and the army served in practice more as a battleground between officers and youth-organization representatives.[75] General Jacques Faure, who became the most notorious antigovernment conspirator of the French Army, attempted as president of the committee to make it an instrument for guiding French youth. His disapproval of the major French student association's ties with a pro-rebel Moslem student association led finally to a crisis. In January, 1957, the representatives of five large youth organizations withdrew from the committee.[76] The committee survived as a liaison tool, but did not succeed in committing French youth organizations to a war to the finish in Algeria. On June 2, 1960, representatives of fifty-three youth organizations expressed their desire "to see ended a war which opposes the youth of two countries." [77] The presence of draftees in Algeria—some one million of them over the years from 1954 to 1962—did not suffice to turn a colonial war into a national war or to seal the breach between the army and civilian society.

Throughout the two colonial wars France remained more on a peacetime than a wartime footing [78]—while over twenty thousand French soldiers from the *métropole*, mostly officers and noncommissioned officers, lost their lives in battle in Indochina, and another nine thousand in Algeria, not to speak of the tens of thousands of Legionnaires, Vietnamese, and Moslems who were killed fighting with the French Army.[79] Though the number of casualties among Frenchmen from the *métropole* was rather limited in comparison with those among non-French troops, French officer and noncommissioned officer ranks suffered heavy losses. In the years 1945 to 1954 almost two hundred officers were killed each year, or the equivalent of three-fifths of an average graduating class at Saint-Cyr.[80] Hundreds more died in Vietminh prison camps.[81] In view of the magnitude of sacrifices among French military cadre, it is not surprising that by the late 1950's officers like one field-grade paratroop officer in Pau, fearful of another defeat in Algeria, cried out in warning to his compatriots, "Halte à l'abandon!" [82]

To the charge of abandonment, the military press joined that of betrayal on the home front, again not without reason. Documents discovered in 1952 and 1953 clearly revealed that the French Communist Party and the Communist-controlled General Confederation of Labor (C.G.T.) were intent upon sabotaging French defenses in Indochina.[83] In fact, the communist position was quite openly stated. Maurice Thorez, secretary general of the French Communist Party, addressed the twelfth congress of the Party in April, 1950, with these words:

> For three and a half years, an unjust war, a criminal war has been carried on against the people of Vietnam. This war of colonial plunder is sowing devastation and death on a people who ask only to live in peace and in fraternal union with the people of France.[84]

On March 3, 1952, the communist parliamentary leader, Jacques Duclos, sent a telegram to the Vietminh leader, Ho Chi Minh, in the name of the French Communist Party, congratulating him on his successes (against the French!) and assuring him of the support of the French working class in this "criminal war." [85]

In May, 1952, Communist Deputy François Billoux urged that "the action of the masses must support and aid the dockers, sailors, and all those who are acting effectively against the transportation and manufacture of war materials." [86] In that same month another prominent Communist Party leader, André Marty, wrote in the party newspaper, *L'Humanité*, "Our duty is to organize the struggle of the masses against the manufacture and transportation of war materials." [87] The Communist Party distributed literature among French troops, and according to General Navarre, commander in chief of French forces in Indochina at the time of the battle of Dien Bien Phu, the Party was also guilty of the sabotage of those motors, ball bearings, batteries, parachutes, and other equipment which arrived in Indochina in defective condition.[88] André Stil, the editor of *L'Humanité*, and Lucien Molino, a C.G.T. leader, were arrested and held for a few months in connection with the communist antiwar campaign.[89] The parliamentary leaders of the Communist Party, however, retained their parliamentary immunity against a government request for their removal in an assembly vote of 302 to 291.[90] General Navarre, by no means the first French military commander to explain military defeat in terms of "betrayal," pointed out quite accurately that 105 Socialists, 13 Radical Socialists, 9 UDSR's, 53 Popular Republicans and even a scattering of conservative Independents joined with 96 Communists and 4 *Progressistes* to protect the communist deputies.[91]

The *rapporteur* for the Parliamentary Immunities Committee viewed the question as one for the government, not the committee, to decide: either the Communist Party should be outlawed as "an enterprise of demoralization and treason," or, if its action and means were considered to be within the framework of "republican legality," its members should be left free to pursue their ends.[92] General Navarre might well have agreed with this analysis, but not with the committee's recommendation against lifting parliamentary immunity. He would have proceeded to the conclusion that in wartime (and France was indeed engaged in war in Indochina in 1953), any party dedicated to the defeat of the nation's armies was obviously beyond the pale of "republican legality." In 1939 the step had seemed obvious enough; but in 1953 public opinion and political leadership, even outside the Communist Party, were so seriously divided concerning war goals that "treason" was exceedingly difficult to define.[93]

And so antiwar propaganda, sabotage, and free circulation of military secrets continued further to impede a military effort in Indochina which was already futile. After the armistice in July, 1954, the army was made aware of the extent of security leaks within the government in the *affaire des fuites* ("leaks"), an affair which prompted a representative of the militant Veterans of Indochina to proclaim: "Now we know that a French Army, on no matter what territory it fights, will always be stabbed in the back." [94] Beginning in July, 1953, it became increasingly apparent that information discussed in meetings of the policy-making National Defense Committee was leaking out. In *France-observateur* of July 30, 1953, there appeared an article by Roger Stéphane entitled, "In a Doubtful Fight," in which General Navarre was quoted (correctly) as having reported that French forces were presently incapable of defending Laos. In September, 1954, police investigations finally revealed that two *progressiste* high civil servants in the Permanent Secretariat of National Defense, Messieurs Turpin (*chef de cabinet* of the director of the Secretariat) and Labrusse (chief of the civil defense service), were guilty of passing out security information for ideological reasons to one André Baranès, a journalist with the *progressiste* newspaper, *Libération*, and also a double agent linked with the Communist Party on the one hand and an anticommunist parallel police system on the other.

Like any proper French *affaire*, this one was bewilderingly complicated and turned into a massive political melée.[95] Baranès was eventually acquitted after the evidence against him proved contradictory; the *France-observateur* case was withdrawn by gov-

ernment decision from the jurisdiction of the military tribunal
which handled the affair; and Turpin and Labrusse went to
prison.[96] In military circles the *fuites* affair was taken as definitive
proof of treason from within and of lack of governmental vigor
in dealing with those responsible.[97] It served as well to reinforce
that long-standing military hostility toward the press which had
already been strengthened in Indochina.[98]

The French Army's battles with the press were only beginning
in 1954. The Algerian revolt which began on All Saints Day in
November of that year had a dual effect on army-press relations.
On the one hand, the French Army developed a concept of revolutionary war and psychological action which required that the press
be cultivated so that it might be used as an instrument in war
for the minds of men. On the other hand, important elements
within the army, in their frustration and eagerness to win, resorted
to summary executions, mass reprisals, and torture of prisoners—
tactics which unleashed upon the military the full fury of a large
segment of the press.[99] The Algerian war was more than two
years old when, in 1957, the Ecole de Guerre added lectures on
the press to its regular curriculum and the military journals opened
their pages to discussion of army-press relations. The *Revue militaire d'information,* published by the Ministry of National Defense
under the direct guidance of the Service of Information and Psychological Action, devoted an entire issue to the problem.[100] Even
when the army put on its courting clothes, however, a lurking
hostility was still evident in its attraction-repulsion posture with
regard to the press.[101]

Repulsion soon gained a clear upper hand when, in the wake
of the infamous "Battle of Algiers," led by the Tenth Paratroop
Division in early 1957, the army faced a barrage of criticism, not
only from the communist press, but also from *L'Express,
Témoignage chrétien, France-observateur,* and the prestigious
Le Monde. On March 21, 1957, Jacques Soustelle attacked these
four newspapers on the floor of the National Assembly as "the
four *'grands'* of French counter-propaganda." [102] Minister of National Defense Maurice Bourgès-Maunoury came to the defense of
his troops, proclaiming:

The attacks of which the Army is the target are only the counter-attacks of the fellagha [rebels] led by certain governmental and intellectual circles. We have entered into battle and we shall continue it to the end.[103]

The minister's identification of critics of the army with enemy "counterattacks" fell on receptive military ears.[104] Yet, despite government seizure in the course of the Algerian war of over 30 books, 265 newspaper editions in the *métropole* and 586 more in Algeria, plus a number of fines levied against offending newspapers, neither the governments of the Fourth Republic nor that of the Fifth Republic suceeded either in ending the antiarmy campaign or in satisfying outraged officers.[105] Government seizure of all unsold copies of a book or article dealing with a delicate subject like torture sometimes had the reverse effect of arousing popular curiosity. Such was the case with *La Question*, Henri Alleg's nauseating description of his treatment at the hands of paratroopers in a "placement center" in Algeria.[106]

The military press reaction to the attacks upon the army for brutality and torture was rapid and violent, especially in *Le Bled*, the military weekly in Algiers with a mass circulation among French troops.[107] There is no question but that frequent attacks on the army in the press and in Left and Left-Center political groups in the *métropole* contributed materially to that angry military state of mind which prevailed in Algeria, and especially in the paratroop units, in the spring of 1958.[108] The state of mind is evident in the interview given by General Jacques Massu, commander of the Tenth Paratroop Division, to an Italian journalist in December, 1957:

It is evident that in Paris an attempt is being made to discredit the army in order more easily to reach an agreement with the F.L.N.; it is an old tactic which I have known since Indochina. Now it must be known that the army will no longer permit the intriguers to betray France. Algeria will remain French, I assure you.[109]

The cause of French Algeria is taken by Massu as unchallengeable. Hence, as other military officers have argued, the "subversive press," "whose every article wounds or kills" through strengthening the enemy, must realize that "every blow struck against the army is struck against the nation itself."[110]

The cry of "treason" in the military press quieted only briefly after the May 13 crisis, to be revived again in 1959 and 1960, focused this time on intellectuals of the Left.[111] A clandestine bulletin entitled *Vérité Pour* began appearing, especially in university circles, in September, 1958, and moved within a year and a half from general opposition to the Algerian war to active support for the F.L.N. (the rebel National Liberation Front).[112] In February, 1960, French security police discovered a network of intellectuals, artists, and students, led by Professor Francis Jeanson, which provided aid of various sorts to the Algerian rebels and was involved in the publication of *Vérité pour.*[113] The "Jeanson trial" provided the occasion, both inside and outside the courtroom, for an impressive number of condemnations of the French position in the Algerian war.[114] On September 6, 1960, a group of 121, soon joined by many others, published a manifesto which encouraged men called to military service to refuse to serve.[115] A week later the party of Mendès-France and of André Philip, the Unified Socialist party, announced its desire to "render homage publicly to the courage and to the disinterestedness of the accused, who have chosen a particularly dangerous form of combat in their struggle against the Algerian War." [116]

In the course of the trial itself a letter from Jean-Paul Sartre was read, a letter affirming the writer's "total solidarity" with the accused, whom he described as working for "a true democracy" and as representing thousands of others who were ready to take up their work. "If Jeanson had asked me to carry letter bags or shelter Algerian militants," Sartre wrote, "and if I had been able to do so without risk to them, I would have done it without hesitation." [117] Another sensational testimony was given by Paul Teitgen, a former director of police in Algiers. Teitgen told the court that he resigned from his position in Algiers because of uncontrolled use of torture and resort to abuses of justice. He did not approve of the actions of the Jeanson group, but "taking into account all that I know and what I learned in Algeria, I excuse them." [118]

Military activists were aroused by the moderate government attitude toward the "121." [119] The meaning of treason was more elusive than ever at a time when Algerian independence was fast becoming government policy.

These numerous examples of public apathy, abandonment, and betrayal in regard to defense of the empire had the effect of deepening the isolation of the French military community, an isolation in which military men, incapable of admitting the futility of their efforts and sacrifices, created their own vision of the world. French military defeats were seen as primarily the result of weakness and treason on the home front; yet military thinkers were at first reluctant to assign primary blame to national decay, for that would mean the end of the grandeur of France. Rather, like General Navarre, many tended to view the "real country," though misled by the "regime," as profoundly healthy.[120] The idea was by no means new to French military men. In the nineteenth and early twentieth centuries—and especially after 1870—aristocratic and antirepublican officers had often distinguished between the regime, which they despised, and the nation, which they served. Weygand, and especially Pétain, demonstrated in 1940 that the distinction could serve praetorian ends. However, it was only after World War II that the dangerous possibilities inherent in the conception were fully revealed. Navarre's analysis added to that revelation:

> It is unfortunately with the "legal country"—that is to say with the oligarchies which dispute the power and profits of the regime— that we must deal. It is the "legal country" which not only is revealing itself to be incapable of arousing within the nation the reactions necessary for salvation, but which also prevents them from being born spontaneously.[121]

From Navarre's distinction between the "legal country" and the "real country," it is only a short step to future premier Michel

Debré's position in 1957: "A legal Government might well be illegitimate; an illegal authority, legitimate." [122]

Just as General Douglas MacArthur, after his removal from the command of American and United Nations forces in Korea, saw the soldier's primary loyalty as due "the country and the Constitution . . . [rather than] those who temporarily exercise the authority of the Executive Branch of government," [123] so Navarre and others like him challenged the legitimacy of the Fourth Republic's legality. In Navarre's eyes the leaders of France's government were "quacks and charlatans" who, if the ailing nation was to be cured, would have to make way for the "great surgeon." [124]

The "great surgeon" arrived in May, 1958, and on the shoulders of the army. The chief of staff of national defense who resigned during the crisis and later was restored by De Gaulle, the man who was often called "the conscience of the Army," General Paul Ely, reviewed the crisis in these terms in the summer of 1958: " . . . While France appeared on the edge of collapse, she [the army] was the one who demonstrated, with the highest discipline, profound respect for a 'genuine legality.' " [125] "Genuine legality," like the "real country," was apparently a concept which the army, in its infinite patriotism, was capable of interpreting. General Maurice Challe apparently thought so when, as leader of the April putsch of 1961, he announced by radio from Algiers:

> The high command reserves the right to extend its action to the *métropole* and to reconstitute a constitutional and republican order which has been gravely compromised by a government whose illegality is manifest in the eyes of the nation.[126]

And this despite the massive "yes" vote for De Gaulle's Algerian policy in the recent referendum of January 8, 1961.

In fact, the notion of the *pays réèl,* as borrowed from the tradition of the antirepublican Right, entailed leadership and education of the nation, as well as its "liberation" from the system which distorted and bound it. The underlying national health of which Navarre spoke increasingly appeared to the abandoned and embittered officer (as it had appeared to the armistice army under

Pétain) as a *potential* health to be recovered only under the care of a pure and strong military physician. The point is made quite boldly in an article entitled "On the Historical Role of the Army" written in 1956 by that curious figure, air force General L. M. Chassin, a prolific military writer, historian, grand strategist, student of Mao Tse-tung, and plotter against the regime.[127] Chassin discusses the stages of civilization in an analysis probably inspired by Toynbee. Following a description of the Eastern Roman Empire in decline, he proposes a remedy obviously intended for his own times:

> Whatever the extent of disorder and internal anarchy, all can be saved so long as one disposes of a solid and sufficiently national army capable of fulfilling two historical functions in a period of disintegration: defend the empire without and place in power within a leader capable of effecting the necessary rectification in re-establishing order and authority.[128]

A wide variety of military writers shared Chassin's view that only the army could save a sick French society, though few couched their argument in such scholarly terms. For one contributor to *Message* the army was the buttress of the nation's unity as well as its conscience.[129] For General Ely (who is apparently then the conscience of a conscience, a responsible position indeed), the army, aided by her obsession for unity, her breadth of social origins, her high conception of the role of France, was not a threat to the nation but rather "an element of wisdom and continuity." [130] For other military writers, including army Chief of Staff André Zeller, the army was a crucial bulwark against communism, a rare remaining embodiment of the values of patriotism, courage, discipline, sacrifice, and solidarity—an example and guide for the nation.[131]

Again as in the wake of the 1940 defeat, military attention turned to French education and its failure to inculcate a civic spirit into French youth.[132] The army's fascination with "psychological action" was largely inspired by the notion that French education and French political leadership had failed, leaving the army a precious remnant of health and vitality with a vital educational and unifying role in a decaying nation.[133] Discussion of that role became particularly frequent in the aftermath of the May 13 crisis of 1958, which placed De Gaulle in power. An editorialist for *Message* was filled with hope and enthusiasm:

> Finally the hour has sounded which we waited for ardently. . . . Finally the Nation as a whole is rediscovering the face of the Army at the same time that it is rediscovering its strength, the grandeur of its destiny, the legitimacy of its cause.[134]

All of this was made possible, he continues, only through the *unity of the army*, an army which responded joyously and spontaneously to the call for abolition of the "system."[135] The army newspaper in Algeria, *Le Bled*, sounded a similar note. The "system" had led France to doubt herself, its editorialist argued, but now "the era of Byzantine discussions is closed. Once again [in the fall referendum] the French soldier will know how to give the Country an Example of Civic Spirit."[136]

One fact received insufficient attention from the military press after *treize mai*: the exemplary unity of the army in May, 1958, was turned *against* the legal government of France, even though officers like Ely may have felt themselves to be respecting a "genuine legality." Ely's resignation and the open sympathy which the Algiers coup provoked in military units in the *métropole* served primarily to leave the government defenseless and with no alternative but De Gaulle or civil war.

How were political actions by military officers to be reconciled with the traditional maxim that "l'armée ne fait pas de politique"? The saving formula was hardly new to the French political scene: "Patriotism knows no politics." General Maxime Weygand, whose critical role in the 1940 armistice we have seen, stated with all seriousness in the Pétain trial in 1945, "I dare anyone to find a political act in my life."[137] Following the May 13, 1958, uprising in Algiers which felled the Fourth Republic, General Jacques Massu, president of the dissident committee of public safety, insisted in similar fashion that he had led an assault on the republic without in any way engaging in politics. General de Gaulle arrived in Algiers on June 4, 1958, as the newly invested Premier of France and heard from Massu's lips that the committee of public safety had wanted only to prevent the abandonment of Algeria and the decadence of France through the "fatal and thoughtless action of irresponsible governments. . . . " [138] Massu, claiming to be "maintaining a strictly apolitical attitude" ["dans un apolitisme absolu"], then urged De Gaulle to "eliminate the remnants of the system and its leaders." [139] Only five months after the events of May, 1958, one military writer argued that the army was eminently suited to direct French "psychological-action" efforts—within the army and, presumably, outside it as well—primarily because of its "apolitical" character, which allowed it to reach above narrow political quarrels to "a correct notion of the 'superior interests of the country.' " [140]

In the April putsch of 1961 open military revolt was explained by General Challe as strictly "apolitical" in nature.[141] When the revolt failed, Challe surrendered, but General Raoul Salan escaped to take the lead of the Secret Army Organization. Salan later told the court in his own trial,

At the moment when I was withdrawing into the night with General Jouhaud, I thought that nothing was more foreign to my life than politics. In agreeing to lead the clandestine struggle, it was not a political decision that I was taking. I was simply recalled to service, not by an official convocation but by the oath which I had taken.[142]

For Weygand, Massu, Challe, Salan, and numerous other military men, patriotic motives and actions placed one above the tainted world of politics. The question now as always was, Whose patriotism? When the official government version strayed from the doctrine of French Algeria in 1959 and 1960, and when the French electorate heartily approved that government version in the referendum of January 8, 1961, hard-core military activists concluded that the army should save the French despite themselves. But the path of military revolt against a popular government led only to failure, disgrace, and a widened gap between the French nation and its embittered and humiliated army.[143]

1. Paxton, "Army Officers in Vichy France," pp. 502–11, 616–19.

2. See below, pp. 107–10.

3. An opinion poll taken shortly after the war found that only 70 per cent of French citizens still wanted an army and these only "because of tradition and a love of swagger" (Edward L. Katzenbach, Jr., "Political Parties and the French Army Since Liberation," in Edward Mead Earle [ed.], *Modern France* [Princeton: Princeton University Press, 1951], pp. 432–33, quoting from *J.O., Déb, A.N.,* December 31, 1945, p. 704).

4. See, for example, Captain L., "Alerte au progressisme," *Message des forces armées,* No. 19 N.S. (February, 1957); and Marc Brouchamp, "Le Progressisme," *RMI,* No. 323 (January, 1961), pp. 16–24.

5. Majority support for retention of French Indochina, as of March, 1947, is evidenced by an opinion survey reported in *Sondages,* the publication of the Institut Français d'Opinion Publique, IX, No. 5 (1947), 59–60.

6. See, for example, Colonel Gabriel Bonnet, "L'Importance du facteur 'moral' dans le complexe 'armée-nation,'" *RDN,* November, 1959, pp. 435–41; Commandant M. Bourgeois, "L'Officier français peut-il faire la guerre révolutionnaire?" (thesis, Ecole Supérieure de Guerre, 73rd promotion, 1960), pp. 11–12; and Michel Déon, *L'Armée d'Algérie et la pacification* (Paris: Plon, 1959), pp. 20–21.

7. See John W. Spanier, *The Truman-MacArthur Controversy and the Korean War* (Cambridge, Mass.: Harvard University Press, 1959), pp. 12, 268–72. Morris Janowitz finds political consensus to be of importance as a buttress to civilian control: "The party neutrality of the military [in the U.S.] has been assisted by the social and political consensus of American society. Until the Korean conflict, generals and admirals had not been confronted with political conflicts in which they were either permitted, or required, to make alliances along partisan lines" (*The Professional Soldier,* [Glencoe, Ill.: Free Press of Glencoe, 1960] p. 233).

8. See the article by an anonymous officer, "Malaise dans l'armée: L'Intégration et l'épuration des cadres officiers," *Etudes,* No. 249 (April-May-June, 1946), pp. 77–85.

9. Several French military officers made this point in conversations with the writer in 1962, stressing that unlike the ordinary *fonctionnaire,* the officer has no right to form unions, to strike, or to express political opinions freely. The same question is discussed in Jean Planchais, *Le Malaise de l'armée* (Paris: Plon, 1958), chap. 3 ("Soldats ou fonctionnaires") pp. 14–19; in Nadine Liber, "La grande frustration du jeune officier supérieure," *Réalités,* May, 1957, p. 40; and in Hubert Bassot's novel, *Les Silencieux* (Paris, 1958), pp. 118–19.

10. In a speech to the National Assembly during the armed forces budget debates on March 17, 1954 (cited in *RMI,* No. 230 [March 25, 1954] p. 7). See also "Les 50,000 officiers français: Qui sont-ils, comment vivent-ils?" *Entreprise,* December 27, 1958, pp. 47–49.

11. Girardet *et al., Crise militaire,* pp. 126–27.

12. *Ibid.,* Table 18, pp. 125–26.

13. *Ibid.*

14. *Ibid.*

15. *Ibid.,* pp. 109–13. A table of sample military allowances is found in *ibid.,* p. 114.

16. *Ibid.,* pp. 115–22. The compulsory retirement age for officers in the combat arms ranged from fifty-two for lieutenants and captains to sixty-one for a full colonel.

17. Liber, *Réalités*, p. 105.

18. Captains T. and A., "Essai sur la structure sociale de l'Armée Française," *La nouvelle critique*, No. 107 (June, 1959), p. 68. The review is Marxist, but this article is informative and carefully done.

19. "La Condition militaire," *RMI*, No. 234 (June 10, 1954), pp. 7–10; and "Les 50,000 officiers," *Enterprise*, pp. 47–49.

20. "Courrier" sec., *Message des forces armées*, No. 42 (April, 1960). This magazine was founded in 1947 as an independent "tribune" for officers of the three services. In 1953, after a lapse of several months, it came under the auspices of the review *Perspectives*, in whose offices it has since been published in mimeographed form. In January, 1962, the name was changed to simply *Message* on the request of the Ministry of Armed Forces, which feared it was being taken as an official publication. Written by, and distributed among, military officers, *Message* concerned itself from the beginning with relations between the army, the government, and the French population. It became an important spokesman for the most militant (and often antigovernment) segment of the officer corps. Since this group was of great importance in the events of 1958–62, and since it could not often speak freely in the official and semiofficial military press, *Message* serves as a valuable documentation of the attitudes of the more militant officers. After February, 1957, each article is separate in pagination; volume numbers from 1953 to the present refer to the "New Series." Almost all articles are unsigned.

21. Captains T. and A., *La nouvelle critique*, p. 68.

22. "Journal de Marche d'un Capitaine en Kabylie," *La nouvelle critique*, No. 107 (June, 1959), p. 14

23. *Ibid.*

24. Girardet *et al.*, *Crise militaire*, Table 14, p. 114.

25. Claude Dufresnoy, *Des officiers parlent* (Paris: René Julliard, 1961), pp. 128–29, quoting a Second Lieutenant N. Others of the seventy officers whom Dufresnoy interviewed did not always agree to this analysis. See the interview with Captain R., *ibid.*, p. 111.

26. This sample of 235 was composed of 161 officers in attendance at the Ecole d'Etat-Major or the Ecole Supérieure de Guerre, 122 officers from organic elements of an army corps stationed in Germany, and 71 officers from an infantry division within that army corps (Girardet [who was a member of the committee] *et al.*, *Crise militaire*, p. 130; and, reporting on the same study, *LM*, December 28, 1960).

27. Girardet *et al.*, *Crise militaire*, pp. 130 n. 22, 141.

28. *Ibid.*, pp. 141–142.

29. "Enquête sur la crise de l'armée," *Message*, No. 18 (December, 1956). The Saint-Cyr class involved was probably that of 1940, which provided many of the contributors to *Message*.

30. "Un programme de 30,000 logements," *RMI*, No. 282 (April, 1957), pp. 35–52.

31. "Les 50,000 officiers," *Entreprise*, p. 49.

32. Liber, *Réalités*, pp. 38, 105.

33. In *Message* see, for example, M. Lombard, "Le Logement des cadres," No. 40 (December, 1952), pp. 31–34; and "Pour une politique du logement dans l'armée" (by "un groupe de Parisiens temporaires"), No. 2 (February, 1954), pp. 7–8. In *RMI* see the source cited in note 30 above and "Le Logement des cadres," No. 291 (February, 1958), p. 67–74.

34. Reboul, *Revue des deux mondes*, pp. 384–88.

35. "Enquête sur la crise de l'armée," *Message*, p. 5.

36. "Courrier" sec., *Message*, No. 42 (April, 1960).

37. *Ibid.*, p. 2.

38. *Ibid.* The rebuttal was not intended to reassure government authorities, for the Gaullist regime, in the eyes of the writers whose work appeared in *Message* in 1960, had "merited" very little indeed.

39. See a discussion of the paratroopers in Chapter 12.

40. Told by Major Robert Lagrange to Liber, *Réalités* p. 38.

41. See Chapter 5.

42. This point was made forcefully in the author's interview in June, 1962, with M. Mialet, a graduate of Saint-Cyr on the eve of World War II and now a *haut fonctionnaire*, who has kept in close touch with his former classmates and a wide range of other officers through the organization Rencontres, of which he is a leader. See also Girardet *et al.*, *Crise militaire*, p. 149; "Les 50,000 officiers," *Enterprise*, p. 48; and Jean Planchais, "L'Armée et la nation: Trois années de rencontre," *LM*, May 17, 1961.

43. Girardet *et al.*, *Crise militaire*, pp. 79-83 and Figure 22; and Captains T. and A., *La nouvelle critique*, pp. 48-50, 64. Judging from data collected in the Girardet volume, Captains T. and A. tend to overstate the problem somewhat. Apparently promotion patterns varied radically from service to service (Girardet *et al.*, *Crise militaire*, pp. 94–100).

44. *Ibid.*, p. 127.

45. The cleavage between age generations within the army is discussed in Chapter 12.

46. Girardet *et al.*, *Crise militaire*, pp. 130 n. 21, 134.

47. *Ibid.*, pp. 134–40; and Captains T. and A., *La nouvelle critique*, p. 51.

48. On this point see General Baillif, "Les Forces armées dans la nation," *RDN*, February, 1960, pp. 220–22; and Girardet *et al.*, *Crise militaire*, pp. 169-77.

49. "Le Mal Jaune" by "a Captain" in *Le Courrier de la nation*, No. 5 (August 14, 1958), p. 20.

50. *Les Centurions* (Paris: Presses de la Cité, 1960), p. 167. Another returned Indochina veteran, portrayed this time by Bertrand de Castelbajac (also a former paratroop officer), finds life at "home" equally distasteful: "Thinking back on it, he had found the stay in France the most upsetting, for now he no longer thought of his 'period in Indochina' but of his 'period in France.' Things made more sense in the war; there he felt at home, and elsewhere he was abroad" (De la Gorce, *The French Army*, p. 391, quoting from Castelbajac, *La Gloire est leur salaire* [Paris: Editions Française et Internationales, 1958]). See also General André Zeller, "Armée et politique," *RDN*, April, 1957, p. 502.

51. The theme recurs most frequently in *Message*: Captain X., "La Crise morale du corps des officiers," No. 12 (February, 1956); "L'Algérie et la volonté de vaincre," No. 42 (April, 1960); and the "Courrier" sec., No. 42 (April, 1960), pp. 5–6. See also Lieutenant Philippe Marchat, "Rappelé en Algérie," *RDN*, December, 1957, pp. 1827–52, especially pp. 1833–34; General Henri Navarre, *Agonie de l'Indochine* (Paris: Plon, 1956), pp. 17, 29–30, and *passim*; "un capitaine," "Le Mal Jaune," *Le Courrier de la nation*, No. 5 (August 14, 1958), p. 20.

52. Thomazo's testimony in the Salan trial (May 21, 1962) in *Procès*

Salan, p. 371. Thomazo's nickname results from the plastic device which he wears on his nose as a result of a serious injury suffered in World War II.

53. Institut d'Opinion Publique, *Sondages*, IX, No. 5 (1947), 59–60.

54. *Ibid.*, IX No. 8 (1947), 90–91.

55. Data as of April, 1947, but reported in *ibid.*, X, No. 17 (1948), 213–14.

56. *Ibid.*, XV, No. 3 (1953), 3–6.

57. *Ibid.*, p. 5.

58. *Ibid.*, XX, No. 3 (1958), 39–46.

59. *Ibid.*, p. 43. For army views on negotiation see below, Chapters 7 and 8.

60. See Captain Moynet's testimony in the Salan trial, *Procès Salan*, p. 164.

61. These examples appear fairly frequently in the military press. See, for example, Navarre, *Agonie de l'Indochine*, pp. 17 n., 29–30.

62. Editorial in *Message*, No. 28 (March, 1958), pp. 1–2.

63. Editorial in *Message*, No. 7 (February, 1955), p. 1.

64. *L'Année politique*, 1956 (Paris: Presses Universitaires de France, 1957), p. 52.

65. Editorial in *Message*, No. 14 (June, 1956), pp. 1–2.

66. See the report of a visit by General Billotte to North Africa and of his press conference on October 21, 1955, in *RMI*, No. 261 (November 10, 1955), pp. 10–11; and the article by Bourgès-Maunoury (who used the term "unshakeable will"), "Nous voulons continuer à écrire notre histoire," which was first printed in *Le Bled*, an army newspaper based at that time in Algiers, and then reprinted in *RMI*, No. 275 (August, 1956), pp. 4–5.

67. De la Gorce, *The French Army*, pp. 426–27; and Colonel Roger Barberot, *Malaventure en Algérie avec le Général Paris de Bollardière* (Paris: Plon, 1957), pp. 58–66.

68. Barberot, *Malaventure en Algérie*. De la Gorce argues that Left-wing student groups and Catholic militants shared leadership with communists (*The French Army*, p. 426).

69. See below, Chapter 11.

70. A graduate of the Institut d'Etudes Politiques in Paris, an antimilitarist in the style of the non-communist intelligentsia of the Left, returned from military service in Algeria convinced of the justice of the French cause there. A number of similar "conversions" are related in *Ceux d'Algérie, lettres de rappelés* (Paris: Plon, 1957). That brilliant and conspiring paratroop colonel and later O.A.S. leader, Antoine Argoud, is often quoted as having said that communists made excellent paratroopers in Algeria (e.g., as quoted in H. Azeau, *Révolte militaire* [Paris: Plon, 1961], p. 167).

71. See the editorials in *Message*, No. 16 (October, 1956), pp. 2–3; and in succeeding numbers.

72. "Témoin d'un 'meneur,'" in Azeau, *Révolte militaire*, p. 185.

73. Xavier Grall, *La Génération du Djebel* (Paris: Editions du Cerf, 1962), p. 20. The question asked, and the responses made, were "en Algérie aviez-vous l'impression d'être: A l'étranger? (359); En France? (177); Les deux? (45); no reply (27)."

74. R. Doumic, "L'Armée et la formation de l'opinion publique," *RMI*, No. 274 (July, 1956), pp. 14–16.

75. Planchais, *Le Malaise de l'armée*, pp. 62–64.

76. Faure intimated to the associations of students attending preparatory classes for military-school entrance examinations that they should apply for membership in the general student association, the Union Nationale des Etudiants Français (U.N.E.F.). U.N.E.F. delayed consideration of the applications, Faure protested to the committee, and the committee split after the military officers on it (now a majority) voted to exclude U.N.E.F. temporarily from the committee. About the same time the original cause of the crisis was erased when the Moslem students' association demanded that U.N.E.F. take a firm political stand, and U.N.E.F. felt compelled to break its ties to the Moslem association (Planchais, *Le Malaise de l'armée*, pp. 63–64).

77. Quoted, disapprovingly of course, in "Ceux qui forment notre jeunesse," *Message*, No. 43 (June, 1960), p. 1. See also "Mourir pour la patrie" in the same issue.

78. In 1953, as the Indochinese war approached its greatest intensity, French military expenditures, including costs of the war, amounted to less than 9 per cent of the Gross National Product—no more than military expenditures in Britain, which was not fighting a war. The United States paid an increasing share of the bill in Indochina in the latter years of the war. In 1956, even with conscripts now in Algeria, that percentage had dropped to 7 per cent of an expanding GNP. See General André Zeller (a leader in the April putsch of 1961), "Le Prix de la défense," *RDN*, August-September, 1957, pp. 1235–49; *L'Année politique*, 1953, pp. 9–10 (for an account of the revealing 1953 budget debates in the National Assembly); Edward L. Katzenbach, "The French Army," *Yale Review*, XLV, No. 4 (June, 1956), 498–513; and Robert Lacoste's remarks to the National Assembly, reprinted in *RMI*, No. 283 (May, 1957), pp. 53–59.

79. Dead and missing among non-French troops fighting with the French Army included 11,620 Legionnaires, 15,229 Africans, and 26,666 indigenous regulars in Indochina, and another 1,200 Legionnaires and 4,000 Moslems in Algeria. In addition, several tens of thousands of associated Indochinese troops were killed or missing (numerous desertions make an accurate count difficult here). Indochinese figures are from Donald Lancaster, *The Emancipation of Indochina* (London: Oxford University Press, 1961), p. 341, citing a publication of the U.S. Information Service, *France: Facts and Figures*, March, 1955, pp. 39–40. See also *NYT*, July 23, 1954, p. 2, Algerian figures are from *LM*, March 9, 1962.

80. Planchais, *Le Malaise de l'armée*, p. 10; and *NYT*, July 23, 1954, citing the French Military Information Service in Hanoi.

81. See Bernard Fall's grim account of death marches and prison camps in Indochina, *Street without Joy* (Harrisburg, Pa.: Stackpole, 1961), pp. 264–79. Vietminh prison camps are also described by Captain de Braquilanges' mimeographed article, "Cours de guerre subversive: Méthodes psychologiques utilisées pour forcer l'adhésion des esprits" (Paris: Ecole d'Etat Major, 1956–57), p. 4.

82. In a text entitled "L'Armée parle aux Français," received by the journalist J.-R. Tournoux and printed in his *Secrets d'état* (Paris: Plon, 1960), p. 437.

83. *L'Année politique, 1953*, pp. 150–51. See also Katzenbach, *Modern France*, pp. 437–38.

84. From the text as found in Monique Lafon, *La Lutte du Parti Communiste contre le colonialisme* (Paris: Éditions Sociales, 1962), pp. 45–46. In the same volume see other statements of party policy on Indochina (pp.

37–84) and especially the bitter assembly speech of Mme. Jeanette Vermeersch (pp. 53–66).

85. One paragraph read: "Le peuple de France, qui a lutté hier et lutte aujourd'hui contre l'occupation étrangère, comprend et soutient la lutte du peuple vietnamien pour sa liberté et son indépendence, il s'élève contre la poursuite de la guerre criminelle faite au peuple vietnamien avec des objectifs contraires aux véritables intérêts de la France" (cited by Roger Duveau, *rapporteur* for the Parliamentary Immunities Committee in the National Assembly, *J.O., Déb., A. N.*, November 6, 1953, p. 4901.

86. *Ibid.*, p. 4902, citing *Cahiers du communisme*, No. 5 (May, 1952), p. 461.

87. *Ibid.*, citing from *L'Humanité*, May 14, 1952.

88. Navarre, *Agonie de l'Indochine*, pp. 112–13, 113 n. See also Katzenbach, *Modern France*, p. 438.

89. *L'Année politique*, 1953, pp. 63, 150.

90. *J.O., Déb., A.N.*, November 6, 1953, pp. 4928, 4944–46.

91. Navarre, *Agonie de l'Indochine*, pp. 113–14, 113 n.; *L'Année politique, 1953*, p. 81; and *J.O., Déb., A.N.*, November 6, 1953, pp. 4928, 4944–46.

92. *Ibid.*, p. 4903.

93. See the public statements of cabinet members Daladier, Monteil, and Naegelin in 1953 and 1954, assembled by Navarre, showing that even within the government many felt (and rightly so) that the war in Indochina was futile (Navarre, *Agonie de l'Indochine*, p. 111 n.).

94. Quoted approvingly by Navarre, *Agonie de l'Indochine*, p. 114. A summary of the affair is found in *L'Année politique*, 1954, pp. 74–78, 98–100.

95. At one point Baranès, the *progressiste* journalist with communist and ultra-Rightist connections, was captured after a cops-and-robbers chase which led to the offices of the moderate conservative paper, *Le Figaro*, where he was hidden by a Radical deputy, André Hugues! (*L'Année politique, 1954*, p. 77). The leader of the parallel police network, which was apparently unknown to Minister of the Interior François Mitterand, was Commissioner Dides, who continued to be a prime figure in extreme Rightist politics until his arrest in November, 1961, for activities in support of the Secret Army Organization (*LM*, November 21, 1961).

96. For four and six years respectively. ("L'Affaire des fuites," *Message*, No. 14 [June, 1956], pp. 20–24).

97. See *ibid.*; and Navarre, *Agonie de l'Indochine*, pp. 114–17.

98. In addition to lack of support in the Left and Left-Center press, many officers were likely angered by legitimate press criticism of the "piastre traffic," in which some officers engaged, and of the "Generals Affair" in 1949–50, when General Revers (chief of staff) and General Mast became involved with a shady civilian intriguer and profiteer, Roger Peyré. See Georgette Elgey, *La République des illusions* (Paris: Fayard, 1965), pp. 467–496. In regard to the general hostility of officers to reporters and the press, see Planchais, *Le Malaise de l'armée*, chap. 12 (entitled "La grande muette et le quatrième pouvoir"), pp. 65–72. See also Planchais, "Journalistes et militaires," *RMI*, No. 287 (September–October, 1957), p. 108; Henri Mongrillon, "L'Attitude de la presse à propos de Dien-Bien-Phu," *Message*, No. 3 (May, 1954), pp. 16–17; and Navarre, *Agonie de l'Indochine*, pp. 54–56, 264–67.

99. See below, Chapter 8, for a fuller discussion of torture and summary executions.

100. *RMI*, No. 287 (September–October, 1957), entitled "La Presse." The *Revue de défense nationale* also printed two articles on the subject in 1957: Pierre Denoyer, "L'Armée et la presse," in the issue of April, 1957, pp. 533–44; and Major Feral, "L'Armée devant la presse," in the issue of December, 1957, pp. 1864–71.

101. See especially the article by Major Feral which is cited above.

102. *J.O., Déb., A.N.*, March 21, 1957, p. 1776. Jean-Jacques Servan-Schreiber of *L'Express* served as a recalled reserve officer in Algeria in 1956, then returned to tell a tale of widespread resort to mass reprisals and summary executions in Algeria (*Lieutenant en Algérie* [Paris: Juillard, 1958], especially pp. 13–45, 48, 65, 68–70, 195). Printed first and widely distributed in *L'Express* in the spring of 1957, then published, the story provoked the Ministry of Defense to bring charges against Servan–Schreiber for attacking the morale of the army. In 1957 Pierre-Henri Simon of *Le Monde* wrote *Contre la torture* (Paris: Seuil, 1957), presenting an impressive number of testimonials as evidence that torture was a widespread practice in the army in Algeria. *Le Monde* first spoke out openly against torture in an editorial introduction of Simon's book (*LM*, March 13, 1957). See also Simon's excellent fictional narrative, *Portrait d'un officier* (Paris: Seuil, 1958), pp. 114–75. *Témoignage chrétien* was blamed in army circles for a consistent policy of defeatism and attack upon the army. See, notably, "Quatres officiers parlent," in the issue of December 17, 1959, in which it was reported that torture was not only common but officially taught in one military school. Minister of Defense P. Guillaumat protested vigorously to this article: see his letter in *L'Armée*, No. 1 (February, 1960), p. 96. Jean-Paul Sartre's review, *Les Temps modernes*, became one center for the antitorture compaign. See, for example, the issue of June, 1960 (Vol. XV, No. 171), which contains four articles on the subject. Among book publishers the Editions de Minuit published a series of "documents" regarding torture in Algeria, the most famous being Henri Alleg's *La Question* (Paris: Les Editions de Minuit, 1958), which was seized by the government, as were several other books in this series.

103. To the Centre Républicain, printed (for the army) in *RMI*, No. 283 (May, 1957), pp. 52–53.

104. See the editorial in *RMI*, No. 284 (June, 1957), pp. 7–11.

105. Martin Harrison, "Government and Press in France during the Algerian War," *American Political Science Review*, LVIII, No. 2 (June, 1964), 273 n. 1, 278, 282; and "L'Armée et les attaques de presse," *L'Armée*, No. 1 (February, 1960), pp. 95–96. According to this article in a semiofficial review (*L'Armée*), fines ranging from twelve dollars to seven hundred dollars were imposed upon seven offending newspapers in September and October, 1959, the heaviest falling upon *La Marseillaise*.

106. *Alleg, La Question*. Alleg was director of *Alger Républicain*, a communist newspaper in Algiers, from 1950 until it was outlawed in September, 1955.

107. See the editorials in the issues of March 16, 1957 (No. 49), pp. 10–12, and April 13, 1957 (No. 53); and France Vilars, "Un Para m'a confié," *Le Bled*, April 13, 1957, pp. 6–7. For 1958 and 1959 see the editorials attacking the "defeatist press" in *Le Bled*, March 12, 1958, p. 3; *ibid.*, May 7, 1958, p. 3; and (again on the antitorture campaign) the articles signed "Narthus" in *ibid.*, September 16, 1959, and *ibid.*, September 26, 1959. See also "Pour comprendre l'armée," *Message*, No. 30 (July, 1958), pp. 1–7, especially p. 7; and "Le Poignard dans le dos," *Message*, No. 44 (July–August, 1960).

108. The hostility of paratroop officers to the political Left and to the press generally is a recurring theme in the two insightful novels by Jean Lartéguy, *Les Centurions* (Paris: Presses de la Cité, 1960) and *Les Prétoriens* (Paris: Presses de la Cité, 1961). See also the testimony of Admiral Ploix in *Procès Salan*, p. 354.

109. Massu then proceeded to argue that only De Gaulle could "resolve" the problem (quoted by J. Ferniot, *Les Ides de mai* (Paris: Plon, 1958), p. 49). Ironically, General de Gaulle personally removed Massu from his command in Algiers two years later after another tempestuous and threatening Massu interview with a German journalist in protest against De Gaulle's method of "resolving" the Algerian problem.

110. Quotations are from Admiral Ploix, testimony in *Procès Salan*, p. 354; Major M. Bourgeois, "L'Officier français peut-il faire la guerre révolutionnaire?" (thesis, Ecole Supérieure de Guerre, 73rd Promotion, 1960), p. 11; and Feral, *RDN*, p. 1871.

111. The long battle between "l'Université" (French education as a whole) and the Army is discussed by Michel Crouzet, "La Bataille des intellectuels français," *La Nef*, Nos. 12–13 (October, 1962–January, 1963), pp. 47–65.

112. De la Gorce, *The French Army*, p. 521.

113. Jeanson was not apprehended. Twenty-three other members of the group were brought to trial for hiding Moslem police suspects, encouraging and aiding French draft-dodgers through the organization *Jeune Résistance*, transporting messages and objects for the F.L.N., etc. (*LM*, September, 1960).

114. See *LM*, September 6, 1960—October 4, 1960. The majority of the defendants received prison terms of three to ten years (*LM*, October 4, 1960).

115. Interestingly enough, the Communist Party disapproved this advice, preferring that communists serve and work within the service (*L'Humanité*, September 9, 1960; and *LM*, October 4, 1960).

116. A statement of the political committee of the P.S.U. later added, however, that it did not approve of evading the draft, though it did approve of refusal to participate in repressive military operations (*LM*, October 4, 1962).

117. The text of the letter is found in *LM*, September 22, 1960, and in Marcel Péju, *Le Procès du Réseau Jeanson* (Paris: Maspero, 1961), pp. 116–19. Sartre's letter is reminiscent of Jeanson's own earlier exposition of his position, written in June, 1960 (*Notre Guerre* [Paris: Les Editions de Minuit, 1960]). Jeanson argues in Marxist terms that in aiding the rebels, in encouraging Frenchmen to refuse military service, he and others like him were serving, not betraying, the "real" (as opposed to the "formal") French community (*ibid.*, pp. 17–18, 81, and *passim*).

118. *LM*, September 20, 1960.

119. On October 3, 1960, six veterans associations demonstrated in protest against the "121" (*LM*, October 4–5, 1960). Few of the signatories were jailed, as many military men thought they deserved to be; yet those actors who signed were banned from radio, television, and state-subsidized theaters, and civil servants (including teachers) were warned by the government that signature could lead to suspension (*LM*, September 20, 1960).

120. Navarre, *Agonie de l'Indochine*, p. 334.

121. *Ibid.* A similar argument is found in "Réflexions sur la discipline," *Message*, No. 40 (January, 1960), p. 3.

122. *Ces princes qui nous gouvernent* (Paris: Plon, 1957), p. 197. This was one of many embarrassing quotations later thrown back at Prime Minister Debré by French Algeria partisans after 1960.

123. In an address to a joint session of the Massachusetts Legislature (*NYT*, July 26, 1951, pp. 1, 12).

124. Navarre, *Agonie de l'Indochine*, p. 335. An anonymous officer, writing in *Message* in January, 1960 ("Réflexions sur la discipline," p. 3), sounded a note very similar to that of MacArthur: "Celles-ci [the armed forces] no sauraient être un jouet docile entre les mains de ceux qui, en général peu nombreux, détiennent provisoirement la réalité du pouvoir."

125. "L'Armée dans la nation," *RMI*, No. 297 (August–September, 1958), pp. 8–9. The article is reprinted in Ely's book, *L'Armée dans la nation* (Paris: Fayard, 1961), pp. 179–92.

126. Jacques Fauvet and Jean Planchais, *La Fronde des généraux* (Paris: Arthaud, 1961), p. 117, quoting Challe, April 22, 1961.

127. *RDN*, October, 1956, pp. 1189–99.

128. *Ibid.*, p. 1195.

129. "Comprendre pour vouloir," No. 29 (April, 1958), pp. 1–2.

130. "L'Armée dans la nation," *RMI*, No. 297 (August–September, 1958), pp. 7–14 (quotation from p. 13).

131. General Boucherie, "Protection du territoire et armée moderne," *RDN*, March, 1955, pp. 255–65; "Enquête sur la crise de l'armée," *Message*, No. 18 (December, 1956), pp. 14–16; Captain Souyris, "L'Action psychologique dans les forces armées," *RMI*, No. 298 (October, 1958), pp. 34–35; Colonel de Metz, "Du rôle national de l'officier," *RDN*, August–September, 1958, pp. 1320–38; Testimony of Colonel Antoine Argoud in the Barricades trial in Comité M. Audin (ed.), *Sans commentaire* (Paris: Editions de Minuit, 1960), pp. 36–37; General André Zeller, "Ordre du jour N° 1," *RMI*, No. 296 (July, 1958), p. 97.

132. A special issue of *RMI*, No. 304 (April, 1959), was dedicated to "L'Enseignment français." In that issue see particularly the introductory note, page 9, by P. Guillaumat, minister of the armed forces; Dean Jean Sarrailh, "Education nationale et civisme," pp. 11–16; and "Armées et université," pp. 75–77. See also G.-P. Jouannet, "Le Maréchal de Lattre: Formateur de la jeunesse," *RMI*. No. 290 (January, 1958), pp. 93–99.

133. See the discussion of psychological action below, Chapter 8. There were also those, unfortunately a rather small minority, who attempted to heal the breach between army and nation, not through indoctrination, but through personal contacts between officers and civilians. Most notable were the efforts of "Rencontre," which brought together over one hundred officers and two hundred fifty civilians for discussion of political, social, and economic questions (interview with M. Mialet [one of the founders of the group], June, 1962). Rencontre is described by J. Planchais, "L'Armée et la nation; Trois années de rencontre," *LM*, May 17, 1961. See also Jean-Maurice Martin "Soldats et citoyens," *RMI*, No. 320 (October, 1960), pp. 39–51; Raoul Perol, "De l'armée de métier à l'armée groupe économico-social," *RMI*, No. 298 (October, 1958), pp. 66–68.

134. No. 30 (July, 1958), p. 1. This was the first issue of *Message* to appear after the May 13 crisis.

135. *Ibid.*

136. Editorial, *Le Bled*, September 13, 1958.

137. *Procès Pétain*, I, 378.

138. Massu's introductory remarks at a gathering at the Palais d'Eté, June 4, 1950, as quoted by Alain de Sérigny, *La Révolution du 13 mai* (Paris: Plon, 1958), pp. 137–38. See also the remarks of a paratroop captain quoted in Tournoux, *Secrets d'état*, p. 338.

139. *Ibid.*

140. Souyris, *RMI* (October, 1958), pp. 38–39.

141. Fauvet and Planchais, *La Fronde des généraux*, pp. 117–18; and the testimony of Colonel Julien Goubard in *Le Procès des Généraux Challe et Zeller* (Paris: Nouvelles Editions Latines, 1961), p. 107 (hereinafter cited as *Procès Challe*).

142. *Procès Salan*, p. 84.

143. After the April putsch the great majority of officers, even those who had remained loyal to the government, were sympathetic to the imprisoned officers and hostile to the government, as testimony in the trials revealed. See Azeau, *Révolte militaire*, p. 6; *Procès Challe; Procès du putsch; Le Procès d'Edmond Jouhaud* (Paris: Michel, 1962); and *Procès Salan*.

Chapter 5

Social Origins and Politics

Among the aspects of democratic society which most concerned Alexis de Tocqueville was its tendency to democratize the military officer corps, to throw open the officer ranks to comers of all social origins.[1] In armies where the officer corps is the near exclusive preserve of a well-defined aristocracy, he observed, the soldier has no hope of one day wielding a marshal's baton and is thereby shielded from dangerous ambitions; similarly, the aristocratic officer's ambition is limited, voluntarily in this case, because his prestige and power stem from his rank in society, rather than in the army.[2] Democratic armies, De Tocqueville feared, would be tempted by unrestained ambition into belligerent and rebellious habits. Probably he would have rejected vigorously the later socialist doctrine, enunciated by Jean Jaurès, that a democratic nation has nothing to fear from an officer corps drawn from all social classes.[3] The restlessness of non-aristocratic armies in under-developed areas in the face of traditional ruling elites would appear to add some credence to De Tocqueville's analysis.[4] Morris Janowitz, in his study of the American military, has voiced a similar concern that democratization of the officer corps may undermine civilian supremacy through weakening professional and traditional restraints on ambition.[5]

The problem of democratization of recruitment deserves attention in the French context, for clearly the French officer corps has lost much of the aristocratic tone which characterized it at the time of the Dreyfus case. It has been argued above that the French officer corps in the nineteenth century formed an order which tended to blur and to dominate the diverse original class loyalties of its members. The same phenomenon is evident in the officer corps since World War II. And yet the question of democratization cannot be ignored.

As we indicated earlier, during the immediate postwar years the army officer corps experienced a heavy personnel turnover. Between 1945 and 1948, 14,000 officers (or close to 50 per cent of all army officers) were released from active duty, and 4,700 new officers, mostly from the French Forces of the Interior (F.F.I.), were integrated into the corps.[6] Yet the impact of this turnover on the army as an institution must not be exaggerated. With few exceptions, newly integrated officers came in as lieutenants or captains at best, and in the case of officers of F.F.I. origin, few got beyond the company-grade ranks.[7] There is good evidence to indicate that in 1946, at least, extremely few newcomers had made their way into the higher grades (from major on up). In that year all 139 of the army's remaining generals had been regular army officers in 1938, as had all but 9 of 259 colonels, all but 18 of 485 lieutenant colonels, and all but 8 of 940 majors in the infantry and 20 per cent of majors in the cavalry, where wartime advancement had been more rapid.[8] In the lower grades, however, the years 1942–48 saw an important influx of new officers, many of them up from the ranks.[9]

The flood of young, new army officers continued through the fifties as a result of combat losses averaging over 130 officers per year, resignations rising from 172 in 1950 to 452 in 1958, retirement losses of some 350 per year, and scattered eliminations of "suspect" elements, especially those of F.F.I. origin.[10] Moreover, the pressure of colonial war, especially in Algeria, pushed the size of the regular army officer corps from a total of 22,500 in 1951 to 31,000 in 1960.[11]

Where were officer recruits found and how did they alter the composition of the officer corps? Restricting our attention to the regular army officer corps, the pattern of recruitment in the years 1950 (after the postwar purges and separations had ended) to

1957 (a few months before the *treize mai*) is shown in Table 1.[12]
The first striking feature in this recruitment pattern is the very
small percentage of Polytechniciens, less than twelve per year, who
chose a regular army career in these years.[13] Graduates of the
prestigious Ecole Polytechnique were still fairly numerous in the
higher grades, though even here their numbers had fallen from 19
per cent of all colonels and lieutenant colonels in 1938 to 14 per
cent in 1958.[14] In the army officer corps as a whole the proportion
of Polytechniciens dropped from 8.4 per cent in 1938 to 2.8 per
cent in 1958.[15] In the lower grades they were disappearing almost

TABLE 1

RECRUITMENT ORIGINS OF REGULAR ARMY OFFICERS, 1950-57*

Origin	Per Cent
Ecole Polytechnique	1.0
Saint-Cyr	27.5
Corps de Troupe (officer-candidate school)	28.0
Reserves	8.0
Ranks	28.5†
Examinations within single branches	7.0

* Girardet *et al., Crise militaire*, p. 27.
† Including 3½ per cent who were commissioned after cursory examinations and
brief training.

entirely, even in the artillery and combat engineers, where they
once constituted a majority.[16] Despite the Ecole Polytechnique's
being a military school, its graduates found little appeal in the
low prestige and guerrilla-warfare tasks of a military career in the
1950's.

A second significant feature of officer recruitment in the 1950's is
the high percentage of direct commissions from the ranks, almost

triple the 10 per cent of all new commissions theoretically reserved for adjutants and chief adjutants.[17] Recruitment from the ranks tends to be high in periods like the mid-nineteenth century and the 1920's, when declining military status reduces the number of academy applicants. In the 1950's as in the 1920's, recruitment from the ranks helped to fill the vacancies left by Polytechniciens who chose more prestigious civilian careers and the vacancies created by combat loss. The great majority of officers up from the ranks had already served several years as enlisted men and could hope to rise only to the rank of captain before reaching the retirement age for their grade.[18] Among captains in the combat arms the proportion of officers up from the ranks rose from 5.4 per cent in 1948 to 35.8 per cent in 1959.[19]

Figures for officers commissioned directly from the ranks, of course, do not include another 28 per cent of officer recruits in the 1950's who passed, after an average of five years of service, from the enlisted ranks into officer-candidate school and then into the officer corps.[20] The several specialized officer-candidate schools, like those of Saumur, Saint-Maixent, and Versailles, were united in 1945 into a single Corps de Troupe division which, along with the Saint-Cyr military academy, made up the Ecole Supérieure Militaire Interarme at Coëtquidan.[21] In October, 1961, the two divisions became separate schools, with the Corps de Troupe division thereafter taking the name Ecole Militaire Interarme, and the Saint-Cyr division that of Ecole Spéciale Militaire de Saint-Cyr. Unlike their less prestigious Corps de Troupe colleagues, who all came from the enlisted ranks, Saint-Cyriens were required to pass both state examinations for the *baccalauréat* (the French secondary diploma) before they were eligible for the competitive admissions examination. Most applicants to Saint-Cyr also spend one to two years beyond the *baccalauréat* attending courses designed specifically to prepare them for the academy's entrance examination. The length and expense of preparation for Saint-Cyr is one factor in discouraging applicants from the lower classes, though preparatory classes within the service are now easing this problem.

Popular disinterest and distaste for things military has again been reflected in a declining number of applicants to Saint-Cyr.[22]

The number of applicants who presented themselves for the entrance examination dropped from an average of 1,616 in the relatively fat years of 1930–38 to an average of 860 in the period from 1945–58; yet even that figure is above the 840 annual average of the 1920's and equal to the 1907–13 average.[23] In order to keep the number of applicants at that level, however, the army was forced to raise the age limit for applicants from 22 to 23 years, allow examination options in history and languages in addition to the science option formerly required of all, and provide preparatory classes for prospective candidates in the enlisted ranks. In view of the small number of applicants and the strong majority view among them that the Saint-Cyr entrance examination was among the easiest of all those numerous *concours* required for admission to civilian and military schools, it is quite unlikely that the quality of applicants accepted declined in comparison with the interwar year.[24]

When one looks at the total officer corps in 1958, it appears rather similar in recruitment origins to the corps of 1938 (Table 2). Yet in 1938 the tide had just turned and Saint-Cyriens and

TABLE 2

COMPARISON OF RECRUITMENT ORIGINS OF REGULAR ARMY OFFICERS*

Year	Ecole Polytechnique	Saint-Cyr	Officer-Candidate Schools	Ranks	Reserve and All Others
1913	12.1	40.0	43.9	4.0	. . . .
1938	8.4	27.5	30.3	24.3	9.3
1958	2.8	31.1	31.5	21.8	12.8

* Girardet *et al., Crise militaire*, pp. 19, 25.

Polytechniciens were beginning to flow into the corps at an accelerated rate, while in 1958 the recruitment crisis continued unabated.

The over-all picture, then—especially when one looks at the recent recruitment pattern—is that of a declining percentage of officers from the *grandes écoles* and an increasing number up from the ranks.

The appearance of "democratization" given by recruitment data is substantiated by postwar trends in the social origins of newly recruited officers.[25] On closer examination, however, the democratization phenomenon proves to be largely the result of increased officer recruitment from within the military community, and especially among sons of noncommissioned officers.

Starting with officers recruited directly from the ranks, a group about which very little is known in regard to social origins, one can assume without too great a risk that the peasantry, the working class, and the lower middle class are more heavily represented here than among school-trained officers. Officers commissioned from the ranks have normally spent over eight years as enlisted men, a role which carries material and status rewards of such a low order that it holds very limited appeal as a career for middle-class youth.

The Saint-Cyr academy has in the past enjoyed considerable prestige and has provided a large majority of the army's generals and field-grade officers.[26] The results of a recent comprehensive study clearly indicate that Saint-Cyr is attracting fewer sons of civil servants and members of the liberal professions: whereas in 1945–48, 21 per cent of the cadets admitted to Saint-Cyr were sons of civil servants (and 8 per cent among these were sons of high civil servants), in the period 1954–58 those figures had dropped to 14 per cent and 4.7 per cent, respectively.[27] The slack was more than taken up by a rapid increase in the proportion of sons of noncommissioned officers, rising from 5 per cent in 1939 to 7.5 per cent in 1945–48 and to 14 per cent in 1954–58. When that 14 per cent is added to another 30 per cent who were sons of officers in the 1954–58 period, the full proportions of self-recruitment within the military community are evident.[28]

The pattern of social origins among cadets in the Corps de Troupe division of the E.S.M.I.A. sits somewhat lower on the status scale, though it is not radically different from the pattern among Saint-Cyr cadets.[29] Again the number of sons of officers and noncommissioned officers rose significantly from 28 per cent in 1945–48 to 36.5 per cent in 1954–58. And again the increase was primarily among sons of noncoms and gendarmes, who constituted 10.5 per cent of all cadets in 1945–48 and 18.5 per cent (or as many as officers' sons) in 1954–58.[30] Sons of civil servants declined in the same years from 22.5 per cent to 14.5 per cent, including a decline in sons of high civil servants from 5.2 per cent to 2.4 per cent.[31] Sons of workers and clerks were slightly more numerous here than at Saint-Cyr, and their numbers increased in both schools in the period 1945–58 to an average of 7.2 per cent at Saint-Cyr and 15.6 per cent at Corps de Troupe.[32]

Students at the Ecole Navale, as opposed to those at Saint-Cyr, and in keeping with the navy's "aristocratic" tradition, are more frequently sons of business and government administrators and members of the liberal professions.[33] The Ecole Navale, moreover, furnishes the navy with all of its regular naval officers. Another distinct corps of "crew officers," composed of officers mostly up from the ranks, performs duties of lesser responsibility. Clearly, the regular naval officer corps draws more heavily from the middle and upper bourgeoisie than does the army officer corps. In direct contrast the air force officer corps, like the U.S. Air Force and the RAF officer corps,[34] has a lower social base of recruitment than either the army or navy. Lacking a bourgeois tradition, the Ecole de l'Air draws more sons of workers and clerks than the other service academies.[35]

In view both of the increasing number of officers recruited from the ranks and of the shifting social composition of military-school classes, it is possible to speak of "democratization" of the French officer corps, though hardly, as at least one French journalist has done, of a "proletarian" officer corps.[36] In regard to social origins the center of gravity for the army officer corps as a whole, following a pattern typical for periods of low military prestige, had probably sunk to the lower middle class by the late 1950's.[37] Yet in the higher grades the middle and upper bourgeoisie, and to a lesser degree the noble aristocracy, were still well represented, though in decline.[38]

Returning to De Tocqueville and Janowitz, two questions must be posed. To what extent can the politicization of the French officer corps in recent years be attributed to the unbridled ambitions of officers from humble social origins? In what degree is military indiscipline and revolt in the late 1950's and early 1960's attributable to a style of "military Poujadism," itself rooted in subaltern and middle-ranking officers drawn from the lower middle class, the frequent breeding ground for fascism?[39]

The causal pattern with which we are dealing is too complex to allow complete and definitive answers to these questions. The weight of the evidence so far available, however, tends to minimize the role of social class as a predominant factor contributing to military disobedience and revolt in contemporary France. Let us examine some of the evidence which can be brought to bear on the democratization hypothesis. The naval officer corps, which recruits from a higher social base than the army officer corps, provided remarkably few of the officer participants in the crises of May, 1958, and January, 1960, or in the putsch during April, 1961, and the ensuing Secret Army Organization (O.A.S.) activities. One of the more aggressive participants in the April putsch, naval Lieutenant Pierre Guillaume, was conspicuous because of the absence of other officers from his branch. Yet class considerations were likely not the primary reason for this general restraint. The navy had been deeply involved in politics during the Vichy regime and had been badly burned: those officers who remained in the navy after the war were understandably wary of another risky political involvement.

More importantly, the navy did not participate so fully as the army in the Indochinese and Algerian wars and hence did not develop as intense a feeling of vain sacrifice and betrayal. Similarly, the air force was not so deeply involved in colonial wars as the army, though more so than the navy. Similarly again, the air force provided relatively fewer military activists than the army, though more than the navy.[40] And the air force, of course, draws from a lower social base than either the navy or the army. Significantly, those air force officers who did participate in military revolt— notably, Generals Maurice Challe and Edmond Jouhaud, both leaders in the April putsch—often had been more deeply involved in the Algerian war than the majority of their colleagues.[41]

Again in defense of the "democratization equals politicization" thesis it might be argued that the strongest antigovernment ferment within the army has come from the middle and lower ranks of the officer corps, and much less often from the normal military elite.[42] Could it be that the greater restraint of the high command is explicable in terms of its more aristocratic class background? This is likely a partial, but hardly a total explanation. The field-grade officers who provided effective leadership for the military activists in this period mostly entered the army in the boom years shortly before and during World War II, hence, before the "democratization" of the postwar years began. If there were ambitious officers of modest social origins among those who flouted the sanctity of military obedience,[43] there were also a considerable number of aristocrats. Among a total of something over one hundred fifty officers arrested as a result of antigovernment activities in the April putsch or in the O.A.S., at least fifteen bore *noms à particule*.[44] Aristocrats were well represented in the camp of military rebellion, since officers with *noms à particule* constituted only approximately 5 per cent of the officer corps in 1958.[45]

In view of the relative isolation of the military community in the years following World War II, it is not surprising that military experiences should continue to shape the political values and perspective of the French officer, whatever his social origins. One of those subordinate officers who returned from Indochina to instruct his colleagues and superiors on revolutionary war describes the French military in these terms:

> No decisive characteristic allows one to fix with certitude the place of the army in the social structure if one tries to integrate it into the usual social stratifications. For this milieu presents a definite diversity and originality. Socially it is a world apart.[46]

And in that "world apart," the army's unrewarded efforts and sacrifices produced bitterness against the bourgeoisie from which most officers had sprung. The point was made forcefully by an editorialist writing for *Le Bled* on the eve of *treize mai* who described French officers in the following terms:

> They feel themselves closer to a proletarian attached to his soil and to his flag than to a capitalist ready to sell his soul to save his money and his prebends.
> To the intellectual masochism of the decadent bourgeois they still prefer the intuitive wisdom of the modest peasant.
> Often sprung from the bourgeoisie, military cadres have long since been without wealth. If they have been fighting, however, for over 20 years, it is in defense of a priceless patrimony: their Fatherland and their Honor.[47]

And yet if the French Army was now a "people's army," it was decidedly not of the sort envisaged by Jaurès or by Guy Mollet, the modern-day leader of the French Socialist party.[48] When the "modest peasant" in France proper, and the urban worker as well, exercised his "intuitive wisdom" and voted in support of Algerian self-determination in January, 1961, officers of the stamp of *Le Bled's* editorialist denounced that decision and turned to their military fellows as the only hope of national salvation.

Where *esprit de corps* was strongest, particularly in paratroop units and in the Legion, common war experiences and remoteness from the concerns of civilian France tended to wean the officer from his former class prejudices and predispositions when these conflicted with military-group interests. We have seen that aristocrats participated in military revolt. One such case is described by Jean Lartéguy, whose personal experience in, and continued familiarity with, the *paras* lends credence to his fictional tale. Captain (and Count) Jacques de Glatigny, a central figure in Lartéguy's *Les Centurions*, returns from a Vietminh prison camp to shock fellow aristocrats in Paris with his defense of a colleague now enflamed with the theory of revolutionary war. A colonel chides him gently:

> My little Jacques, I don't doubt the value of your judgment, but perhaps it has been distorted by the ambiance of the camps and that incessant propaganda to which you were subjected. The army

is one thing, politics is another, and the word revolutionary war is the negation even of all our tradition.

Every war, sir, [Glatigny retorts] will become political, and an officer who has no political education will soon lose all effectiveness. Often the word "tradition" serves only to hide our indolence.[49]

De Glatigny went on to plot against the Fourth Republic and to assist in its overthrow before finally returning to the disciplined path of the traditional officer.

De Glatigny, of course, was not representative of all aristocrats in uniform. Those at the higher echelons, and especially those who held mostly staff, rather than combat assignments, were often loyal to the traditional maxim that the military man in politics cannot safeguard his honor. The aristocratic military tradition very likely bolstered the discipline of soldiers such as General (and Marquis) Henri de Pouilly, who was one important reason why the putsch of April, 1961, failed to win over western Algeria.[50]

Even among the most traditional officers, however, the army's new role of maintaining order posed challenges to discipline. The case of General Paris de Bollardière is particularly interesting for the light it sheds on traditional military honor.[51] As a combat commander in Algeria in 1956 and early 1957, Bollardière protested against summary executions and the use of torture by the army and approved the publication of Servan-Schreiber's account of these abuses.[52] The traditional sense of honor of this Breton nobleman led him knowingly to an act of indiscipline and then to a punishment of two months of fortress arrest.[53] It is quite likely that the "dirtiness" of the army's role in counterrevolutionary war was a factor in the growing disaffection of the French titled aristocracy for the military.[54] In view of the number of titled officers who ignored the requirements of traditional military discipline, however, it would appear that once a man had become an officer, the common experiences of an isolated military community and military *esprit de corps* were frequently more powerful factors than traditional class ties.

Of related interest here are the findings of Kurt Lang in a study of those German generals who conspired against Hitler during World War II. Class factors, he found, were less important than civilian contacts and career involvement in political tasks in distinguishing conspirators from the non-committed.[55] Similarly again, Janowitz finds:

> In the United States, to an even greater extent, differences in political behavior between services or within services cannot be accounted for by social background. . . . Analysis of social origins of the military elite demonstrates that there has been a progressive decline in the importance of social heritage and a rise in the importance of organizational experiences.[56]

In the case of French Army praetorians, one can hardly overestimate the importance of the peculiar and political nature of recent French military experiences, a topic to which we will turn in the following two parts.

What is most important for military politics in the shifting social composition of the French officer corps is not so much the phenomenon of democratization, but rather that of recruitment from within. In the years from 1954 to 1958, it will be recalled, 44 per cent of Saint-Cyr cadets and 36 per cent of those at Corps de Troupe were sons of professional soldiers; moreover, officer recruits outside the two military schools were almost all taken from the ranks of noncoms with several years' service. The phenomenon of self-recruitment seems to appear most clearly in periods of low military prestige, when the number of qualified applicants from outside the military community declines. Though no complete data are available for the interwar years, the noted British military writer, Captain B. H. Liddell Hart, noted in 1928 that 50 per cent of Saint-Cyr cadets were then sons of officers.[57] By the fatter recruiting years 1937–39 the proportion of sons of career military men at Saint-Cyr (sons of noncoms as well as officers) had dropped to 30 per cent.[58] Again, and more permanently this time, recruitment patterns in the postwar years tended to intensify (as well as to demonstrate) the separation of the military community from French civilian society.

The social cleavage between French military and civilian communities in the period after 1945 is similar in many respects to the estrangement of the two communities in the nineteenth century and, to some degree, in the 1920's and early 1930's. In all of these periods social isolation of the military community was accompanied by instability in the French political system. Yet in the nineteenth century, we have argued, the army reacted with disciplined political neutrality, rather than with bitterness, anger, and finally revolt, as in the years after 1945. Why was the military reaction so different in the two cases? The essential differences seem to lie in the following conditions: first, the threatened loss after 1945 of the colonial outlet for military ambition, which has been discussed above;[59] and second, the extent of the army's *dependence* upon the support of the government and of public opinion. From 1815 until 1870 the French Army fought only in limited wars which required little sacrifice from the population at home. When major wars finally came in 1870 and 1914–18, an aroused population united behind its army. Following World War II, the French Army in Indochina and again in Algeria met a new style of warfare which made victory even in remote colonial wars dependent as much on political strength and decisiveness as on military skill. It is to that style of warfare, which turned military isolation into bitterness and revolt, that we must now turn.

1. *Democracy in America*, II, chaps. 22–23, 279–89.

2. *Ibid.*, p. 280. In the aristocratic Prussian Army of the early eighteenth century under Frederick Wilhelm, only generals bore designation of rank, and the king wore the same uniform as captains and lieutenants (Craig, *The Politics of the Prussian Army*, p. 11).

3. Jean Jaurès, *L'Armée nouvelle*.

4. Edward Shils, "The Military in the Political Development of the New States," in John J. Johnson (ed.), *The Role of the Military in Underdeveloped Countries* (Princeton, N. J.: Princeton University Press, 1962), pp. 17, 24; H. Daalder, "The Role of the Military in the Emerging Countries," Institute of Social Studies (The Hague: Mouton, 1962), p. 13; and Edwin Lieuwen, *Arms and Politics in Latin America* (New York: Praeger, 1961), pp. 190–200, 122–28, especially p. 126.

5. *The Professional Soldier*, pp.10–11, 254.

6. By the end of 1948, 658 officers had been "purged," 12,679 "separated," and another 604 had resigned. Also by the end of 1948, 3,585 F.F.I. officers and 1,134 others, mostly Free French officers, had been integrated into the army officer corps. See the reply of the army secretary of state to a written parliamentary question in *J.O., Déb., A.N.*, May 19, 1949, pp. 2704–5; and Chapter 3 n. 119, above.

7. Only one-third of all officers who entered the regular army from the F.F.I. (Forces Française de l'Intérieur) were still on active duty in 1960. Of these, 80 per cent were still captains, and none held a permanent grade of higher than major (Girardet *et al.*, *Crise militaire*, p. 69).

8. Paxton, "Army Officers in Vichy France," pp. 12–13. The data were taken from the *annuaires* of officers for 1938 and 1946.

9. Girardet *et al.*, *Crise militaire*, pp. 65–66. Girardet and Thomas (p. 22) also assert that from 50 to 60 per cent of the victims of the postwar purges were graduates of Saint-Cyr or the Ecole Polytechnique, thus lowering the proportion of this elite in the officer corps. Yet Paxton's perusal of the *annuaires d'officiers* for 1938 and 1946 revealed that the proportion of Saint-Cyriens in the middle grades (major to colonel) had *increased* from 1938 to 1946 in the infantry and had declined only slightly in the cavalry ("Army Officers in Vichy France," Table 1). Of course the purges continued until 1948, and most F.F.I. officers were integrated at lower grades.

10. Girardet *et al.*, *Crise militaire*, pp. 23 and 69. Combat-loss figures are undoubtedly low since they do not include those numerous officers who died from wounds or in prison camps. Officer casualties were higher in Indochina than in Algeria.

11. Jacqueline Bernard, "L'Origine sociale des officers," *LM*, December 28 and 29, 1960. These two articles report on a study of officer recruitment and social origins done by the Commission de Sociologie Militaire created at the Ecole de Guerre. That same study also served as the basis for the thesis by Prost, "Le Recrutement des officiers," and for much of the material in Girardet *et al.*, *Crise militaire*.

12. All of the figures which follow exclude conscripted and recalled reserve officers. Reserve officers who remain on active duty as a career are normally absorbed into the regular army, contrary to frequent American practice.

13. A larger number of Polytechniciens, up to seventy per year, chose one of the technical common services, which are quite distinct from the combat arms and are normally not included in army-strength figures. In contrast to the pattern in the 1950's, just before World War II more than one hundred Polytechnique graduates each year stayed in the army as regular combat officers (Bernard, *LM*, December 29, 1960; and Girardet *et al.*, *Crise militaire*, p. 30).

14. Girardet *et al.*, *Crise militaire*, p. 83.

15. *Ibid.*, p. 25.

16. Among artillery captains the percentage of Polytechniciens dropped from 53 per cent in 1913 to 11 per cent in 1939, 5 per cent in 1953, and to .5 per cent in 1958. Among captains in the combat engineers the figures for the same years are 61 per cent, 23 per cent, 2 per cent, and 1.5 per cent (Captains T. and A., *La nouvelle critique*, pp. 55–56).

17. The highest French noncommissioned ranks, above *sergent and sergent-chef*.

18. In 1954 officers up from the ranks within the combat arms of the army stationed in the *métropole* made up 21.5 per cent of all second lieutenants, 30.2 per cent of all lieutenants, and 34.8 per cent of all captains; but in contrast, only 1.7 per cent of all majors, .7 per cent of all lieutenant colonels, and 1.2 per cent of all colonels (Girardet *et al.*, *Crise militaire*, Table 4).

19. Captains T. and A., *La nouvelle critique*, p. 55.

20. Girardet *et al.*, *Crise militaire*, p. 56.

21. It was hoped that unification of military schools would help unify the officer corps. The specialized schools continued to be used for the one-year

Ecole d'Application training which followed a more academic program at Coëtquidan of two years for Saint-Cyriens and one year for Corps de Troupe students (or "Interarmes," as they were sometimes called).

22. The "Saint-Cyr crisis" is often commented upon in the military press. See especially General Jean Malgré, "Recrutement des officiers et structure sociale: Le Crise de Saint-Cyr et ses remèdes," *Revue politique et parlementaire*, No. 657 (April, 1956), pp. 21–29.

23. Girardet *et al., Crise militaire*, p. 34.

24. *Ibid.*, 34–38; and Malgré, *Revue politique et parlementaire*, No. 657, pp. 21–29.

25. The most valuable source here is Girardet *et al., Crise militaire*, which reports on a study of military-school students from 1945 to 1958. More general discussions of the "democratization" trend include the following: J.-R. Tournoux, "A Proletarian Army," *Reporter*, February 18, 1960, pp. 19–21; J.-M. Lombard, "La grande démission" (desertion of the wealthier classes), *Message*, No. 39 (October, 1952), pp. 29–32; "Les 50,000 officiers français," *Entreprise*, December 27, 1958, pp. 47–49; and Katzenbach, *Yale Review*, pp. 498–513.

26. In 1958 Saint-Cyriens made up 41.2 per cent of all second lieutenants, 28.7 per cent of lieutenants, 22.8 per cent of captains, 39.8 per cent of majors, 45 per cent of lieutenant colonels, and 57.3 per cent of colonels (over 80 per cent in the infantry). When Polytechniciens are added to these figures (0.3 per cent of captains, 3 per cent of majors, but 11.2 per cent of lieutenant colonels and 17.4 per cent of colonels), one finds that 56.2 per cent of all lieutenant colonels and 74.7 per cent of all colonels were graduates of one of the two major academies (Girardet *et al., Crise militaire*, pp. 24, 101). These figures, nevertheless, represented a serious decline from those of 1913 (Liber, Réalités, p. 105).

27. Girardet *et al., Crise militaire*, pp. 46, 51; and Bernard, *LM*, December 28, 1960. For the years 1945–58 the fathers of Saint-Cyr cadets were classified as follows: officers and noncoms, 40 per cent; industry, 12.5 per cent; civil servants, 17.5 per cent (7 per cent with the additional designation of "cadre supérieure" and 4 per cent, "ouvriers et employés"); liberal professions, 7 per cent; commerce, 9 per cent; agricultural, 5 per cent; and miscellaneous and unknown, 9 per cent (Girardet *et al., Crise militire*, p. 41).

28. *Ibid.*, pp. 39, 44, 46.

29. For the years 1945–58 the fathers of Corps de Troupe cadets were divided by occupation in the following manner: officers and noncoms, 32 per cent; civil servants, 19 per cent (3.7 per cent with the additional designation of "cadres supérieurs" and 5.4 per cent, "employés et ouvriers"); industry, 12.5 per cent; liberal professions, 4.5 per cent; commerce, 13 per cent; agriculture, 6.5 per cent; and miscellaneous and unknown, 12.5 per cent (*ibid.*, p. 41).

30. *Ibid.*, pp. 45, 48–50, 58.

31. *Ibid.*, pp. 45, 48, 58.

32. A comparison of the averages for the years 1945–48 with those of 1954–58 indicates that sons of clerks and workers in the *public* sector of the economy declined slightly from 4.6 per cent to 3.8 per cent at Saint-Cyr, and from 9.7 per cent to 6.8 per cent at Corps de Troupe. But sons of clerks and workers in private industry increased from .9 per cent in 1939 to 1.2 per cent in 1945–48 and to 3.4 per cent in 1954–58 at Saint-Cyr, while at Corps de Troupe they composed 3.8 per cent in 1945–48 and 8.8 per cent in 1954–58 (*ibid.*, pp. 46, 58.)

33. The fathers of one-third of the students at Navale were in these occupations in the 1945–58 period, as opposed to slightly over one-fifth at Saint-Cyr. At Polytechnique, the comparable proportion was almost one-half (Bernard, *LM*, December 29, 1960; and Prost, "Le Recrutement des officiers," p. 17).

34. Janowitz, *The Professional Soldier*, pp. 90–91; and Philip Abrams, "Democracy, Technology, and the Retired British Officer," in Samuel P. Huntington (ed.), *Changing Patterns of Military Politics* (New York: Free Press of Glencoe, 1962), pp 153–54.

35. Bernard, *LM*, December 29, 1960; and Centre d'Etudes et d'Instruction Psychologiques de l'Armée de l'Air, "Attitudes et motivations des candidats aux grandes écoles," *Revue française de sociologie*, II, No. 2 (April–June, 1961), 135.

36. Tournoux, *Reporter*, pp. 19–20.

37. Caution is still in order because of incomplete data regarding the social origins of officers who were recruited before 1945 and all officers recruited directly from the ranks.

38. Relying again upon *noms à particule* as a rough indication of nobility, Captains T. and A. found that the 6 per cent of the entire officer corps in 1949 with noble-type names had dropped to 5 per cent in 1958 (and among captains, from 6 per cent to 4 per cent). In the aristocratic stronghold—the armored cavalry and the armored corps—the percentage of those with noble-type names dropped in those same years from 38 per cent to 32 per cent of all field-grade officers, from 25 per cent to 14.5 per cent of captains, and from 16 per cent to 6 per cent of lieutenants and second lieutenants (*La nouvelle critique*, p. 57).

39. The term "military Poujadism" has been used both in reference to the lower–middle class origins of most officers and in reference to officer protests against technical modernization. In the judgment of the writer the two problems are largely distinct and will be treated so here. The air force officer corps, for example, includes more officers from the lower and lower middle classes than the army officer corps; yet air force officers are more technical-minded. For discussion of the "modernization crisis," see Chapter 10 below.

40. See below, Chapter 12.

41. Challe was supreme commander of French Forces in Algeria—mostly land forces—from December, 1958, to April, 1960; Jouhaud, born in Algeria himself, was commander of French aviation there in 1958. Lieutenant Guillaume, moreover, one of the navy's rare representatives in the ranks of the military rebels, had a brother who was killed at the head of commando group in Algeria (Fauvet and Planchais, *La Fronde de généraux*, pp. 113–14).

42. See below, Chapter 12. "Front" leaders were usually, but not invariably, generals, but the impetus and organization came from colonels and lower ranking officers, especially in 1960 and 1961.

43. Colonel Bigeard, the famous paratroop colonel who come up from the ranks, comes immediately to mind, though he only hovered on the margins of legality.

44. Among the participants in the events of May 13, 1958, one finds the following *noms à particule*: Colonel de la Borderie and Colonel de Lachenal, who accompanied General Dulac on a secret visit to General de Gaulle on May 28, 1958; General de Roncourt, who reportedly was in charge of aviation for operation "Resurrection," the unused plan for invasion of Paris; and Colonel de Vismes, commandant of the paratroop school at Pau, who was charged with taking the Paris Prefecture of Police and the city hall in operation "Resur-

rection." During the Rennes trial, involving the use of torture by paratroopers during the "Battle of Algiers" in early 1957, Captain Yves de la Bourdonnage refused to testify as a witness unless placed under arrest himself. Colonel Georges de Boissieu was a member of the "soviet of colonels" during the Barricades week. In the April putsch important roles were played by Colonel Ogier de Baulny, Colonel Charles de la Chapelle, Major Elie Denoix de Saint-Marc, and Captain Philippe de Saint-Rémy, all of whom received prison terms. Officers who received suspended sentences included Captain Rubin de Servens and Lieutenants Picot d'Aligny and de Firmas de Péries. Among officers arrested for O.A.S. activities, for example, were Lieutenant Colonel le Barbier de Blignières, Colonel Bertrand de Sèze, Colonel de Sarrazin, Major Bertrand de la Bigne de Villeneuve, Captain des Rieux, Captain du Breil de Pontoriand, Captain Bertrand de Gorostarzu, Lieutenant de la Bigne, Lieutenant Jean Rozier de Linage, and Lieutenant Picot d'Aligny d'Assignies.

45. See note 38 above.

46. Captain Souyris, "Les Cadres de l'armée dans la société française," *Les Cahiers français*, No. 23 (November, 1957), p. 2.

47. "Le Message de Jeanne" (Joan of Arc), *Le Bled*, May 14, 1958, p. 3. Though dated May 14, this edition was obviously written before the uprising of the evening of May 13. See also Planchais, *Le Malaise de l'armée*, pp. 6, 20–21.

48. See Mollet's comments on the isolation of the army from civilian society (which he regretted) collected in a pamphlet, "L'Armée et la nation," (Arras: Société d'Editions du Pas-de-Calais, 1960).

49. *Les Centurions*, p. 200. Lartéguy's two novels on the army in Indochina and Algeria, *Les Centurions* and *Les Prétoriens* follow primarily the recent history of Colonel Bigeard and his regiment of paratroopers. In addition to his personal service as a paratroop officer and long experience as a war correspondent, Lartéguy enjoyed personal friendships with a number of them. See Colonel Gardes' testimony in the Barricades trial, in Alain de Sérigny (ed.), *Un Procès* (Paris: La Table Ronde, 1961), p. 54.

50. Fauvet and Planchais, *La Fronde des généraux*, pp. 131–32, 173.

51. The story is told by Barberot, commander of a half-brigade under Bollardière, in *Malaventure en Algérie*.

52. The text of Bollardière's letter to Servan–Schreiber is in *ibid.*, p. 220. Another letter, longer and more personal, is found in Servan-Schreiber, *Lieutenant en Algérie*, pp. 261–62.

53. Barberot, *Malaventure en Algérie*, p. 234. Bollardière was released from active duty on his request, October 1, 1961 (*LM*, October 3, 1961). The same aristocratic repulsion for the police and political tasks of the army in Algeria is described dramatically in Simon's narrative, *Portrait d'un officier*, pp. 124–31.

54. Evidenced by (Count) Bertrand de Jouvenel in conversation with the writer in September, 1961, and by figures cited above, note 38.

55. Conspirators and the pro-Nazi faction had more quasi-political assignments than the uncommitted (as had many French Army praetorians in the 1950's and early 60's). The pro-Nazi group, however, more often than the other two groups were from lower–middle class backgrounds in southern Germany, as were most Nazi Party leaders ("Tradition, Skill, and Politics in the German Army," unpublished manuscript).

56. Janowitz, *The Professional Soldier*, p. 292.

57. *The Remaking of Modern Armies* (Boston: Little, Brown & Co., 1928), p. 260.

58. Bernard, *LM*, December 28, 1960; and Girardet, *Crise militaire*, pp. 39, 42. In the U.S. Army the proportion of sons of officers among generals dropped from 23 per cent in 1935 to 11 per cent in 1950. Self-recruitment probably was on the increase by 1960, however, when 25 per cent of the graduating class at West Point were officers' sons. In the German Army interwar military expansion dropped the proportion of officers' sons among generals from 52 per cent in 1925 to 30 per cent in 1939 (Janowitz, *The Professional Soldier*, p. 96).

59. See above, pp. 10–11, 45–46. See also Chapter 10 below.

Part III

The Political Demands of Revolutionary-Guerrilla War

Chapter 6

Political Challenge and Military Response

When the leaders of the January, 1960, uprising of European settlers in Algiers were finally brought to trial, one of the paratroop
officers who had given them tacit support, Colonel Joseph Broizat,
took the stand as a witness and told the court:

> . . . If we, the officers of 1939–1945, who almost led assaults in
> white gloves and *casoar* [the plumed cap of Saint-Cyr cadets], if we,
> in short, became interested in the political problem, it was not be-
> cause of a taste for politicking; it was because of the demands of
> our professional duty.[1]

The colonel's defense of the army's political ventures in Algiers
cannot be dismissed as apologetics pure and simple. As Broizat
himself never ceased to explain, from 1946 onward the French
Army had been engaged in a new and unorthodox style of war
in which military and political questions were inextricably intertwined.

If one is to comprehend the reasons for the French Army's political role in Indochina and especially in Algeria, he must understand
something of the rebel foes who forced French officers to question
those military values associated with the "Great Mute." The purpose
of this and the following chapter will be to examine the essential
character of "revolutionary-guerrilla war," especially in Indochina
and Algeria, and then to view the new political roles of the French
Army in these two wars in the context of that highly political style
of combat.

In all modern Western nations clean-cut lines between the political and military realms have been increasingly difficult to trace in this century of total war and cold war. For the officer newly engaged in revolutionary-guerrilla war, however, that distinction appears almost irrelevant: down to the level of the squad commander, political and human considerations often must be given priority over tactical military considerations. And no army in the world has as much experience against this style of warfare (or has suffered as serious a politicization from it) as has the French Army.

The style of war which the French faced in Indochina and in Algeria belongs to a sizeable category of wars, variously styled "subversive," "brushfire," "unconventional," "irregular," "revolutionary," and (most commonly) "guerrilla." Since 1945 wars of this style have raged in China, Greece, Malaya, the Philippines, and Cuba, in addition to Indochina and Algeria. What are the common and distinguishing features of what will here be called "revolutionary-guerrilla war"?[2] All depend upon the use of guerrilla tactics, especially in the early phases. In this sense, and in their rural or mountainous bases of operation, they are essentially different from the urban revolutions in France in 1789 and in Russia in 1917.[3] But guerrilla forces have often been employed simply as an adjunct to regular armies, or as a means of defense against an invader after the defeat of regular forces (as in Spain in 1803–13 against Napoleon, and in Russia in World War II against Hitler). In the Chinese Communist revolutionary war, and in other similar recent wars, guerrillas were used as a revolutionary offensive weapon which was coupled with intense psychological warfare aimed at subverting the defending regime and building a strong popular revolutionary front.

Revolutionary-guerrilla war of the Communist Chinese style had a number of historical precursors, among them the slave revolt led by Spartacus against the Roman Republic in 73–71 B.C. and, in modern France, the Protestant Camisard rebellion of 1702–4 and the Catholic Vendéen uprising against the revolutionary government after 1793.[4] It was only in the twentieth century, with the British Colonel T. E. Lawrence and his Arabian guerrillas of World

War I, however, that revolutionary-guerrilla war began to be a
systematic, self-conscious weapon.[5] Far more important as a mentor
to modern rebels was Mao Tse-tung, who combined an excellent
comprehension of the age-old rules of guerrilla warfare with an
intelligent communist's organizational talent and ideological zeal.[6]

Mao's numerous writings on the subject of revolutionary-guerrilla
war return again and again to a central theme: guerrilla war, a
tool of the militarily weak, can be successful only if it is also a
people's war.

> Many people think it impossible for guerrillas to exist for long in
> the enemy's rear. Such a belief reveals lack of comprehension of
> the relationship that should exist between the people and the troops.
> The former may be likened to water and the latter to the fish who
> inhabit it. How may it be said that these two cannot exist together?
> It is only undisciplined troops who make the people their enemies
> and who, like the fish out of its native element, cannot live.
>
> .   .   .   .
>
> Because guerrilla warfare basically derives from the masses and
> is supported by them, it can neither exist nor flourish if it separates
> itself from their sympathies and cooperation.[7]

Mao's successful pupils in Indochina, Algeria, and Cuba all understood this pre-eminent principle of revolutionary war: the most
crucial immediate task is not defeat of the government army (an
unrealistic objective in the early years) but development of support
from, and control over, the civilian population.[8] Once the "water"
is safe from pollution, the revolutionary-guerrilla movement is virtually assured of eventual victory. The rebels will watch the enemy's
every move through millions of civilian eyes and, when outnumbered by enemy troops, will melt unseen into a protective civilian
population. Though rebel losses may far outnumber government
casualties, as they did in Indochina and in Algeria, a supporting
native population produces an inexhaustible supply of replacements.
On the other hand, if the rebellion does not succeed in winning-
over a large portion of the civilian population, it will shrivel and
die, as it did in Greece in 1949 and then in Malaya after 1953–54.

Three qualifications are in order with regard to popular support
for revolutionary-guerrilla war. First, particularly in the early stages
of the war, strong support in certain base areas may be sufficient to

launch the movement and eventually to win more general active support, e.g., Fidelist support in Cuba's Oriente Province. Second, the revolutionary movement rarely can hope for the support of the total population, even in an anticolonial war, for inevitably there will be an older native elite fearful of losing all privilege and wealth to the revolution. Third, a revolutionary movement which does not embody an already existing national sentiment, nor one which easily can be aroused by propaganda, usually turns to terrorism on a mass scale in an attempt to coerce "traitors" within the target group to rally to the revolutionary cause. In Kenya, Algeria, and Malaya rebel terrorism struck the indigenous population far more often that it struck European civilians or security forces.[9] Yet the true stakes of revolutionary-guerrilla war remain support from the population, for if the target population cannot be brought to believe that the revolutionary cause is just and right, terrorism may well produce alienation rather than support. Such was the case in Malaya in the early 1950's and in Kenya after the Larbi Massacre in 1953.[10]

The term "guerrilla warfare" alone describes only one of the tactics and one of the phases (albeit the longest one) of revolution on the Chinese Communist model. Though no fixed chronological sequence of phases fits all wars on this model,[11] in very general terms it may be said that a successful revolutionary-guerrilla movement must accomplish the following tasks: (1) develop a political-military organization which eventually extends its control over a majority of the population; (2) organize guerrilla units to harass and eat away at enemy defenses and morale; (3) develop a secure territorial base for training, for escape from pursuing enemy troops, and for the seat of a provisional government (either in a mountainous or remote area where the population is sympathetic, as in Cuba and China, or in a bordering country, as in Vietnam after 1949 and in Algeria); (4) finally, if the enemy's strength and determination are too great to be broken by a long guerrilla war of attrition, develop a regular army and launch a conventional campaign to defeat his armies. The most frequent developmental tendency for a successful revolutionary movement is from an early stage of organization, propaganda, and often terrorism, to expand guerrilla activities, and finally to primary reliance upon a regular revolutionary army.

In the course of a revolutionary-guerrilla war an appeal is usually made for aid from foreign countries, and that aid may be a vital factor in the outcome of the war. Following the Chinese Communist conquest of all of mainland China in 1949, the Vietminh received Chinese war materials, which allowed the development of the large and powerful army that was more than a match for crack French paratroop regiments at Dien Bien Phu in 1954. The process worked in reverse in Greece, where Tito's break with the Cominform in 1948 led to withdrawal of Yugoslav aid and shelter to Greek Communist guerrillas, thus contributing heavily to their defeat a year later.[12] Yet foreign aid or its lack is not necessarily crucial, for guerrillas notoriously supply themselves by disarming prisoners and by raiding enemy depots and arsenals. The Chinese Communists supplied themselves primarily with equipment stolen, captured, and bought from Chiang Kai Shek's troops, and Fidel Castro overthrew the Batista regime without important foreign aid.[13]

The Indochinese and Algerian rebellions are of course of greatest interest here, for they occupied the French Army for sixteen years. Each deserves a brief description.

During World War II Ho Chi Minh, alias Nguyen Ai Quoc, founder of the Communist Party of Indochina, succeeded in taking the lead of the newly created League for the Independence of Vietnam, popularly known as the Vietminh.[14] When Japanese troops overthrew the French Vichyite administration in Indochina on March 9, 1945, former schoolteacher Vo Nguyen Giap and his Vietminh guerrillas extended rebel control—first over the Tonkin countryside, and then, following Japanese surrender in August, 1945, over the whole of that northernmost province. Free French troops moving in from the south on the heels of the British were able to re-establish control in Hanoi, capital of Tonkin, only after heavy fighting with Vietminh forces. The Vietminh retreated to the countryside, leaving the cities to the French, and strengthened

their organizational hold over a population already favorably disposed toward independence.

The war, of course, was then only beginning. The French gradually and painfully learned of the skilful manner in which the
Vietminh organized and controlled the Vietnamese population,
leaving the French administration, especially outside the larger
cities, nothing but a hollow shell cut off from its nominal charges.
The Vietminh's chief revolutionary strategist, General Giap, gave
clear priority to political over military activities in the early stage
of what he termed "armed propaganda" led by Vietminh political-
military units.[15] Using non-communist nationalists as well as communists placed in key positions, the Vietminh employed threats
along with persuasion in creating a powerful system of "parallel
hierarchies," as French military writers have labeled it, composed
of an "associational hierarchy" and a "territorial hierarchy." [16] The
Vietminh progressively organized the entire population in its stronghold areas and a large part of the population outside those areas
into a series of specialized associations for youth, peasants, non-
peasants, women, elderly people, and so forth, according to the
natural groupings of the local population. Alongside the associational hierarchy, which rose from village to canton to subprefecture
to prefecture to nation, was a territorial hierarchy composed of
governing committees for the entire population at each of the same
levels, responsible always to the unit above. Alongside these two
hierarchies was still a third, this one more selective in composition
—the Party. Throughout this overlapping organizational structure,
personal responsibility was clearly assigned, and safeguards against
disloyalty were multiple and overlapping. A leading French military
expert on the Vietminh, Colonel Charles Lacheroy, writes: "We
hardly have an example of an agent who lasted over three months
in enemy territory." [17]

Though often forced to operate clandestinely, Vietminh territorial committees were capable of administering justice, enforcing
decisions through a Vietminh police force, gathering information,
and generally undermining effective French control even in areas
where French military superiority was undeniable. The Vietminh
often succeeded in realizing the full totalitarian possibilities of this

system of overlapping structures. The cause of independence became a glorious national mission; its defenders were patriots and its opponents—and often the uncommitted as well—could only be traitors. The pure, hard Vietminh movement dealt violently with "traitors," especially those who collaborated with and informed the French. Vietnamese who were tempted to provide information to French troops when they moved into a village in force could rest assured that the Vietminh would survive any French repression and, when French troops moved on, would claim its revenge.

And so the French controlled the cities and the roads—during daylight hours [18]—while the Vietminh controlled the countryside and built a powerful military system composed of local guerrilla and self-defense units, larger regional units, and a powerful regular army. While the Vietminh watched their every move, French forces rarely could decipher the nature and movements of their enemy through the dense screen of popular silence and widespread hostility. As France hesitated to concede independence to a noncommunist Vietnamese government, then did so only in form after 1949, the Vietminh built up a political-military machine which, with Chinese Communist military equipment and tens of thousands of bicycle-pushing civilians to carry it, attacked and defeated an important French fortress at Dien Bien Phu. Indigenous troops fighting with the French, soldiers whose morale had never rivaled that of the Vietminh, all but disintegrated as negotiations at Geneva led finally, in July, 1954, to an armistice and partition of the country at the seventeenth parallel. Again as in China five years before, a powerful modern army, with air power and armor, had been defeated by a revolutionary enemy equipped initially and primarily only with small arms—and with the loyalty of the civilian population.

The victory of the National Liberation Front (F.L.N.) in Algeria is even more impressive in some respects, for French interests were greater there, French forces and colonists were more numerous, and F.L.N. military strength, even at its height, considerably less than that of the Vietminh.[19] When a group of impatient young rebels, encouraged by Colonel Nasser of Egypt, broke with the older, factious Algerian nationalist groups in March, 1954, and created the embryo of what was to become the F.L.N. and its military twin, the National Liberation Army (A.L.N.), they benefitted from no such power vacuum as Ho Chi Minh enjoyed in 1945. The French government, in fact, saw no reason for serious alarm on November 1, All Saints Day, 1954, when seventy terrorist attacks in Algerian cities, followed by rebel guerrilla raids in the Aurès Mountains, announced the beginning of what was to be a futile eight-year war for France.[20] The obstacles to an F.L.N. victory seemed great indeed. Algeria had been French since the 1830's. Her three departments were considered parts of the French Republic. Over a million Europeans had made their homes on Algerian soil, in contrast to the scant ten to fifteen thousand European residents in Indochina at the outset of the war there.

When the strength of the F.L.N. rebellion grew to serious proportions, the brunt of French defense was no longer left largely to native troops, as it had been in far-off Indochina, where all but some 175,000 men (many of these Africans and Foreign Legionnaires) out of the 500,000 defending troops had been uninspired Indochinese.[21] A French defending army of similar size in Algeria after 1957 was composed largely of draftees from the *métropole*.

Against such a formidable French Army the A.L.N. probably never had more than 30,000 to 40,000 men in arms within Algeria itself, far fewer than the Vietminh's estimated 350,000 troops in 1953.[22] Militarily the French were relatively stronger in Algeria than they had been in Indochina and the rebels considerably weaker. In eight years of war in Algeria, French military forces lost only 9,000 men while killing 141,000 rebels.[23] Though rebel forces were able to replenish their ranks indefinitely and continue a prolonged war of harassment and terrorism, it was not military defeat which forced out the French. In fact, the military operations led by Commander in Chief Maurice Challe in 1959–60 were quite successful against rebel *military* forces. If one looked only at the strength of the rebel army within Algeria, there was some truth to the claim of army Chief of Staff André Zeller in June of 1959: "The victory thus acquired by the military in Algeria is taking a form unknown until now. All that is left is to conclude it politically." [24]

Yet military means proved incapable of breaking the F.L.N. political-military organization and its control over a broadening segment of the population; nor, so long as that organization remained intact, could they halt terrorist attacks and scattered guerrilla raids, despite the considerable success of the French (especially after 1957) in cutting off rebel supplies and reinforcements from abroad and from A.L.N. bases in Tunisia and Morocco.[25] The war came to an end in March, 1962, when it had become apparent to De Gaulle and to the majority of Frenchmen that the only alternative to Algerian independence was interminable war.

The F.L.N. owed its victory·against apparently strong odds, not so much to foreign aid (as French official and military opinion often held),[26] as to terrorism, political organization, and widespread underlying resentment against the privileged European *colons.* F.L.N. tactics were similar in many respects to those of the Vietminh, although the Algerian rebels, as Arab nationalists, had little love for the Algerian Communist Party, which was predominantly European in composition and initially opposed to Algerian independence.[27]

Since the position of the F.L.N. was much weaker than that of the Vietminh had been at the outset of the war, terrorism played a more important role (probably a necessary one from the rebel point of view) in tightening F.L.N. control over a wavering population.[28] General or systematic terrorism, usually in the form of bomb and grenade explosions in buses, cafés, theaters, and other public places, was designed to pose the "Algerian problem" and to create a climate of fear and lack of confidence in French protection. Shortly the F.L.N. turned as well to selective terrorism aimed at Moslem public officials and, generally, to those Moslems and Europeans who formed a bridge between the two communities. Notes threatening death or mutilation went out to Moslem notables who sat on municipal councils, to shopkeepers who refused to contribute to the F.L.N., and to many others, even strong Moslem nationalists, who refused to accept F.L.N. authority. For those who did not comply, punishment was immediate, cruel, and widely publicized, as in those cases where the victim was returned to his village alive, but with his nose, lips, ears, or sexual parts savagely cut off.[29] If "treason" was a collective act on the part of a whole village, the F.L.N. on occasion resorted to a general massacre in which women and children were not always spared—for example, in the village of Melouza, where the entire male population of three hundred was slaughtered in May, 1957, for co-operating, not with the French, but with the rival Algerian National Movement.[30]

In Algeria, as in Indochina, the heart of the rebel movement was not the rebel army but the solid political-administrative organization which again pulled the native population out from under an undermanned French administration. Though somewhat unsystematic in the early stages, the F.N.L. gradually by mid-1956 had extended its organization from mountain strongholds to the whole of Algeria.[31] The official F.L.N. weekly, *El-Moudjahid*, later explained that the fundamental mission of early guerrilla bands was not military activity but "above all the organization of the people and the diffusion of patriotic passwords. These groups organized successful ambushes, lightning attacks, spectacular assaults. But their primary task consisted of setting up the F.L.N. organization." [32] Only then could the A.L.N. be built and supported on this organizational base.

Constructed on a communist-type cellular principle and building from the village or district level up to the six "Willayas" (plus the autonomous zone of Algiers), into which all of Algeria was divided, the F.L.N. organization consisted at most levels of a governing committee of three to five members. At middle and higher levels a political-military chief had the assistance of a political executive, a military executive, an executive for liaison, and another for intelligence. Each of these four executives belonged also to a parallel (and watchdog) system of functional hierarchies, according to their special responsibility.[33] Alongside the territorial and functional hierarchies were, as in Indochina, a number of professional associations, notably the powerful General Union of Algerian Workers formed in February, 1956. Though there existed a national liberation army (the A.L.N.), political considerations generally took precedence over military considerations, according to the guiding principle adopted by the rebel congress held in August, 1956, in

the valley of Soummam. Once the F.L.N. political-military organization was in place, repeated military defeats could not destroy
the rebel movement.

Underlying much of the effectiveness of F.L.N. terrorism and
organization was the vulnerability of Algerian society. An uneven
pace of social and economic modernization, coupled with rapid
population growth after 1930, had disrupted the traditions and
restraints of Arab family and communal life, creating an uprooted
and poverty-stricken urban working class, a frustrated educated
elite, and a peasantry newly aware of its misery. The French
sociologist, Pierre Bourdieu, described the war accurately when
he wrote:

> Its underlying causes may be found in a bitterly real drama: the
> overthrow of a vital order and the collapse of a whole world of
> values.
>
> .   .   .   .
>
> To claim that the war was imposed upon the Algerian people by
> a handful of ringleaders who resorted to compulsion and trickery
> is to deny the fact that the struggle was able to draw on strong
> popular sentiment for its vital strength and purpose, a sentiment
> inspired by an objective situation.[34]

In Algeria (as in Malaya, for example) [35] rebellion attracted those
who had broken with the traditional way but had been refused
self-fulfilment within the framework of Western colonial society.
The F.N.L. drew strong support from Moslem intellectuals (who
were aware of their subordinate social and professional status in a
colonial society) and from Moslem youth (who through education, mass media, physical mobility, and especially urbanization
were torn from traditional family and communal restraints).

Clearly, one cannot explain the determination, the sacrifice, the
fighting spirit of the Algerian rebellion, its hold over Moslem intellectuals and youth, nor the mass of Moslem demonstrators it finally
called out on the streets of Algiers in December, 1960, without
reference to Algerian nationalism, without mention of the bitterness of an awakening and disoriented native population subordi-
nated socially and economically to a European community only a
tenth its size. The failure of French psychological warfare and

its theme of "integration" of the two communities is further evidence that not just any goal will do. Lawrence of Arabia once remarked that a rebellion can be made by an active 2 per cent of the population, if only—but only if—the bulk of the remaining population is "passively sympathetic" to the rebel cause.[36]

Here, then, was the kind of enemy against which the French Army battled so frustratingly for sixteen years. Shunning the open field of battle, at least in the early stages, this rebel adversary gave clear priority to political organization and control of the population above all purely military objectives. Once having achieved control over the majority of the target population through a blended campaign of propaganda, terrorism, and organization, he could not be rooted out by military action alone.

The varied responses of the French Army to such an unorthodox foe are significant in that all of them in some way contributed to the erosion of effective civilian control. What were those responses? Throughout the Indochinese war and in the initial years of the Algerian war, French officers generally failed to understand the nature of the war being waged against them and riposted ineffectually (and worse) with an old-fashioned military attempt at repression. A second type of response was proposed (and occasionally attempted) by numerous military specialists in *la guerre révolutionnaire*, who urged that the French turn back against the rebels their own totalitarian techniques of organization and thought reform. Yet neither the French government nor the majority of French officers were willing to turn the whole of Algeria into a totalitarian state, though most agreed that effective means had to be found to deal, not only with rebel bands, but also with the rebel political-administrative organization. Hence, thirdly, government and army devised other political activities in which military personnel played a leading role, notably "psychological action" and organization and administration at the local and regional levels. Fourthly, once fully involved in the political character of revolutionary-guerrilla war, key French officers became increasingly impatient with the flagging determination of French governments and the French population. It seemed to these officers that, if Algeria were not to be lost, the army would have to focus its new political and ideological leadership, not only on the Algerians, but on the French government and the metropolitan French population as well.

The civil-military tensions which arose from all of these responses were in good measure the result of the new political demands of revolutionary-guerrilla war and deserve further consideration in that context in this and the following chapter. Those tensions were also aggravated, however, by the feeble authority of the Fourth Republic, which delegated wide powers and failed to control their exercise. Such was particularly the case with psychological action and military use of torture, both of which will be mentioned only briefly here and then discussed in more detail in a succeeding section under the rubric "political authority and civilian control."

The initial and instinctive reaction of most French officers to colonial rebellion was to call for more troops and more police in order to crush the enemies of France. Colonial uprisings as recent as those in the Algerian city of Sétif on V-E Day in 1945 and in Madagascar in 1947 had been snuffed out quickly with a ruthless campaign of repression which killed several thousand Moslems in the first instance and some thirty thousand Malagache rebels in the second.[37] Yet the French predicament in Indochina after 1946 and in Algeria after 1954 was infinitely more complex than in these and earlier colonial rebellions. Whereas harsh official suppression of revolts at Sétif and in Madagascar had been almost ignored by the French population at home and by the world outside, by the 1950's general and rapid social change in French colonial countries, modern communications, and anticolonialist sympathy both at home and abroad all conspired to publicize colonial revolts and the official reaction to them. Moreover, the enemy was now better organized, more widely dispersed, and skilled in the techniques of revolutionary-guerrilla war.

Like their more aristocratic predecessors of the early eighteenth century against the Camisard rebellion, French officers in Indochina and Algeria soon discovered that against a popular, well-organized, and determined rebellion, a tactic of bloody repression often succeeds only in spreading and intensifying the fire.[38] French troops in Indochina and then in Algeria unthinkingly fell headlong into the trap intended by rebel terrorists to alienate the native population from the French and their army. Upon seeing Frenchmen and their native supporters slaughtered and mutilated by rebel terrorists and guerrillas, who could not be distinguished from the ordinary urban worker or rural peasant and who hid behind a general conspiracy of silence, French soldiers rather naturally came to look upon all natives as rebels until proven otherwise. French reprisals against supposedly rebel villages and summary executions of suspects, practices already rather familiar in Indochina, became commonplace in Algeria.[39]

Given the unorthodox and total character of revolutionary-guerrilla war, it is not surprising that atrocities on both sides usually abound. A French platoon which arrived in an Algerian village to find the gruesomely mutilated bodies of their ambushed comrades not infrequently vented their horrified anger in burning the village and massacring its inhabitants—or by requesting an air raid upon the village as a rebel stronghold.[40] In some units (certainly not all) the cycle of terror, reprisal, and increased terror produced an attitude of strong suspicion and hostility with regard to all Moslems. Troops moving into a village often fired at all who ran from them, although many who fled did so only from fear aroused by past reprisals.

Arbitrariness in reprisals and repression was partly the result of the pitiful weakness of French intelligence. Following the 1954 armistice, General Giap is reported to have told French officers, "I won notably because the French were not informed. The French were always an average of a year behind in their evaluation of our strength." [41] The same problem plagued the French in Algeria, where frequent resort to beatings, electric shock, and the "water treatment" (forced ingurgitation or repeated near drowning), in the "interrogation" of suspects often picked up almost at random could not compensate for the absence of a co-operative and sympathetic local native population.

In Algeria those officers who understood the requirements of lasting pacification, particularly those assigned after 1955 to political-military "Specialized Administrative Sections" (SAS), were usually aware that random and uncontrolled brutality was self-defeating rather than "realistic." [42] Hence, despite military objections that "the armed forces are one," [43] tension developed between most SAS officers, on the one hand, and combat (especially *para*), intelligence, and security-unit officers, on the other. The primary task of the former was to win over the population; that of the latter, to ferret out the rebels and destroy them. One successful commander of an SAS unit, vexed by the brutality of troops passing through his sector, reported to his superiors in this manner: "At a time when the population is more and more coming back over to us and when it is important to convince them that French troops are there to protect them, such incidents must absolutely be avoided."[44]

The problem was well stated by another French officer deeply engaged in pacification efforts, an officer said to be none other than Colonel Antoine Argoud, later a key leader in military revolt:

> Incapable by their own means of distinguishing rebels from peaceful citizens, they [the forces of order] are forced by lack of information to lead a blind repression, and they amass abuses of justice. Each false *fellagha* struck down is replaced by ten real ones; until the day when our forces, finding before them the totality of the population, will be forced to practice a policy of extermination—an hypothesis excluded by definition—or give up. . . .[45]

Similar sound advice was given the French by Adjoul-Adjoul, a captured rebel leader:

> Those people who flee at the sight of French troops because they have learned of or seen with their own eyes summary executions carried out by the troops, or because the fellaghas have forbidden all contact with the French, are so many recruits ready to rejoin the ranks of the outlaws.[46]

Violence and counterviolence increasingly split the Moslem and European communities, throwing more and more of the hesitant into the rebel camp. Moslems continually suspected of being rebels became vitally aware of their alienation from the dominant European community and eventually fulfilled suspicions about them.[47]

The rising cycle of violence and counterviolence had at least two deleterious effects on military morale and, ultimately, on civilian control. Reports of atrocities committed by the French Army made their way to the *métropole*, where many good republicans as well as communists registered disapproval, and politicians and journalists from the extreme Left to the Left-Center launched a series of stinging attacks on the behavior of the nation's army.[48] Within Indochina and Algeria themselves the angry heavy-handedness of many army units tended to cut off the French from the very populations which they would have had to win over if the rebellions were to be crushed. By contributing in this manner to the certainty of French defeat, such tactics had a part in producing that deep sense of frustration and humiliation among officers which played so important a role in the breakdown of civilian control in 1958.[49] If French attempts at military repression of revolutionary-guerrilla war produced some threat to civilian control, more serious civil-military tensions arose, as will be shown in the following chapter, after the French Army began to wage a broader and more political counterinsurgency campaign in Algeria.

1. Testimony of Broizat in De Sérigny (ed.), *Un Procès,* p. 29.

2. Depending upon the criteria of selection, one might also include Indonesia, Cyprus, Kenya, Morocco, Tunisia, etc. In these cases, however, rebellion either lacked the sophisticated political-military organization and development seen in the other examples cited and/or succeeded without need for guerrilla action beyond the terrorist stage.

3. Some use was made of guerrilla tactics in the American Revolution, especially in the South. But from 1775 onward the Continental Congress and General Washington gave strong priority to the creation of a regular army (Walter Millis, *Arms and Men* [New York: Mentor, 1958], pp. 22–30).

4. Colonel Gabriel Bonnet, *Les Guerres insurrectionnelles et révolutionnaires* (Paris: Payot, 1958), especially pp. 53–55, 60–62, and 69–92; Fernand Theibaut, "Par–delà les normes de la guerre conventionnelle . . . les leçons de l'histoire," *RDN,* February. 1960, pp. 296–317; Léonard, *L'Armée et ses problèmes au XVIIIᵉ siècle,* chap. 4 ("La Guerre des Camisards, exemple de 'guerre à fond' "); and Colonel André Montagnon, *Une Guerre subversive: La Guerre de Vendée* (Paris: La Colombe, 1959).

5. T. E. Lawrence, *Seven Pillars of Wisdom* (Garden City, N.Y.: Doubleday, 1935); and Lawrence, "The Evolution of a Revolt," *Army Quarterly,* XLI (October, 1920) reprinted in his book, *Oriental Assembly* (London: Williams & Norgate, 1939), pp. 103–34.

6. Mao's principal writings on revolutionary-guerrilla war are to be found in the following: General S. B. Griffith (ed.), *Mao Tse-tung on Guerrilla Warfare* (New York: Praeger, 1961); and Mao Tse-tung, *Selected Works* (New York: International Publishers, 1954————), including "Strategic Problems of China's Revolutionary War" (I, 175–253), "Strategic Problems of the Anti-Japanese Guerrilla War" (II, 119–56), "On the Protracted War" (II, 157–243), and "Problems of War and Strategy" (II, 267–281).

7. Mao Tse-tung, *Mao Tse-tung on Guerrilla Warfare*, pp. 44, 92–93.

8. General Vo Nguyen Giap, *People's War, People's Army* (Hanoi: Foreign Languages Publishing House, 1961), reprinted in a facsimile edition by Praeger (New York, 1962), pp. 78–79, 124; E. Che Guevara, *Guerrilla Warfare* (New York: Monthly Review Press, 1961), p. 17; *El-Moudjahid* (the official weekly journal of the F.L.N.), No. 46 (July 20, 1959), as quoted in André Mandouze (ed.), *La Révolution algérienne par les textes* (3rd ed. Paris: Maspero, 1962), p. 33.

9. Samuel P. Huntington, "Patterns of Violence in World Politics," in S. P. Huntington (ed.), *Changing Patterns of Military Politics*, p. 25.

10. Brian Crozier, *The Rebels* (Boston: Beacon Press, 1960), pp. 168, 179.

11. Colonel Rocolle, "Les Constants de la guerre subversive," *RDN*, February, 1958, pp. 245–64.

12. Colonel J. C. Murray, "The Anti-Bandit War," *Marine Corps Gazette*, XXXVIII, Nos. 1–5 (January-May, 1954), reprinted in Lieutenant Colonel T. N. Greene (ed.), *The Guerrilla—And How to Fight Him* (New York: Praeger, 1962), pp. 65–111; and Jacques Dinfreville, "La Victoire de l'Armée Grecque sur la guérilla communiste," *RDN*, October, 1955, pp. 323–33; and *ibid.*, November, 1955, pp. 442–53.

13. Dickey Chapelle, "How Castro Won," in Lieutenant Colonel T. N. Greene (ed.), *The Guerrilla—And How to Fight Him*, pp. 229–30.

14. The best general sources on the Indochinese War are: Philippe Devillers, *Histoire du Viet-Nam de 1940 à 1952* (Paris: Seuil, 1952); Jean Lacouture and Philippe Devillers, *La Fin d'une guerre* (Paris: Seuil, 1960); and Donald Lancaster, *The Emancipation of French Indochina* (London: Oxford University Press, 1961).

15. Giap, *People's War, People's Army*, pp. 78–79.

16. The first and foremost French analyst of "parallel hierarchies" is Colonel Charles Lacheroy, who became head of the Service d'Information et d'Action Psychologique in the Ministry of Defense, and later joined the O.A.S. in its futile crusade for French Algeria. See, for example, his articles, "Une Arme du Viet-Minh: Hiérarchies parallèles" (Paris: Section de Documentation Militaire de l'Union Française [hereinafter SDMUF], 1954; mimeo.); "La Campagne d'Indochine, ou une leçon de guerre révolutionnaire," (Paris, SDMUF, 1954; mimeo.), and his lecture, "La Guerre révolutionnaire," in Centre des Sciences Politiques de l'Institut d'Etudes Juridiques de Nice (ed.), *La Défense nationale* (Paris: Presses Universitaires de France, 1958). See Colonel Nemo, "La Guerre dans le milieu social," *RDN*, May, 1956, pp. 605–23; "La Guerre du Viet-Minh," by "un groupe d'officiers," in *RMI*, No. 281 (February-March, 1957), pp. 23–39; and Lancaster, *The Emancipation of French Indochina*, pp. 418–28.

17. *La Défense nationale*, p. 314.

18. As Lacheroy puts it "Nous exerçons à peu près la 'Royauté du jour'

dans notre zone, mais le Viet y partage très largement avec nous la 'Royauté du la nuit' " ("Une Arme du Viet-Minh: Hiérarchies parallèles," p. 4).

19. The Algerian war has already been the subject of an extensive literature. Of particular interest are: Jacques Soustelle, *Aimée et souffrante Algérie* (Paris: Plon, 1956); Germaine Tillion, *L'Algérie en 1957* (Paris: Editions de Minuit, 1957); Serge Bromberger, *Les Rebelles algériens* (Paris: Plon, 1958) (hostile to the F.L.N.); Charles-Henri Favrod, *La Révolution algérienne* (Paris: Plon, 1958) (favorable to the F.L.N.); Mandouze (ed.), *La Révolution algérienne par les textes* (excerpts from F.L.N. documents and publications); Michael Clark, *Algeria in Turmoil* (New York: Praeger, 1959) (a well-documented "French Algeria" viewpoint expressed by a former *New York Times* reporter); R. le Tourneau, *Evolution politique de l'Afrique du Nord Musulmane, 1920–1961* (Paris: Colin, 1962); Roger Trinquier, *La Guerre moderne* (Paris: La Table Ronde, 1961) (pp. 115–21 for a description of the F.L.N. organization); Lucien Poirier, "*Un instrument de guerre révolutionnaire: Le F.L.N.*," RMI, No. 289 (December, 1957), pp. 7–34, and *ibid.*, No. 290 (January, 1958), pp. 69–92; Raymond Aron, *La Tragédie algérienne* (Paris: Plon, 1957); and Aron, *L'Algérie et la république* (Paris: Plon, 1958).

20. The events of that All Saints Day are described in Clark, *Algeria in Turmoil*, pp. 3–5. See also General C. R. Cherrière, "Les Débuts de l'insurrection algérienne," RDN, December, 1956, pp. 1450–62. Cherrière was commander of French military forces in Algeria in 1955–56.

21. Figures are for 1953 (Navarre, *Agonie de l'Indochine*, p. 46).

22. The Vietminh estimate is by Navarre, *Agonie de l'Indochine*, p. 46. Estimates of F.L.N. guerrilla strength in the Aurès Mountains in the fall of 1954 vary from 350 (Cherrière, *RDN*, p. 1454) to 2,000 (Clark, *Algeria in Turmoil*, p. 122). By March, 1956, French intelligence estimated rebel armed strength at 8,000 regulars and 21,000 auxiliaries (*ibid.*, p. 299). F.L.N. sources claimed as many as 100,000 rebel troops in the fall of 1957, while a Tunisian newspaper close to the F.L.N., the *Petit Matin*, put the figure at 42,000 (Bromberger, *Les Rebelles*, 248–49). The actual figures, though impossible to determine exactly, were probably between 25,000 and 40,000 in 1957. Completion of an electrified barrier on the Tunisian border in September, 1957, thereafter limited A.L.N. access and probably held armed rebel forces within Algeria to about the same limits.

23. *LM*, March 9, 1962, quoting "official sources." Very likely the figure for rebel casualties includes many Moslems who had little or no connection with the F.L.N., but who were killed in French raids on rebel villages. See below, pp. 61–62.

24. "L'Armée de terre liée à la nation," RDN, June, 1959, p. 963. See also General Challe's testimony in *Procès Challe*, p. 26 (" . . . En 1960 les rebelles étaient pratiquement défaits . . . ").

25. Arms, probably from Egypt, came into Algeria across the Tunisian border in the early years of the war. Yet a French intelligence report of March, 1956, estimated rebel armament to include primarily hunting rifles, which were probably of domestic origin (18,000 hunting rifles as against 3,200 army rifles and 606 small automatic weapons [Clark, *Algeria in Turmoil*, p. 299]). Two ships carrying heavier military equipment intended for the rebels were captured by the French—the Greek ship "Athos" bearing arms from Egypt, in October, 1956, and the Yugoslav ship "Slovenija," in January, 1958. In the latter years of the war the A.L.N. maintained regular bases in Tunisia and Morocco.

26. In regard to foreign responsibility for the war, see, for example, Cherrière, *RDN*, p. 1451; Soustelle, *Aimée et souffrante Algérie*, p. 21; and Déon, *L'Armée d'Algérie et la pacification*, p. 36. With respect to French military disregard for rebel goals and ideology, see Chapter 11 below.

27. After the Sétif uprising in 1945 the central committee of the Communist Party for North Africa announced: " . . . Il faut tout de suite chatier rapidement et impitoyablement les organisateurs de troubles, passer par les armes les instigateurs de la révolte et les hommes de main, qui ont dirigé l'émeute" (*Liberté* [organ of the Parti Communiste Algérien], May 17, 1945, as quoted by Guy Mollet, *13 Mai 1958, 13 Mai 1962* [Paris: Plon, 1962], p. 140). When again in 1954 the French and Algerian communist parties initially opposed Algerian independence, the F.L.N. condemned them in its Soummam Valley platform of 1956 (Mandouze, *La Révolution algérienne par les textes*, pp. 94–95). On the subject of F.L.N.–Communist Party relations see also *LM*, March 23, 1957; Jean Glories, "Quelques observations sur la révolution algérienne et le communisme," *L'Afrique et l'Asie*, No. 41 (1958), pp. 16–44; *ibid.*, No. 42 (1958), pp. 3–23; and (from a writer closer to the French *guerre révolutionnaire* school) Déon, *L'Armée d'Algérie et la pacification*, pp. 38–52, 178–87, 183–93.

28. The role of terrorism was more important, I would argue, than suggested by Crozier in *The Rebels*, p. 191. But terrorism alone is hardly capable of establishing community support, as suggested by writers such as Virgil Ney, "Guerrilla War and Modern Strategy," *Orbis*, II, No. 1 (Spring, 1958), 75; and Colonel Trinquier, *La Guerre moderne*, pp. 40–44.

29. See Bromberger, *Les Rebelles algériens*, pp. 40, 81; Soustelle, *Aimée .et souffrante Algérie*, pp. 23–24, 215–17, 299 (photographs of victims after pp. 88 and 136); and Crozier, *The Rebels*, pp. 170–75.

30. C. L. Sulzberger, "The Nationalist Strategy of Terror in Algeria," *NYT*, June 5, 1957. One French reserve lieutenant, who favored independence for Algeria told the writer of finding dozens of Moslem men, women, and children killed and mutilated as the result of a punitive F.L.N. raid in 1958. See the internal F.L.N. directive ordering mass reprisals by burning of villages and massacre of male inhabitants in cases where villagers asked for French protection, in *L'Année politique 1957* (Paris: Presses Universitaires de France, 1958), p. 231.

31. Poirier, *RMI*, No. 289 (December, 1957), pp. 25–26.

32. No. 53–54, November 1, 1959, as excerpted in Mandouze, *La Révolution algérienne par les textes*, p. 40.

33. Poirer, *RMI*, No. 290 (January, 1958), pp. 72–83.

34. See Pierre Bourdieu, *The Algerians*, trans. Alan C. M. Ross (Boston: Beacon Press, 1962, pp. 144–45; see also pp. 134–44. This book was originally published in 1958 and revised in 1961 as *Sociologie de l'Algérie* ("Que sais-je" series [Paris: Presses Universitaires de France]).

35. Lucien Pye, *Guerrilla Communism in Malaya* (Princeton, N. J.: Princeton University Press, 1956), pp. 7, 343–44.

36. T. E. Lawrence, *Oriental Assembly*, p. 134. On the same point see also Griffith, *Mao Tse-tung on Guerrilla Warfare*, p. 43.

37. Moslem casualties at Sétif have been estimated at figures ranging from 1,300 (by official French sources) to 45,000 (by the F.L.N.); 10,000 is perhaps a reasonable estimate. See Crozier, *The Rebels*, pp. 197–99 (and, with regard to the Madagascar revolt, pp. 199–201); Clark, *Algeria in Turmoil*, pp. 29–38; and Le Tourneau, *Evolution politique de l'Afrique du Nord*, p. 350.

38. Similar experiences were had by the French in the Vendéen rebellion, by the Germans in Russia and Yugoslavia in World War II, and by the Japanese in China in the late 1930's and early 40's. See Léonard, *L'Armée et ses problèmes au XVIIIe siècle*, pp. 71 and 76 (Camisards); Montagnon, *Une guerre subversive: La Guerre de Vendée*, pp. 16, 116, 120, 122, and *passim*; Danila Grujic (ed.), *The Liberation Struggle of the Yugoslav Peoples, 1941–1945* (Belgrade, 1961), p. 53; Chalmers Johnson, *Peasant Nationalism and Communist Power* (Stanford, Calif.: Stanford University Press, 1962), pp. 31–70; and Johnson, "Civilian Loyalties and Guerrilla Conflict," *World Politics*, XIV, No. 4 (July, 1962), 651–52.

39. Instances when suspects were tortured and shot in Indochina were related to the writer in 1956 in Saigon by former French Legionnaires. Napalm air attacks against entire villages in Indochina, ordered as punitive measures, are described by Fall, *Street without Joy*, pp. 104–5, 108, 253–55; Lancaster, *The Emancipation of French Indochina*, p. 224 n. 3; Devillers, *Histoire du Viet-Nam*, pp. 251–52; and Barale, *La IVe République et la guerre*, p. 489. In regard to mass reprisals and summary executions in Algeria, the evidence is weighty. See Dufresnoy, *Des Officiers parlent*, pp. 5, 6, 12, 56; Simon, *Contre la torture*, 84–93; Barberot, *Malaventure en Algérie*, 108–16; Servan–Schreiber, *Lieutenant en Algérie*, 13–45, 48, 65, 68–74, 157, 195, 197; J.-M. Darboise, "L'Echec de la pacification," in J. M. Darboise, M. Heynaud, and J. Martel, *Officiers en Algérie* (Paris: Maspero, 1960), 28–29; R. B. Bruno, "Soldat en Algérie," *Les Temps modernes*, XV, No. 171 (June, 1960), 1835–36; Pierre Leulliette, *Saint Michel et le dragon: Souvenirs d'un parachutiste* (Paris: Editions de Minuit, 1961), p. 220, and *passim*. A vivid account of French Army arson, massacre, pillage, rape, and torture is found in the work of a former French commando, Benoist Rey. The account is exaggerated and representative of relatively few units, but it is worthy of note (*Les Egorgeurs* ["The Cutthroats"] [Paris: Editions de Minuit, 1961]). A large collection of letters, cables, and petitions from Moslems protesting against French brutality and summary executions is found in Patrick Kessel and Giovanni Pirelli, *Le Peuple algérien et la guerre: Lettres et témoignages, 1954–1962* (Paris: Maspero, 1962), especially pp. 29–31; 36–45; and 299–306. Like the work of Benoist Rey, this collection describes only the most violent aspects of French pacification. For a fictional account of counterterrorism in Algeria see Lartéguy, *Les Centurions*, 294–95. In regard to the generalized and imprecise French concept of the enemy, we have the testimony of Governor-General Jacques Soustelle to the effect that the indiscriminate arrest of supposed Algerian nationalists who had nothing to do with the rebellion of November 1, 1954, only served to feed the rebellion (*Aimée et souffrante Algérie*, p. 28).

40. In an interview with the writer in April, 1963, Reserve Lieutenant J. recalled finding the bodies of French soldiers in 1957 with their sexual organs cut off and stuffed into their mouths. Lartéguy, *Les Centurions*, pp. 294–95, describes a similar incident. Such acts were likely intended as provocations. Mass reprisals are described or mentioned in Servan–Schreiber, *Lieutenant en Algérie*, p. 72; Lieutenant de P. in Dufresnoy, *Des officiers parlent*, p. 12; Darboise, *Officiers en Algérie*, p. 28, Rey, *Les Egorgeurs*, *passim.*, and Lieutenant Philippe Marchat, *RDN*, pp. 1832–33.

41. Tournoux, *Secrets d'état*, p. 16 n.

42. In *Malaventure en Algérie*, Colonel Barberot argues convincingly that as the army unknowingly (and often despite contrary intentions) assumed the role of protecting the European minority and its privileges, it destroyed its effectiveness as a pacifying force (pp. 115–17 and *passim*).

43. See the editorial in *Message,* No. 21 (April, 1957), p. 2, for a defense of the unity of the army. In the preceding issue of *Message,* however (No. 20, March, 1957: "D'Algérie: Une opinion sur le moral des officiers"), one finds an officer denouncing the use of torture and the army's police role generally (pp. 1–4). The realities and unrealities of army unity are discussed in Chapter 12 below.

44. Lieutenant Morin, commander of a subsection near Algiers, as quoted in Barberot, *ibid.,* p. 109.

45. A "report" of Major "Marcus" (pseudonym), commander of a regiment including a harki, or Moslem, unit (quoted by Servan-Schreiber, *Lieutenant en Algérie,* p. 70). "Marcus" is identified as Argoud by Jacques Fauvet and Jean Planchais in *La Fronde des Généraux,* p. 93. See Argoud's recommendations of 1960 regarding "adapted justice," below, Chapter 9.

46. Quoted in Barberot, *Malaventure en Algérie,* p. 113.

47. See Bourdieu's discussion of the Moslem reaction to being permanent suspects (*The Algerians,* pp. 153–54).

48. See Chapter 4 above and Chapter 9 below.

49. See Chapter 10 below.

Chapter 7

Counterinsurgency and Military Politics

Many of those French officers who returned home from Indochina and from Vietminh prison camps reflected lengthily on their defeat and particularly on the unorthodox character of their victorious adversary. It was clear to all that French military repression had been pitifully ineffective against the Vietminh. For some, like General Navarre, a weak and vacillating French government was almost entirely to blame; but in the minds of a growing number of captains, major, and colonels, it gradually became clear that the army itself had failed to understand the political nature of revolutionary-guerrilla war. And so in the early years of the Algerian war, a whole doctrine of *la guerre révolutionnaire* was developed and diffused within the army until it became official policy.[1] Detailed discussion of that doctrine will be deferred to a later chapter; suffice it to say here that theorists of *la guerre révolutionnaire* looked, not to military action, but to psychological warfare and organization of the population as primary weapons against a revolutionary-guerrilla enemy. In many respects they were right. Unfortunately for civilian control of the French military, their conception of the political demands of counterrevolutionary-guerrilla war drew them eventually into conflict with civil authorities.

One strong wing of the *guerre révolutionnaire* school insisted that only by abandoning temporarily the restraints of a liberal democracy, only by resorting to totalitarian tactics, could France possibly defeat a totalitarian enemy.[2] The rebel political-administrative apparatus (the core of the rebel movement) could never be crushed, it was argued, if France gave more attention to individual rights than to victory. One of the earliest and most influential military theoreticians of this persuasion was Colonel Charles Lacheroy, a close student of Vietminh organizational tactics. In November, 1953, as the Indochina war still continued, he wrote:

> On the one side, an *easy-going justice* in a *venal and relaxed democracy*; on the other, a *popular-political-military dictatorship, relatively pure*, always *hard*, and, when necessary, *cruel*. . . . One replies to war gas with war gas, to "strategic" bombing with "strategic" bombing, to the atomic bomb with the atomic bomb; otherwise, one gives up hope of winning and goes home.[3]

Lacheroy's plan was to meet the enemy's organizational efforts with a massive French campaign to establish its own "parallel hierarchies" to control the native population. The colonel was fully aware of the totalitarian character of such a plan. "Every living being" must be forced to "engage" himself, he writes:

> It is necessary that all forms of complicity, including those of abstention and silence, be rendered impossible or treated, in the same manner as the crime of treason, by special courts and an expeditious procedure.[4]

Lacheroy's proposal was taken up and applied in a few cases in Algeria, notably by Colonel Yves Goddard and by Colonel Roger Trinquier. In February, 1957, the Tenth Paratroop Division under General Jacques Massu was called into Algiers and given full police powers; the F.L.N. organization, officially estimated at only two hundred terrorists supported by some five thousand militants, was killing two hundred civilians per month while local police stood by virtually helpless.[5] Thousands of suspects were picked up by Massu's *paras*, interrogated, often tortured, and sometimes executed without a trial.[6] Paratroopers stood ready to utilize all information in surprise raids against the F.L.N. organization. From February to October the F.L.N. apparatus and its terrorist campaign were largely crushed; then they succeeded in self-regeneration from April to June; but, finally, both were torn down again from June to October as high F.L.N. leaders were killed (Ali la Pointe), captured (Yacef Saadi), or forced to flee.[7]

In the course of the "battle" Massu's executive officer, Roger Trinquier, worked with Sector Commander Colonel Godard in creating an hierarchical organization which extended down to districts, *ilots*, and groups of houses, subjecting every resident to the control and scrutiny of carefully selected leaders.[8] A careful census and a system of identity cards indicating the exact district of residence of the bearer facilitated tight control of all movement of persons into and within the city. Under the control of Colonels Godard and Trinquier this "organization of the population," as Trinquier refers to it, served largely as a channel for collecting information without fully realizing the indoctrination potential which Lacheroy had envisaged for it.[9] Nevertheless, during the dramatic May days of 1958 following the army-supported French Algerian uprising in Algiers, Colonel Trinquier (whose troops had been instrumental in the revolt's success by failing to halt it) went back into the Casbah, renewed contacts with what remained of his "organization of the population," and in co-operation with French military urban-administration and psychological-warfare officers on the scene, brought thousands of Moslems onto the Algiers Forum on May 16 for a massive fraternization festival with the European population.[10]

The organization of the European population, unlike the organization of Moslems (where Frenchmen held the higher posts), was *pied noir* (European settler) throughout. It facilitated later French Algeria crusades, from that of May 13, 1958, to the Secret Army Organization.[11] So long as military officers could control these "organizations of the population" (both Moslem and European), they had at their disposal a political weapon which could as easily be turned against the Paris government as against the F.L.N.

To the despair of French revolutionary-war theorists the organization created in Algiers in 1957 was not maintained, nor was it used as a model for pacification elsewhere.[12] Officers such as General Massu and his guiding colonels (Argoud, Broizat, Godard, and Gardes) received little more satisfaction concerning the "adaptation" of procedures of justice, despite their repeated pleas.[13]

As we shall see more fully in the following chapter, Massu and his staff went far toward "adapting" justice on their own initiative, without waiting for changes in the law. What is important here, however, is the rather widespread (though far from universal) military belief—especially in paratrooper, military-security, and intelligence circles—that summary executions and torture were essential tools in defense against a terrorist and guerrilla enemy.[14] "One does not fight a revolutionary war with the Napoleonic code," argued Colonel Lacheroy, one of the more cautious exponents of "adapted" justice.[15] From the *Message des forces armées* during the battle of Algiers came the warning, "Legality is bad when it no longer protects the victim from the murderer."[16] And, again from the *Message* a year later, "Either France and the French will die in legality, or they will save themselves . . . with new laws." [17]

And what manner of new laws were thought to be required? To paraphrase Colonel Broizat, who finds in the battle of Algiers a high percentage of "unusual and even illegal procedures" but "a very high percentage of just solutions," "adapted" justice must be: decentralized, rapid, with penalties geared to *war* and not to peace, often secret in testimony but public in execution, applicable to all who aid the rebellion in any way, without appeal to higher courts, and with allowance for exceptions.[18] As for Colonel Argoud, another of the army's political colonels, justice (as defined in French law) applied in Algeria is seen as

profoundly unjust, since, save in exceptional circumstances, it strikes only the little man; it is totally ineffective, since, in the place of a severe, simple, immediate, exemplary justice which the Moslem people and the circumstances call for, we have had for six years, alas, a justice of criminal weakness, desperate slowness, and Byzantine complexity, justice often delivered almost in secret.[19]

And what does Argoud understand by "severe, simple, immediate, exemplary justice"? If the published text of his secret testimony at the Barricades trial is authentic, he there provided the answer in relating his personal experience as commander of a sector at Arba during the battle of Algiers:

. . . I decided, of course after mature reflection and without hiding from myself the disadvantages of the system, I applied this justice personally under my own responsibility; that is to say that after a precise, tight investigation, aided by inspectors from the judicial police, I shot the murderers and rebel leaders on the public square.[20]

Justice in the fashion of Colonel Argoud, coupled with torture of suspects, unquestionably broke the F.L.N. in Algiers, at least temporarily, and henceforth stood for Massu, Broizat, Argoud, Trinquier, and others as a model of counterterrorism.[21] But there were others for whom torture and summary executions were dishonorable and completely unacceptable; among these were General Paris de Bollardière, whose protests led him to two months of fortress arrest,[22] and former minister of defense, General Pierre Billotte. Billotte and Massu carried on a heated exchange in 1957, during which the military master of the Algiers area replied to Billotte in the following terms in a circular sent to his officers and to selected politicians:

The soldiers who, in Algiers, arrested hundreds of killers know that there are few cases indeed where the killers have not been able to give the name and address of their cell leader, of other killers of the cell. How does the general believe that we arrested these killers? By subtle reasoning? . . . Does he believe that one can afford the luxury of waiting weeks, or just days, for a bomb setter to give the address of the cache where bombs are hidden? . . . General B. is ready to suffer the misfortune of others with the greatest abnegation and the greatest nobility. . . . Let hundreds of people perish (and we are saying hundreds) rather than dirty our hands![23]

To pose the problem in dramatic terms, as does the novelist Jean Lartéguy, suppose the capture of a terrorist known to have planned and supervised the planting of bombs set to explode in crowded stores in mid-morning.[24] The terrorist refuses to divulge the location of the bombs. Shall his interrogator force out the secret by torture, or shall he be indirectly responsible for the death and maiming of dozens of innocent civilians? The moral problem is a difficult one, especially for the man who is directly responsible for the safety of his civilian and military charges;[25] yet, of course, the dilemma is not fairly stated in Lartéguy's fictional account, nor by protagonists of the "hard" line generally.[26] Given the French Army's tenuous contacts with the Moslem population, given the frequency of denunciations which were simply acts of personal vengeance,[27] one can understand the alarm of French liberals when Massu could announce that ". . . . the rights of the innocent are superior to those of the guilty." [28]

Purely on grounds of expediency, the case for "adapted" justice to allow summary executions and regulated torture is far from clear. If such tactics were effective temporarily in the rebel autonomous zone of Algiers, it is not at all likely that they would have succeeded over the whole country—*unless*, it must be added, France had been willing and able to renounce outright its constitutional tradition and to organize the entire population in a totalitarian state. As one of Massu's critics put it:

> . . . If we continue to defend French civilization in Algeria by torture, even against an enemy who never hesitates to play the butcher, torture will install itself in Algeria, but French civilization there will be destroyed.[29]

In view of the reaction of the free press and of the political opposition in metropolitan France, it is quite likely that the cause of French Algeria was damaged, rather than strengthened, as a result of the battle of Algiers. The cases of Maurice Audin, Henri Alleg, Djamila Bouhired, and other victims of the *paras* served as powerful symbols reminding Frenchmen of their guilty conscience and undermining their faith in the justice of the French position.

The Gestapo-like police activities of certain army units in Algeria contributed significantly to those civil-military tensions which finally erupted in May, 1958. On the one hand, the battle of Algiers produced the strongest attacks yet voiced in French political and press circles against the army and further revealed the isolation of many French officers from the mainstream of French opinion. With regard to specific military grievances against governmental officials, militant colonels like Argoud, Gardes, Godard, Trinquier, and Broizat (all key figures in later military revolt) were disgusted and embittered by the abandonment of experiments of the Algiers variety and by government investigations into military behavior during the battle of Algiers.[30]

Even though the French government and probably most army officers shied from a totalitarian solution to the problem of pacification in Algeria, many (but not all) civil and military officials gradually became aware of the need for a positive political response to what was viewed, by 1956–57, as a predominantly political challenge. Largely as a result of the growing influence of the *guerre révolutionnaire* school,[31] more and more military officers and civil administrators came to conceive of their task as had the famous colonizer, Marshal Gallieni, in his too-long-forgotten directive of May 22, 1898:

> . . . We must remember that in colonial struggles we must destroy only in order better to build. . . . Each time that incidents of war require one of our officers to act against a village or an inhabited center, he must not lose sight of the fact that his first concern, once the inhabitants have submitted, will be to reconstruct the village, to create a market there, to establish a school there. It is from the combined action of force and politics that the pacification and eventual organization of the country will later result. Political action is much more important. It draws its greatest strength from the organization of the country and its inhabitants. . . .[32]

To be sure, the guerrilla bands had to be defeated and the rebel political-administrative organization destroyed. Yet if the crucial support of the civilian population was to be won and held, the French, it was beginning to be understood, would need a political *program* of reforms aimed at the satisfaction of real grievances, *propaganda* to put across that program, and political *organization* capable of both interpreting the appeal and implementing reforms. In fact, in all of the most striking recent instances in which a revolutionary-guerrilla movement has been defeated (in Greece, Malaya, and the Philippines), government military efforts were strongly seconded by an effective economic and political appeal.[33]

A series of official statements in 1956 evidences a firm governmental decision to vest the army with important political and administrative responsibilities in an attempt to renew French contact with the Moslem population and to win it over through propaganda and organization. In the summer of 1956 Minister of National Defense Bourgès-Maunoury remarked:

> It has become almost a commonplace to speak of psychological war and revolutionary war. . . . We now have not only an Army of soldiers; we have an Army of builders, an Army of doctors, an Army of pioneers, I could almost say an Army of propaganda, an Army of "contact" with the population.[34]

At about that same time (in June, 1956) the resident minister in Algeria, Robert Lacoste, issued a general directive to military personnel in Algeria impressing upon them their obligation to help rebuild general confidence in France, to rejoin the Moslem and European communities, and to sell the government's reform program of local self-government, industrialization, improvement of agriculture, and opening of the civil service to more Moslems.[35] In a follow-up statement printed in the July, 1956, issue of the *Revue militaire d'information* under the heading "The Role of the Army in Psychological Action," Lacoste argued:

> Military action is nothing without action on opinion. . . . The Army must play the role of the connecting link in acting both on the Moslem population and on the French population to break this sort of complicity in mutual ignorance and, if something is not done rapidly, in hatred.[36]

Even more indicative of shifting military roles was Lacoste's General Directive Number Three of November 30, 1956:

> . . . I know what you are today being asked to do: protect the population, care for them, teach them, sometimes administer them. I beg of you now to help them in their local politics since, in this strange form of conflict, psychological and political action are juxtaposed tightly with military action. . . . The purely military phase of your action in Algeria is ending in effect and is tending to be progressively replaced by a political-military phase where the search for contact with the French Moslems through specific institutions will be the conducting wire.[37]

Specifically, what were the army's new political responsibilities? Of the three major aspects of the counterinsurgency campaign— a political program, propaganda, and organization—only the formulation of a program was intended to remain a totally civilian responsibility, and even there the military progressively moved to fill a civilian vacuum. The story of French military "psychological action" and its abuses will be left to the following chapter, where it can be better understood in the context of the *immobilisme* and waivering authority of the Fourth Republic. Discussion here will focus on French military efforts at winning over local communities and mobilizing them against the rebels.

A few scattered attempts at organization and mobilization of local communities against the Vietminh had been made in Indochina, even though, with few exceptions (Colonel Lacheroy and a few others), the French were as yet quite ignorant of the more political aspects of revolutionary-guerrilla war.[38] One notable exception to the general pattern was the relatively systematic policy in Cambodia after 1952 of relocating threatened communities and organizing them for self-defense.[39] Another was the successful pacification of Ben Tre Province at the mouth of the Mekong River where, armed with full powers, a Eurasian colonel in the French Army, Jean Leroy, skilfully combined military action with agrarian and political reform.[40] Beginning with the Catholic minority, Leroy built a twelve-thousand-man militia, the "Mobile Units for the Defense of the Christian Communities." He protected the peasant against the landowner and moneylender, combining a veritable social revolution with local self-government. His mode of operation was similar to that of the Vietminh: armed bands moved into a community in strength, forced out the enemy, indoctrinated and organized the population for self-defense, economic reconstruction, local self-government, and community development (schools, infirmaries, sports). But when Leroy was assigned to a larger, but strictly military, command in November, 1952, the nominally independent Vietnamese government in Saigon was eager to diminish the strength of his militia. The Vietminh quickly moved back into the province, and Leroy's embryonic organization largely collapsed.

Other less thorough attempts at political-military organization on the local level included the brief efforts in Tonkin in 1952 by "Mobile Administration Groups for Operational Purposes," composed mostly of Vietnamese,[41] and the more strictly military work of the French military *Section Action,* which raised some thirty thousand anti-Vietminh guerrillas among mountain people in Tonkin and Laos.[42]

With the exception of the Cambodian self-defense policy guided by Premier Norodom Sihanouk and the work of Colonel Leroy, organizational efforts against the Vietminh stopped short of effective mobilization of popular support. In both of these exceptional cases it is interesting to note the following: first, vigorous native leaders (quasi-native in the case of Leroy) played an important role; and second, the character of mobilization was positive and reformist, more than it was repressive.[43] Would community political-military organization throughout Indochina have defeated the Vietminh? Most probably not, for the weakness and vicissitudes of French policy and its feeble political appeal in Indochina would have limited the success of such an enterprise, except perhaps in the strong Catholic areas within North Vietnam.

The program of community organization and mobilization launched in Algeria in 1955 was far more systematic than anything attempted in Indochina. Given the serious shortage of civil administrators in Algeria,[44] the high proportion of *pieds noirs* in the Algerian civil service, the reluctance of civil servants in France to go to a war-torn country,[45] the dominance of narrow colonialist interests in local government councils,[46] and the constant threat of terrorist and guerrilla attacks, government officials had little choice but to call on the military for help, at least in rural areas. Governor General Jacques Soustelle, the anthropologist turned politician, began what was, in effect, a revival and an expansion of a century-old institution—the Bureaux Arabes. It was in 1833, three years after the French conquest of Algiers, that Captain Lamoricière had headed the first Bureau Arabe, an early effort to spread French administration into the hinterland.[47] Eleven years later the Bureaux Arabes were extended to the whole of occupied Algeria by

Marshal Bugeaud. They were later subjected to attack and revision, but they survived to serve as the model for a similar system of military administration in Tunisia after 1881 and Morocco after 1911.[48] The Bureau Arabe officer was expected to do more than simply maintain order with the aid of his small body of native troops: he was expected to take the lead as well in directing economic and hygienic improvements within his district—all with due regard for local tradition. Within Algeria the system continued in force under various names until 1945, when it was dismantled everywhere but in the Saharan regions.

"Saharan Affairs Officers" had dropped in number to only 75 by 1950;[49] but the still-familiar concept of the officer-administrator facilitated the creation in September, 1955, of Specialized Administrative Sections (SAS), designed to extend an effective local French administration to threatened areas.[50] According to official figures, the corps of SAS officers increased from 160 in January, 1956, to 1,287 by the end of 1959.[51] Alongside 661 noncoms and 2,921 civilian specialists, these officers manned a total of 660 sections in Algeria in that year.[52] Aided by a doctor (often a military doctor), a social assistant, a small security force recruited locally (the Maghzen), and sometimes a few civil servants, the SAS officer put men to work on road construction and other public projects, opened schools (often with the help of military personnel as teachers), expanded medical assistance, and began to rebuild community life. By the end of 1958, 1,023 soldier-teachers were teaching 58,641 pupils in 752 schools; over 400 military doctors and a number of civilian doctors under the SAS handled 940,000 free medical visits each month; a thousand Moslem sports directors had been trained; and 407 public-works projects were operating under military direction.[53] Even many of those who are generally most critical of French pacification in Algeria have kind words for SAS officers and their efforts in education, medical care, and community development.[54]

SAS officers necessarily gave attention to the collection of intelligence and to the registration and control of all local residents. Under the guidance of the Fifth (psychological-action) Bureau, they also created and maintained numerous organizations within

the Moslem population, notably among youth, women, and veterans.[55] As a rule, however, SAS officers were inspired less by the
theory of "parallel hierarchies" than by the tradition of Gallieni and
Lyautey, the two most famous French colonial generals of the late
nineteenth and early twentieth centuries. In Indochina from 1893–96
and then in Madagascar from 1896–1905, Gallieni perfected the
"splash of oil" (*tâche d'huile*) strategy of pacification, whereby
through arming loyal villagers, winning the confidence of the local
population, and increasing economic prosperity in the pacified zone,
he prepared the population in progressively larger areas in turn to
accept French authority. Lyautey described the "Méthode Gallieni"
(which Lyautey made his own) as consisting "less in military operations than in an organization in movement." [56] This tradition
was undeniably paternalistic and authoritarian; but it was infinitely
more humane than either military pacification—or rather repression
—in Algeria or the parallel-hierarchies school.

There is good reason to believe that the work of the French
Specialized Administrative Sections in outlying areas, and that of
the similar Urban Administrative Sections after 1957, was aimed
accurately at one of the major roots of rebellion. If Professor Bourdieu is correct, as he very likely is, if rebellion in Algeria was fed
by "the overthrow of a vital order and the collapse of a whole world
of values" [57]—if the rebel, more than the non-rebel, was uprooted
and adrift—then it appears inescapable that pacification could succeed only by integrating rebels and potential rebels into a modernizing community.[58]

Clearly, the task of the SAS was immeasurably complicated by
(a) the presence in Algeria of over a million European settlers
intent on preserving their privileges, (b) uncontrolled military repression, and (c) the majority population's being of a different race
and culture. Many French officers, and especially those in the
SAS, were quite aware that if the army was to win, it would have
to lead its own social and economic revolution in Algeria to bring
education, health, dignity, and a greater measure of prosperity to
the Algerian masses. For example, a commander of a pro-French
Moslem commando unit conceived in this manner of the motivations of his men, all of whom were former rebels:

> We do not hide it; we all are revolutionaries. These men joined
> the ranks of the rebellion pushed by a revolutionary will which,
> though badly defined, was singularly violent. The rebellion disap-
> pointed and deceived them. With us, they know that they will
> carry out that revolution which the FLN is incapable of accom-
> plishing.[59]

The vast resettlement program which emptied well over a million
people from mountainous and border areas into fortified villages
was inspired, not only by military considerations, but also by the
desire to organize and integrate the Moslem masses into tightly-knit,
modernizing communities.[60] Unfortunately for the French, the most
uprooted and educated elements of Moslem society, i.e., those most
eager for modernization, had for the most part either emigrated
to the cities or joined the rebels. As Bourdieu discovered, French
officers too often attempted rigidly and unsuccessfully to impose
a more modern, Western style of life (built around uniform houses,
on straight streets, with a war memorial in the village center)
upon the most traditional people in all of Algeria.[61]

Yet, despite Bourdieu's uniform condemnation of military authoritarianism and intolerance in the resettlement program, SAS
officers were very different in their approaches to the problem.[62]
Some were career officers, others reservists. All were left with wide
local initiative. Their styles ranged from totalitarian to liberal
reformist. All in all, the work of the Specialized Administrative
Sections provided a number of bright spots in a pacification effort
that was otherwise depressingly gloomy. One early practitioner and
student of community organization for "self-defense" in Cambodia,
Captain André Souyris, is probably correct when he argues that
organization on a community level is the ideal point of entry in
combining a strong political appeal with economic and political
reforms and eventually with a local self-defense organization. In
this manner, Souyris concludes, ". . . the vicious circle in which
a government is caught: reestablish order before granting reforms
or grant reforms before reestablishing order, can be broken." [63]
Restoration of order can proceed together with supporting reforms
to meet real grievances and to reintegrate wavering elements of
the community.

Despite the extension of military control to the fields of administration and propaganda, especially after May 13, 1958, the French pacification effort never achieved that unity of conception and command which is crucial in war against a revolutionary-guerrilla enemy.[64] Conflict rather frequently arose between officers intent upon exercising ever broader powers and civil administrators jealous of authority which they often had no means to enforce. Once involved in administrative responsibilities themselves, officers like Colonel Roger Barberot (who also clashed with the military high command over its resort to strong-arm police tactics) often became impatient with the civil administration for its red tape, its eternal procrastination, and its excessive centralization.[65] There was, for example, the captain who wrote in 1959 that ". . . mention of a civilian administration is enough to bristle the hairs of any soldier." [66] Beyond their frequent differences in basic outlook and operating procedure, military commanders and civil administrators often clashed on such specific questions as judicial restraints, civilian-run detention centers, and the government's social-welfare program, with its *centres sociaux*.[67]

While it is undeniable that pacification suffered from a lack of unity of command and a lack of clear policy goals and guidelines from Paris, the unification of civil and military powers under General Salan in May, 1958, produced no miraculous improvement.[68] When General Maurice Challe replaced Salan in December, 1958, the rebel bands were as strong as ever.[69] In fact, pacification suffered, not only from civil-military rifts, but also from confusion in *military* circles regarding proper strategy against the F.L.N. and the absence of tight, unified controls over units in the field. One of the problems, as Gallieni and Lyautey had warned over half a century before, lay in the Bureaux Arabes concept, which called for separation of territorial military administrators from regular troop commanders and, hence, the establishment of a troublesome dualism within the army.[70] Again, in Algeria as in Indochina, military operations often cleared out rebel bands but in doing so alienated the local population to the extent that the rebel organization and military effort soon reappeared stronger than ever.

It was probably inevitable that the political assignments of a great number of officers in Algeria—SAS officers, psychological-action officers, officers engaged in police duties (like those of the Tenth Paratroop Division), and many regular combat officers—would further erode the traditional value of political neutrality among professional officers. The objectives of war have always been political. Now the means as well had become deeply political as each officer—indeed, each soldier—was called upon to be a government propagandist and a jack-of-all-trades. The old military values associated with the traditional cavalry commander seemed almost beside the point to officers like Captain Estoup of the First Foreign Legion Paratroop Regiment. When brought to trial for his participation in the military revolt of April, 1961, Estoup replied:

> I was never taught at Saint-Cyr to organize the provisioning of fruits and vegetables for a city like Algiers. On January 2, 1957, I received the order to do so.
>
> I was never taught at Saint-Cyr to do the work of a police inspector. In February, 1959, in September and October, I received the order to do so.
>
> I was never taught at Saint-Cyr how to exercise the functions of Prefect of Police for a population of about 30,000 inhabitants. In January, February, March, 1957, I received the order to do so.
>
> I was never taught at Saint-Cyr to set up the embryo of a municipality, to open schools, to open a market. In the Fall of 1959 I received the order to do so.
>
> I was never taught at Saint-Cyr to disperse insurgent citizens by political means. In February, 1960, I received the order to do so.
>
> I was never taught at Saint-Cyr to defy my comrades or my leaders.[71]

With new functions came an evolution in military values: if war could no longer be won militarily, then was not the officer allowed, even obligated, to exert political pressure when necessary to fulfil his original mission—the protection of the national territory? So it seemed to many.[72]

Clearly, the deeply political nature of the army's assigned tasks in Algeria tended to draw military men into the political realm. Yet the mixture of military and political roles was not in itself sufficient to produce a praetorian army. The officer-administrator was less prominent than were paratroop, Foreign Legion, and psychological-action officers in the April putsch of 1961, when military sector commanders in Algeria were almost unanimous in their loyalty to the government.[73] Paratroop and psychological-action officers had also been assigned political tasks in Algeria and had been deeply marked thereby. Yet war against a revolutionary-guerrilla enemy presents other political demands, which will be considered next, which placed greater stress upon civilian control in France.

Revolutionary-guerrilla war, we have seen, is pre-eminently war for the "conquest" of the population, as the *guerre révolutionnaire* school often put it. And since lasting "conquest" must rest on consent as well as on force, at least outside a totalitarian setting, it is of critical importance that adversaries convince the population of their unflinching determination to carry the battle to victory and to honor all commitments made. The least indication that the existing government might abandon its friends, renege on its promises, even give in to the rebellion, will immediately cast doubt over the whole pacification effort. For members of the target population it would be more than unwise to be caught in the camp of treason after a rebel victory. In the Algerian war in particular one might have hoped for leniency or even clemency if the French were to win; the rebel record left the Moslem friend of France with little such hope of mercy in case of an F.L.N. victory.

In his testimony to the Barricades trial, paratroop Colonel Joseph Broizat told of his experience in visiting a village in Algeria where a French second lieutenant had just been killed. "I was able to question the men," Broizat related:

> They told me, "What do you want us to do? We are forced to help them. If France remains, we will always manage! If they come back, they will cut off our heads!" And they told me, "You, you

don't give a damn! You will leave for Paris with your wife and children. It isn't your wife who will have her head sliced off, it isn't your house that will burn, it isn't your children who will have their throats cut, it's mine!"[74]

Hence, the vital importance of a clear show of strength and consistent determination to win if the French were to rally the population to their active support.

Especially when the defending government is a colonial government, the vision of a bright tomorrow *within* the government program must be supported with consistent statements and actions if it is to hold any lasting appeal. The colonial government has less to lose than a native defending government and will be more subject to suspicions of a weakening will. As Brian Crozier has put it, "When the question, 'Is it worth it?' begins to be asked, the terrorists are winning. When the answer is 'No,' they have won." [75] The British were "defeated" in Palestine, in the Suez Zone, and in Cyprus by terrorist tactics alone—simply because the prize was not worth greater sacrifice to them. The French in Algeria did not lose so much as they failed to win and finally tired of the costs of interminable war. Mao warned that revolutionary victory could be achieved only after regular rebel armies entered the fray.[76] He was correct only when the defending government is relatively strong and determined. Victory in any war is psychological, as well as military, in that it comes when one side feels the fight is no longer worth the likely rewards and gives up. This psychological factor is much more important in revolutionary-guerrilla war, where the visible signs of who is winning are obscure and difficult to read. Huntington has expressed it concisely and well: "Whichever side can convince the target group that it is winning is in fact winning."[77]

Promises of reform and even reform action are of little avail unless the government succeeds in building public confidence in its word, its good will, and its determination to win. The successful experience of Marshal Papagos against the Greek communist rebellion and, especially, that of Ramon Magsaysay against the Huks in the Philippines demonstrate the key role of credibility and determination in defense against a revolutionary-guerrilla enemy. In these instances credibility was in good measure the product of a dynamic, even a charismatic style of leadership, which was rare in the French camp after 1945.[78] The political system must be strong enough and stable enough to produce and support such a leader.

Resident Minister for Algeria Robert Lacoste fully understood the crucial importance of credibility in revolutionary-guerrilla war when he issued his General Directive Number Five of August 12, 1957:

> Confidence, that is the key word of this summer of 1957. . . . [With it, all is saved.] On the other hand, if we should falter, if the French by their behavior, their attitude, their statements allow it to be believed that a tired France is refusing the effort imposed upon her, is betraying her duties by desertion, then we will see our adversaries renew their hopes, their intrigues, their efforts, and multiply their crimes.[79]

Such a warning from the pen of the government's socialist minister in Algeria was aimed at Paris, as well as at the army in Algeria.[80]

Given the retention of French sovereignty in Algeria as a fixed goal, Lacoste's warning was both logical and necessary. Though it is likely that such a goal was no longer realistic in 1957,[81] at least so long as France remained a liberal, democratic society, the internal logic of Lacoste's position was sound. In order to carry out an original government policy of permanent French sovereignty in Algeria, Lacoste was obliged to convince his civilian and military subordinates, as well the Moslem population, that French determination was boundless and the goal was worthy of all sacrifices. He had no difficulty in convincing the bulk of the French officer corps of the high stakes involved. The greater difficulty came in persuading all concerned, and particularly the Moslems, that the rumblings of the antiwar party at home did not mean a weakening of French determination. Even though the official goal of French Algeria remained intact, at least until 1959, domestic political attacks on this official French position could only serve to strengthen the rebel hold over the Moslem population.

In view of the primacy of consistent determination in building public confidence in the government against a revolutionary-guerrilla enemy, it is now easy to understand the fury of a large segment of the French Army at the noisy antiwar and antiarmy campaigns being waged in French political and press circles.[82] As early as 1962 a celebrated French officer, Colonel M. de Crèvecoeur, insisted on the primacy of determination in counterrevolutionary war before an audience of Ecole de Guerre officer-students:

> In the light of this psychological fact, the restrictions placed on us by our allies and the campaigns of abandonment in France appear to be much graver mistakes than those which may be made by leaders and subordinates in striving for victory.[83]

General Vo Nguyen Giap, the Vietminh military commander, might well have agreed with Colonel Crèvecoeur on this point, though the two military leaders would have clashed on the meaning of "justice." In his book, *People's War, People's Army*, Giap writes of his French enemy of many years: "His weak point lay in the unjust character of his war. As a result, he was internally divided, not supported by the people of his own country and did not enjoy the sympathy of world opinion." [84]

Again in Algeria the French Army was accused on all sides of fighting an "unjust" war. Again, more ferociously this time, army spokesmen retorted with charges of "treason" and "subversion" against those Frenchmen who weakened French confidence and determination and gave moral support to the Algerian rebellion.[85] Among the more moderate statements were those by General Jacques Allard, commander of the Algiers Army Corps, and Commandant Jacques Hogard, a prominent theoretician of *la guerre révolutionnaire*. In November of 1957 Allard told a SHAPE conference:

> The fact that the FLN can say that there is no national unanimity in France for the maintenance of French Algeria is, in my opinion, along with aid from abroad, one of the principal causes of the prolongation of the struggle in Algeria.[86]

Writing in the November, 1958, issue of the *Revue militaire d'information*, Hogard was more direct:

> Who does not see that the "turning point" of the Algerian War would be reached decisively the day when the rebels would cease to be encouraged, aided by certain Frenchmen of France, the day when the Algerian populations would finally have the *certitude*

that France will never capitulate, will never abandon them to their executioners.[87]

The day when the French Army could fight in distant lands and win without great support or sacrifice from the French government and population at home was now past. Given its political character and frequent setting in a spotlight of world attention and contention, war against a revolutionary-guerrilla enemy does not allow victory without sustained political determination.

In view of the capital importance of clear and consistent determination in winning such a war, it is understandable that French officers were alarmed whenever it appeared that the French government was about to negotiate with rebel leaders on grounds other than surrender. It was felt that no matter what the outcome, such negotiations would have the effect of raising doubts and, hence, of jeopardizing the government's pacification efforts. As a case in point, the announcement of an impending Geneva conference on Indochina in early 1954 had the dual effect of demoralizing and disintegrating the Vietnamese government units fighting with the French on the one hand, and of rallying and strengthening the Vietminh military effort on the other.[88] French Commander in Chief Henri Navarre, who in a cable to Paris characterized the decision to call the Geneva conference as "catastrophic," claims that he was neither informed nor consulted regarding the government's intention to negotiate.[89] Even after eight years of war with the Vietminh, either French government officials had not yet learned that political and military questions could not be treated in separate and water-tight compartments, or they felt that civilian control could be assured only by presenting the army with a *fait accompli*. French negotiators at Geneva had the painful experience of watching the French outpost at Dien Bien Phu crumble and fall as the talks proceeded. France was fortunate indeed to save all of Vietnam below the seventeenth parallel from the Vietminh control. Negotiation with the Vietminh was the only means by which the war could be ended as the French desired. Yet resort to negotiation was above all an admission that the war could not be won, or at least that France was weary of trying to win it.

Reflecting upon the French experience at Geneva in 1954, French military theorists of *la guerre révolutionnaire* concluded that one must avoid negotiations with a revolutionary-guerrilla enemy. "To negotiate as an equal with the totalitarian revolution does not end its venture; it only facilitates and hastens its success," wrote Major Hogard as his eleventh rule of counterrevolutionary war.[90] Hogard's statement is particularly significant in that it appeared in June of 1958 and likely was written before or during those stormy May days of 1958, when the army helped to overthrow the Fourth Republic precisely because a new Prime Minister, Pierre Pflimlin, was on record as favoring negotiations with the F.L.N.[91]

، And, of course, the De Gaulle solution to the *treize mai* crisis only delayed the issue of negotiation. But first came De Gaulle's speech of September 16, 1959, in which he proposed "self-determination" as a goal of French Algerian policy: the Algerian population was to be given an option between independence, association with France, or integration into France. In the army, and especially in paratroop and psychological-action circles, such a policy was frequently taken to mean the first step toward another abandonment. Again, one of the most vigorous spokesmen for the militant French Algerian element in the army was Colonel Broizat, whose attitude led him eventually into the preparation of the April putsch and then into the O.A.S. At the Barricades trial he testified:

> What does it mean to obtain self-determination from the French Government if one puts himself within the framework of revolutionary war? It means essentially that the enemy, that is to say France, has agreed to envisage an outcome wherein she could be beaten; that is to say that she has envisaged as possible the independence which is the objective of the FLN. Consequently, one can say that victory is won, for the enemy has ceased wanting to win at all cost since he accepts the hypothesis that he might be defeated.[92]

At that same trial General Jacques Faure was equally hostile to the self-determination policy:

> . . . September 16, 1959, marks the date, the point of departure of all the uncertainties and all the fears, and one has to have lived

through that period as we have, in positions of responsibility, to measure its difficulties.[93]

In fact, neither the French government nor the majority of the French population were willing to win "at all cost." The results of the referendum of January 8, 1961, were convincing proof of a majority will to end the war, even at the sacrifice of French sovereignty over Algeria.

Yet Broizat was right so long as the French war goal remained the retention of French Algeria. As General Challe claimed in his own trial after the April putsch of 1961, De Gaulle's admission of an "Algerian Algeria" on November 4, 1960, was undoubtedly taken in Moslem circles as evidence of waning French determination.[94] A French government policy of self-determination and negotiation finally allowed the F.L.N. to extend its control over virtually the whole of a long-hesitant Moslem population. When the F.L.N. staged massive street demonstrations and riots in Algiers in December, 1960, the green and white flag of the rebellion was allowed to wave virtually undisturbed by a French administration which had almost ceased to wage war.[95]

In the Challe trial and again briefly in the Salan trial, the accused and their defenders made much of the still mysterious Si Salah affair in 1960 and its implications for negotiations in revolutionary-guerrilla war.[96] Colonel Si Salah was the commander of "Wilaya 4," the province-sized F.L.N. administrative area which surrounded a smaller F.L.N. administrative area labeled the "Autonomous Zone of Algiers." In March, 1960, he and his colleagues apparently contacted French authorities in the hope of ending the war. Si Salah, his executive officer (Major Si Mohammed), and Captain Si Lakdar all are said to have visited Paris in June, 1960, to arrange for a peace settlement within the context of De Gaulle's earlier offer of amnesty to the rebels—all without the approval of the F.L.N. provisional government in Tunis. No word was heard from them after their return to Algeria. Then, according to Challe, the French learned that Si Mohammed had reversed his position, killed Si Salah and many of his supporters, and taken control of Wilaya 4.[97] Challe and other French military officers involved in the exchange were convinced that De Gaulle's appeal of June 14, 1960, to rebel leaders in Tunis for negotiations, and subsequent announcement of a forthcoming French-F.L.N. conference at Melun, had in effect undermined the position of Si Salah and precluded a major, and perhaps a conclusive, French victory.[98]

Despite the tribunal's reply to Challe that the F.L.N. provisional government in Tunis simply caught up with Si Salah,[99] it is most probable that a French policy of negotiation with the provisional government gave courage to his enemies within the A.L.N. and disheartened his supporters. An appeal for negotiation on grounds other than surrender could only strengthen the rebel hand. That fact was well understood by angry and militant French Algerian partisans in the army.[100]

One final political characteristic of revolutionary-guerrilla war which merits attention is the vital importance of political commitment among troops on either side. Characteristically, rebel troops are strongly indoctrinated in the cause for which they are fighting. General Giap's statement regarding political commitment is of particular interest in view of the fanatical fighting spirit of his Vietminh troops:

> Profound awareness of the aims of the Party, boundless loyalty to the cause of the nation and the working class, and a spirit of universal sacrifice are fundamental questions for the Army and questions of principle. Therefore, the political work in its ranks is of the first importance. *It is the soul of the army.* [101]

Must a defending army be similarly indoctrinated and dedicated? The answer must depend upon two major factors: the kind of troops in question, particularly the extent of their professional training and the strength of their *esprit de corps*, and the degree to which they are given political responsibilities. Well-disciplined, highly professional troops (e.g., the U. S. Marines or the French paratroopers in Indochina) will usually fight well out of *esprit de corps*, with no need for ideological commitment—so long as they are confined to action against rebel bands. Even here, of course, troops unaware of the *political* stakes involved may do serious harm by alienating the native population.

If the troops in question are not highly professional, they most probably will need a strong political commitment, even if they are confined to strictly military tasks. To be sure, the experience of World War II (despite the strong ideological overtones of that struggle) demonstrated that troops often derive their fighting spirit more from small peer-group support and pressure than from ideological commitment.[102] In the intense political conflict of revolutionary-guerrilla war, however, the experience of defending troops in Greece, the Philippines, Cuba, and Indochina (both under the French and more recently) demonstrates that in order to face up to an inspired enemy, in order to weather the storm of his psychological-warfare attacks (your war is unjust, criminal, imperialist), the non-professional defending soldier must have a fairly clear notion of why he is fighting. Often dispersed in relatively small, unmechanized units in difficult terrain, he may shy away from combat and retreat when attacked unless, like his adversary, he has some of the qualities of the crusader as well as those of the soldier.

The true novelty of revolutionary-guerrilla war, of course, lies not in its highly ideological and propagandistic character, but in its primary target—the population. If, as in the Algerian war, defending soldiers are asked by their government also to be political organizers and propagandists, they must understand the political goals of the war and believe fervently in them. How else can they hope to compete with the rebel soldier-militant in appealing for popular loyalty and confidence and in guiding their own actions in terms of political as well as military goals? [103]

In the early days of the Algerian war military students of revolutionary-guerrilla war began insisting that the French Army could not be effective against the F.L.N. without a doctrine, a faith, or at the very least, a deep attachment to clear and consistent political goals for which it supposedly was fighting.[104] Even an early critic of French Algerian policy, Raymond Aron, found the "politicization" of the French Army quite normal: " . . . Perhaps this is the essential: one cannot lead a war against a nationalist rebellion without a political conception." [105] Aron's conclusion is correct, though his statement would have been more accurate had he insisted on the revolutionary-guerrilla style of the F.L.N., rather than its nationalist fervor. Support for the same argument (as applied to revolutionary-guerrilla war) comes from Samuel P. Huntington, the staunch defender of "objective civilian control" of a strictly apolitical military establishment. In "domestic war," Huntington agrees, the only effective solution is "subjective civilian control," whereby the soldier is motivated primarily by belief in the political cause which he is defending, rather than simply by his professional sense of duty.[106] The recent history of revolutionary-guerrilla war points to the rather clear conclusion that defense against a revolutionary-guerrilla enemy cannot be effective and lasting unless political action is combined with military action. And defending troops will fail in their political-military missions, or will ruin the political work of civilian organizers and propagandists, unless they know why the war is being fought and what promise victory holds.

It is obvious, especially in a liberal democracy, that political indoctrination of defending troops raises serious problems concerning the delineation of an official "doctrine" and then control over its uses and abuses. As will be seen in the following chapter, such problems helped to undermine civilian control of the French Army in Algeria.

Convinced that the army's political work in Algeria was insufficient so long as the French population and the French government seemed unwilling to maintain French Algeria at all costs, spokesmen for a growing military faction began pleading that the army should now play a leading political role *within France herself.* As indicated earlier,[107] the demand for a new political role for the army arose in part from a widespread military belief that the French civilian population was defeatist and sick, "rotted" (*pourri*) by communist and *progressiste* propaganda, leaving the army as the sole remaining guardian of the national patrimony. At least as significant as a reason for changing military attitudes in this respect, however, was the political nature of revolutionary-guerrilla war, which rendered public support and determination of vital importance to the counterrevolutionary campaign. General Jean Valluy put it aptly: "I am told, 'Let the Army do its job and be victorious.' But precisely, success has become political." [108]

One of the earliest and boldest pleas came from the pen of General L. M. Chassin in an article written in 1954 entitled "On the Ideological Role of the Army."

> It is time that the Army ceased to be the Great Mute. The time has come for the free world, if it is not to die a violent death, to apply certain of the methods of its enemy. But one of these methods—and without doubt the most important—resides in the ideological role which, behind the iron curtain, is given to military forces.[109]

Lacking effective civic education from other institutions, Chassin argued, the citizen-soldier must be prepared by the army for ideological warfare through a three-month period of civic instruction in the strengths of Western values (justice, liberty, the rights of man) and the evils of communism (its effects on family and on individual liberty).

As we shall see later, the preoccupation with a Western political and philosophical *doctrine* and with the army's role in spreading that doctrine, a preoccupation seen in Chassin, in army Chief of Staff André Zeller, and in the growing *guerre révolutionnaire* school generally, stemmed not only from the political nature of revolutionary-guerrilla war, but even more from a tendency to identify all revolutionary anticolonial enemies with international communism.[110] Nevertheless, apart from the communist threat, revolutionary-guerrilla war in itself demanded clear objectives on the part of the defending government and a strong political consciousness on the part of defending troops. This theme is a central and recurring one in the French military press, as well as in the court testimony of a host of officers.[111] Had the French Army not experienced long and direct involvement in a highly political form of war, other factors pushing toward politicization would not have produced military disobedience and revolt.

By rendering impossible clearcut military victories, by finally forcing the transformation of French officers into policemen, propagandists, civil administrators, political organizers, and ideologists, France's revolutionary-guerrilla adversaries of sixteen years seriously undermined the power of that old and usually respected adage that "l'officier ne fait pas de politique." What lessons for civil-military relations are suggested by the French experience with revolutionary-guerrilla war?

Clearly, an effective response to a revolutionary-guerrilla enemy must join with military action a determined, concerted, and consistent program of political action, including reforms to meet real grievances, political propaganda, political organization, and frequently, troop indoctrination. In the midst of terrorism and guerrilla activity it is probably unrealistic to expect that civilian civil servants in sufficient numbers can handle all of even the most obviously political aspects of the government's counterinsurgency campaign. Two critical problems arise as a result of the inevitable involvement of the defending army in such a political program. The first problem involves changes in government goals as the war proceeds. As we have seen, war goals must not only be clear, consistent, and backed with determination; they must also be accepted and believed by the defending army, which must spread public confidence in them. If the government later changes those goals, as Pflimlin was suspected of intending in May, 1958, and as De Gaulle actually did after September, 1959, the army may well reply with wrathful charges of defeatism, abandonment, and betrayal. When a large segment of the army believes the original goals to be vital to the preservation of the nation as they conceive of it, wrath may turn to disobedience and revolt, as in France. Those French officers who were most deeply affected by the Indochinese and Algerian wars have often argued that once the army has been assigned its mission, the government must desist from tampering with that mission until the war is won.[112]

There is no easy solution to this problem, certainly not a return to the notion of a completely non-political military sphere. On the contrary, as a beginning the defending government might provide military leaders and cadre with an early and continuing exposition of government goals and their relative priority, allowing for the possibility of future change. Admittedly, great care would have to be exercised to avoid weakening general confidence in the government and its will to win. Moreover, such an approach assumes a certain stability and continuity in policy formulation.

A second difficult problem arising out of the political nature of revolutionary-guerrilla war, one which will be explored in the following chapter, involves a situation (such as that in France from 1946–58) where government is too weak and too unstable to formulate a clear, coherent, and determined policy, complete with specific operational objectives for the army. Once the defending army realizes the importance of clear and consistent objectives, it will be sorely tempted to fill the vacuum with objectives of its own conception. Such was the case in France. When former army Chief of Staff André Zeller presented the case for a more active political role for the army in April, 1957, he dismissed the danger of praetorianism, but added significantly: "In any case, military dictatorship results less from the ambition of a leader than from the infirmity of existing institutions." [113] There is some truth in Zeller's words, despite their inappropriateness from the pen of an eminent military leader at a time when the "infirmity" of the Fourth Republic was already being discussed in military circles.[114] In order to view the political demands of revolutionary-guerrilla war in an explosive French setting, we must turn in the following chapter to an examination of French political weakness, instability, and immobilism in the conduct of recent colonial wars.

1. The term *guerre révolutionnaire* will be left in the French since as a French military doctrine it pertains, not only to revolutionary war, but also to a broader set of political and military propositions. See below Chapter 10.

2. Among the proponents of parallel hierarchies and/or "adapted justice," see the writings of Lacheroy (Chapter 6, note 16, above); Lieutenant Commander X., "La 3ᵉ Guerre Mondiale n'aura pas lieu," *Message,* No. 11 (December, 1955), p. 12; Trinquier, *La Guerre moderne;* "La Guerre subversive à la lumière des expériences d'Algérie," *Message,* No. 27 (February, 1958), p. 10; Broizat, letter in *LM,* January 20, 1961; Argoud, testimony in the Barricades trial, *Sans commentaire;* and Massu, testimony in the same trial, *Un Procès.*

3. Lacheroy, "Une arme du Viet-Minh: Hiérarchies parallèles," p. 6. See also Trinquier, *La Guerre moderne,* p. 188.

4. *Ibid.,* p. 8.

5. Figures are from the December, 1957, report of Colonel Godard, commander of the Algiers-Sahel sector, as found in Déon, *L'Armée d'Algérie et la pacification,* Annex 4, pp. 194–204.

6. With regard to the battle of Algiers see Bromberger, *Les Rebelles algériens,* pp. 139–204; Crozier, *The Rebels,* pp. 202–3; Broizat, letter to *LM* January 20, 1961; G. Perrault, *Les Parachutistes* (Paris: Seuil, 1961), pp. 175–76; Lartéguy, *Les Centurions,* pp. 359–410 (a fictional account, but close to the facts); and *Sans commentaire,* esp. pp. 34–35, 84.

7. Colonel Godard's report in Déon, *L'Armée d'Algérie et la pacification,* pp. 200–201.

8. The organization was the model for that described in Trinquier's surprisingly frank book, *La Guerre moderne*, pp. 50–58 (in the English translation entitled *Modern Warfare* [New York: Praeger, 1964], pp. 29–35). It is also described in a short article by the liberal Algiers attorney, Pierre Popie, "Comment fut préparé la journée du 13 mai à Alger," *LM*, May 30, 1958.

9. French propaganda in Indochina, as Lacheroy saw it, had been inadequate and ineffective: "Par ailleurs, et c'est un point sur lequel on n'insistera jamais assez, la propagande sur un fond de démocratie débonnaire, vénale, et détendu, perd les neuf dixièmes de ses chances alors qu'au contraire elle atteint à son efficacité maximum sur le fond d'organisation pure et dure des hiérarchies parallèles" ("La Campagne d'Indochine," p. 21).

10. Interview with Colonel Trinquier, April, 1962.

11. *Ibid.*

12. Trinquier was recalled to the *métropole* in November, 1957 (because the government was afraid of his power as head of the organization of the population, he told me). He returned to Algeria as a combat commander and participated in the *treize mai;* then, as commander of the El Milia sector after July, 1959, he created another "organization of the population" before his recall to France in July, 1960, and his retirement in January, 1961.

13. See Massu's testimony in the Barricades trial: *Un Procès*, especially p. 81; Argoud's secret testimony in the same trial, *Sans commentaire*, pp. 30–34; and Broizat's letter to *LM*, January 20, 1961. Argoud was cited as a defense witness in the Jeanson trial (see above, Chapter 4) on the basis of his reported belief that summary justice was necessary for the fight against the F.L.N. (Merry and Serge Bromberger, Georgette Elgey, and J.-F. Chauvel, *Barricades et colonels* [Paris: Fayard, 1960], pp. 15, 28). Argoud declined to testify, realizing of course that the defense hoped to prove that draft evasion was justified; but in a letter to the court he stated that his positions had been "assez fidèlement rendues" by the Brombergers *et al.* (LM, September 24, 1960).

14. The British Army units facing the non-uniformed terrorists of the Irish Rebellion from 1916–22 called for relief through martial law from similar legal frustrations, though their reaction was less violent than that of the French Army (Robin Higham, *Armed Forces in Peacetime: Britain, 1918–1940*, a *Case Study* [London: G. T. Foulis, 1962], pp. 50–54).

15. In *La Défense nationale*, p. 330.

16. "Milites" (pseudonym), "Morale de la guerre et morale de l'armée," *Message*, No. 21 (April, 1957), p. 3.

17. "La Guerre subversive à la lumière des expériences d'Algérie," *Message*, No. 27 (February, 1958), p. 10. Quoting a "rebel document," the writer states: "Since the arrival of the paratroopers in Algiers, one can no longer even count on legality for an escape" (*ibid.*, p. 10).

18. Letter to *LM*, January 20, 1961.

19. Argoud, in secret testimony to the Barricades trial, as quoted in *Sans commentaire*, p. 30. This book is presented as a verbatim report of Argoud's testimony, a copy of which had fallen into the hands of the Comité Audin. It was seized by the French government, but, to my knowledge, Argoud never denied its authenticity. (Used by permission of the publisher, Editions de Minuit.)

20. *Ibid.*, pp. 34–35. (Used by permission of the publisher.)

21. See Trinquier, *La Guerre moderne*, pp. 39–42. Coming from the creator of the "Organization of the Population," Trinquier's general recommendation for the interrogation of terrorist suspects is particularly interesting: "For that interrogation, he will certainly not be assisted by a lawyer. If he gives the information asked for with no difficulty, the interrogation will be quickly termi-

nated; if not, specialists will tear his secret from him. He, like the soldier, will then have to confront suffering and perhaps the death that he has so far managed to avoid" (*ibid.*, p. 39).

22. See above, Chapter 5.

23. As found in J. C. Bloch-Michel and Jean Bloch-Michel, "La Discipline des généraux: Des lois de la guerre et la torture," *Preuves*, No. 83 (January, 1958), p. 51. In this article the authors provide extensive excerpts from the Billotte-Massu exchange and comments upon it.

24. Lartéguy, *Les Centurions*, pp. 400–406.

25. And so one officer writing in *Message* finds the whole Massu-Billotte exchange to be abstract, unreal: "Aucun de ces 'témoins' n'a suivi ce dur chemin de crête où sont mis en balance dans un conflit inexpiable, la souffrance d'un homme, souvent criminel de droit commun, et la vie de centaines d'autres" ("La Fin et les moyens" ["Ends and Means"], *Message*, No. 26 [December, 1957], p. 2).

26. For example, the article by "Milites" in *Message*, No. 21 (April, 1957), p. 3.

27. Adjoul-Adjoul, a captured rebel leader, made the following statement, which was mimeographed and distributed by French military authorities: "Les militaires qui ne connaissent pas la population se laissent induire en erreur par des agents qui assouvissent une vengeance. Et je peux vous affirmer que, la plupart du temps, ces agents de renseignements, qui servent les unités française en campagne, sont des agents doubles des fellaghas, qui prennent un malin plaisir à faire supprimer des gens n'apportant aucune aide aux hors-la-loi" (quoted in Barberot, *Malaventure en Algérie*, p. 115).

28. Quoted in Bloch-Michel, *Preuves*, p. 52.

29. *Ibid.*, p. 56.

30. See below, Chapter 9.

31. See Chapter 11 below.

32. As quoted in Lyautey, *Lettres du Tonkin et de Madagascar*, p. 638. See also the statement of General Lazare Hoche, who defeated the Vendéen rebellion, in Bonnet, *Les Guerres insurrectionnelles et révolutionnaires*, pp. 132–33.

33. Pye, *Guerrilla Communism in Malaya*, esp. pp. 102–4; Papagos, *Foreign Affairs*, January, 1952, pp. 219, 230; Dinfreville, *RDN*, October, 1955, p. 331; Crozier, *The Rebels*, pp. 208–20 (Malaya and the Philippines); Lieutenant Colonel Uldarico S. Baclagon, *Lessons from the Huk Campaign in the Philippines* (Rizal: Philippine Army Training Command, 1956; mimeo.) pp. 27–29.

34. To the Cercle Militaire in Paris, as printed in *RMI*, No. 274 (July, 1956), p. 7.

35. *RMI*, No. 273 (June 25, 1956), pp. 12–16.

36. *RMI*, No. 274 (July, 1956), pp. 10–11. See also Lacoste's general directives Nos. 1 and 2 (May 19, 1956, and August 18, 1956), reprinted in Déon, *L'Armée d'Algérie et la pacification*, Annex V, pp. 205–20.

37. *Ibid.*, p. 227.

38. Colonel Nemo, "La Guerre dans le milieu social," *RDN*, May, 1956, pp. 608–9; and Navarre, *Agonie de l'Indochine*, p. 129.

39. See the excellent article by Captain André Souyris, "Un procédé de contre-guérilla: l'Auto-défense des populations," *RDN*, June, 1956, pp. 686–99. See also the novel, likely written by the same author under the pseudonym of Pierre Rolland, *Contre-guérilla* (Paris: Editions Louvois, 1956).

40. The Ben Tre case is described by Leroy himself in *Un homme dans la Rizière* (Paris: Editions de Paris, 1955), especially pp. 109–92. Graham Greene and Jean Lartéguy have added laudatory prefatory remarks.

41. Lancaster, *The Emancipation of French Indochina*, p. 254.

42. Interview with Colonel Roger Trinquier, April 2, 1962. Trinquier was head of the Tonkin branch of Service Action after December, 1951, and in May, 1953, took charge of that service for all of Indochina. He was given a handsome silver necklace by a Meo chief who wore one like it.

43. Captain Souyris' description of resettlement in Cambodia—a resettlement which later became a model for self-defense and resettlement programs in Algeria—is replete with references to social mobilization: "Le reserrement de la population a été l'occasion d'une véritable révolution à l'intérieur du Cambodge" (*RDN*, June, 1956, p. 692). "Le travail collectif occasionné par le regroupement créa les sentiments de solidarité, de confiance et de force que donnent la masse et le nombre; il fit naître les conditions indispensables pour engager la population dans la lutte" (*ibid.*, p. 693). See also *ibid.*, pp. 693–96 for discussion of social and economic reforms and propaganda.

44. Soustelle, *Aimée et souffrante Algerie*, pp. 25–27.

45. See above Chapter 4.

46. In December, 1956, the Guy Mollet government dissolved municipal councils, hoping thereby to neutralize conservative *pied noir* resistance to governmental reforms. Most Moslem councilors had already resigned their posts by that time (*J.O., Lois et decrets*, December 13, 1956, as cited in *L'Année politique*, 1956, p. 231).

47. Jacques Weygand, "L'Officier des affaires indigènes," *RMI*, No. 269 (March 25, 1956), pp. 63–66; and General M. Boucherie, "Les Bureaux arabes: Leur rôle dans la conquête de l'Algérie," *RDN*, July, 1957, 1052–66.

48. Weygand, *op. cit.*, p. 64.

49. *Ibid.*, p. 66.

50. Le Tourneau, *Evolution politique de l'Afrique du Nord*, p. 396.

51. *Le Bulletin d'information* of the Ministry of the Armed Forces, March 20, 1959, summarized in *LM*, March 21, 1959; for the figure for late 1959 see *Rapport sur l'activité de l'administration* (Algiers: Délégation Générale du Gouvernement en Algérie, 1959), p. 52, as cited by Peter Paret, *French Revolutionary Warfare from Indochina to Algeria* (New York: Praeger, 1964), pp. 50, 147–48.

52. *Ibid.*; and Déon, *L'Armée d'Algérie et la pacification*, pp. 147–50.

53. *Bulletin d'information*, as summarized in *LM*, March 21, 1959. One recalled reserve lieutenant who served as head of an SAS in North Constantinois in 1956–57 has related his successful experience in a book which reveals many of the roots of French military rebellion (Jean-Yves Alquier, *Nois avons pacifié Tazalt* [Paris: Lafont, 1957]).

54. Darboise *et al.*, *Officiers en Algérie*, pp. 29–30, 81; and Servan-Schreiber, *Lieutenant en Algérie*, p. 66.

55. Colonel Goussault, in "Les Principes de 'l'action psychologique' et de la 'guerre subversive' décrits par deux de leurs practiciens" (*LM*, July 10, 1958). Goussault was head of the Fifth Bureau in Algeria at the time of the May 13, 1958, uprising. See also Déon, *L'Armee d'Algérie et la pacification*, pp. 130–47.

56. Lyautey, Conclusion (entitled, "Du rôle colonial de l'armée"), *Lettres du Tonkin et de Madagascar*, p. 632. For a description of the method in action see *ibid.*, pp. 119–72, 457–68, 628–47.

57. *The Algerians*, p. 144. See also the April, 1958, issue of the F.L.N. organ, *El-Moudjahid* (entitled, "L'Afrique en marche vers l'unité"), extracts from which are included in the collection of documents edited by Mandouze, *La Révolution algérienne par les textes*, pp. 85–86.

58. For a similar conclusion with regard to Malaya, where voluntary associations are seen as an answer to a similar problem, see Pye, *Guerrilla Communism in Malaya*, p. 348. See also *ibid.*, pp. 243–63.

59. "Captain Georges" to Raoul Girardet during a visit of the latter to western Algeria in 1960 (Girardet, "Victoires et servitudes des capitaines," [Paris: *Combat*, 1960]). This pamphlet is a reprint of articles by Girardet which appeared in *Combat*. See also *Contacts*, March, 1958, pp. 2–4.

60. See note 43 above. French Delegate General in Algeria Jean Morin estimated the number of displaced persons at over two million in June, 1961 (*LM*, June 18–19, 1961). Not all of these however, went into resettlement centers.

61. Bourdieu, *The Algerians*, pp. 163–84. A much more favorable view of resettlement, by a "French Algeria" partisan, is found in Déon, *L'Armée d'Algérie et la pacification*, pp. 153–58. Déon describes the combined military-political pacification of the region of Dahra east of Mostaganem, where the F.L.N. had been in full control in 1956 and 1957. The Fifth Half-brigade under Colonel Cazelles moved into the area, drove out rebel bands, launched an intensive campaign to win over the population, and finally organized eighty villages as self-defense units. The pacification program here was taken as a model by Commander in Chief Challe (Déon, pp. 155–58).

62. One battalion commander in Kabylia who had five SAS officers (mostly draftees) under his command found that each had a quite different attitude and approach toward his job (interview with Colonel Bourdis, June, 1962).

63. *RDN*, June, 1956, p. 699.

64. The argument for unity of command—in either military or civilian hands—is a very common one among students of revolutionary-guerrilla war. See Major J. Hogard, "Tactique et stratégie dans la guerre révolutionnaire," *RMI*, No. 295 (June, 1958), pp. 30–32; and Hogard, "L'Armée Française devant la guerre révolutionnaire," *RDN*, January, 1957, p. 82; Captain A. Souyris, "Les Conditions de la parade et de la riposte à la guerre révolutionnaire," *RMI*, No. 281 (February–March, 1957), pp. 100–102; Maurice Megret, *L'Action psychologique* (Paris: Fayard, 1959), pp. 42–43; Captain H. Martin, "Guérilla, guerre en surface, guerre révolutionnaire," *RMI*, No. 288 (November, 1957), p. 62; "Quelques réflexions sur les pouvoirs civils et militaires en Algérie," *Message*, No. 34 (February, 1959), pp. 1–6; General Raoul Salan, interview in *Le Bled*, June 18, 1958, p. 4; General Jacques Massu, testimony in *Un Procès*, p. 115; Barberot, *Malaventure en Algérie*, pp. 86–87, 95–96, 114–15; Huntington, *Changing Patterns of Military Politics*, p. 28; Paret and Shy, *Guerrillas in the 1960's*, pp. 21–24; and Papagos, *Foreign Affairs*, p. 227.

65. Barberot, *Malaventure en Algérie*, pp. 86–87, 95–97. See also Cherrière, *RDN*, p. 1462; and Marchat, *RDN*, p. 1834.

66. "Journal de marche d'un capitaine en Kabylie," *La nouvelle critique*, No. 107 (June, 1959), p. 11.

67. See Argoud's testimony in the Barricades trial, *Sans commentaire*, pp. 11–12, 80–82; and Massu's testimony in the trial, *Un Procès*, pp. 114–15.

68. Delegation of powers is discussed in Chapter 8 below.

69. See Challe's testimony in *Le Procès des Généraux Challe et Zeller, texte intégral des débats* (Paris: Nouvelles Editions Latines, 1961), pp. 24–25 (Hereinafter cited as *Procès Challe*).

70. Lyautey, *Lettres du Tonkin et de Madagascar*, pp. 632–33.

71. From the excerpts of Estoup's testimony, *Procés du putsch*, p. 80

72. See Chapter 7 below.

73. The one notable exception was Colonel Roca, commander of the Fort National sector in Kabylia, who rallied to Challe and on his orders replaced (loyalist) General Simon as commander of the East Algerian zone. There were also some SAS officers in the Challist ranks, notably Captains Hurtaix and Oudinot, both assigned in Kabylia (*Procès du putsch*, pp. 123, 126, 130). See also Planchais and Fauvet, *La Fronde des généraux*, pp. 133, 139. See also Chapters 9 and 12 below.

74. Testimony of Broizat, *Un procès*, p. 39.

75. *The Rebels*, p. 191.

76. *Mao Tse-tung on Guerrilla Warfare*, p. 62.

77. *Changing Patterns of Military Politics*, p. 26.

78. Marshal de Lattre de Tassigny produced a new and more confident spirit during his brief tenure as commander in chief and high commissioner in Indochina, and General Challe had some similar success in Algeria in 1959–60, though primarily among French troops. De Gaulle might have been capable of retaining stronger French influence, if not sovereignty, in Algeria, but it was far too late to save that province by the time he arrived on the scene.

79. In Déon, *L'Armée d'Algérie et la pacification*, appendix, pp. 245–46.

80. Like his socialist predecessor, Marcel-Edmond Naegelen, and like many other French governors general in Algeria, Lacoste was intoxicated by the *pied noir* ambiance of Algiers. Lacoste did not participate in the May 13 uprising which overthrew the Fourth Republic; but on the other hand, he may well have toughened army resistance to any basic changes in the government's Algerian policy.

81. See below Chapter 8.

82. See above Chapter 4.

83. "Le Problème français en Indochine," a lecture given at the Ecole Supérieure de Guerre in April, 1952, mimeographed by the Section de Documentation Militaire de l'Union Française, p. 26. See also, on the theme of determination, the letter from "V. O.," "Faisons la point," *Message*, No. 24 (September, 1957), pp. 2–6, in the "Courrier des lecteurs" section; Major R. de la Tousche, "Déterminisme et Détermination," *RMI*, No. 311 (December, 1959), pp. 32–38; Jean Barale, *La IVe République et la guerre* (Aix-en-Province:La Pensée Universitaire, 1961; mimeo.), p. 24; and the testimony of Colonel Broizat in the Barricades trial, *Un Procès*, pp. 28–39, especially 29, 37, and 39.

84. Pp. 98–99.

85. De la Tousche, *RMI*, p. 35 ("N'est-ce pas de la subversion que de travailler à la défaite de l'Armée partout ou elle se bat?"); the letter of a *para* officer found in Tournoux, *Secrets d'état*, p. 435; and Trinquier, *La Guerre moderne*, p. 48. See also Chapter 4 above.

86. "Vérités sur l'affaire algérienne," *RDN*, January, 1958, p. 227.

87. "Tactique et stratégie de la guerre révolutionnaire," *RMI*, No. 295 (June, 1958), 35 n.

88. Navarre, *Agonie de l'Indochine*, pp. 140, 255, 298–99; and Dejean, French Commissaire Général in Saigon, cable 3873/92 to Paris, as quoted by Tournoux, *Secrets d'état*, 32.

89. *Agonie de l'Indochine*, pp. 296–97 n.

90. *RMI*, June, 1958, p. 24. Hogard earlier made the same point in *RDN*, December, 1956, pp. 1509–10, and in *RMI*, January, 1957, p. 14.

91. In recent articles, especially one in *Le Nouvel Alsacien* of April 23, 1958, and in a speech on May 2, 1958, to the Conseil Général du Bas Rhin. See Tournoux, *Secrets d'état*, p. 246.

92. *Un Procès*, p. 37. During the Barricades crisis Colonel Georges de Boisseau, chief of staff to the French military commander in Algeria, General Maurice Challe, is reported to have told Premier Michel Debré, "On ne peut pas se faire tuer pour une possibilité. Il faut nous donner des raisons de nous battre" (Brombergers *et al.*, *Barricades et colonels*, p. 287). General Challe was not quite so completely hostile to the self-determination policy, though he feared it had confused the Moslems and disturbed the army. See his testimony, *Procès, Challe*, pp. 27–28.

93. *Un Procès*, p. 44.

94. "Je pense qu'aussi longtemps que les armes ne se sont pas tues et que les passions ne sont pas apaisées, les populations prennent encore cela pour de la faiblesse, et en pays d'Islam, le faible n'a qu'à disparaître, le résultat est d'habitude inverse de celui escompté."—*Procès Challe*, p. 35.

95. De la Gorce, *The French Army*, pp. 534–35.

96. *Procès Challe*, pp. 30–35 (on the first day of the trial a closed session was agreed upon to air the Si Salah affair, but it never materialized); *Procès Salan*, pp. 226–27; Fauvet and Planchais, *La Fronde des généraux*, pp. 263–64; and Claude Paillat, *Dossier secret de l'Algérie* (Paris: Le Livre Contemporain, 1961), pp. 434–38, 455–56.

97. Fauvet and Planchais, *La Fronde des généraux*, p. 264, report that both Si Salah and Si Mohammed were killed by French troops in July and August, 1960.

98. Challe testified, "Nous venions à ce moment-là de passer à côté de la paix que nos armes nous avaient conquise. Pourquoi? L'Armée n'a pas encore compris, semble-t-il, comment le Gouvernement avait pu faire une erreur pareille" (*Procès Challe*, P. 32).

99. *Ibid.*, p. 198.

100. See the editorial in *Message*, No. 43 (June, 1960), denouncing negotiation feelers in De Gaulle's speech of June 14, 1960.

101. *People's War, People's Army*, p. 55. See also *Mao Tse-tung on Guerrilla Warfare*, pp. 43–44, 88–91, especially p. 90 (" . . . The basis for guerrilla discipline must be the individual conscience"); and Lawrence, *Oriental Assembly*, pp. 128–31.

102. Samuel A. Stouffer, *The American Soldier* (Princeton, N.J.: Princeton University Press, 1949); and E. Shils and M. Janowitz, "Cohesion and Disintegration in the Wehrmacht in World War II," *Public Opinion Quarterly*, Summer, 1948, pp. 280–315.

103. "Si l'on accepte le schéma 'action psychologique = transformation de l'esprit de la troupe = transformation des rapports franco-musulmans,' on voit donc l'importance extrême du facteur intermédiaire" ("Contacts," "L'Action psychologique plaide non-coupable," *Contacts*, No. 7 [1959], p. 19).

104. Jacques Hogard, "Le Soldat dans la guerre révolutionnaire," *RDN*, February, 1957, pp. 212–13; "Salus Populi suprema Lex esto," *Message*, No. 44 (July–August, 1960), pp. 4–5; "Pourquoi l'Indochine," *RDN*, June, 1954, pp. 645–55; Zeller, *RDN*, April, 1957, pp. 509–14; testimony of Thomazo, *Procès Salan*, p. 371. See also Part V below, regarding military attitudes and ideology.

105. *L'Algérie et la république* (Paris: Plon, 1958), p. 97.

106. *Changing Patterns of Military Politics*, p. 22.

107. Chapter 4 above.

108. "Armée Française, 1961," *Revue des deux mondes*, June 15, 1961, p. 579.

109. *RMI*, No. 239 (October 10, 1954), p. 13. This article drew hostile cries of "brain-washing," to which an anonymous author replied in a later issue of *RMI* that the civic education which Chassin proposed that the army give to its charges was a far cry from communist-style indoctrination ("A propos du rôle idéologique de l'armée," *RMI*, No. 242 [November 25, 1954], pp. 19–21).

110. See below, Chapter 11.

111. As far back as 1952 *Message* had concerned itself with developing a greater political consciousness among officers. This concern heightened as a result of the Indochinese and Algerian wars. See "A nos lecteurs," in No. 39 (October, 1952), p. 2; the editorial in No. 40 (December, 1952), p. 3; and the editorial in No. 3 (New Series) (May, 1954). The theme of the army's political and ideological responsibilities reaches a high point of intensity in an article in *Message* in July–August, 1960, "Salus populi suprema lex esto." In *Le Bled* see notably the fighting editorials in the March 12, 1958, and September 13, 1958, issues. The theme of the political demands of revolutionary war is central in Thierry Maulnier, "Du 13 mai au 28 septembre," *RDN*, November, 1958, pp. 1655–63; in the Ecole Supérieure de Guerre thesis of Major Bourgeois, "L'Officer français peut-il faire la guerre révolutionnaire?"; and in most of the *guerre révolutionnaire* literature discussed below in Chapter 11. The same theme was present in the testimony of the following officers: in the Barricades trial (see *Un Procès*, containing long extracts from the verbatim record), Colonel Joseph Broizat, pp. 28–41; Colonel Charles Lacheroy, pp. 72–74; General Jacques Massu, pp. 79–81, 100. In the trial of Generals Challe and Zeller (see *Procès Challe*, the complete verbatim record), General Challe, p. 23; Colonel de Boissieu, pp. 138–40; General Valluy, p. 162. In the trial of other officers involved in the April, 1961, putsch and the concurrent "Paris Plot" (excerpted in *Procès du putsch*), Major Denoix de Saint-Marc, p. 10; Captain Estoup, pp. 79–82; Colonel Emery, p. 119. On this same theme see Girardet *et al.*, *Crise militaire*.

112. For example, see General Challe's testimony, *Procès Challe*, p. 23 and *passim*. Colonel Roger Trinquier told the writer that the government must set the objectives of the war and then give up all right to change them. A very similar argument was made by Douglas MacArthur in reference to a more traditional war in Korea (Spanier, *The Truman-MacArthur Controversy*, p. 6).

113. *RDN*, April, 1957, p. 516.

114. At the time of writing Zeller was still on active duty, though he had resigned as army chief of staff in February, 1956, after clashing with Army Secretary of State Max Lejeune and Minister of Defense Maurice Bourgès-Maunoury over their plan to break up modernized units in Germany and send them to Algeria. Curiously enough, his resignation in protest did not involve the defense of French Algeria (for which he five years later became a leader of military rebellion); rather, it involved the preservation of French mechanized units in Germany. Zeller was recalled as army chief of staff in July, 1958, was retired shortly after De Gaulle's September 16, 1959, speech, and was one of the four generals at the lead of the April putsch of 1961, for which he received a fifteen-year prison sentence.

Part IV

**Political Authority and
Civilian Control**

Chapter 8

"Immobilisme" and Delegation of Power

In no area of public policy were the legendary weakness and instability of the French Fourth Republic more dangerous than in the field of colonial policy. The general story of that instability is too well known to bear lengthy retelling here.[1] In brief, a system of multiple, doctrinaire parties resting on a political society which lacked broad political consensus, combined with a traditional parliamentary suspicion of strong popular executives, produced a series of hamstrung coalition governments with an average longevity of eight months. Public policy under "le système," or "le régime des partis," as its opponents referred to it, was characterized, not so much by discontinuity, as by procrastination and immobility. There were occasional breakthroughs, among them the successes of Pierre Mendès-France in ending the Indochinese war and setting Tunisia and Morocco on the road to independence, and the decision (in 1957) to join the Common Market. In the main, however, the system rewarded cautious diplomats and temporizers like Henri Queuille and banished dynamic and popular leaders like Mendès-France (who as Prime Minister ignored the rules of the parliamentary game in appealing directly for popular support).

The fragmented French National Assembly followed a pattern often typical of factious parliaments: negative agreement came easily, but positive agreement on an alternative government or policy was extremely difficult to attain. Colonial wars in Indochina and Algeria deepened the persistent divisions between parties, opened new cleavages within parties, and played a direct or indirect part in the fall of sixteen of the Fourth Republic's eighteen governments.[2] Civil servants carried on as governments rose and fell, but administrators could not initiate the bold new policies which alone could have avoided lengthy and futile wars in Indochina and Algeria. In the absence of vigorous governmental leadership from Paris, local French settlers and administrators in Indochina and Algeria tended to wield disproportional influence in shaping French policy in those areas. The French political system was not conducive to the organization of potential majorities capable of challenging vested colonial interests.

Within this picture of hobbled governmental authority and lengthy colonial wars must be fitted an additional element—the French tradition of rather extensive autonomy for the army in colonial service. Such famed military colonizers as Lyautey and Gallieni left behind a legacy of independence and occasional disobedience of governmental authorities. De Gaulle, the greatest of modern French military rebels, had that legacy in mind when he wrote in the early 1930's, " . . . Those who accomplish something great often must pay no heed to the appearances of a false discipline." [3] The memory of such a legacy facilitated military challenges to civilian control during the Algerian war, when civil-military tensions were great and governmental authority dangerously weak.

One of the most striking and tragic features of the Indochinese war was the complete inability of the French government to decide upon the objectives for which the war was being fought. To be sure, De Gaulle had suggested limited local autonomy in March, 1945, and on March 6, 1946, French representatives recognized a "free" Republic of Vietnam within the Indochinese Federation and the larger French Union.[4] Yet the crucial question of the limits of local freedom remained unanswered by a chain of virtual caretaker governments in Paris. The policy vacuum left by indecision and weakness in Paris had two effects: it encouraged unauthorized initiatives by French officials in Indochina, and it frustrated a

French Army which could not defeat its revolutionary-guerrilla enemy without a clear alternative political program.

Soon after French representatives arrived in Indochina in the late summer of 1945, there emerged two divergent points of view in official French circles on the scene. The new high commissioner and commander in chief, Admiral Georges Thierry d'Argenlieu, was a Gaullist of 1940 who now came under the influence of local French administrators intent upon turning back the Indochinese clock to 1939 and unchallenged French supremacy.[5] In contrast, the commander of French Army forces in Indochina, General Philippe Leclerc, and the French commissioner for North Indochina, Jean Sainteny, were convinced that a new form of Vietnamese–French association was needed to respond to a genuine and widespread Vietnamese nationalist sentiment.[6]

Rather than launch a war which they feared would be long and bitter, Leclerc and Sainteny preferred negotiation with the government of Ho Chi Minh on the basis of Vietnamese self-government. Summarizing the situation as of April 30, 1946, Leclerc reported:

> Nonetheless, negotiations and agreements are necessary; it is no longer a question at this hour of imposing ourselves by force on masses who desire evolution and change. If not, no slackening of our military effort will be possible for a long time.[7]

The prospect of Vietnamese self-government struck terror in the hearts of the French administrators in Saigon, who encouraged D'Argenlieu to undermine and sabotage a negotiated settlement.[8] The admiral proceeded to do just that, especially after the agreement of March 6, 1946, was concluded between Sainteny and Ho Chi Minh.[9] Though that agreement clearly called for an eventual referendum to determine the fate of Annam (Central Vietnam) and Cochin China (Southern Vietnam), D'Argenlieu considered it to be a strictly local North Vietnamese accord and won the agreement in principle of Overseas Minister Marius Moutet for the creation of a "free state of Cochin China."[10] On May 30, 1946. D'Argenlieu acted without instructions in recognizing the creation of the "Republic of Cochin China," thereby presenting the French government in Paris and its expected guest, Ho Chi Minh, with a serious *fait accompli*.[11] Delay and indecision in Paris had prompted the admiral's move, which went unpunished and almost unnoticed.

In the course of the Fontainbleau conference, held with French and Vietnamese representatives in the summer of 1946, Pham Van Dong asked, with good reason, who spoke for France—her representatives in Saigon or those in the *métropole?*[12] Negotiations at Fontainbleau all but collapsed over the definition of "independence" and the fate of Cochin China. Finally, on September 14, 1946, Ho Chi Minh signed a limited, desperation agreement which bound the Vietminh to end the hostilities which had broken out in the south and to safeguard French economic interests and customs control.

In Vietnam the absence of firm policy guidance from Paris worked to the advantage of the D'Argenlieu group. The French Expeditionary Corps, which the admiral had long wished to throw against the Vietminh,[13] at last had its chance in late November, 1946, when a clash between French troops and Vietminh militia over French customs control led to a general French bombardment of Haiphong. Part of the responsibility for the generalization of that conflict—the actual beginning of the Indochinese war—must be assigned to the local French commander, Colonel Dèbes, who first sent tanks against Vietminh militia and then refused to apply a truce agreement reached by his superiors in Hanoi.[14] Yet if General Morlière, acting French commissioner in Tonkin, was fearful of the consequences of Dèbes' actions, the Haiphong commander received full support and encouragement from Saigon. On November 22 the order came from the French expeditionary corps commander and acting high commissioner, General Jean Valluy, that "by all means at your disposal you must make yourself the complete master of Haiphong and bring the commanders of the Vietnamese [Vietminh] Army to repentence."[15]

Admiral d'Argenlieu was at that time absent from Indochina, leading a vigorous anti-Vietminh campaign in press and political circles in Paris, where the French elections of November 10, 1946, had left the government headed by Georges Bidault in a temporary caretaker position. On November 23, D'Argenlieu persuaded the Interministerial Committee for Indochina to support the use of force, if necessary, against any breech of faith. But that very day French naval artillery was already flattening large sections of Haiphong (on orders from Dèbes) and killing an estimated six thousand persons.[16] A further French ultimatum to the Vietminh followed, and when Jean Sainteny returned from Paris to his post as French commissioner for Tonkin in early December, 1946, the Haiphong bombardment had created a situation in which compromise was impossible and general war inevitable.

Lest D'Argenlieu, Valluy, and their civil-servant advisers be taken too readily as the villains of the piece, it need be added that they were quite right in asserting that the Vietminh was under communist leadership. Nor should these events of 1945-46 be taken as clear evidence of military ascendancy in political affairs. Leclerc, the first French Army commander in Indochina, vigorously opposed D'Argenlieu, who, as high commissioner, was inspired and supported primarily by civilian civil servants.[17] It would not be fair to say that it was the French Army which chose to fight a war in Indochina.[18] What is of greatest interest here is the manner in which local French officials committed the nation to war while the Paris government remained virtually a passive spectator, incapable of setting guidelines for French policy in Indochina.[19]

If in hindsight D'Argenlieu must be credited with understanding the communist nature of Vietminh leadership and the ultimate futility of negotiations aimed at preserving an important degree of French influence,[20] he must equally be saddled with major responsibility for French failure to envisage a viable alternative to Vietminh rule. Puppet Vietnamese governments would hardly do; yet that was the best the admiral and his advisers had to offer.[21] Leclerc spoke wisely in January, 1947, when he said, "Anticommunism will be a lever without a fulcrum so long as the national problem goes unresolved." [22] In the years after 1946, division and hesitation in Paris combined with strong pressure from colonist and administrative circles in Saigon to delay and impede movement toward Vietnamese independence under a non-communist government; that goal alone would have made victory over the Vietminh possible. As a result, French policy in Indochina was the slave of events, rather than their master. When the prospect of Vietnamese independence began to take on greater reality in the early 1950's, it was too late: the French had already thoroughly discredited Emperor Bao Dai by starring him in a futile attempt at puppetry.

In the context of revolutionary-guerrilla war the absence of attractive French war goals (in fact, the absence of any clear goals), division and evasion of responsibility in guidance and conduct of the war,[23] and profound political dissension in Paris concerning French policy in Indochina—all served to make the French Army's assigned task a hopeless and frustrating one. To be sure, despite Navarre's apologies, French military commanders (Navarre included) were far from brilliant in their comprehension and conduct of the war. After the fall of Dien Bien Phu a government-appointed investigation commission headed by General Catroux apparently concluded in its secret report that immediate responsibility for that critical defeat lay with General Navarre and his errors of strategy.[24] In a subsequent book, however, Catroux hastened to add that the Laniel government and its predecessors were equally responsible for defeat in Indochina—responsible, among other things, for failure to define French objectives there.[25] Taking "victory" to mean the creation of an independent Vietnam under a non-communist government closely allied with France, rather than under the Vietminh, Brian Crozier is correct when he writes: "In terms of results . . . the conduct of the war was almost irrelevant, for political action had created the conditions of defeat, not victory."[26]

The French experience in Algeria after 1954 followed a similar pattern. By November, 1954, the goal of a modernizing Algeria tied closely and permanently to France was perhaps already unattainable. Again, as in Indochina, local colonial pressures and *immobilisme* in Paris were key factors in French failure to provide an attractive alternative to anti-French nationalism. On September 20, 1947, when the French National Assembly adopted the Algerian Statute, there seemed to be hope for greater Moslem political participation within legal institutions.[27] A newly created Algerian Assembly gave equal representation to the two electoral "colleges," one primarily European and the other totally Moslem.[28] In practice, however, after a frightening display of nationalist strength in the municipal elections of October, 1947, the exercise of the ballot was rigged by the administration to exclude all but a few Algerian nationalists.[29] The Algerian Assembly, now a tool of European settlers and Moslem "beni-oui-ouis" (yes men), exercised none of the special reform powers delegated to it in regard to local government, women suffrage, teaching of Arabic in the schools, and elimination of state controls over the Moslem religion.[30] At a time when the Moslem population was beginning to stir under the pressures of urbanization, rapid population growth, agricultural depression, and budding nationalism, the European population in Algeria and the administration which it largely dominated fought off all challenges to their privileged position. Rigged elections and an immobile French government left ambitious and embittered Moslems with little hope for a legal enactment of the social revolution which alone could begin to relieve mounting frustrations.[31]

The outbreak of rebellion on November 1, 1954, failed to rouse Paris and Algiers out of their lethargy, though it produced a chorus of declarations that "Algeria is forever French" from Prime Minister Pierre Mendès-France and others who lived to regret their words.[32] To be sure, there were the announced reforms mentioned above:[33] easier access for Moslems into the administrative ranks, greater involvement of Moslems in local self-government, extension of educational opportunities, economic development, and the whole SAS community-development concept. Nevertheless, the French government failed to resolve a long-standing confusion between the goals of assimilation and federation, and it left the Moslem population with no clear notion of how the new Algeria was to differ from the colonial society of old. Continuing dissension and instability in Paris were demonstrated, for example, by the failure of the Edgar Faure government and the National Assembly to agree on anything more than short-term reforms in October, 1955.[34] And, after Faure took the fatal step on December 1, 1955, of dissolving the French National Assembly for the first time since 1877, the newly elected legislature was more hobbled than before by Communists on the Left and Poujadists on the Right.

A new government under the Socialist Guy Mollet, which was to last for eighteen months, rapidly proved itself as weak as its predecessors in facing up to the demands of the European population in Algeria. Mollet and his intended resident minister for Algeria, General Georges Catroux, were suspected in Algiers of dangerously liberal and even capitulatory intentions.[35] A hostile crowd of European settlers and a barrage of stones and ripe tomatoes directed at Mollet during a visit to Algiers on February 6, 1956, convinced the new Prime Minister that his plans for Algeria would need revision. Catroux was allowed to withdraw (to avoid embarrassment to the government) and was replaced by Robert Lacoste. By capitulating to the European community in Algeria, Mollet lost whatever chance there might have been for a viable solution to the Algerian problem and thereby set the stage for May 13, 1958.

Mollet and his government lasted until May, 1957, when he was eventually replaced by Maurice Bourgès-Maunoury, who himself was defeated over Algerian reforms on September 30, 1957. Never was the colonial-policy paralysis of the Fourth Republic more evident than in the last year of its life, when Bourgès-Maunoury and his successor, Félix Gaillard, attempted to gain legislative approval for a "basic law" which would grant a degree of local autonomy to Algeria and political equality to its Moslem majority. The National Assembly eventually accepted a diluted basic law for Algeria on November 29, 1957; but it was only after bitter opposition from within the government, notably from Bourgès-Maunoury's defense minister, André Morice, and a final admission of executive helplessness in an appeal to an extra-constitutional "round table" of parties and politicians. The final legislative product was hedged with so many safeguards for the privileges of the European minority that it was incapable of producing an effective impact on Moslem opinion.[36]

French officers who began to understand something of revolutionary-guerrilla war after 1954 became increasingly impatient with the procrastination, confusion, and general weakness of French

Algerian policy. As usual, the *Message des forces armées* was most violent in its commentary. One captain wrote in February, 1956:

> We have the disarming impression that all action has become vain henceforth because it is sabotaged by a political "System" which is incapable of awakening the national consciousness and gives itself up to unreal games at a time when the country is in danger of foundering.[37]

Later that same year an arrest was made which previewed the gravity of the threat which angry and impatient officers were soon to pose to the French political system. As executive officer for operations in the Algiers division in 1956, General Jacques Faure had become convinced that only by taking power directly by means of a coup could the army convince the Moslem population that France was in Algeria to stay. He contacted Colonel Robert Thomazo and his *pied noir* territorial units and Poujadist friends, conferred with Michel Debré and others in Paris (but got little encouragement), and finally, with surprising naïveté, revealed his plans to the secretary-general of police in Algiers, Paul Teitgen. Teitgen tape-recorded his conversation with Faure, who was recalled to Paris, relieved of his command, and sanctioned with sixty days' fortress arrest.[38]

In the aftermath of Faure's arrest the editors of *Message* remarked that now, perhaps, the government would pay more heed to the moral crisis in the army. Claiming to speak for their fellow officers as well, the editorialists found

> on the part of governmental leaders a complete bankruptcy in the definition of war goals, in the elaboration of a general policy adapted to these goals, in the supply of means necessary for the battle, in the repression of defeatism and even of treason and in the formation of opinion.[39]

A *Message* editorial of August, 1956, was more threatening in tone:

> Charged for ten years with accepting in its flesh the responsibility for our political errors, tossed about at the mercy of events which were easily foreseeable, but in which one pretended not to believe, badly adapted to badly defined missions, fighting all of that time

with more abnegation than faith, the Army, ignored in Indochina, humiliated in Morocco and Tunisia, will it be able to stand another forfeiture?[40]

For many of those officers who were now interested in politics, governmental weakness was not only a fact to be stressed and protested, but also an additional and sufficient reason for the army to move to fill a policy vacuum.[41] A *Message* editorial stated that position quite clearly in November, 1957:

> . . . Fearing that at this hour and for a long time yet nothing positive can still come from Paris, the Army is driven to finding *by itself* the roads to total victory, and not only to the military victory which is now within its grasp.
>
> As an instrument of times of crisis, the Army has the duty to compensate at all echelons in Algeria for a wavering authority. Why, for example, would it allow disembodied politicians or judges to impose upon it a political statute stemming more from intellectual acrobatics than the concrete facts of the problem?[42]

A year later *Message* looked back at May 13, 1958, as an example of governmental failure to defend the nation; the army had only restored a "saving authority": "If this role was played by the Army last May it was uncontestably because she was more vividly aware [than other public bodies] of the gravity of the situation." [43] Clearly, governmental weakness and immobility under the Fourth Republic were critical factors in preparing military opinion for that pattern of delegation and usurpation of power which developed in Algeria after 1956.

Temporary delegation of power was a time-honored custom for the French National Assembly whenever the consequences of legislative immobility became too grave. The law of March 16, 1956, was in this tradition when it empowered the Mollet government to act as it saw fit in restoring order in Algeria.[44] What was new, however, was the absence of the necessary administrative means in Algeria to make these powers effective. Outside the cities an undermanned civil administration stopped well above the local level, leaving in the villages only a few Moslem *caïds*, or local administrators, who lacked prestige and authority. Governor General

Jacques Soustelle remarked after a tour of the Algerian hinterland in 1955:

> . . . At each step I was conscious of how great a void we had allowed to hollow itself out behind the decor of the regular administration, which hovered too high while it should have clung at ground level with those who lived and suffered in these expanses.[45]

On November 1, 1954, when the rebellion began, the sixty-five thousand scattered inhabitants of the Aurès region were served by only one administrative post and fourteen gendarmes.[46]

Understandably, Resident Minister Lacoste and the Mollet government leaned ever more heavily upon the army to administer Algeria. Well before the Algerian uprising of May 13, 1958 (when all Algerian prefects and underprefects were replaced by military officers), the army had been delegated full police and administrative powers on the local level in almost all parts of Algeria. Specialized Administrative Sections (SAS) officers were under orders from the Directorate of Algerian Affairs, which answered directly to the Government General in Algiers; but they were also under the orders of those military-sector commanders who had joined, and sometimes superseded, civilian underprefects in rural districts. At each administrative level above the local community (where most often there were no French civilian administrators), a military territorial hierarchy was constructed paralleling the civil administration from *arrondissement* (underprefect and military-sector commander) to department (prefect and zone commander) to region (administrative inspector general on extraordinary mission—the "I.G.A.M.E." or "superprefect"—and corps commander) to Algeria as a whole (minister or governor general and supreme joint commander).[47] In a number of *arrondissements*—and even in a few remote departments—the army assumed primary responsibility in 1956 and 1957, with the civilian administrator staying on as deputy to the military commander.[48] Even in Algiers itself, General Massu and his Tenth Paratroop Division had been given full police powers and extensive administrative functions.[49]

Delegation of power, however, did not constitute an Algerian policy. Lacoste still faced barriers in many directions: the French political milieu which kept Mollet's government in power, local vested interests (including the local administration), and now the army itself.[50] The directives received by military administrators at the local and sector levels continued to be "vague, hesitant, contradictory." [51] Moreover, despite his long tenure as resident minister (February, 1956, to May, 1958),[52] Lacoste was helpless to suppress the doubts and fears about Algeria's future stirred up by political dissension in Paris. Within this context of chronic uncertainty, the delegation of propaganda responsibilities to the army in 1956–57 was to prove an exceedingly dangerous act.

Unlike the Americans and the British, the French had no special psychological-warfare service during World War II.[53] Even in Indochina there were only a few French psychological-warfare specialists, and these relied upon rather standard propaganda techniques. Mention has already been made, however, of the horrendous impact of Vietminh prison camps upon those French officers who were hardy enough to survive them. Military schools and the military press gradually began to take interest in their accounts of self-criticism sessions, carrot-and-stick conditioning, and "conversion" through forced progressive compromise of the prisoner.[54] An "Introductory Course in the Study of Psychological Warfare" was created in the Ecole de Guerre (the French war college) in September, 1954, though its purpose was primarily to provide British and American specialists in allied headquarters with trained French colleagues.[55] More significant were the innovations of 1956–57. A group of forty "itinerant officers" was recruited from among Vietminh prison-camp veterans to teach psychological-warfare techniques in the various military units stationed in Algeria.[56] A Psychological-Warfare Instruction Center (Centre d'Instruction de l'Arme Psychologique) was created in Paris in 1956 to train specialized officers, and, in the following year, courses on psychological warfare were introduced in all military schools.[57] In Algeria, Resident Minister Lacoste created a Psychological-Action Committee to study reform plans within the framework of counterrevolutionary-war objectives.[58] Most important of all, in 1957 a Fifth Bureau was created in all military headquarters in Algeria to advise commanders on the use of "psychologal action." [59] The

Defense Ministry's information service became the Information and Psychological-Action Service, under Colonel Charles Lacheroy.

An official "provisional order" on psychological action, which appeared in July, 1957, under the signature of Prime Minister Maurice Bourgès-Maunoury, announced its object as being "to form, develop, and sustain morale and to immunize personnel against enemy psychological attacks."[60] The term "psychological action" was customarily thought to apply to defensive action on one's own population and military forces, as opposed to psychological warfare which one waged against the enemy.[61] In practice, however, the difficulty of distinguishing friend from foe in Algeria encouraged the use of the term ("psychological action") to describe such diverse techniques, wherever applied, as information, propaganda, conditioning of the masses, organization of the population, parallel hierarchies, and "brainwashing" (or intensive individual or group indoctrination).

From the standpoint of civilian control the most formidable of all parallel hierarchies created in Algeria was that composed of Fifth Bureau officers themselves. To be sure, on paper the itinerant officers and the loudspeakers and tract companies (C.H.P.T.) which formed the embryo of the Fifth Bureau were securely controlled through regular command channels.[62] In practice, however, the military high command and the commanders of units to which psychological-action officers were assigned frequently left them alone through lack of interest or knowledge. Fifth Bureau officers naturally turned for advice to fellow psychological-action officers at higher levels, thus forming a hierarchy separate from the regular chain of command.[63] French political objectives in Algeria, we have seen, were ambiguous and uncertain; hence, in order to do its job, the Fifth Bureau picked up elements of government policy regarding Algeria, expanded upon them, and laid them out as a permanent, irrevocable statement of French intentions.[64] Those objectives which would seem necessary to success in the eyes of the Fifth Bureau are easily predictable in terms of the revolutionary-guerrilla-war setting. First and foremost was the unnegotiable affirmation that Algeria was forever French; second was the assurance that the Moslem population could expect equality and social and economic progress. The military newspaper in Algiers, *Le Bled*, returned to these themes again and again in 1957–58.[65] Other elements of French psychological action were more strongly ideological and less generally accepted; these will be reserved for later discussion.[66]

The Fifth Bureau directed its campaigns at French Army officers and enlisted men, at the Moslem population, and eventually at the French government and population. On the national level Colonel Lacheroy stated in July, 1957, that the tools of psychological action included the *Revue d'information militaire* and *Le Bled*, the latter then having a circulation of three hundred and fifty thousand in four editions, including one in Arabic.[67] *Le Bled* repeatedly featured French victories, French determination and reforms, the rallying of Moslems to the side of the French, and attacks upon the F.L.N. and the "Egyptian dictatorship" behind it.[68] Basic-training centers and military schools generally (especially the Ecole de Guerre) now gave more attention to French values, rights, and objectives in Algeria.[69] In order to reach into the French civilian population Colonel Lacheroy suggested in 1957 that younger reserve officers within the National Union of Reserve Officers (U.N.O.R.) devote serious study to *la guerre révolutionnaire*. There followed, beginning in 1958, the emergence within the U.N.O.R. of a "young Turk" movement, which held a series of army-financed conferences, taking upon itself the task of interpreting the army's present actions to the French population and educating the population to an awareness of the high stakes involved in the defense of Algeria and the deadly menace of "subversives" who would give up the fight.[70] Meanwhile, psychological-action training officers in Algeria urged recalled reserve officers to carry on the fight for French Algeria after their release from active duty.[71]

All newly arrived officers in Algeria received instruction in "why we fight" from Fifth Bureau officers at the Joan of Arc training camp and later at the Arzew training camp.[72] Itinerant officers spread the message effectively throughout the army in Algeria and guided a program of tracts, meetings, and organization designed to win over the Moslem population.[73] In some internment camps techniques were introduced—probably by subordinates—which strikingly resembled brainwashing of the Chinese and Vietminh variety. According to a secret psychological-action circular, Moslem internees were to be subjected to a group method of thought reform in three phases, revealingly entitled: "Disintegrate the Individual"; "Creation of a Collective Conscience: Reindoctrination"; and "Creation of the Collectivity: Reaction of the Collectivity on the Individual." [74] This circular and the techniques it outlined were suppressed after a draftee and former Catholic seminarian, Christian Bloc, sent a copy to his, clerical superiors, who apparently gave it to the press. (Bloc, however, was arrested for divulging state secrets.) [75] A number of officers continued to resist the Fifth Bureau's new-fangled notions about war. Yet, as Jean Planchais put it in 1959, "Without falling into a paradox, one could write that 'indoctrination' succeeded best on a part of the military community." [76]

All went relatively smoothly between the Fifth Bureau and the government so long as Mollet, Lacoste, and others of their persuasion in official positions agreed with the goal of a new French Algeria. It was only in the spring of 1958 that the psychological-action monster revealed that he was unleashed. *Le Bled's* searing attack on the "defeatist press" on March 12, 1958, was aimed as well at prospective government leaders who favored negotiation with the F.L.N.[77] The Fifth Bureau went on to exploit and direct the *pied noir* uprising of May 13, as we shall see in the following chapter. By its inaction and excessive delegation in the public-information field, the government in Paris had encouraged the monster to grow.[78] Governmental leaders had failed to listen to—of all people—the then Captain Antoine Argoud, who in discussing psychological warfare in 1948 had warned: "It is up to it [the government] to take this weapon well in hand, in such a manner as to prevent that it be misused." [79]

No aspect of the war in Algeria produced more passionate controversy, more violent attacks on the French Army, than the extensive use of torture by government forces. Again, local initiative and weakness of governmental controls led to a clash between the army and "the system." The fact of torture in Algeria is beyond refutation, though the number of victims is still impossible to determine. It is certainly safe to say that thousands of persons underwent torture by electric shock, beatings, hanging from the feet, repeated near drowning, and forced bloating with water.[80] Already in 1954 and 1955 torture was rather commonly used by the *gendarmerie* and police in Algeria and was largely unpunished by the administration. One inspector general of administration, Roger Wuillaume, reported on March 2, 1955, after a trip to Algeria, that forty of the sixty-one prisoners whom he had interviewed there had been tortured. Many had scars to prove it.[81] The inspector concluded, however, that limited and regulated use of torture was justified in some cases. Therefore, he argued: "It is fitting to raise the veil of hypocrisy with which these police procedures have been covered. That is the only way of giving the police the necessary confidence in their activity." [82]

Torture by army personnel was begun on the initiative of information-hungry subordinate officers in the field. In 1956 and especially 1957 it became a frequent and even systematic practice in some units, notably in the Algiers area, where the special powers delegated to the army by the Mollet government were exercised to allow suspects to be held by paratroopers in "placement centers." In Algiers, as in other cities and towns where French troops were assigned security duties, the primary objective of torture was not to extract information about rebel bands. Rather, the information sought, information denied the French by an unco-operative Moslem population, concerned the activities and personnel of the F.L.N. political-administrative organization, which was responsible for terrorist attacks.

The best known of the placement centers run by the paratroopers in Algiers was the one in the El-Biar district. It was there that Henri Alleg and Djamila Bouhired were tortured, Maurice Audin disappeared, and Ali Boumendjel committed "suicide"—all in the spring and summer of 1957.[83] Some twenty-four thousand persons were "assigned to residence" in Algiers between January and September, 1957, and passed into the hands of the *paras*.[84]

When accusations, testimonials, and pleas filled the French press as the battle of Algiers got underway in 1957, it appeared that either the administration and the military high command were permitting the use of torture or that they had lost control over their charges. In fact, both alternatives applied, depending on the individual official involved. Civilian administrators in Algiers like Paul Teitgen, secretary-general of police in Algiers, and Jean Reliquet, prosecutor general, were quite helpless to protect suspects after police powers in Algiers were given over on January 7, 1957, to General Massu, who delegated them to his subordinates. Teitgen resigned in protest in September, 1957, over the manner in which justice was being abused. He was particularly concerned with "the anonymity and irresponsibility which can only lead to war crimes." [85] Reliquet stayed on until September, 1958; but later, in the Audin case at Rennes in the fall of 1960, he described the impotence of civilian control during the battle of Algiers.[86]

Other more highly placed members of the Mollet government in 1957 left Massu's organization a free hand, not so much because civilian control was impossible, as because the army was at last destroying the F.L.N. terrorist network in Algiers. The names of three ministers of the Fourth Republic usually arise when antitorture campaigners talk of civilian "cover" for army torture: Robert Lacoste, Maurice Bourgès-Maunoury, and Max Lejeune (resident minister for Algeria, defense minister, and secretary of state for the army, respectively, in the spring of 1957).[87] Official government statements continued to affirm that the use of torture was forbidden, rare in actual practice, and secretly punished whenever proven. Prime Minister Mollet asserted in April, 1957, that "reprehensible acts" were so few they "could almost be counted on one's fingers." [88]

Mollet's personal attitude is difficult to fathom, though his defense of the army won him enemies on the liberal Left. In regard to the three ministers mentioned above, however, the lack of written evidence of official approval of torture does not disprove the existence of a tacit or verbal cover for the use of torture.[89] The secret testimony of Prosecutor General Reliquet and General Jacques Allard to an examining magistrate at Rennes is significant here, though unfortunately that testimony is known only through the copy made by a hardly disinterested party, Madame Audin, widow of Maurice Audin, whose disappearance was the subject of the trial.[90] According to Madame Audin's report, Reliquet testified that despite numerous reports of torture, Lacoste did nothing to disavow, forbid, or punish the use of violence against suspects and prisoners. In fact, Reliquet reported hearing from General Jacques Allard, Algiers corps commander, that Lacoste, Bourgès-Maunoury, and Lejeune had *encouraged* such practices.[91] The examining magistrate proceeded to call upon Allard, who testified that the ministers in question had placed no restriction on their orders to destroy the F.L.N. and the Algerian Communist Party "whatever the cost." [92] Recalling a visit in the company of a minister to the headquarters of the celebrated paratroop colonel, Marcel Bigeard, Allard told of the minister's praise for the colonel's success and the latter's reply: "*Monsieur le ministre*, don't think that one gets such results with choirboy procedures." Allard added, "To which he was told only to be careful that there were no marks." [93]

Even if torture was never explicitly approved by representatives of the government (and this cannot be determined with certainty), their failure to take vigorous action to stop the practice lends some truth to the charge made by Pierre Mendès-France at the Radical congress of May 3–4, 1957: "The errors [torture] are not imputable to the Army, but to our political and governmental leaders. . . ." [94] The Mollet government had indeed created a Permanent Commission for the Safeguard of Individual Rights and Liberties on April 5, 1957. Despite the obstacles which were thrown up against the commission's investigation in Algiers, the report of the secretary-general, Parisian barrister Maurice Garçon, contained evidence of illegal detention, extensive use of torture, and mysterious disappearances of detained persons.[95] Yet the report was withheld from the public until it leaked out and was printed by *Le Monde* on December 14, 1957. Apparently very little government action was taken as a result of the commission's findings.[96]

A second Commission de Sauvegarde, created in August, 1958, was equally without effect, though the Audin trial and that of Djamila Boupacha were transferred from Algeria to France on its request. In fact, there is good reason to wonder if the commission itself did not approve of "adapted justice." Colonel Antoine Argoud testified in the Barricades trial that the president of that commission, Maurice Patin, approved of summary executions and insisted only that they not be allowed in written instructions. Patin was most concerned about a Massu-Argoud directive which sanctioned summary executions. According to Argoud, Patin said to him on this subject:

> I understand perfectly your anguish; I understand perfectly the importance which this problem has assumed for the army. But, for the sake of God, cancel your directive, make up good dossiers for us, even create false witnesses; I will do everything to help you, but cancel, for heaven's sake, cancel your directive.[97]

Argoud's impressive argumentative powers apparently won over the commission which was sent to control him and his colleagues.

If the Commission de Sauvegarde exercised no effective supervision over the army in Algeria, neither did the committees of the National Assembly. In mid-March of 1957, in the heat of the battle of Algiers, an investigating committee composed of seven members of the Interior Committee reported with one dissenting voice (a Radical) that it had found no substantial evidence of torture in Oran. The committee added, suspiciously, that ordinary means were inadequate against the F.L.N.[98] The National Defense Committee in the National Assembly was no more effective as a controlling organ in this field, either under the Fourth of Fifth republics. Drawn from those elements in the various parties which were more favorable to the military than their colleagues (a number of them were former officers themselves), committee members usually directed their efforts to the defense, rather than the control, of the army. The subject of torture was rarely, if ever, mentioned in committee meetings. If anything, the National Defense Committee probably encouraged the army to stand up to the "defeatists" in and out of the government.[99]

Massu and his paratroopers did not ask for police powers in Algiers. Massu apparently assumed them with some reluctance,[100] though some of his colonels were probably pleased at the opportunity to take on the F.L.N. organization in Algiers. Once deeply involved in a brutal pacification effort, Massu and his officers understandably believed themselves covered by ministers who knew and did not object. Government officials, eager to end terrorism in Algeria, yet aware of the political dynamite involved in the use of torture, apparently failed either to take full responsibility for, or to call an early halt to, interrogation by electric shock and other such practices. Would civilian control have been better assured had those officials issued clear orders to end the use of torture and then acted to back up that order? Clearly, as in the case of "adapted justice," Massu and his officers would have been angered by such limitations. Nevertheless, clearcut governmental action would have helped to break that pattern of military usurpation of powers in which the army—not the government—was setting the pace in Algeria.

As it was, the battle of Algiers and its aftermath of accusation and investigation clearly heightened the resentment of officers in Algeria, particularly those paratroop officers directly involved. Lacoste, Bourgès-Maunoury, and Lejeune could not bind other present and potential ministers, nor could they control the antiarmy campaign being conducted from Paris. Despite resistance from military authorities, several officers accused of torture during the battle of Algiers (including the often mentioned Lieutenant Charbonnier of the El-Biar center) were called before civilian examining magistrates.[101] As the anti-torture campaign mounted in the *métropole,* the government replied, both before and after the *treize mai,* that when suspects were mistreated " . . . disciplinary or judicial sanctions are always imposed. Obviously no publicity is given to them, for it is easy to see how they could be exploited to the ends of a dismal propaganda." [102] In fact, it appears that by 1962 sanctions of some variety (mostly quite light, in all probability) had been imposed in approximately 125 cases of this variety.[103]

Officers who felt they had been "covered" often blamed a weak and hypocritical government for throwing their colleagues to the wolves.[104] As early as March, 1957, when the anti-torture writings of J. J. Servan-Schreiber and P.-H. Simon had just begun to appear, an unnamed officer stationed in Algeria wrote in *Message.*

Civil authorities were incapable of assuring the functioning of the judicial system and the collection of political intelligence and found it convenient to have these sordid jobs done by soldiers, remaining free to accuse them next of cruelty. . . . [105]

This officer declared that the "moral elite" of the officer corps would leave the army if not relieved of such "degrading" tasks. Among most officers in the Tenth Paratroop Division, however, the inclination was not to give up so easily. Colonel "Raspeguy," a thinly disguised Colonel Bigeard, is made to say (in former paratrooper Jean Lartéguy's bestseller, *Les, Centurions*):

However "they" told us to use all means to win it, this battle of Algiers. . . . Each time that ministers or deputies came to our Headquarters, I told them: "It takes place on the side. . . . We do it because your government has ordered us to, but it disgusts us, it sickens us." They pretended not to understand or believed I was only joking. Others replied with a little unctuous gesture of the hand: "It is for France." Now these same bastards *[salopards]* want to send us before their courts. Hold fast to the stocks of your machine guns, then no one will come to bother *[emmerder]* us.[106]

The colonel stretches the facts when he shifts the responsibility for the initial decision to use torture from military to civilian shoulders. Yet here again, diffusion, delegation, and evasion of responsibility contributed to the anger and disgust which most officers felt toward the Fourth Republic. Nor did the overthrow of the Fourth Republic end the rancor of Massu and his officers, for investigations continued. Massu is said to have complained of De Gaulle in January, 1960, "He made me a grand officer of the Legion of Honor for having won the Battle of Algiers. And now he brings my officers before the examining magistrate." [107]

Two specific incidents, both of which had grave consequences, serve to demonstrate the pattern of unchecked military initiative which developed in Algeria during the Fourth Republic: the capture of Ben Bella and other F.L.N. leaders in October, 1956, and the bombing of the Tunisian border town of Sakiet Sidi Youssef on February 8, 1958. In the night of October 21, 1956, French intelligence in Morocco learned that the leader of the F.L.N., Mohammed Ben Bella, and several of his associates were to fly across Algerian soil en route to Tunis.[108] Resident Minister Lacoste was in France at the time, and Defense Minister Bourgès-Maunoury was in London. The French commander in chief in Algeria, General Henri Lorillot, finally got through by phone to Max Lejeune, secretary of state for the army and for Algerian affairs. Lejeune approved a plan for the capture of the rebel leaders. But then the French crew of the Moroccan plane carrying Ben Bella changed plans and landed at Majorca, thereby avoiding an overflight of Algerian soil. At that point, without civilian approval, someone within the air force hierarchy in Algeria ordered that the kidnap plan be carried through. The pilot was told by radio whom he had aboard and persuaded to land in Algeria. Lacoste returned to Algiers when the plane was already over Algerian soil and agreed to carry out the capture plan.[109]

Prime Minister Guy Mollet and President of the Republic René Coty are said to have reacted with sharp disapproval upon hearing of the incident. Alain Savary, secretary of state for foreign affairs, protested vigorously, called for the release of the rebel leaders, and finally resigned when Mollet decided to accept responsibility for the kidnapping.[110] Lejeune's authorization of the kidnap plan and Lacoste's belated approval remove this incident from the realm of clear military usurpation, though apparently military authorities alone decided to carry out the plan over international waters.[111] Already in October, 1956, a serious cleavage was evident *within* the government, a cleavage which was to widen in succeeding governments and which facilitated and encouraged military initiative. As for the effectiveness of the Ben Bella coup, F.L.N. terrorism in Algiers continued mounting and the F.L.N. as an organization was not seriously hurt, though the Moroccan government was badly offended.

Early in 1958, in retaliation for F.L.N. raids launched from Tunisian bases, the French joint commander in Algeria, General Raoul Salan, approved of a proposed air attack on the Tunisian border town of Sakiet. The raid killed seventy-five persons and wounded over a hundred more.[112] Intended as a warning to the Tunisian government, the bombing was ordered without the approval of the French government, then headed by Félix Gaillard.[113] Military authorities had become virtual masters in Algeria and were apparently unwilling to risk a governmental veto on the Sakiet raid. Foreign Minister Christian Pineau told Joseph Alsop on February 11 that the bombing was "a deplorable mistake" which had not been authorized by the government.[114] Yet, perhaps fearful of the army reaction to a denunciation, Prime Minister Gaillard decided to accept responsibility for the Sakiet raid and apparently persuaded Pineau to deny the remarks made in his interview with Alsop. Gaillard went so far as to accept the very doubtful French Army story that most of the victims had been Algerian rebels.[115]

The consequences of the raid were (1) an angry Tunisian protest placing in doubt the future of French bases in Tunisia; (2) an American "good offices" mission led by Robert Murphy; (3) a hostile French popular reaction against Murphy and American interference generally; (4) a further weakening of the authority of the Paris government; and (5) a strong additional impulse to military and civilian activists [116] in Algeria to stand up to Paris.[117]

In the spring of 1958, when its enemies struck, the Fourth Republic was divided within itself, lacking authority in the nation, and helpless to control its nominal subordinates in Algiers, to whom it had delegated great power. As for the armed forces, chief of staff of national defense, General Paul Ely, later explained that by May, 1958, the army " . . . had been led to exercise activities far superior to those which had formerly been assigned to it. . . . It was therefore in a position, faced with a new situation, to expand still further its field of activity." [118] The expanded "field of activity" of which General Ely speaks included decisive military support of the insurrection which felled the Fourth Republic.

With the picture of the Fourth Republic's policy paralysis and extensive delegation of powers in Indochina and Algeria now in mind, can it be said that civilian control would not have been menaced in the spring of 1958 had the French government, backed by a more united nation, been able to lay out and carry through a clear and vigorous colonial policy? Military apologists often have replied with an unqualified yes.[119] In fact, the answer must depend upon the following conditions: first, the time at which such a policy might have been attempted; and second, the aims of that policy with regard to French sovereignty in Algeria. Had there been clear, consistent, and vigorous civilian leadership from 1946 onward— even from 1954 onward—the army could have been held in check, despite its anger, even by a government intent upon independence for the colonies. By 1957 and 1958, however, once the army had been allowed (and even encouraged) to step into a civilian power vacuum in Algeria, once military honor, prestige, and self-esteem had been heavily invested in the defense of French Algeria, it was probably too late for any government of the Fourth Republic, no matter how vigorous, to abandon French Algeria without serious obstruction from the army. By the last years of the Fourth Republic, as the *treize mai* crisis revealed, the French Army in Algeria clearly preferred to be left a free hand in Algeria by a weak government in Paris, rather than to receive firm but unacceptable directives from a more vigorous government.[120] Had the Pflimlin government in May of 1958 been capable of rallying the firm support of the bulk of the French population behind a policy of negotiation with the F.L.N. (it was not), it probably could have saved the Fourth Republic, but it could not have avoided a clash of some sort with its army in Algeria.

1. See, for example, Philip Williams, *Politics in Postwar France* (2d ed.; London: Longmans, Green & Co., 1958); Herbert Leuthy, *France against Herself*, trans. E. Mosbacher (New York: Meridian, 1957); Nathan Leites, *On the Game of Politics in France* (Stanford, Calif.: Stanford University Press, 1959); Jacques Fauvet, *La IVe République* (Paris: Fayard, 1959); and Edgar S. Furniss, Jr., *France, Troubled Ally* (New York: Praeger, 1960).

2. Barale, *La IVème République et la guerre*, pp. 291, 294–318. Barale examines in some detail the interrelationship between French colonial wars, legislative weakness, and governmental instability (*ibid.*, pp. 35–336).

3. De Gaulle, *Le Fil de l'épée*, p. 58. De Gaulle continues: "Ainsi Pélissier à Sebastopol, empochant les dépêches comminatoires de l'Empereur, pour les lire seulement quand l'affaire serait terminée. Ainsi Lanrezac, sauvant son armée après Charleroi en rompant le combat malgré les ordres reçus. Ainsi

Lyautey, conservant tout le Maroc en 1914 en dépit des instructions supérieures. Aprés la bataille navale du Jutland et l'occasion manquée par les Anglais de détruire la flotte allemande, Lord Fisher, premier Lord de l'Amirauté, recevant le rapport de l'amiral Jellicoe, s'écriait avec chagrin: 'Il a toutes les qualités de Nelson, sauf une: il ne sait pas désobéir!' " (*ibid.*, p. 58–59).

With regard to military independence and disobedience in the colonies, see above, Chapter 1.

4. Devillers, *Histoire du Viet-Nam de 1940 à 1952*, pp. 144–45, 225–28 (hereinafter cited as *Histoire du Viet-Nam*). The text of the agreement, signed by the French representative, Jean Sainteny, Ho Chi Minh, and Vu Hong Khanh, is found on p. 225. Devillers was a reporter for *Le Monde* and press attaché on the staff of General Leclerc in Vietnam in 1945–46. His history of the war up to 1952 is the best general work available and an impressive condemnation of French indecision in Indochina. In English, the best general work is Lancaster, *The Emancipation of French Indochina*. Again, General Navarre's book, *Agonie de l'Indochine*, though polemical, is useful in tracing French political errors of omission and commission in Indochina.

5. Devillers, *Histoire du Viet-Nam*, pp. 149, 170, 211, 243, and 246; and Navarre, *Agonie de l'Indochine*, pp. 15–16.

6. Devillers, *Histoire du Viet-Nam*, pp. 207–8, 214, 238–40; Lancaster, *The Emancipation of French Indochina*, p. 142; and Tournoux, *Secrets d'état*, p. 4 (excerpts from Leclerc's report of April 30, 1946, are given on pages 453 and 457).

7. Tournoux, *Secrets d'état*, appendix, p. 453, quoting from Leclerc's report of April 30, 1946. For a slightly later and much more fearful view of negotiations with the Vietminh, see Leclerc's letter of June, 1946 to Maurice Schumann, found in Georgette Elgey, *La République des illusions* (Paris: Fayard, 1965), pp. 161–62.

8. D'Argenlieu's conservative legal adviser, Albert Torel, seems to have been particularly influential (Devillers, *Histoire du Viet-Nam*, pp. 170, 211, 257 n., 327).

9. Devillers, *Histoire du Viet-Nam*, pp. 241–71. The text is found on *ibid.*, pp. 225–26.

10. Devillers, *Histoire du Viet-Nam*, p. 244, and Lancaster, *The Emancipation of French Indochina*, pp. 170–71.

11. Devillers, *Histoire du Viet-Nam*, pp. 269–70; Lancaster, *The Emancipation of French Indochina*, pp. 156–57. The Bidault government in 1950 recognized the illegality of this and other acts of D'Argenlieu and had a surprisingly passive National Assembly validate them retroactively (Barale, *La IVème République et la guerre*, pp. 94–95).

12. Devillers, *Histoire du Viet-Nam*, pp. 295–308, especially p. 300.

13. On March 8, 1946, D'Argenlieu had told General Valluy, then Leclerc's representative: "Je m'émerveille, oui mon général c'est le mot, je m'émerveille que la France ait en Indochine un si beau corps expéditionnaire, et que ses chefs préfèrent traiter que de se battre . . . (as reported by Devillers, *Histoire du Viet-Nam*, p. 242).

14. Devillers, *Histoire du Viet-Nam*, pp. 332–34.

15. Quoted by Devillers, *Histoire du Viet-Nam*, p. 336, citing *France et Viet-Nam: Le Conflit franco-vietnamien d'après les documents officiels* (Geneva: Institut Franco-Suisse d'Etudes Coloniales, 1947), p. 42.

16. Devillers, *Histoire du Viet-Nam*, p. 337; and Lancaster, *The Emancipation of French Indochina*, pp. 170–71.

17. Leclerc left Indochina in July, 1946; but in November, 1946, the acting commissioner for Tonkin, General Morlière, and his staff worked just as diligently to avoid war as Leclerc might have done (Devillers, *Histoire du Viet-Nam*, pp. 335–38).

18. One very able French officer, Lieutenant Colonel A., told the writer that after World War II the feeling was quite general in the officer corps that France should not attempt to re-establish full control in Indochina and that to do so would only serve narrow French economic interests. Yet once thrown into the war, he argued, the army felt betrayed when it was not supported (interview, June 26, 1962).

19. See Devillers' excellent summary of this situation in *Histoire du Viet-Nam*, p. 359.

20. The Vietminh leadership looked upon negotiations simply as a first step toward the complete elimination of French influence. Giap said as much in a public rally in Hanoi on March 7, 1946, the day after the signing of the Sainteny–Ho Chi Minh agreement: "La liberté, ce n'est pas l'autonomie, c'est plus que l'autonomie, mais ce n'est pas encore l'indépendance. Une fois la liberté atteinte, nous irons jusqu'à l'indépendance, jusqu'à l'indépendance complète" (quoted by Devillers, *Histoire du Viet-Nam*, p. 228). See also Tournoux, *Secrets d'état*, pp. 6–7 n.

21. The first President of the Republic of Cochin China, Dr. Nguyen Van Thinh, hanged himself on November 10, 1946, after realizing that he was powerless and lacked public support (Devillers, *Histoire du Viet-Nam*, pp. 324–25, 327). His successor, Colonel Nguyen Van Xuan, was a naturalized French citizen and French Army officer who spoke no Vietnamese. Lancaster, *The Emancipation of French Indochina*, p. 165 n.

22. Quoted in Devillers, *Histoire du Viet-Nam*, p. 367. See also Tournoux, *Secrets d'état*, p. 457, for a similar statement attributed to Leclerc by one of his staff officers.

23. In regard to the lack of synthesis in French Indochinese policy and the confusion of command responsibility, see (in addition to the Devillers and Lancaster books) Navarre, *Agonie de l'Indochine*, pp. 3–4, 8–9 (and especially pages 91 and 94); "Les Forces armées françaises," *RMI*, No. 232 (May 10, 1954), pp. 15, 19; *ibid.*, No. 233 (May 25, 1954), p. 16 (regarding the division of responsibility for French forces in Indochina between the minister of overseas France and the secretary of state for armed forces–war); P. Gerbet, "Les Rapports entre pouvoir civil et pouvoir militaire en France dans l'élaboration de la politique de défense" (paper presented to the Fifth Congress of the International Political Science Association, Paris, September, 1961), pp. 9–14; General Catroux, *Deux actes du drame indochinois* (Paris: Plon, 1959), pp. 111–235; Tournoux, *Secrets d'état*, pp. 19, 28 n.; and "Quand aurons nous une véritable hiérarchie?" *Message*, No. 3 (May, 1954), pp. 10–14.

24. See excerpts from the report in Tournoux, *Secrets d'état*, pp. 460–62; and Catroux, *Deux actes du drame Indochinois*, pp. 215, 226, and *passim*.

25. *Ibid.*, pp. 226–35. Among Catroux's other charges against French governments: failure to rally public support for the war; failure to provide necessary men and material; failure to eliminate confusion in command responsibility. The Catroux commission apparently recommended sanctions against Navarre, as well as against Generals Castries and Cogny. When General Pierre Billotte became minister of defense in 1955, he refused to act on those recommendations because the responsibilities of particular *government* officials had not been investigated thoroughly. The investigation was dropped and no sanctions were levied (interview with Billotte, June 27, 1962).

26. *The Rebels*, p. 117.

27. The Algerian Statute and its application are described in sympathetic fashion by Le Tourneau, *Evolution politique de l'Afrique du Nord*, pp. 359–82; and in a hostile manner by Clark, *Algeria in Turmoil*, pp. 44–50.

28. In 1947 the first college included 469,023 Europeans (88.1 per cent) and 63,194 Moslems (11.9 per cent); the second college was composed of 1,301,072 Moslems (*ibid.*, p. 46).

29. *Ibid.*, pp. 48, 50–56; and Le Tourneau, *Evolution politique de l'Afrique du Nord*, pp. 365–66.

30. *Ibid.*, p. 367; and Clark, *Algeria in Turmoil*, p. 50.

31. See Governor General M. E. Naegelen's indictment of both *pied noir* and Parisian resistance to reform, *Mission en Algérie* (Paris: Flammarion, 1962), pp. 148–59; and Le Tourneau's excellent summary of the Algerian situation in 1954 (*Evolution politique de l'Afrique du Nord*, pp. 379–83).

32. Mendès-France told the National Assembly on November 13, 1954: "Les départements d'Algérie constituent une partie de la République française. Ils sont français depuis longtemp et d'une mannière irrévocable. . . . Entre elles et la métropole, il n'y a pas de sécession concevable. Cela doit être clair une fois pour toutes et pour toujours, aussi bien en Algérie et dans la métropole qu'à l'étranger. Jamais la France, aucun gouvernement, aucun Parlement français, quelles qu'en soient d'ailleurs les tendances particulières, ne cédera sur ce principe fondamental" (*J. O., Déb., A.N.*, November 12, 1954, p. 4961). M. François Mitterand, minister of the interior, was equally firm: " . . . L'Algérie, c'est la France. Et qui d'entre vous, mesdames, messieurs, hésiterait à employer tous les moyens pour préserver la France?" (*ibid.*, p. 4968).

33. Chapter 7 above.

34. "For three days and a night the Assembly debated the Algerian question, but the only reflection in the mirror it held up to the nation was: indecision" (Clark, *Algeria in Turmoil*, p. 230, in his chapter entitled, "Debate and Indecision").

35. *Ibid.*, pp. 268–79.

36. The story of the formulation of the Algerian *loi cadre* is told by William G. Andrews, who sees therein "the portrait of a regime in full disintegration" (*French Politics and Algeria* [New York: Appleton-Century-Crofts, 1962], p. 90). See also *ibid.*, pp. 75–91, and 136–63.

37. Captain X. "La Crise morale du corps des officiers," *Message*, No. 13 (February, 1956), p. 5.

38. See Tournoux, *Secrets d'état*, pp. 197–98; and Planchais, *Le Malaise de l'armée*, pp. 39–42. Faure was later involved in the Paris plot of April, 1961, and sentenced to ten years imprisonment (*Procès du putsch*, pp. 207–35).

39. Editorial, *Message*, No. 19 (February, 1957), p. 1. See also, on the same theme, "Sommes-nous condamnés à toujours improviser?" *Message*, No. 13 (April, 1956), pp. 22–23; "Enquête sur la crise de l'armée," *Message*, No. 18 (December, 1956), p. 14; and J. Perrin, "L'Impuissance à choisir," *RDN*, February 18, 1958, pp. 165–76.

40. *Message*, No. 15 (August, 1956), before p. 1.

41. See the following quotations in Dufresnoy, *Des officiers parlent:* "L'Armée n'a jamais reçu de véritable directives. Elle a donc du en forger et toute la 'politisation' de l'Armée vient de là" (Major de P., p. 116); "On ne peut pas en vouloir au 5ᵉ Bureau d'avoir donné un sens et un but à une guerre à

laquelle aucun de nos gouvernments n'en a jamais donné. Leur carence doctrinale a permis toutes les initiatives et tous les excès. On ne peut pas demander à une armée de se battre pour rien . . . " (Lieutenant de L., p. 94). See also General Baillif, "Les Forces armées dans la nation," *RDN*, February, 1960, p. 222; Raoul Girardet, "Pouvoir civil et pouvoir militaire en France sous la IV° République" (paper presented to the International Political Science Association roundtable, September, 1959); Girardet, "Pouvoir civil et pouvoir militaire dans la France contemporaine," *Revue française de science politique*, X, No. 1 (March, 1960), 5–38.

42. Editorial, *Message*, No. 25 (November, 1957), pp. 1–2.

43. L. L., "Du rôle politique de l'armée," *Message*, No. 31 (October, 1958), p. 3.

44. *L'Année politique*, 1956, p. 504. Mollet largely delegated these powers to Resident Minister Lacoste (Barale, *La IV° République et la guerre*, p. 454).

45. Soustelle, *Aimée et souffrante Algérie*, p. 26. The question of "under-administration" was also mentioned by Prime Minister Guy Mollet before the National Assembly on March 27, 1957 (*J. O., Déb., A.N.*, p. 1911); by the *Bulletin d'information du ministère des armées*, March 20, 1959; by Chief of Staff of National Defense Paul Ely in *RMI*, No. 297 (August–September, 1958), p. 8; and by Cherrière, *RDN*, December, 1956, p. 1459.

46. R. Van Geffen, "La Pacification, tâche primordiale," *Message*, No. 11 (December, 1955). This article is an extract from the bimonthly, *Connaissance de l'Algérie*.

47. General Allard, "Verités sur l'affaire algérienne," *RDN*, January, 1958, pp. 24–25. See also Déon, *L'Armée d'Algérie et la pacification*, pp. 147–48.

48. In 1955 Generals Parlange and Vanuxem were given full civil powers in the Aurès; in 1956 General Olie in Kabylia, Colonel de Bollardière (later succeeded by Colonel Argoud) in the Atlas Mountains area, and a paratroop colonel in Philippeville received a similar delegation of powers (P. Vidal-Naquet, *La Raison d'état* [Paris: Editions de Minuit, 1962], p. 21; Soustelle, *Aimée et souffrante Algérie*, p. 125; and Barberot, *Malaventure en Algérie*, p. 95–97).

49. Déon, *L'Armée d'Algérie et la pacification*, pp. 202–3; Girardet, "Pouvoir civil et pouvoir militaire en France," pp. 32–33; and above, Chapter 9.

50. Servan-Schreiber tells of the colonel who implored Lacoste as minister for Algeria and director of the pacification campaign to remove several generals responsible for brutality. Lacoste is said to have replied: "Mon cher, je ne demanderais que ça! Mais je ne peux pas. Ce n'est pas de moi que ça dépend." The colonel then added, "Ses collègues à Paris m'ont dit exactement la même chose: c'est pas d'eux non plus que ça dépend . . . " (*Lieutenant en Algérie*, p. 154). See also *ibid.*, p. 155; and Barberot, *Malaventure en Algérie*, pp. 96–97.

51. "Major Larsan" in Pierre-Henri Simon's excellent *Portrait d'un officier* (Paris: Seuil, 1958), p. 117.

52. After July, 1957, he was officially known as "minister for Algeria."

53. General Baillif, "Forces armées et psychologie," *RDN*, May, 1960, p. 821.

54. Mayor Grand d'Esnon and Captain Prestat, "L'Endoctrinement des prisonniers de guerre dans les camps du Vietminh," *Revue des forces terrestres*, No. 6 (October, 1956), pp. 35–40; Captain de Braquilanges, "Cours de guerre subversive: Méthode psychologique utilisée pour forcer l'adhésion des esprits," Ecole d'Etat-Major-Armée. 1956–57, XVIII° Promotion (Paris, no date;

mimeo.), 18 Pp.; and Captain R., "Ma captivité chez les Viets," *Message*, printed in serial form in Nos. 15 through 22 (August, 1956—June, 1957).

55. Baillif, *RDN*, May, 1960, pp. 821–22.

56. The group of "officiers itinérants" was created on a trial basis in 1956 by Major Dadillon and then formally organized by the resident minister (Tournoux, *Secrets d'état*, p. 125; and "Les Officiers itinérants," *Message*, No. 25 [November, 1957], pp. 1–7).

57. Girardet, "Pouvoir civil et pouvoir militaire en France," pp. 27–28.

58. Major Cogniet, "Fondements idéologiques et principles d'emploi de l'action psychologique" (lecture at the Ecole Supérieure de Guerre, January 6, 1960; mimeo.), p. 55.

59. Like the U.S. Army, the French Army has a *1er Bureau* (the American G–1) for personnel, a *2e Bureau* (G–2) for intelligence, a *3e Bureau* (G–3) for training and operations, and a *4e Bureau* (G–4) for logistics.

60. From the order as extracted in Jean Planchais, "L'Action psychologique, hier et aujourd'hui," *LM*, April 3, 1959.

61. Souyris, "L'Action psychologique dans les forces armées," *RMI*, No. 298 (October, 1958), p. 37.

62. The itinerant officers originally received their instructions from the General Directorate of Political Affairs in Algiers ("Les Officiers itinérants," *Message*, p. 3).

63. Maurice Megret, *L'Action psychologique* (Paris: Fayard, 1959), pp. 172–78. I am also indebted for information concerning the *5e Bureau* to Colonel Bourdis, director of the Service d'Information, Ministère des Armées, himself a "psychological-action" officer while the term was still in use (interview, June 25, 1962).

64. The voice of Raymond Aron might be added to those already cited on this point: "Ainsi, l'armée d'Algérie fut contrainte de se donner une conception politique de la pacification, faute d'en recevoir une de Paris et de crainte que les politiciens choisissent finalement l'abandon" (*L'Algérie et la République* [Paris: Plon, 1958], p. 97).

65. See, for example, "L'Algérie nouvelle se construit," in No. 39, January 4, 1957, pp. 3–4, and the editorial in the issue dated February 12, 1958, p. 3. See also the March, 1958, issue of *Contacts*, a review which was nominally independent but was in fact an organ of the tenth military region with its headquarters in Algiers.

66. Chapter 13 below.

67. Lacheroy in *La Défense nationale*, p. 327.

68. In regard to the attacks on Nasser, see the issues of January 12, 1957, pp. 3–4, and January 26, 1957, pp. 3–4. French victories and Moslems newly rallied to the French cause were featured in virtually every issue from 1957 to 1960.

69. See the description of the psychological-action program in basic-training centers which was set up in April, 1958, and revised at the end of 1958, in Planchais, "L'Action psychologique, hier et aujourd'hui," *LM*, April 3, 1959.

70. Azeau, *Révolte militaire*, pp. 61–68.

71. Maurice Megret, "L'Officier de réserve, la défense et la nation," *LM*, June 25, 1959; *ibid.*, June 27, 1959.

72. Maurice Heynaud, *Officiers en Algérie*, pp. 46-49.

73. "Les Officiers itinérants," *Message*, p. 6.

74. Excerpted in *LM*, January 23, 1958. The similar Chinese method is described in Robert Lifton, *Thought Reform and the Psychology of Totalism* (New York: Norton, 1961).

75. *LM*, January 23, 1958; and J. Planchais, "Petite histoire de l'action psychologique," *Signes du temps*, No. 1 (January, 1959), pp. 13–14. General Massu and Colonel Argoud later protested, with some truth, that under civilian control after 1957 these internment camps became "veritable seminaries for the rebellion" (Massu, *Un Procès*, p. 114; and Argoud, in *Sans commentaire*, pp. 80-83).

76. *LM*, April 4, 1959.

77. Editorial, p. 3.

78. This is the central theme of Megret's *L'Action psychologique*. See especially pp. 172–78, 184, 196.

79. Argoud, "La Guerre psychologique," *RDN*, April, 1948, p. 470. Argoud's role, after January, 1960, as grand strategist of military revolt is discussed in the following chapter.

80. The most complete documentation on the subject of official torture in Algeria is found in Vidal-Naquet, *La Raison d'état*. Vidal-Naquet is a member of the Comité Audin, the committee named for a communist from Algiers who disappeared under mysterious conditions while in paratrooper hands. A wide literature by victims and observers of torture includes: Alleg, *La Question* (the account of a communist victim in the battle of Algiers); G. Arnaud and J. Vergès, *Pour Djamila Bouhired* (Paris: Editions de Minuit, 1957), (a book concerning two Moslem victims, one a girl, in the battle of Algiers); P. Vidal-Naquet, *L'Affaire Audin* (Paris: Editions de Minuit, 1958); *LM*, January 4, 1960 (the summary of an International Red Cross report of its investigation); Leulliette, *Saint Michel et le dragon* (by a former paratrooper); testimony of Leulliette and others, *Provocation à la désobéissance* (Paris: Editions de Minuit, 1962), especially pp. 47–53; Simon, *Contre la torture* (a collection of incidents involving torture and other abuses of justice); Rey, *Les Egorgeurs* (by a former Moslem member of a French commando unit); Barberot, *Malaventure en Algérie*, especially pp. 180–86, 195–203, 220–21 (General Bollardière's clash with Massu and the high command over the unbridled use of torture); Hafid Keramane, *La Pacification: Livre noir de six années de guerre en Algérie* (Lausanne: La Cité Editeur, 1960), (a collection of statements and documents indicating the extent of the use of torture in Algeria); Kessel and Pirelli, *Le Peuple algérien et la guerre* (another large collection of letters and statements, mostly by victims and witnesses); Dufresnoy, *Des officiers parlent* (torture is mentioned by interviewed officers on pages xix, 6, 7, 29, 31–33, 45, 51, 56, 86–87, 130, 138–39); Laurent Schwartz, "Le Problème de la torture dans la France d'aujourd'hui," *Les Cahiers de la république*, VI, No. 38 (November, 1961), 17–31; Simone de Beauvoir and Gisèle Halimi, *Djamila Boupacha* (Paris: Gillimard, 1962; New York: Macmillan, 1962), (the torture in February, 1960, of a girl accused of setting bombs for the F.L.N.); *LM*, January 17, 19, and 20, 1962 (the surprising acquittal by a military tribunal of three officers accused of torturing a Moslem woman to death); and Grall, *La Génération du Djebel*, pp. 28–31, 34–35. For fictional accounts see Georges Buis, *La Grotte* (Paris: Julliard, 1961), pp. 17–19 (a short, simple incident during a combat operation in the mountains, illustrative of a common pattern); Lartéguy, *Les Centurions*, 387–93, 401–6, and *passim*.

81. Wuillaume's entire report is printed in Vidal-Naquet, *La Raison d'état*, pp. 57–68. It was first published by the Comité Audin as No. 11 of its publi-

cation, *Vérité-Liberté*. According to Vidal-Naquet, Governor General Soustelle rejected Wuillaume's suggestion that torture be officially sanctioned, but agreed not to punish those responsible for acts of torture committed before February 1, 1955 (*La Raison d'état*, p. 57).

82. *Ibid.*, p. 68.

83. The El-Biar center was still being used for the same purpose in February, 1960, as the case of Djamila Boupacha revealed.

84. Schwartz, *Les Cahiers de la république*, p. 19.

85. Quoted from his first letter of resignation (which was rejected) of March 24, 1957, as found in *LM*, October 1, 1960. Teitgen's revealing statement of September 1, 1957, to the Commission de Sauvegarde (as found in Vidal-Naquet, *La Raison d'état*, pp. 187–202) concludes with the charge that " . . . nous sommes bel et bien engagés dans la voie d'une systématisation de la torture que l'on ne craint plus de justifier" (p. 202). Commissioner Teitgen later testified (on January 11, 1962) in the Davezies trial that 3,024 of the 24,000 persons assigned to residence in the battle of Algiers disappeared altogether (*ibid.*, p. 200 n. 20).

86. Reliquet's statement in the Rennes trial, as reported by Mme Audin, is found in *ibid.*, pp. 270–73.

87. See the "Déclaration solennelle du Comité Maurice Audin" in *Sans commentaire*, p. 104; Schwartz, *Les Cahiers de la république*, p. 20; and the testimony of Reliquet and General Jacques Allard at the Rennes trial in Vidal-Naquet, *La Raison d'état*, pp. 268–75.

88. In a speech at Chalons-sur-Marne on April 14, 1957, as quoted in *L'Année politique*, 1957, p. 40. See also Mollet's statement to the National Assembly, March 27, 1957 (*J.O., Déb., A.N.*, p. 1911).

89. As early as July 29, 1955, Minister of the Interior Bourgès-Maunoury told the National Assembly that investigations to date had shown no evidence of torture of the type denounced by the opposition. Yet the Wuillaume report was dated March 2, 1955 (Vidal-Naquet, *La Raison d'état*, pp. 57, 69).

90. The text of testimony by Reliquet and Allard, as provided by Mme Audin, who had access to the dossier, is given in Vidal-Naquet, *La Raison d'état*, pp. 270–75.

91. *Ibid.*, pp. 272–73.

92. *Ibid.*, pp. 273–74. In turn, Massu's instructions in the battle of Algiers left his charges with a free hand: "La vitesse est primordiale. Inutile d'intérroger longuement les membres d'un groupe d'action (tuers, guetteurs) si l'on tient le chef de groupe, ce qui doit amener par un *intérrogatoire serré* les noms des membres du groupe . . . " (quoted in the report of Maurice Garçon, President of the Commission de Sauvegarde, June, 1957, as found in Vidal-Naquet, *La Raison d'état*, p. 1953). In a later directive, Massu went so far as to authorize summary executions (Brombergers *et al.*, *Barricades et colonels*, p. 15).

93. Vidal-Naquet, *La Raison d'état*, p. 274. General Massu was also questioned at Rennes and confirmed that these three ministers had been his strongest supporters (Schwartz, *Les Cahiers de la république*, p. 20).

94. Quoted in *L'Année politique*, 1957, p. 45. This congress was torn by a sharp clash between Mendès-France and his fellow Radical, Bourgès-Maunoury, even though some of the most strongly "French Algeria" Radicals—André Marie, André Morice, Pascal Arrighi—had already broken off and formed a dissident Radical party in October, 1956. The Socialists were also divided over Algerian policy (*ibid.*, pp. 36–40).

95. The report, dated June 12, 1957, is printed in full, apparently for the first time, in Vidal-Naquet, *La Raison d'état*, pp. 133–67. Obstacles to the commission's investigation are detailed in *ibid.*, p. 165, and in another book by the same author (*l'Affaire Audin*, pp. 44–45).

96. Schwartz, *Les Cahiers de la république*, p. 26.

97. Argoud, in *Sans commentaire*, p. 32. See also Brombergers *et al.*, *Barricades et colonels*, p. 15.

98. *LM*, March 17, 1957; *ibid.*, March 18, 1957; and M. Duverger, "Absence française," *LM*, March 22, 1957.

99. The discussion here of the role of the National Defense Committee is based largely on interviews with former Defense Minister General Pierre Billotte (June 27, 1962) and with Joël le Theule, deputy from Sarthe and Rapporteur of the National Defense Committee, June 21, 1962. M. le Theule suggested to the writer that the committee likely *encouraged* the military revolt of April, 1961, through giving officers the false impression that the cause of French Algeria had mass support in the National Assembly. When the committee chairman, François Valentin, died in the fall of 1961, *Message* published a tribute to him as a true friend and one who had encouraged the efforts of that volatile military journal ("Notre ami François Valentin," *Message*, No. 49 [January, 1962], n.p.). In the spring of 1962 the committee clashed repeatedly with the government over the latter's refusal to allow committee member Colonel Robert Thomazo (who was known to be in sympathy with the O.A.S.) to leave metropolitan France on committee inspection tours. See *LM*, March 1, 1962; *ibid.*, April 8, 1962; and *ibid.*, April 9, 1962.

100. Testimony of Prosecutor General Reliquet at Rennes, in Vidal-Naquet, *La Raison d'état*, pp. 271–72.

101. For accusations against specific officers, see Alleg, *La Question*; Vidal-Naquet, *L'Affaire Audin*; and Vidal-Naquet, *La Raison d'état* (especially p. 23). Investigations in the Audin case are discussed in *ibid.*, p. 25; and Brombergers *et al.*, *Barricades et colonels*, p. 32.

102. P. Guillaumat, ministre des forces armées, in *L'Armée*, No. 1 (February, 1961), p. 96.

103. General Pierre Billotte in an interview, June 27, 1962. Despite De Gaulle's reported statement that Charbonnier deserved five years of hard labor (Brombergers *et al.*, *Barricades et colonels*, p. 32), the lieutenant not only escaped imprisonment but was soon promoted to the rank of captain. The amnesty of March 22, 1962, absolved most military personnel guilty of torture in Algeria (Vidal-Naquet, *La Raison d'état*, pp. 321–25).

104. According to Jean-Louis Guillard, the accusation of torture against Charbonnier inspired a group of paratroop officers to assemble a dossier of orders and cables which indicated the civil authorities' acceptance, and even encouragement, of the use of torture ("Les Soldats perdus," *La Nef*, No. 19 [October, 1962–January, 1963], p. 120). See also Jean Planchais, "Atteint au moral de l'armée," *LM*, March 20, 1957.

105. "D'Algérie: Une opinion sur le moral des officiers," *Message*, No. 20 (March, 1957).

106. Lartéguy, *Les Centurions*, p. 411. Servan-Schreiber tells a related story of a general and operational-zone commander who refused to order summary executions as Algiers wished (without a written order). As he told Servan-Schreiber: "A Alger, on me dit qu'on ne veut pas le savoir, et qu'on fermera les yeux. . . . Tiens! Bien sur! On fait faire le sale boulot par les militaires, on est débarassé des meneurs nationalistes, et ensuite on se retournera, un jour,

contre l'Armée pour dire que c'est de la boucherie; ces messieurs auront les mains propres. Je ne marche pas!" (*Lieutenant en Algérie*, p. 157). The general acted wisely.

107. Brombergers *et al.*, *Barricades et colonels*, p. 33. See also Massu's testimony in the Barricades trial, *Un Procès*, p. 108.

108. The incident is described in Tournoux, *Secrets d'état*, pp. 127–36, 464.

109. *Ibid.*, p. 133; and Richard and Joan Brace, *Ordeal in Algeria* (Princeton: Van Nostrand, 1960), p. **145.**

110. Tournoux, *Secrets d'état*, pp. 138–39, 145.

111. It is also curious that Mollet was not contacted during the period of almost twenty-four hours which elapsed from the time when French intelligence heard of the flight until the plane's eventual landing at Cherchell Airport near Algiers (*ibid.*, pp. 127–34).

112. Alexander Werth, *The De Gaulle Revolution* (London: Robert Hale, 1960) p. 18.

113. *Ibid.*, and Le Tourneau, *Evolution politique de l'Afrique du Nord*, p. 426. In a National Assembly debate on February 11, 1958, the Socialist Party spokesman, M. Deixonne, suggested that Defense Minister Chaban-Delmas had approved the raid without informing his ministerial colleagues (Werth, *The De Gaulle Revolution*, p. 20).

114. The interview appeared in the *New York Herald Tribune* and is excerpted in Werth, *The De Gaulle Revolution*, p. 19.

115. In his speech to the National Assembly on February 11, 1958 (*ibid.*, p. 20).

116. The term "activist" is used here as it has been used in French in the context of the Algerian war: to refer to militant partisans of French Algeria, who were often willing to resort to insurrection when necessary to prevent Algerian independence. It will be used here in preference to another label— "ultra"—which is also frequently attached to *pied noir* activists.

117. *Ibid.*, pp. 18–45. Werth refers to the Sakiet raid, and especially the Murphy mission, as " . . . decisive in precipitating the Algiers *putsch* of May 13" (*ibid.*, p. 22). The influential publisher of the *Echo d'Alger*, Alain de Sérigny, agrees with that analysis in his book, *La Révolution du 13 mai*, pp. 3–4. The groundwork of revolt had already been laid, however.

118. Ely, "L'Armée dans la nation," *RMI* (August–September, 1958), p. 8. In the same article Ely remarked that during the May, 1958, crisis " . . . il n'y avait ni à Alger ni à Paris de pouvoir civil réellement efficace . . . " (*ibid.*, p. 7).

119. In April, 1957, it will be recalled, former Army Chief of Staff André Zeller had strongly implied that military discipline depended upon strong government: "'Armée n'est pas un 'instrument' ni un 'moyen': C'est une expression, l'un des aspects de la Nation. Que celle-ci apparaisse vivante et ferme, l'Armée, éprouvée mais forte par nature, y reprendra toute sa place" ("Armée et politique," *RDN*, April, 1957, p. 517). See also the statement of defense attorney Paul Arrighi, drawing upon the writings of R. Girardet, in *Procès Challe*, p. 253.

120. On this point see Edgar S. Furniss, Jr., *De Gaulle and the French Army* (New York: Twentieth Century Fund, 1964), pp. 68–69.

Chapter 9

Political Authority and Civilian Control
in the Praetorian Years

May, 1958, marks the official entry into politics of the French Army as an institution. Isolated individuals—notably General Jacques Faure—had toyed with revolution in the preceding years; but only in 1958 did the army, virtually as a unit, reject the crumbling authority of the Fourth Republic. General Massu, who became president of the insurrectionary Committee of Public Safety, later explained publicly his role on May 13, 1958, when demonstrators stormed the Government General Building in Algiers: "I was not in on any plot; I boarded a 'moving train,' if I may put it that way, and I tried to reach the locomotive to prevent it from going to a catastrophe." [1] The same may be said of most of those officers who were to play leading roles in the fatal May days of 1958. Raoul Salan, joint military commander in Algeria, Colonel Charles Lacheroy, Colonel Roger Trinquier—none of these were originally parties to the revolt; yet all contributed to its success and direction. Lest the "moving train" analogy be taken too seriously, however, it must be noted that the initial civilian conductors of the *treize mai* train had acted largely because of an expectation of army support, without which the revolt could not have succeeded.

There were exceptions to the general rule that civilians, not officers, plotted the uprising of May 13.[2] Gaullists, Poujadists, and other enemies of the Fourth Republic in both Algiers and Paris hoped to capitalize upon the Algerian war and the embitterment it had produced among French settlers in Algeria and among the army cadre. A nameless and clandestine "counterrevolutionary" organization in the *métropole* had as its leader and potential dictator of France a former French commander in Algeria (now retired), General Paul Cherrière, who was assisted by the familiar General L. M. Chassin, who remained on active duty until shortly before May 13 as NATO co-ordinator of aerial defense.[3] Within metropolitan France, Cherrière and Chassin had the co-operation of the volatile Veterans of Indochina (of whom Chassin was honorary president).[4] In Algeria they claimed the support of the activist North African French Union, under the leadership of an Algerian winegrower and former Cagoulard, Robert Martel. Among military officers on active duty, Chassin and Cherrière won the sympathy and latent support of General Roger Miquel, commander of the Toulouse military region, and Colonel Robert Thomazo, head of the auxiliary territorial units in the Algiers area, both of whom were also recruited by Gaullist conspirators.[5]

The Gaullist forces, who eventually won control of the rebellion, could claim the services of a number of influential former leaders of the Gaullist Rally of the French People (R.P.F.), among them the French Algerian attorney J. B. Biaggi, Senator Michel Debré, Jacques Soustelle (still a popular hero in Algeria and leader of the Union for the Safety and Renewal of French Algeria [U.S.R.A.F.]), and Minister of Defense Jacques Chaban-Delmas. Chaban-Delmas, or more precisely, Léon Delbecque, the head of a Defense Ministry "antenna" or delegation in Algiers, played a double game of helping to overthrow the government and even the republic in which he served. Aided by Guy Ribeaud, the secretary-general of the Social Republicans (the remnants of the R.P.F.), and by two army officers, Major Poujet and Captain Lamouliatte, Delbecque canvassed and organized military officers and civilian activists, preparing them for a Gaullist coup.[6] Delbecque inspired the creation of the activist Vigilance Committee in Algiers, which united Gaullists, veterans, Poujadists, Martel and his followers, and Colonel Robert Thomazo. Then, on April 26, 1958, despite protests from Lacoste and Salan, he directed a mass demonstration against a possible investiture in Paris of René Pleven as the next Premier.[7]

The Fourth Republic, like the Third, harbored its own grave-diggers: a Defense Ministry representative was stirring up rebellion in Algiers while the resident minister himself, Robert Lacoste, was telling friends and associates that only a "government of public safety" could save Algeria from a "diplomatic Dien Bien Phu." [8] As for the military high command in Algeria, on May 9, 1958, General Salan issued a virtual ultimatum to present and potential governments. His message to President of the Republic René Coty, sent through the chief of staff for defense, General Paul Ely, indicated that he would accept an appeal to the rebels for surrender with guaranteed amnesty—but nothing more. [9] He continued:

> The Army in Algeria is troubled by the consciousness of its responsibility:
>
> —in regard to the men who are fighting and risking a vain sacrifice if national representatives are not determined to maintain French Algeria, as the preamble of the basic law stipulates [the basic law of January 31, 1958];
>
> —in regard to the French population of the interior which feels itself abandoned and the French Moslems who, each day more numerous, have again placed their confidence in France, confidence in reiterated promises never to abandon them.
>
> The French Army, in a unanimous fashion, would feel the abandonment of this national patrimony to be an outrage. One could not predict its reaction of despair.
>
> I ask you please to call the attention of the President of the Republic to our anguish, which can only be erased by a government firmly determined to maintain our flag in Algeria. [10]

Paris was now duly warned that if an "acceptable" government was not forthcoming, the army was prepared to turn against its civilian masters in a "reaction of despair."

When the big day finally arrived, neither Delbecque, Cherrière, nor those few other military officers who were *dans le coup* had much control over things. A day of demonstrations ordered by the Vigilance Committee was to culminate in a ceremony at the monument to the dead. Generals Salan, Jouhaud, Allard, Massu, and Admiral Auboyneau appeared briefly about 6 P.M. amid cries of "the Army to power" and "Massu to power." [11] At that point, without the knowledge of the Gaullist contingent of the Vigilance

Committee, Robert Martel and student and Poujadist leaders in the committee launched an attack on the Government General Building (the "G.G."). Pushing aside security police and a handful of paratroopers, who hardly resisted, a few hundred demonstrators smashed in the G.G. gate with a paratrooper truck and took the building by storm.

The deed was done against the protests of Colonel Ducourneau, Lacoste's military aide, Colonel Godard, commander of the Algiers-Sahel sector since early 1957, and Colonel Thomazo, who only felt that the time was not ripe, nor the army yet fully committed.[12] Yet the few hundred activist storm troops could easily have been halted if either the security police (the Compagnies Républicaines de Sécurité) or the "Bigeard Regiment" (the Third Colonial Paratroop Regiment), now on security duty under its new commander, Colonel Roger Trinquier, had been at all serious about the defense of the G.G.[13] That paratroop regiment had been recalled from the Tunisian border a few days earlier, and, as veterans of the battle of Algiers, its members were most unlikely to deal harshly with a French Algerian uprising.[14] Moreover, Premier Félix Gaillard had apparently ordered that police and paratroopers should not fire on the crowd.[15] The point is not crucial, since the *"paras"* likely would not have fired if so ordered, and a successful defense of the G.G. by security police on May 13 would not have prevented a more powerful popular rebellion in succeeding days.

Once the G.G. had fallen to activist besiegers led by student leader Pierre Lagaillarde, General Massu soon arrived, vented his fury at the activist leaders,[16] and then proceeded to negotiate a settlement. In order to "prevent the locomotive from going to a catastrophe," Massu agreed to preside over the Committee of Public Safety, which joined Delbecque (a late arrival), local activist leaders, and those military officers who were most acceptable to the European community—Colonels Trinquier, Ducasse (Massu's chief of staff), and Thomazo, and as "candidate members," Captains Engels, Marion, and Renauld.[17] The committee drafted a historic cable to Paris which Massu sent in his own name:

REPORT CREATION CIVIL AND MILITARY COMMITTEE PUBLIC SAFETY IN ALGIERS, PRESIDED OVER BY MYSELF, GENERAL MASSU, BECAUSE GRAVITY SITUATION AND ABSOLUTE NECESSITY MAINTENANCE ORDER,

AND THIS TO AVOID ALL SPILLING OF BLOOD. DEMAND CREATION PARIS
OF A GOVERNMENT OF PUBLIC SAFETY, ALONE CAPABLE OF RETAINING
ALGERIA INTEGRAL PART OF METROPOLE.[18]

Early the following morning, after a National Assembly with its back to the wall had invested Pierre Pflimlin as Premier, Massu produced another stronger message beginning, "we are announcing to the population that the government of abandonment led by M. Pflimlin has just been invested with the participation of communist votes." [19]

Massu faced a rebellion which was not directly of his making; yet he was in full agreement with its intent, and, rather than repress it with violence, he preferred to become an insurgent himself. By recognizing the Committee of Public Safety, General Salan as well placed one foot in the camp of rebellion.

In the night of May 13–14 General Salan was vested with full civil powers in the city of Algiers by Gaillard and then, the following morning, by Gaillard's successor, Pierre Pflimlin, after the latter had been invested as Premier. Salan then proceeded to balance delicately between legality and rebellion, moving progressively toward the latter. The military commander continued to report to Paris and assure the Pflimlin government of his loyalty. Yet he asserted full power over the whole of Algeria without authorization from Paris;[20] he called for a government of public safety in Paris;[21] he publicly added his voice to the cries of "Vive De Gaulle" on May 15 before a crowd at the G.G.;[22] he gave legal sanction to Massu's insurrectionary Committee of Public Safety;[23] he secretly contacted De Gaulle;[24] and finally, he took command of "Operation Resurrection," designed to overthrow the Fourth Republic by force, if necessary.[25] On the other hand, Delbecque was never certain that Salan was not about to arrest him.[26] Salan, or the "Mandarin," as he was sometimes called, played a complex and subtle game, hopeful perhaps both of avoiding violence and of covering himself in any eventuality.[27] Yet he must be credited with maintaining that veneer of legality which facilitated a bloodless transition to the Fifth Republic.

General Salan, in fact, was an enigma in many ways. A former intelligence officer, said to be a republican, perhaps a socialist, and (more doubtfully) even a Free Mason, he arrived in Algiers with a not altogether undeserved reputation of having favored looser French ties in Indochina. He was thought by Algiers activists to be so much of a threat to French Algeria that his assassination was attempted. That still mysterious bazooka attack of January 16, 1957, killed Salan's aide and set off a spectacular investigation in which an alleged "committee of 6," including Michel Debré, was accused of inspiring the deed.[28] In contrast to the popular Massu, General Salan was regarded with suspicion and hostility by Europeans in Algeria; the Mandarin stepped out on the balcony of the G.G. on the night of May 13 to address the crowd and was met with angry cries of "Indochine," "Vive Massu," and "Foutez le camp" (roughly, "Get the hell out of here!").[29] It took public pleading by Colonel Thomazo and probably some behind-the-scenes work by Martel and by army psychological-action and security officers to produce a more favorable popular reaction to Salan when he addressed the crowd again on May 15.[30] The successful outcome of the May 13 uprising and Salan's newly found popularity led the cautious and enigmatic Mandarin into quite a new type of existence: total commitment to a passionate and violent crusade, that of French Algeria.

May 13 was the work of activist leaders of the local European population; yet these men were responsible for neither of the two major themes which *treize mai* came to represent—Gaullism and integration. The Gaullist turn of the insurrection must be credited to Delbecque, a skilful manipulator, to Massu, a "Gaullist of 1940," to Jacques Soustelle, who arrived in Algiers on May 17 after an escape from police surveillance in Paris, and to De Gaulle himself, who spoke and acted discreetly and in time, and who, though not immensely popular among career officers, was nevertheless a military man. Generals Cherrière and Chassin quickly lost any control they might have had over the uprising.[31]

"Integration," with its radical political equality of Moslems and Europeans in Algeria, was the price *pied noir* leaders were forced to pay for critical army support.[32] Integration as a theme was largely the product of the Fifth Bureau in Algiers. Working with Colonel Godard's networks within the European and Moslem populations in Algiers, seizing especially upon contacts with reservists, veterans, and local auxiliary territorial units, the Fifth Bureau helped to develop a climate of opinion which facilitated the *treize mai* uprising and turned it toward integration as a dominant theme.[33] In defense of integration, psychological-action officers, Colonel Trinquier, Colonel Godard's agents, and officers of the Urban Administrative Sections all co-operated in staging one of the most dramatic events of the May crisis. Trinquier and Godard, the creators of the organization of the population in 1957, personally went into the Casbah to negotiate and organize a Moslem demonstration for May 16. Thousands of Moslems flooded out of the Casbah to join more thousands of Europeans in a delirious festival of integration.[34] Here was the greatest success which French psychological action in Algeria was to achieve. Moslems and *pieds noirs* were sincerely moved at the time; but Algerian nationalism on the one hand and racism and privilege on the other were too deeply rooted to be overcome for long by a revival-meeting conversion.

Soustelle arrived on May 17, met a cool reception from Salan, but stayed on to confirm the theme of integration.[35] The Fifth Bureau under Colonel Charles Lacheroy became, henceforth, the primary carrier of that message. *Le Bled* blossomed forth in its issue of May 21 with headlines announcing the permanence of French Algeria and describing the integration miracle of May 16.[36] Working more with the Committee of Public Safety than with Joint Commander Salan, the Fifth Bureau displayed an open independence and power which were to end only with its dissolution in February, 1960.

The attitude of the army was quickly apparent. Minister of Interior Jules Moch later told a Socialist Party conference, "Out of nine officers commanding military regions [in the *métropole*], at least four—with authority over forty departments—did not hide the fact that they were in sympathy with Algiers." [37] On May 15 General Maurice Challe, deputy chief of staff for defense, visited Guy Mollet to inform him that the armed forces as a whole were in sympathy with the dissident generals in Algeria.[38] Defense Minister Pierre de Chevigné then shuttled General Challe off to assigned residence in

Brest for having ordered twelve paratroop planes to Algeria on May 11, though Challe insisted the planes were necessary reinforcements and not intended to support a paratroop attack on Paris.[39] The Chief of Staff of National Defense, Paul Ely, had urged Pflimlin to resign on several occasions; on the 16th he submitted his own resignation, purportedly because of the action taken against General Challe and another air force General, André Martin, who was expedited to Metz.[40] Ely's post was refused by two generals, Blanc and Gouraud, before the government finally found a taker— army chief of staff and former joint commander in Algeria, General Henri Lorillot. And even Lorillot cabled Salan that he was accepting only in order to support the army in Algeria and maintain the unity of the army.[41]

The government's few firm supporters in the army were badly outnumbered.[42] Operation Resurrection, the plan for an armored and paratroop assault on Paris, was more than a bluff, though government officials in Paris were indeed the object of a well-orchestrated "intoxication" campaign of mysterious radio messages, anonymous telephone calls, and rumors of impending invasion—all designed to frighten them into abdication.[43] Command of the operation was given by Massu and Salan to General Miquel, to be supported by French paratroopers under his command as head of the Toulouse military region, by more paratroopers to be flown from Algeria, and by Colonel Gribius and his armored group at Rambouillet, near Paris.[44] Had De Gaulle agreed to the landings (he did not),[45] or had he not been invested by the National Assembly on June 1, Operation Resurrection probably would have gone into effect.[46] In fact, General Miquel testified in the Salan trial that even after the investiture of De Gaulle as Premier, the presence in his cabinet of men associated with the "system" prompted a military directorate in Algiers to consider again the appropriateness of a coup.[47] According to Miquel, Salan opposed a military coup on the grounds that De Gaulle had been invested and now had to be trusted.[48]

Army officers were patently unwilling to come to the defense of *le système.* Some of the reasons for that unwillingness have been suggested above;[49] others will be explored in detail below.[50] Here it is sufficient to say that the defense of French Algeria had become for a large segment of the army a sacred cause, integrally linked with safeguarding not only the French nation (for some, the entire Western world) but also military honor, prestige, and power. The most serious military grievance against *le système* (which, through its weakness, had magnified the army's stake in French Algeria) was its lack of determination in waging the holy battle across the Mediterranean. On June 4, 1958, when De Gaulle arrived in Algiers as Premier, General Massu introduced him to the Committee of Public Safety for Algeria with these words:

> The rush of the Algiers crowds toward the Government General Building was intended to express refusal to continue to accept successive capitulations, the abandonment which appeared unavoidable, the acceleration of French decadence through the fatal and thoughtless action of irresponsible governments subject to the haggling and incompetence of the party politicians who made up the Parliament.[51]

For Massu, as for numerous other military spokesmen, the Fourth Republic had long since lost its legitimacy.[52]

The behavior of the army in May, 1958, was not simply an obedient response to a few dissident commanders at the top of the military hierarchy. On the contrary, hostility toward *le système* was probably greatest among younger officers, especially in Algeria, who held positions below the highest command posts.[53] In Algeria it was not Salan who formally joined the insurrection but Massu, whose captains, majors, and colonels had facilitated the organization of the European settlers for direct political action during the battle of Algiers.[54] In the *métropole* General Ely and others like him leaned toward Algiers largely because of a fear of splitting the army. In July, 1958, *Message* editorialists, spokesmen for many of the more politically aggressive officers in the lower and middle ranks, wrote:

> Some have talked of plots and conspiracy. Blind are those who have not been able to see that the cry which burst forth from Algiers had long burned the lips of virtually all of us, and that our agreement was such that there was no longer any need for either passwords or instructions.[55]

Two months later *Le Bled* added its joyous benediction to "the era of Byzantine discussions." [56]

If the great majority of French officers had lost respect for the Fourth Republic, most probably would have hesitated to turn on their civilian masters had it not been for two factors: (a) the choice forced on them by the action of Massu and his officers in Algiers, and (b) the general disaffection of civilians as well as military officers toward *le système*. In 1958 the Fourth Republic found its authority in an advanced stage of disintegration, not only with respect to the army, but also with respect to police, gendarmes, some civil administrators, and the French population generally. Here, as is often the case, political authority (and its collapse) was of a piece.

Even if Operation Resurrection had been launched, there probably would have been no civil war. Police and security troops in the *métropole* were strongly antiparliamentary in outlook, particularly in the case of the influential "Dides network" within the police force.[57] Minister of the Interior Jules Moch soon became aware of "the most humiliating weakness of the reliable means at my disposal." [58] He received devastating proof of his helplessness on May 24, 1958. A delegation was dispatched to Corsica by Massu and Salan and on that day succeeded in rallying the support of Captain Ignace Mantei and the two hundred fifty paratroopers of his First Shock Batallion stationed there. Mantei and his paratroopers were sent to the departmental capital of Ajaccio, where police and gendarmes put up no opposition as civilian demonstrators invaded public buildings and formed a committee of public safety.[59] Reinforcing gendarme units sent by air from Nice arrived only to place themselves under the orders of dissident military authorities.[60] The prefect of Corsica resisted, as did the deputy mayor of the city of Bastia; yet all but one of the six underprefects rallied to Algiers.[61]

Where were the republicans in May, 1958? In effect, the Left could not arouse much popular passion over the survival of the Fourth Republic. To be sure, a belated mass demonstration in Paris on May 28 attracted over 100,000 people. Moreover, Pflimlin deliberately refrained from appealing for working-class support, fearing the Communist Party might come out the winner, rather than the Fourth Republic.[62] Nevertheless, it is noteworthy that work stoppages ordered by the communist-led General Confederation of Labor (C.G.T.) were almost totally ignored. In a referendum organized by the C.G.T. in the Paris area, only 20 per cent of the workers favored a general strike in the event that De Gaulle were invested as Premier.[63] Near the height of the crisis, on May 25, meters on the Freeway of the West counted 36,463 automobiles leaving Paris for the weekend—3,126 more than in the preceding year. As Tournoux puts it, "The weekend triumphs." [64] More eloquent yet are the results of an opinion poll taken in August, 1958. When a national sample was asked whether the army's role in the *treize mai* had been useful or harmful, 55 per cent of all respondents answered useful, as against only 17 per cent who replied harmful.[65]

Might the Pflimlin government have turned the tide and saved the Fourth Republic if, instead of hedging and temporizing, it had condemned categorically the insurrection and had appealed vigorously to the French people to defend the republic, at the barricades if necessary? Three years later, such vigorous executive leadership threw hesitant army officers behind Paris, rather than Algiers, and helped to squash the April putsch. In May of 1958, however, Pflimlin (who was no De Gaulle) represented a republic which had allowed its authority to erode away, both with regard to military and police forces and with regard to a civilian population which found little to be proud of in *le système*. The most likely alternative to De Gaulle was not pure republicanism, but military dictatorship. Incapable of rallying the nation behind it, unable to act effectively and in time, helpless at the hands of foes within its ranks, the government of the Fourth Republic was indeed an easy prey for its civilian and military enemies.

Reinstalled as chief of staff of national defense in the summer of 1958, General Paul Ely addressed a call to obedience to the armed forces in an article published in the August–September issue of the *Revue militaire d'information*. He lavished praise on the army for having prevented a cleavage between Algeria and the *métropole* in May, 1958, and then dismissed the fears of those who saw the army as a threat to civil authority: "The Army always remains in its place with a strong government and when it knows it is being commanded." [66] Unquestionably, De Gaulle was a strong political leader with firm popular and parliamentary support. Yet in the first three years of the Fifth Republic, he was to face the following opposition: first, in January, 1960, a muted repeat performance of the *treize mai;* and then, in April, 1961, an open and aggressive military revolt. Why did military indiscipline continue to be a problem despite vigorous governmental leadership? Of course, all of those interrelated politicizing factors discussed in earlier and succeeding chapters were still at work; nevertheless, one must ask why renewed governmental strength was inadequate to check their effect. A brief review of the "Week of the Barricades" and the April putsch of 1961 will be necessary in answering that question.

Until September 16, 1959, De Gaulle and the army in Algeria coexisted without great mutual trust, but also without serious conflict. Government officials were at times annoyed by a tendency of military authorities in Algiers (especially the Fifth Bureau) to act on policy matters without government authorization.[67] And among officers in Algeria there were undoubtedly some, like Massu, who felt De Gaulle was wrong in ordering military personnel out of all committees of public safety in September, 1958, and in transferring a number of key officers out of Algiers, among them General Salan, who was recalled to Paris in December, 1958.[68] However, a climate of latent military revolt began to form only after De Gaulle's announcement on September 16, 1959, that the Algerian population was to be allowed to choose independence, "association," or integration with France.

Shortly after that announcement, the chief of the Fifth Bureau for Algeria, Colonel Jean Gardes, persuaded Salan's successor, General Maurice Challe, to call together representatives from all army corps, zones, and sectors. Again on Gardes' urging, the group was informed that the army would continue to campaign for French Algeria.[69] Challe must have been aware that such an order probably would not have met with official approval in Paris. We have the testimony of Colonel Gardes, to whom Challe said, "You will not write it. These orders are only verbal, and you will give these instructions yourselves verbally." [70] In the next several months, until his transfer in April, 1960, however, Challe publicly continued to defend the goal of French Algeria in his speeches and even in his formal directives.[71] He was never rebuked by De Gaulle for taking that line, though in his own pronouncements the President of the Republic clearly shied from a commitment to integration.

De Gaulle was understandably hesitant to clash with the army unnecessarily; yet his reluctance to halt the army's campaign for French Algeria allowed officers and their defenders to claim they had been tricked and betrayed by a government which was only awaiting a chance to renege on French commitments in Algeria.[72] On the basis of Challe's verbal orders that "we will continue to work for the 'most French solution'" among the three alternatives, Massu could later defend French Algeria partisans of the Week of the Barricades on grounds that they were within the bounds of discipline.[73] But, of course, the issuance of the orders themselves had been an act of indiscipline.

De Gaulle increased anxiety in military circles in Algeria when in his press conference of November 10, 1959, he called for negotiations with rebel leaders leading to a cease-fire and promised that the self-determination referendum would be "entirely free" and open to *all* Algerians.[74] By mid-January, 1960, General Massu was in an explosive state of mind. As "superprefect" of Algiers (since June, 1958), in addition to his role as commander of the Algiers Army Corps, Massu felt that "it was difficult for me not to engage in politics. That was the role of civil authorities . . . which I was." [75] The general apparently was unaware that, in principle at least, the prefect's job is not to *faire de la politique*. And, of course, Massu's view of politics was no longer that of General de Gaulle. Massu's fury was unleashed in an interview with a German journalist, Hans Ulrich Kempski of the *Suddeutsche Zeitung*.[76] Remarking that "we no longer understand his policy," Massu, the strong Gaullist of the *treize mai* crisis, went on to suggest that "he was the only man at our disposition. But perhaps the Army made a mistake there." [77] Not content with lamenting past errors, the Victor of Algiers added: "The first question to be asked is to know when a successor to General de Gaulle will arrive. . . . The Army has the strength. It has not shown it so far. The occasion has not presented itself; but, in a certain situation, the Army would establish its power." [78]

Understandably enough, Massu was recalled to Paris and relieved of his command. With Massu gone the only key military figure of the *treize mai* still left in Algiers was Colonel Yves Godard, now Directeur de la Sûreté for all of Algeria. Among those who had been transferred out were: the joint commander in Algeria, General Raoul Salan, who was given the "up and out" treatment with a nonexistent post as "inspector general of defense"; the air commander for Algeria, General Edmond Jouhaud, who retired on request after Salan's recall; the commander of the Algiers Army Corps, General Paul Allard, who became commander in chief of French forces in Germany; the one-time president of the Committee of Public Safety for Algiers, Colonel Roland Vaudrey; Colonels Lacheroy and Goussault of the Fifth Bureau; the commander of the *gendarmerie* in Algiers, Colonel Crazafor; and Colonel Trinquier, whose paratroopers had done so little to halt the *treize mai* assault on the G.G.

Deprived of the last of their military defenders of the *treize mai*, leaders in Algiers rallied the auxiliary territorial units in that city and launched what was intended to be a repeat performance in republic-busting. [79] Military authorities in Algiers refused to allow an assault on public buildings; yet paratroopers ordered to the scene conveniently (and purposefully) arrived too late on January 24, 1960, to assist security guards in a move to clear armed demonstrators from Boulevard Laferrière in central Algiers. [80] A fierce battle ensued between the well-armed demonstrators and the security police, whose weapons initially had been unloaded, as ordered. [81] Civilian casualties totaled 6 dead and 24 wounded, as against 14 dead and 123 wounded among the security guards. [82] Thereafter the paratroopers moved in as arbitrators, more interested in forcing Paris to retract its self-determination policy than in routing armed demonstrators out of their barricaded retreats. De Gaulle held firm, and a week after the crisis had begun, paratroop commanders on the scene finally began reacting as disciplined soldiers, rather than as arbitrators and negotiators. Shorn of tacit military support, the rebellion crumbled.

As in May, 1958, the leaders of the immediate uprising were not military officers but local civilian activists, this time Pierre Lagaillarde (as on May 13) and Joseph Ortiz, the neo-fascist leader of the ten-thousand–member French National Front (F.N.F.).[83] But even more than on the *treize mai*, army officers, and especially those of the Fifth Bureau, were in large measure responsible for creating the means and the will for revolt. It was the auxiliary and locally recruited territorial units which provided the weapons and most of the manpower which were turned on the gendarmes on January 24.

The period of a year and a half from May 13, 1958, to January, 1960, was the heyday of psychological action in Algeria. The French military doctrine of *la guerre révolutionnaire* was officially accepted in military schools and in most military headquarters in Algeria, despite De Gaulle's preference for more classical warfare.[84] The Fifth Bureau was blocked abruptly after May 13, when it attempted to propagandize the metropolitan French population with films and recordings glorifying the themes of French Algeria and fraternization of Europeans and Moslems.[85] Colonels Lacheroy, Goussault, and Feaugas of the Fifth Bureau in Algiers were rebuked and transferred in the fall of 1958 after *Le Bled* published an article attacking various men of *le système*.[86] So long as the Fifth Bureau in Algiers stuck to propaganda and political organization within Algeria, however, it was generally left free to campaign for French Algeria and for integration.[87] And even within the *métropole* the cause of French Algeria found vigorous military and quasi-military propagandists in Marshal Juin (who long purported to be an interpreter of De Gaulle's intentions) and in the "Young Turk" movement within the official National Union of Reserve Officers.[88]

The "pilot Bureau" in counterrevolutionary war, as General Massu had described the Fifth Bureau,[89] succeeded in producing no more than surface reactions among Moslems, who had reason to be disillusioned by a rapid *pied noir* retrenchment into their Afrikander mentality after May 16, 1958. Psychological-action officers then made the fatal error of attempting to swim in the European, not the Moslem sea. To be sure, in the fall of 1959 the chief of the Bureau in Algiers, Colonel Jean Gardes, attempted to create a massive Moslem and European organization comparable to the "political-administrative organization" of the rebel F.L.N. and based on European territorial units and Moslem self-defense corps.[90] But the European population in Algiers was more receptive than the Moslem population.

In practice, the Federation of Territorial Units neither joined Moslems with Europeans nor assured army control over *pied noir* activists; on the contrary, it served as a tool and an arsenal of those it was intended to control—notably of Joseph Ortiz, who placed the commander of his personal four-thousand-man F.N.F. army, Captain Ronda, as secretary-general of the federation. "Control," however, was not the only aim of military authorities in Algiers. Local activist organizations served as a useful and indirect weapon against the government in Paris. Alongside representatives from Massu's headquarters, Colonel Gardes worked closely with Ortiz, giving his F.N.F. a quasi-official status.[91] Ortiz, in return, promised to consult Massu before "launching anything" in Algiers.[92] The relationship between the army in Algiers and the F.N.F. could be characterized better as one of complicity, rather than army control, as Massu claimed.[93]

In the afternoon of January 23, 1960, after a stormy interview with De Gaulle, Massu telephoned his chief of staff, Colonel Argoud, to rescind earlier orders to hold tight.[94] Argoud took this to mean an approval of activist demonstrations.[95] Local activist leaders were soon informed. A number of territorial units had been mobilized mysteriously during the night of January 22–23, "on order from Colonel Gardes" their officers were told.[96] Gardes likely did not give the order, but he was clearly sympathetic, if not to a repeat performance of the *treize mai*, at least to a rousing demonstration designed to put pressure on De Gaulle.[97] That sympathy was shared by a number of other officers in Algiers, notably Colonel Argoud and Colonel Broizat, commander of the First Chasseurs Paratroop

Regiment, which showed such little enthusiasm for maintaining order in face of activist insurgents.[98]

Gardes and Argoud, however, could not speak for Massu's successor as commander of the Algiers Army Corps, General Crépin, who was in no mood to give over the city to Ortiz, or for Colonel Fonde, commander of the Algiers-Sahel sector. Even General Challe apparently concurred in the order to use troops to clear armed demonstrators off the streets, though earlier on the 24th he had given Ortiz permission to carry out a *peaceful* demonstration.[99] Elsewhere in Algeria, the army generally remained loyal to Paris. In Oran, General Gambiez disarmed the territorial units and put his tanks into action.[100] Clearly, despite the government's "self-determination" policy and rumors of impending negotiations with the F.L.N., the mood of most elements within the officer corps was not revolutionary: De Gaulle could not be scorned so easily as Pflimlin.

It so happened, however, that the psychological-action and paratroop colonels then in Algiers were among the army's most violent partisans of French Algeria, despite the transfers of the past eighteen months. Most of those colonels who later planned the April putsch of 1961 and then built the Secret Army Organization were assembled there. There was Colonel Jean Gardes, who had been deposed as chief of the Fifth Bureau for his political adventures two weeks before the barricades went up,[101] but was still on hand on January 24 to appear in uniform with Ortiz on the balcony on the Territorial Unit Building, which had become the F.N.F. command post.[102] There was Colonel Antoine Argoud, regarded as "one of the best brains of the Army," [103] a Polytechnicien who had not served in Indochina, but who had, of late, become a theorist of *la guerre révolutionnaire* (as were all of these men).[104] There were the paratroop colonels, especially Colonel Joseph Broizat, an intellectual, a former Catholic seminarian, and a dedicated anticommunist crusader; and Colonel Dufour, commander of the First Foreign Paratroop Regiment, which later provided the shock troops for the April putsch of 1961.[105]

These were the men who in fact controlled Algiers for the Week of the Barricades, with Argoud the leader among them. On the night of January 24, General Challe and Resident Minister Delouvrier called in two battalions of the Twenty-fifth Paratroop Division (under General Ducourneau) from the Constantine area to add to the Tenth Paratroop Division (under General Gracieux, who was now given Colonel Fonde's post as commander of the Algiers-Sahel sector). This attempt to quiet the uprising gently with the beloved *paras* failed completely. Gracieux became the tool of his colonels, whose troops fraternized with the demonstrators and allowed them to enter and leave the barricaded areas at will. Colonel Gardes, in fact, before his recall to Paris on January 27, even attempted to effect a reconciliation between the leaders of two rival activist camps—Lagaillarde and Ortiz.[106]

When Premier Michel Debré arrived in Algiers on the night of January 25, he was told by the generals on hand (Crépin among them) that the troops would never fire on the demonstrators.[107] The colonels were even more blunt and rude. Argoud, by his own testimony, announced that Challe would have to take charge if De Gaulle refused to renounce his self-determination policy. "If he refuses?" Debré asked. "Monsieur le premier ministre," Argoud replied, "at that moment it will be an affair for the colonels, whatever their names may be." [108] Debré returned to Paris thinking that Algiers was in the hands of a soviet of colonels.[109]

Thereafter the insurgents' position weakened as a result of a series of developments. The army attempted to organize another massive Moslem-European rally on the model of May 16, 1958, and met with complete failure.[110] Delouvrier persuaded Challe to join him on January 28 in an escape from the city which neither now controlled. Chief of Staff Paul Ely arrived in Algiers and talked severely with the colonels, though earlier the same day he had urged Debré to make firm promises regarding the future of Algeria.[111] Finally, and most important, De Gaulle addressed the nation and the army on January 29, conceding to the latter the right to supervise future elections in Algeria and to select the proper means for restoring order in the present crisis. He was firm and convincing, however, in regard to those officers who wished to formulate the nation's Algerian policy. His warning was clear enough: "No soldier may associate himself at any time, even passively, with the rebellion without committing a grave mistake." [112] His words had a powerful effect on a hesitant officer corps in Algeria.[113] Shortly after the broadcast of his address in Algeria, while the Algiers colonels were realizing that it was all over (for the moment), telegrams from unit commanders and SAS officers flowed into Delouvrier's office proclaiming army loyalty to the head of the state.[114]

In contrast to the *treize mai* crisis, this time the army elsewhere in Algeria had remained loyal, with few exceptions. Now, after the master had spoken, Gracieux broke with his political colonels, the Tenth Paratroop Division was replaced by regular infantry troops (including many draftees), the territorial units were called to active duty, and activist forces were left only to surrender (as did Lagaillarde) or flee (as did Ortiz). De Gaulle's strong public support in the *métropole*, his firmness and self-assurance, his commanding manner in addressing the army and the nation—all these contributed to the realization that this time the unity of the army could be preserved only through loyalty to the government.[115]

The Barricades crisis served as a warning to De Gaulle that the army's loyalty could not be assured through generous delegation of civil powers. Prefects and underprefects gradually were given back their civil powers wherever possible.[116] The whole structure of the Fifth Bureau was dissolved.[117] *Le Bled* offices were moved to Paris in early May, 1960, and the very term "psychological action" soon became taboo in official military circles. However, a number of psychological-action specialists continued their activities under other services, particularly under the Second and Third bureaus.[118] Officers who had encouraged the insurrection or attempted to profit from it were removed from their posts. Among them were Colonels Gardes, who was the only officer to be tried (he was acquitted), Argoud, Broizat, Godard, and Bigeard (who had sent a message of support to the insurgents), and Generals Mirambeau (Bigeard's superior at Saïda) and Faure (the eternal conspirator).[119] General Challe himself was transferred in April, 1960, likely because he was not thought to have been firm enough with his colonels and with the insurgents in January.[120]

Transfers could not halt a renewal of anti-Gaullist conspiracy, however, as the President of the republic spoke progressively of a future "Algerian Algeria," [121] and then of an "Algerian Republic." [122] The group of military conspirators led by Colonel Argoud acted on a sentiment that was widespread in the army, as evidenced by the impressive array of spokesmen who renewed the cry of "halte à l'abandon" in the winter of 1960–61. General Challe resigned from active duty in December, 1960, in protest over De Gaulle's Algerian policy. Shortly before the referendum of January 8, 1961, on that policy, statements of opposition were made by Marshal Juin on December 28, by General Valluy on December 31, and then by General Zeller and sixteen other retired generals on January 4.[123]

In October, 1959, and again in January, 1960, Right-wing conspirators in Paris had hoped. for the co-operation of Generals Zeller, Salan, and Jouhaud.[124] Now, for the first time, a purely military conspiracy was bred and implemented by the colonels—Argoud, Gardes, Broizat, Lacheroy, Godard—and the four generals whom they succeeded in recruiting to lead the coup—André Zeller, Edmond Jouhaud, Raoul Salan, and Maurice Challe.[125] As in May, 1958, the professional officer corps as a whole was favorably disposed toward another military crusade to prevent Algerian independence, now more imminent than ever.[126]

If military sentiments had not changed, however, there had been a great change in the willingness of officers to act on their convictions in defiance of a vigorous, self-confident governmental leader who rapidly won the active support of the French population. Pflimlin had temporized with the peaceful and admittedly ambiguous insurrection of May 13; De Gaulle quickly labeled insurgents as such. On April 23, 1961, a day after Challe and his forces had staged a palace revolution in Algiers with the aid of First Foreign Paratroop Regiment, De Gaulle addressed the nation and the army by radio, warning that "I forbid all Frenchmen, and above all all soldiers, to execute any of their orders." [127] In effect, De Gaulle was saying that, by entering into a state of insurrection, those officers who had rallied to Challe had lost all command authority, leaving their subordinates under the orders of loyal superiors, or of the President as commander in chief. Again, as on January 29, 1960, it was difficult for officers to ignore such a commanding voice. To be sure, "loyalist" officers refused to arrest their Challist colleagues, though a number of arrests were made in the other direction.[128] Few officers were ready to oppose the Challists outright; yet few outside the Tenth and Twenty-fifth paratroop divisions were willing to throw their lot with the putsch against the express orders of De Gaulle. As a result, Challe was forced to send a few paratroop regiments scampering all over Algeria to press local military commanders to join him.[129] With very few exceptions, military zone and sector commanders remained loyal to the government.[130]

The final blow to the mutineers was the response of thousands of conscripts, who had posed no barrier to the *treize mai* uprising. In the *métropole* De Gaulle's pleas of "Françaises, Français, Aidez-moi!" met with a hearty response from trade unions (including police unions), political parties (except for the extreme Right), and the population generally;[131] in Algeria citizen soldiers in many units pressed their commanders to declare against Challe and ceased obeying orders if those commanders refused. In a few cases, as in the La Calle sector, conscripts went so far as to arrest their officers.[132] The putsch might well have collapsed eventually even without the obstruction of the conscripts; nevertheless, their attitude and passive disobedience clearly hastened its demise.[133]

Challe's surrender on April 25 ended the immediate crisis, but not the smoldering threat to military discipline. Generals Salan and Jouhaud and almost all of the soviet of colonels fled after disagreeing with Challe's refusal either to call on the armed support of European settlers or to launch the nation into civil war. The Secret Army Organization (O.A.S.), which had played a minor role in the putsch, under the leadership of General Salan now became the central organ of a clandestine and insurrectionary movement aimed at joining the army and civilian partisans of French Algeria in a desperate campaign to prevent Algerian independence. In hopes of forcing the army into alliance with the *pieds noirs* through provoking a bloody racial war between the Moslem and European communities in Algeria, the O.A.S. proceeded to kill twelve hundred Moslems and two hundred Europeans by April, 1962.[134]

It soon became clear, however, that if a military leader as prestigious as Maurice Challe could not outbid the Fifth Republic for the army's obedience, neither could the less popular Salan. The April putsch had revealed that again military disobedience was to be considered a crime, despite the grandeur of its motives. On March 5, 1962, as negotiations between the F.L.N. and the De Gaulle government were reaching a successful conclusion, army forces in Algiers finally opened fire on European demonstrators. Unable to persuade the army to join with it, the O.A.S. turned its terrorists on unco-operative army personnel, killing fourteen officers and sixty-two enlisted men by mid-June, 1962.[135] These assassinations only served to widen the rift between the O.A.S and the majority of officers.

In spite of the now obvious risks involved, however, a number of officers did desert the army to join the ranks of the O.A.S. By the end of 1962 some two hundred officers were in prison for antigovernment activities,[136] and perhaps another hundred deserters and purged officers were still active within, or on the fringes of, the O.A.S.[137] A general reduction in officer personnel provided the opportunity for releasing from active duty over a thousand officers, many of whom undoubtedly were purged for disloyalty to the government. Almost all of those released from active duty against their will were from the *armée de terre,* rather than the navy or air force.[138] An increased rate of voluntary resignations and a large number of unpublicized sanctions within the service completed the picture of a purge which could strike only at the most obvious activists in a generally disaffected officer corps.

With the circumstances of the Week of the Barricades and the April putsch of 1961 now in mind, it is possible to shed a bit more light on the French Army's indiscipline in the face of a solid, popular, and effective political regime. The explanation seems to be threefold. First, as the French political scientist Maurice Duverger put it in 1958 (writing as a Frenchman as well as a political scientist): "It is said that there are women who have never had a lover, but few indeed who have had only one lover."[139] Once crossed, the Rubicon could more easily be recrossed. The first crossing had been simple enough and had won public acclaim for the army; why should military men stop at a second political venture to save French Algeria from abandonment?

Second, De Gaulle took power at a time when the army in Algeria was the effective governing and administrative power in that province. He could not easily or quickly withdraw delegated powers. In fact, the constitutional referendum and elections of the fall of 1958 forced him to call on additional military aid in order to conduct an election in a war-torn country where the F.L.N. was circulating threats to candidates and voters.[140] Officers attending the Ecole de Guerre in Paris were sent to Algeria to help officers there in the conduct of the election.[141] The army helped to produce a massive affirmative vote in Algeria for the De Gaulle Constitution, but in the process, military commitment to French Algeria was further extended.

Third, the *treize mai* did not end the ambiguity which had long surrounded the objectives of the French government in Algeria. Thirty years earlier, De Gaulle himself had recognized the importance of clear directives when he wrote:

> In the last resort exaggerations of initiative are caused primarily by the absence or laxity of decisions by the superior echelon. An enterprising spirit in a leader is never a danger in itself.[142]

Yet now in office, despite his early and continuing doubts about the feasibility of ending the war by "integrating" Algeria and France, De Gaulle was after all indebted to, and limited by, the military and civilian king-makers of the *treize mai*—most of whom were devoted partisans of French Algeria. One of the reasons for his recall to power and for his widespread popularity in 1958 was that the defenders of French Algeria and their opponents in France each felt that De Gaulle was in agreement with them. Coupled with De Gaulle's own pragmatic search for terms on which the war might be ended, these limitations lent a mysterious oracular quality to pronouncements on Algeria by the chief of state. Even the historic "self-determination" speech of September 16, 1959, failed to end all ambiguity. Initially, De Gaulle pronounced neither for "integration" nor for "association" with France.[143] His preference for "association" gradually became apparent; yet this notion was itself so ambiguous that it might include anything from limited local autonomy to complete independence under the F.L.N. —the form it finally took in the Evian agreement of March, 1962.

De Gaulle probably could not have moved more rapidly toward Algerian independence without stirring up even worse opposition than he actually met.[144] Military attacks on De Gaulle's "double game" in Algeria, such as that made at the Salan trial, must not be taken at face value.[145] It is not true, as one lieutenant colonel argued in 1962, that "de Gaulle had only to tell us what he intended back in 1958 and all the trouble would have been avoided." [146] Gardes, Argoud, Challe, and others were quite aware that De Gaulle never fully committed himself either to "integration" or to "French Algeria." Nevertheless, whatever the causes, an absence of clear policy goals, especially in the first two years of the Fifth Republic, again encouraged uncontrolled military initiatives in the domain of policy formulation and allowed the army's commitment to French Algeria to deepen before the goal of an "Algerian Republic" was finally declared.[147] The army's long-standing fears of "betrayal" and "abandonment" were intensified as De Gaulle's firm promises of September, 1959, and January, 1960 —no political negotiations with the F.L.N. alone and none whatsoever until after a full cease-fire—were eventually broken.[148]

In the last analysis, French military behavior since 1958 appears to support, rather than to disprove, the theory that firm, well-rooted governmental authority, buttressed by a general belief within the civilian population in the legitimacy of the existing government, is the strongest single deterrent to military disobedience and revolt. The army in Algeria in April, 1961, had all the reasons for disobedience which had inspired it in May, 1958. De Gaulle was now more committed to an independent Algeria than Pflimlin had ever been. The army was still the object of abuse in the metropolitan press. The F.L.N. had more and bolder supporters in the *métropole* than ever before. The paratroopers had gained in political aggressiveness since 1958, and the army as a whole was more convinced than ever of the political demands of revolutionary-guerrilla war. The army still hungered for a victory, and the war seemed all but won militarily. Military honor was at stake in regard to innumerable pledges to France's Moslem and European supporters in Algeria that they would never be abandoned. Nevertheless the putsch rallied only a minority of officers, just as the "soviet of colonels" in Algiers had failed to draw general army support in January, 1960. To be sure, some officers most probably were disheartened by the massive F.L.N. demonstrations of December, 1960, and by the *pied noir* Arab hunts which followed. Yet the major novelty in the situation was undoubtedly De Gaulle, who brought to the French political scene a firm authority rooted in a wide, charismaticly based consensus.

French experience since 1939 in general seems to support the thesis that political authority stemming from consensus is the single most powerful guarantor of civilian control.[149] The recent experience of underdeveloped countries reveals even more dramatically the frequent praetorian consequences of feeble political authority.[150] Especially in the West, however, solidity of political authority is not the only significant defense against praetorianism, nor is it always sufficient. As mentioned earlier, the French Army in the nineteenth century remained obedient, for the most part, despite the instability and uncertain authority of the French political system during most of that period. The French Army under the Fourth Republic probably would have behaved similarly had it not been for the strains of decolonization and revolutionary-guerrilla war.

It is the relatively weak government with shallow roots which needs be most wary of the assignment of political tasks to its army. During the French Revolution the Directorate sealed its own fate when, on the one hand, it left Napoleon with full powers outside France and, on the other, came to rely upon army support for defense against its domestic political enemies.[151] The Corsican responded to a Directorate alarm in 1799, only to gobble up his civilian masters.[152] As for that very recent period since World War II, it is obvious that uncontrolled delegation of political powers helped to undermine civilian control.

Judging from recent French experience, it would appear that even a more powerful government enjoying considerable authority may find itself unable to control power delegated to the military if one of two conditions are present: first, if a tradition of civilian control is absent or if it has been recently weakened by a serious and successful challenge; and second, if military leaders have been allowed to acquire the habit of largely uncontrolled exercising of political power. Both conditions prevailed in the early years of the French Fifth Republic. One of the first acts of the Challists, once in power in Algiers in April, 1961, was to restore full civil government powers to territorial military commanders.[153] The second condition seems also to have played a considerable part in producing American civil-military tensions in Korea in 1950–51 and in West Germany from 1949–55.[154]

1. In the Barricades trial, *Un Procès*, p. 87.

2. The complexities of the plots leading up to the *treize mai* will not be described here. The reader is referred to the detailed description in Merry and Serge Bromberger, *Les 13 complots du 13 mai* (Paris: Fayard, 1959), pp. 11–164 (hereinafter cited as *13 Complots*); and Tournoux, *Secrets d'état*, pp. 180–206, 219–80. In English, see Werth, *The De Gaulle Revolution*, pp. 1–69. Other works on the *treize mai* generally include de Sérigny (an activist leader and editor of the Algiers daily, *Echo d'Alger*), *La Révolution du 13 mai*; P. Gérin, *L'Algérie du 13 mai* (Paris: Gallimard, 1958); Ferniot, *Les Ides de mai*; James Meisel, *The Fall of the Republic* (Ann Arbor, Mich.: University of Michigan Press, 1962); and Roger Trinquier, *Le Coup d'état du 13 mai* (Paris: Editions l'Esprit Nouveau, 1962).

3. The original organizer of this "counterrevolutionary" organization (the Brombergers call it the "Grand O") was apparently a mysterious Dr. Martin, a militant in the 1930's of the clandestine and antirepublican Cagoule. Martin and the "Grand O" are discussed in Brombergers, *13 Complots*, pp. 78–84; and Tournoux, *Secrets d'état*, 121–24, 180–92.

4. The association popularly known as the Anciens d'Indochine was originally created in 1947 as the Association des Anciens du Corps Expéditionnaire d'Extrême-Orient, and was later renamed the Association des Combattants de l'Union Française. With a membership of twenty-eight thousand under Secretary-General Yves Gignac, they were primarily responsible for a demonstration at the Etoile in Paris on April 4, 1954, when Prime Minister Laniel and Minister of Defense Pleven were mobbed and jostled by a hostile crowd shouting "Vive l'armée" and "Vive Juin." (Marshal Juin had just been relieved of his post as permanent government adviser for his public opposition to the European Defense Community plan.) See *L'Année politique, 1954*, pp. 19–22. See also Tournoux, *Secrets d'état*, pp. 78–79. Gignac was arrested during the Week of the Barricades and again in March, 1962—this time for conspiratorial activities with the O.A.S. (*LM*, March 6, 1962).

5. Tournoux, *Secrets d'état*, pp. 186, 189–91; and Brombergers, *13 Complots*, pp. 69, 123–24. Thomazo apparently kept General Salan informed of activist

plans, though Salan was not directly involved in them (Tournoux, *Secrets d'état*, pp. 257, 259).

6. *Ibid.*, pp. 219–20, 239, 265–66; and Brombergers, *13 Complots*, pp. 105–14. Delbecque and his group won over Colonel Thomazo and contacted, among others, Colonel Gribius, commander of the armored unit stationed at Rambouillet, near Paris (Tournoux, *Secrets d'état*, pp. 239, 265).

7. De Sérigny, *La Révolution du 13 mai*, pp. 14–15; Brombergers, *13 Complots*, pp. 107–8, 111–12; and Tournoux, *Secrets d'état*, pp. 275, 478.

8. De Sérigny, *La Révolution du 13 mai*, pp. 26–28, and Brombergers, *13 Complots*, pp. 129–39.

9. Salan's deputy commander, General Jacques Allard, testified in the Salan trial that he and General Edmond Jouhaud, air force commander in Algeria, together with Salan, drafted the message, and then Lacoste agreed to its expedition (*Procès Salan*, p. 188). The text is found in Ferniot, *Les Ides de mai*, p. 9; and in de Sérigny, *La Révolution du 13 mai*, pp. 30–31.

10. Ferniot, *Les Ides de mai*, p. 9.

11. De Sérigny, *La Révolution du 13 mai*, p. 57; and Brombergers, *13 Complots*, p. 171, 174.

12. Brombergers, *13 Complots*, p. 168; and de Sérigny, *La Révolution du 13 mai*, p. 65.

13. Brombergers, *13 Complots*, pp. 174–79.

14. Pierre Popie, a liberal Algiers lawyer, reported soon after the *treize mai* that Trinquier's regiment had been ordered to Sidi-Ferruch (near Algiers) on May 11 by Defense Minister Chaban-Delmas, who had little interest in defending the G.G. or the Fourth Republic ("Comment fut préparé la journée du 13 mai à Alger," *LM*, May 30, 1958). Yet the transfer may have been made without conspiratorial intention, since Trinquier's regiment apparently had no part in Delbecque's plans and, according to Trinquier, the unit was overdue for rotation (Trinquier, *Le Coup d'état du 13 Mai*, pp. 65–85; and Tournoux, *Secrets d'état*, p. 279 n. 47). The regiment was ordered into Algiers on May 13 by General Massu (de Sérigny, *La Révolution du 13 mai*, p. 47).

15. Ferniot, *Les Ides de mai*, pp. 19–29, and Brombergers, *13 Complots*, p. 177. On the fourteenth, however, Salan felt called upon to explain to Paris that the order to fire was not given because of the density of the crowd and the presence of women and children. See his report to the new Defense Minister Pierre de Chevigné in Tournoux, *Secrets d état*, pp. 479–81.

16. Clark, *Algeria in Turmoil*, p. 377; Tournoux, *Secrets d'état*, p. 281; and Brombergers, *13 Complots*, pp. 183–84, 186, 198.

17. See de Sérigny, *La Révolution du 13 mai*, pp. 164–68 for complete lists of members of the various committees of public safety. Massu described his role at the G.G. on May 13 in a press conference on May 14, 1958, excerpts from which are found in Clark, *Algeria in Turmoil*, pp. 378–79, and Ferniot, *Les Ides de mai*, pp. 33–36.

18. *LM*, May 15, 1958.

19. The Communists abstained, and in fact Pflimlin had a majority even if the Communist abstentions were counted as negative votes. The text of Massu's statement is found in Ferniot, *Les Ides de mai*, pp. 31–33 (quotation from pp. 31–32).

20. De Sérigny, *La Révolution du 13 mai*, pp. 78–83; and Tournoux, *Secrets d'état*, pp. 481–83.

21. *Ibid.*, p. 288.

22. Some have suggested that Delbecque was just behind him and prompted

the "Vive De Gaulle" (Brombergers, *13 Complots*, p. 232; Ferniot, *Les Ides de mai*, p. 45; and Tournoux, *Secrets d'état*, p. 29). Salan was not a Gaullist, but he probably felt that de Gaulle was the best available alternative to the Fourth Republic if civil war was to be avoided.

23. De Sérigny, *La Révolution du 13 mai*, pp. 145, 169–71.

24. Ferniot, *Les Ides de mai*, p. 155.

25. General Miquel, in *Procès Salan*, p. 216; Brombergers, *13 Complots*, pp. 305–6; Tournoux, *Secrets d'état*, pp. 373–74.

26. *Ibid.*, pp. 294, 313; and Claude Paillat, *Dossier secret de l'Algérie* (Paris: Le Livre Contemporain, 1961); pp. 171–72.

27. See Minister of Interior Jules Moch's report of Salan's messages affirming his loyalty and republicanism after May 17, 1958, cited by Tournoux, *Secrets d'état*, p. 317.

28. After many delays a few of the "little men" in the plot were finally convicted, but many questions remained unanswered. In the Salan trial in 1962 the defense attempted with inconclusive results to show that Debré was behind the attempt on Salan's life and now was in no position to accuse him (*Procès Salan*, pp. 230–37, 275–303 [Debré's testimony], 375–79, 420–31, 432–39). See also Werth, *The De Gaulle Revolution*, pp. 223–28, 249–50, 343–48; Tournoux, *Secrets d'état*, pp. 198–99, 249; and Paillat, *Dossier secret*, pp. 521–22.

29. Brombergers, *13 Complots*, p. 185.

30. *Ibid.*, pp. 185, 232; and Ferniot, *Les Ides de mai*, p. 18.

31. Yves Gignac, secretary-general of the Anciens d'Indochine, and a few others were arrested in Paris on the night of May 13 (Tournoux, *Secrets d'état*, p. 289). Cherrière and Chassin escaped arrest orders that were out for them. Cherrière got to Switzerland, then to Algeria on May 18, but found himself helpless and finally joined the Gaullists (*ibid.*, p. 328). Chassin went to Saint-Etienne in central France, attempted an abortive attack on the prefecture building with his small revolutionary band, and escaped into the mountains to form the "premier maquis de France," unsupported by an intended Poujadist uprising (*ibid.*, pp. 322–23, 372, 404 n., 416).

32. See Ferniot, *Les Ides de mai*, pp. 37–40, regarding De Sérigny's opposition to liberal reform and the hatred Massu had for him as a result.

33. See Colonel Thomazo's revealing testimony in *Procès Salan*, p. 373. See also Ferniot, *Les Ides de mai*, pp. 34, 47, 50-54. *Le Bled* had long been an instrument of propaganda for integration. See, for example, the issue dated February 12, 1958, and that dated May 14, 1958, which was written before the *treize mai*. See also de Sérigny, *La Révolution du 13 mai*, p. 55; and Brombergers, *13 Complots*, p. 172.

34. Colonel Trinquier showed the writer his personal notebook from that period wherein the order for a demonstration was recorded. The demonstrations were described in Brombergers, *13 Complots*, pp. 257–61, whose account explains the role of Godard and the S.A.U. but neglects somewhat the contrived and ephemeral character of the whole affair.

35. De Sérigny, *La Révolution du 13 mai*, p. 112. In its first motion, on May 20, the Comité de Salut Public announced that 'tous les citoyens de cette Province sont des Français à part entière" (*ibid.*, p. 131).

36. On the cover of that issue in large print was the headline: "Mission No. 1 de l'Armée: Garder l'Algérie à la France." Other headlines in that issue included: "16 mai 1958: Une grande date dans l'histoire de l'Algérie et de la France" (p. 7) and "Une Journée Mémorable" (p. 11).

37. To the S.F.I.O. (Socialist Party) Conférence Nationale d'Information,

meeting at Issy-les-Moulineaux on July 6, 1958, as cited by Ferniot, *Les Ides de mai*, p. 140. The four were probably General Miquel at Toulouse (the appointed commander of "operation resurrection"), General Descours at Lyon, General Lecoq at Bordeaux, and General Manceaux-Desmiaux at Rennes (Brombergers, *13 Complots*, pp. 250–51). The others were mostly hesitant and not unreservedly loyal to the government.

38. *Ibid.*, pp. 235–37.

39. *Ibid.*, p. 237.

40. *Ibid.*, pp. 246–48. In a final order of the day, Ely explained that "ne pouvant admettre que ma présence à ce poste risque de donner une caution à des measures qui iraient à l'encontre de ce que je tiens pour essentiel, j'ai remis ma démission au ministre de la Défense Nationale. Ressentant profondément pour l'éprouver moi-même l'angoisse qui est votre aujourd'hui, je vous demande pour le plus haut intérêt de la France, de maintenir, chacun à sa place, la cohésion et l'unité des forces armées françaises, gage suprême de l'unité nationale" (*ibid.*, p. 249).

41. De Sérigny, *La Révolution du 13 mai*, p. 139. Apparently under strong pressure from army officers, De Gaulle later removed Lorillot, who was blamed for agreeing to replace Ely, both from his post as chief of staff of national defense and from his former post as chief of staff of the army (Brombergers, *13 Complots*, p. 40).

42. The Brombergers cite General Jacquot, commander in chief of French forces in Germany and General Morlière, military governor of Paris as firm government supporters (*ibid.*, p. 252). See also Tournoux, *Secrets d'état*, p. 374 n. Among those in high positions who were particularly hostile to the "system" (in addition to those already mentioned) were Deputy C.O.S. General André Petit (a Gaullist who went to Algiers on May 13); General Cogny, former French military chief in Morocco; and France's only living marshal, Alphonse Juin, who told the government in late May that army garrisons in the *métropole* would folllow Algiers (Brombergers, *13 Complots*, pp. 145–47, 253–54; and Ferniot, *Les Ides de mai*, p. 119).

43. Tournoux, *Secrets d'état*, pp. 340–42; Ferniot, *Les Ides de mai*, p. 139; and Brombergers, *13 Complots*, pp. 431–32.

44. Brombergers, *13 Complots*, pp. 305–14, 378; Tournoux, *Secrets d'état*, pp. 373–80; and the testimony of General Miquel, *Procès Salan*, pp. 216–18.

45. De Gaulle's surprising and inaccurate announcement of May 27 ("J'ai entamé hier le processus régulier nécéssaire à l'ètablissement d'un gouvernement républicain") was prompted in part by information that a military coup was scheduled for the next day (Tournoux, *Secrets d'état*, pp. 342–51; and Brombergers, *13 Complots*, pp. 377–86).

46. *Ibid.*, pp. 418, 432, 435, 438; and Tournoux, *Secrets d'état*, p. 390.

47. On May 18, 1962, Miquel told the Haut Tribunal Militaire that he met in Algiers on June 2 or 3, 1958, with Generals Salan, Jouhaud, Massu, Dulac (Salan's Chef de Cabinet), and Lennuyeux. Tournoux suggests that it was Miquel himself who brought up the question at that point (*Secrets d'état*, pp. 399–406). Miquel's testimony is found in *Procès Salan*, pp. 217–18.

48. *Ibid.*

49. Chapters 6, 10, and 11.

50. Part V, "Attitudes and Ideology."

51. Quoted in de Sérigny, *La Révolution du 13 mai*, p. 137.

52. See above, pp. 113–17, 214–16, and *passim*.

53. See Chapter 12 below.

54. Popie, *LM*, May 30, 1958.

55. Editorial, *Message*, No. 30 (July, 1958), p. 1.

56. Editorial, *Le Bled*, September 13, 1958.

57. Werth, in *The De Gaulle Revolution*, pp. 26–28, describes the angry demonstration of French police in Paris on March 13, 1958. Former Police Commissioner Dides had created a parallel police network which was involved in the Affaire des Fuites in 1953–54. In 1958 he was an extreme Rightist deputy, still with considerable influence in the Paris police. See Chapter 6 above.

58. Moch, writing in *Midi libre* in June, 1958, quoted by Tournoux, *Secrets d'état*, p. 322 n. 1. See also Moch's statement to the Journées Nationales de la S.F.I.O., July, 1958, quoted in *ibid.*, p. 326 n. 2 ("la police, je le dis à ma honte, car j'ai été profondément humilié de ce que j'ai constaté, la police elle-même était gangrenée").

59. Brombergers, *13 Complots*, pp. 341–56; Werth, *The De Gaulle Revolution*, p. 126; De Sérigny, *La Révolution du 13 mai*, pp. 118–19; Tournoux, *Secrets d'état*, pp. 332–38; Ferniot, *Les Ides de mai*, p. 106.

60. De Sérigny, *Le Révolution du 13 mai*, pp. 118–19; and Brombergers, *13 Complots*, pp. 345–46.

61. *Ibid.* pp. 345–46, 349–54; Tournoux, *Secrets d'état*, p. 333; and Moch, as cited in *ibid.*, p. 334.

62. Tournoux, *Secrets d'état*, p. 323.

63. *Ibid.*, p. 324; and Ferniot, *Les Ides de mai*, p. 82.

64. Tournoux, *Secrets d'état*, pp. 337–38.

65. Thirteen per cent replied "neither," and 15 per cent gave no opinion (Institut Français d'Opinion Publique, *Sondages*, XX [1958], No. 4, 25). Forty-seven per cent were found to be satisfied with General Salan's being governor of Algeria, while 17 per cent were dissatisfied (*ibid.*, p. 25). The same issue of *Sondages* reported that in response to the question, "Will Algeria still be French in 10 years?" the following results had been found in other national polls: In January, 1958—27 per cent, yes; 22 per cent, no; 51 per cent, undecided. In June, 1958—42 per cent, yes; 18 per cent, no; 40 per cent, undecided (*ibid.*, p. 19). Apparently more Frenchmen felt confident of the army's usefulness in overthrowing the "system" than in fighting the Algerian war.

66. *RMI*, No. 297 (August–September, 1958), p. 11. A similar interpretation is made by Professor Maurice Duverger, who cannot be accused of sympathy for the *treize mai* coup: "S'il y avait eu un exécutif fort le 13 mai 1958, les généraux révoltés eussent été promptement ramenés à obéissance. Que dis-je? Les généraux ne se fussent point révoltés" (*Demain la république*, pp. 145–46).

67. For example, Salan's last order of the day in December, 1958, called upon the army to help the civilian administration in Algeria. That order brought a retort from Defense Minister Guillaumat (Paillat, *Dossier secret*, 147–48). See also Planchais, "L'Action psychologique, hier et aujourd'hui," *LM*, April 3, 1959.

68. See Massu's testimony in the Barricades trial, *Un Procès*, pp. 76–77.

69. See the testimony of Massu and Gardes in *ibid.*, pp. 62, 90. See also the Brombergers *et al.*, *Barricades et colonels*, pp. 295–96.

70. To Gardes and two other officers on September 18, 1959 (Gardes, in *Un Procès*, p. 62).

71. Paillat, *Dossier secret*, pp. 328–29, 388–93.

72. See, for example, *Procès Salan*, especially pp. 507–48.

73. *Un Procès*, p. 90.

74. Brombergers *et al.*, *Barricades et colonels*, pp. 67–68.

75. In *Un Procès*, p. 79.

76. The published version of the interview is found in Brombergers *et al.*, *Barricades et colonels*, pp. 34–36. Massu's comments on the interview are found in *Un Procès*, pp. 96–103.

77. Brombergers *et al.*, *Barricades et colonels*, pp. 34, 35.

78. *Loc. cit.*

79. The Week of the Barricades is described in detail in Brombergers *et al.*, *Barricades et colonels*. The more important testimony in the Barricades trial has been assembled by Alain de Sérigny in *Un Procès*. Colonel Argoud's secret testimony in that same trial was published by Comité Audin in *Sans commentaire*. See also Jean-André Faucher, *Les Barricades d'Alger* (Paris: Editions Atlantic, 1961); André Euloge and Antoine Moulinier, *L'Envers des Barricades* (Paris: Plon, 1960); and Bernard Brown, "The Army and Politics in France," *Journal of Politics*, XXIII, No. 2 (May, 1961), 262–78.

80. In *Un Procès* see the testimony of General Coste (especially p. 212), Colonel Debrosse (pp. 202–15), Lieutenant Colonel Ceccaldi (pp. 218–24), Colonel Dufour (pp. 224–33), Colonel Broizat (pp. 234–45), and Major Lafargue (pp. 245–48). See also Brombergers *et al.*, *Barricades et colonels*, pp. 226–46.

81. Brombergers *et al.*, *Barricades et colonels*, p. 227; and the testimony of Major Tardy (director of *Le Bled* and an eyewitness), *Un Procès*, p. 191.

82. Brombergers *et al.*, *Barricades et colonels*, pp. 243–44.

83. *Ibid.*, p. 106.

84. Tournoux reports that De Gaulle once told General Jacques Faure, "Je n'y crois pas à votre guerre subversive!" (*Secrets d'état*, p. 441). See also *ibid.*, p. 420; Paillat, *Dossier secret*, pp. 76–77.

85. Captain Bernard Moynet, testimony in *Procès Salan*, p. 164; and Paillat, *Dossier secret*, pp. 75–76.

86. See Gardes' testimony in *Un Procès*, pp. 53, 67; and Paillat, *Dossier secret*, p. 119.

87. Gardes' testimony, in *Un Procès*, pp. 56–59; and Paillat, *Dossier secret*, 237–38. Gardes does not emphasize enough the role that he and Colonel Argoud played in laying out policy guidelines.

88. Azeau, *Révolte militaire*, pp. 61–70; Megret, *LM*, June 25, 1959; and *ibid.*, June 27, 1959.

89. It was likely their blind defense of privilege, as well as their factionalism, which prompted Gardes to say of the *pieds noirs* in the summer of 1959: "Ce ne sont pas les musulmans qui ont besoin de l'action psychologique mais les Européens. Chaque jour ils nous rendent le travail de plus en plus difficile" (Euloge and Moulinier, *L'Envers des Barricades*, p. 47).

90. Brombergers *et al.*, *Barricades et colonels*, pp. 106–10; Paillat, *Dossier secret*, p. 330; and Gardes' testimony in *Un Procès*, pp. 64–66.

91. Gardes and Massu were assisted by Captain Filippi, Major Navarro, and Lieutenant Sanne—all three from Massu's headquarters rather than from the Fifth Bureau, which belonged to Challe's headquarters. Sanne left active duty in October, 1959, but as a civilian continued thereafter to act as liaison between Massu's headquarters and the F.N.F. See Massu's testimony in *Un Procès*, p. 93; and Brombergers *et al.*, *Barricades et colonels*, pp. 94, 98, 104–5.

92. Massu, in *Un Procès*, p. 84.

93. "Je le contrôlais par liaison directe, humaine" (*ibid.*, pp. 84–85).

94. Brombergers *et al.*, *Barricades et colonels*, pp. 174–76. Colonel Gardes, who should know, took issue with the Brombergers on one point at the Barricades trial, but added, "En général, ils sont d'ailleurs fort bien renseignés . . . " (*Un Procès*, p. 67).

95. Brombergers *et al.*, *Barricades et colonels*, p. 176.

96. *Ibid.*, pp. 168–69.

97. *Ibid.*, pp. 171–72.

98. *Ibid.*, pp. 198–99, 214; and Colonel Broizat's testimony in *Un Procès*, p. 236. There may well have been some officers who assured Ortiz of full army support. See Euloge and Moulinier, *L'Envers des Barricades*, p. 87.

99. Argoud, in *Sans commentaire*, p. 49; and Brombergers *et al.*, *Barricades et colonels*, p. 211.

100. *Ibid.*, p. 193. A few days later, however, the territorial units gained control of the city hall in Oran (*ibid.*, p. 350).

101. *Ibid.*, p. 170. In October, 1959, Minister of Defense Guillaumat asked that Gardes, whom he regarded as imprudent, be transferred out of the Fifth Bureau. Challe kept him in place and gave rather little attention to his activities (*ibid.*, p. 113). On the scene in Algiers, Gardes was under the surveillance of Sûreté agents for a few days as a result of his involvement with activist leaders. A series of "workshops" joining these leaders with military officers produced an order from Delouvrier to Gardes to cease meetings of this nature (*ibid.*, p. 106).

102. *Ibid.*, p. 207. Gardes was tried and acquitted in the Barricades trial ·and then was a key figure behind the April putsch, as were Argoud, Godard, Broizat, and Lacheroy (the only one of the five who was not then in Algiers), (Fauvet and Planchais, *La Fronde des généraux*, pp. 65–78). After the attempted putsch failed in April, 1961, he fled, became a leader in the O.A.S., led an abortive guerrilla uprising in Algeria, and finally took refuge in Spain. In March, 1963, he was deported to Argentina (*LM*, March 6, 1963). For a biographical sketch see Fauvet and Planchais, *La Fronde des généraux*, pp. 71–73.

103. *Ibid.*, p. 92.

104. Transferred to a staff position in Metz after the Week of the Barricades, Argoud became the leading force in preparation for the April putsch (*ibid.*, p. 95) and then the principle organizer and strategist of the O.A.S.-C.N.R. (Conseil National de la Résistance) until he was kidnapped in Munich and brought to Paris in late February, 1963, probably by French government agents (*LM*, February 28, 1963). A biographical sketch is contained in Fauvet and Planchais, *La Fronde des généraux*, pp. 92–95.

105. Dufour himself was transferred out of Algeria in November, 1960, and kept under careful surveillance in Germany during the April putsch. He deserted from the army in April, 1962, and became a leader of the C.N.R., successor to the O.A.S. (*LM*, February 28, 1963). Broizat was one of the five colonels who prepared the April putsch.. Along with Colonels Argoud, Gardes, Godard, and Lacheroy, he fled when the putsch failed and, like them, was sentenced to death in absentia on June 1, 1961.

106. Brombergers *et al.*, *Barricades et colonels*, pp. 342, 313.

107. *Ibid.*, pp. 282–83. General Gracieux is said by the Brombergers to have told Debré he would not obey an order to attack the barricades (*ibid.*, p. 283).

108. Argoud, testimony in the Barricades trial, *Sans commentaire*, p. 65. See also *ibid.*, p. 66; and Brombergers *et al.*, *Barricades et colonels*, pp. 283–88.

109. *Ibid.*, pp. 268, 291, 293.

110. *Ibid.*, p. 353. Faucher, in *Les Barricades d'Alger*, claims that the failure was due in part to the lack of co-operation of Colonel Santini, an Urban Administrative Sections officer assigned to the Casbah (pp. 259–261).

111. Brombergers *et al.*, *Barricades et colonels*, pp. 348, 388.

112. *LM*, January 31—February 1, 1960 (text on p. 3). Another noteworthy passage: "L'armée française, que deviendrait-elle, sinon un ramas anarchique et dérisoire de féodalités militaires, s'il arrivait que des éléments mettaient des conditions à leur loyalisme?"

113. *Ibid.*; Euloge and Moulinier, *L'Envers des Barricades*, pp. 144–46; and Faucher, *Les Barricades d'Alger*, 288–89.

114. Brombergers *et al.*, *Barricades et colonels*, pp. 388–96.

115. In Paris General André Zeller, now already a potential rebel leader, is said to have remarked that the army was powerless if not supported by a part of public opinion in the *métropole* (ibid., p. 303).

116. The transfer of powers was almost completed when on March 1, 1961, the remaining thirty-nine arrondissements in which military-sector commanders exercised police powers were cut to only seventeen, these being in mountain and border areas (*NYT*, March 2, 1961). General Challe, for one, was disturbed by this "premature" restoration of civil administrators. (*Procès Challe*, p. 29).

117. In a press conference on May 4, 1960, the dissolution of the Fifth Bureau was discussed by the new defense minister, Pierre Messmer, who replaced Guillaumat after the Week of the Barricades. He explained: "Dans tous les cas les questions d'action psychologique sont à chaque échelon du ressort du commandement alors que dans le passé les 5ᵉ Bureaux travaillaient souvent en franc-tireurs et avaient constitué des sortes de hiérarchies parallèles . . . " (*LM*, May 6, 1960).

118. *Message* commented bitterly in June, 1960: "L'Emploi du terme d'action psychologique est désormais interdit à l'Armée, mais le pays tout entier est soumis quotidiennement à un traitement auquel il ne manque que le nom" ("Les nouveaux collaborateurs," *Message*, No. 43 [June, 1960], p. 3). The military press and military-school courses henceforth dealt more with "human problems" or "public relations." (See Lieutenant Colonel Etienne, "Problèmes humaines," *RMI*, No. 326 [April, 1961], pp. 48–66; and "Les Armées forment des officiers des relations publiques," *LM*, November 22, 1962.) In regard to continued psychological-action activities after the Week of the Barricades, see Jean Daniel, "La Dossier Numéro Un," *L'Express*, March 3, 1960, pp. 10–11; and De la Gorce, *The French Army*, p. 523.

119. *NYT*, February 6, 1961; Paillat, *Dossier secret*, p. 362; and Brombergers *et al.*, *Barricades et colonels*, pp. 375–79.

120. Fauvet and Planchais, *La Fronde des généraux*, p. 55. Challe was resentful at his removal before his pacification plan had been completed. See his testimony in *Procès Challe*, p. 29.

121. On March 5, 1960 (*LM*, March 8, 1960).

122. On November 4, 1960 (*LM*, November 6–7, 1960).

123. Fauvet and Planchais, *La Fronde des généraux*, pp. 40-42. See also the issues of *Message* after September, 1960, wherein the cry of "treason" mounted fiercely.

124. Brombergers *et al.*, *Barricades et colonels*, pp. 44–50, 67, 70–71, and *passim*.

125. The April putsch of 1961 is best described by Fauvet and Planchais (both of *Le Monde*), *La Fronde des généraux*. See also Azeau, *Révolte militaire*, and the court records of the major trials, available in complete published form: *Procès Challe*; *Procès Salan*; and *Le Procès d'Edmond Jouhaud*. The trials of other officers involved in the putsch have been excerpted and summarized (with a strongly Challist bias) by Maurice Cottaz in *Procès du putsch*.

126. On December 31, 1960, a brilliant retired air force general, Jean Valluy, who took no part in the April putsch, made public a message in which he said of the army: "Aujourd'hui, dans sa quasi-totalité et par ses éléments les meilleurs qui représentent toutes les familles sociales et spirituelles de la nation, elle est au bord du désespoir, peut-être de la révolte, certainement du mépris" (*LM*, January 1–2, 1961).

127. From the text as found in Azeau, *Révolte militaire*, Annexe 4, p. 274.

128. Fauvet and Planchais, *La Fronde des généraux*, p. 134.

129. See the discussion of the paratroopers, below, Chapter 12.

130. Fauvet and Planchais, *La Fronde des généraux*, pp. 133, 139; and Azeau, *Révolte militaire*, p. 142. Among those officers who remained loyal to the government were General Gambiez, commander in chief of French forces in Algeria, General Vézinet, commander of the Algiers army corps, General de Pouilly, commander of the Oran army corps, and even General Saint-Hillier, commander of the Tenth Paratroop Division (Fauvet and Planchais, *La Fronde des généraux*, pp. 104–12, 131–32). Of the three corps commanders in Algeria only General Gouraud in Constantine wavered in his loyalty to the government. Gambiez, Vézinet, and Saint-Hillier were arrested by the Challists, but De Pouilly retreated from Oran to Tlemcen and blocked the putsch in western Algeria.

131. Azeau, *Révolte militaire*, pp. 162–66. A massive and symbolic strike was held on Monday, April 24, to evidence popular support for De Gaulle (*ibid.*, pp. 165–66).

132. Testimony of Colonel Bouchoud, commander of the La Calle sector, in *Procès du Putsch*, p. 112. See also *ibid.*, pp. 152, 167–68, 177.

133. The role of conscripts in crushing the putsch is especially emphasized (in fact, somewhat overemphasized) by Azeau, *Révolte militaire*, pp. 168–96. See also Fauvet and Planchais, *La Fronde des généraux*, pp. 145–48, 218, and 234.

134. Testimony of René Janin, director of the Sûreté Nationale in Algeria, *Procès Salan*, pp. 149–50.

135. *LM*, June 16, 1962.

136. *LM*, January 19, 1963, note added, probably by Jean Planchais, to a report of C.N.R. leader Georges Bidault's statement that "half" of all French officers were in prison or "repos forcé."

137. Guillaud, *La Nef*, p. 116.

138. Numbers are difficult to determine because political reasons were rarely given for involuntary retirements. In 1961 alone, six hundred officers were involuntarily retired from the armed forces, compared to only twenty or less in each of the three preceding years (*ibid.*, p. 117). Moreover, on June 7, 1961, De Gaulle made use of his emergency powers under Article 16 of the constitution to create a "special leave" status for officers. According to figures from the Ministry of the Armed Forces, 534 officers and 574 noncoms were, in effect, retired in this manner, most against their wills and, undoubtedly, most for political reasons (*LM*, October 13, 1961).

139. Duverger, *Demain la république*, p. 146.

140. See Jean Meyre, "L'Algérie après les élections," *RDN*, April, 1959, pp. 588–603. Meyre understands the artificiality of elections in Algeria under the conditions of war and the widespread lack of education, but he underemphasizes the army's guiding role in the outcome of the referendum. In regard to F.L.N. threats see Paillat, *Dossier secret*, pp. 86–90.

141. Colonel Bourdis, who was among those sent (interview, June, 1962).

142. *Le Fil de L'épée*, p. 36.

143. In his speech of January 29, 1960 (during the Barricades uprising), De Gaulle declared that " . . . rien ne causerait plus de joie à la patrie et à de Gaulle que de les [the rebels] voir choisir, entre telle ou telle solution, celle qui serait la plus française" (from the text as found in Brombergers *et al.*, *Barricades et colonels*, p. 393).

144. Dorothy Pickles, *Algeria and France* (New York: Praeger, 1963), pp. 139–47.

145. *Procès Salan*, especially pp. 507–8. See also Paillat, *Dossier secret*, p. 393.

146. Lieutenant Colonel A., interview, June, 1962.

147. On November 4, 1960 (*LM*, November 6–7, 1960). Regarding the link between policy ambiguity and military revolt in the Fifth Republic, see the provocative, if somewhat overstated argument of Maurice Duverger, "L'Armée et les procès," *LM*, June 11–12, 1961.

148. The promises were made in the speech on September 16, 1959, renewed in his speech of January 29, 1960, and partially renewed again in his statement of September 5, 1960. In April, 1961, shortly before the putsch occurred, the French government was preparing for negotiations at Evian with the F.L.N. alone, before conclusion of a cease-fire. See the summary of the Algerian war in *LM*, March 20, 1962; and Pickles, *Algeria and France*, p. 131.

149. That thesis is expounded in Finer, *The Man on Horseback;* Rapoport, "Praetorianism: Government without Consensus"; and Rapoport, *Changing Patterns of Military Politics*, pp. 71–100. A similar but less global argument is made by Jean Meynaud, "Les Militaires et le pouvoir," *Revue française de sociologie*, II, No. 2 (April–June, 1961), 85–86.

150. Daalder, "The Role of the Military in the Emerging Countries," p. 16; and Johnson (ed.), *The Role of the Military in Underdeveloped Countries*, pp. 4, 40, and *passim*.

151. "Au delà des frontières naturelles, le Directoire avait laissé Bonaparte créer un dangereux précédent par la formation de la Cisalpine; il l'avait imité à Rome et à Naples, s'était installé en Piémont et avait fait du Valais une république pour tenir les routes alpestres; il s'était comporté en maître dans la Hollande et la Suisse" (Lefèbvre, *Napoléon*, p. 55).

152. Before the 18 Brumaire the army had been called in for support by the Convention on 13 Vendemiaire of the year IV (October 5, 1795) and by the Directorate on the 18 Fructador of the year V (September 4, 1797), (*ibid.*, p. 60; and G. Chevrier, "Les Rapports du pouvoir civil et du pouvoir militaire de la Chute de l'empire romain à la fin du Ier Empire," in *La Défense nationale*, pp. 83–84).

153. Fauvet and Planchais, *La Fronde des généraux*, p. 118.

154. Spanier, *The Truman-MacArthur Controversy*, pp. 65–67, 271, and *passim;* Harold Zink, "American Civil-Military Relations in the Occupation of Germany," in Coles (ed.) *Total War and Cold War*, pp. 211–37.

Part V

Attitudes and Ideology

Chapter 10

The Rivals of Discipline

Professional military officers in France are almost as diverse in political and religious beliefs as the nation which they represent. Non-believers as well as devout Catholics are to be found among them, socialists and radicals as well as conservatives and fascists. Yet there are attitudinal patterns which tend to distinguish most professional officers from their civilian compatriots. With the earlier discussion of professional military attitudes before 1939 as a backdrop,[1] the present chapter will examine some of the most relevant of these typical military attitudes in the period from 1945 to 1962. The army's closest approach to a consistent military ideology in these years—the *guerre révolutionnaire* doctrine—will be reserved for discussion in the following chapter.

In view of the grave damage suffered by the French professional military tradition of discipline and political neutrality in World War II and the decade and a half of revolutionary-guerrilla wars thereafter, it might be argued that praetorianism in France from 1958 to 1961 was simply the result of a collapse of professional restraints. Indeed, the *guerre révolutionnaire* school had nothing but scorn for the traditional, white-gloved cavalry officer, who symbolized strict military obedience and warfare of a more noble and gentlemanly genre than the battle of Algiers. Yet, in fact, much of the rationale for military rebellion was found *within* the body of traditional military values, among which discipline was often difficult to reconcile with such ideals as honor and military effectiveness.

Again, the absence of systematic attitude-survey data complicates the task of piecing together the postwar character of the French "military mind." On the basis of the rather sketchy evidence available it would appear that, with the exception of political neutrality, all of the traditional "functional-requisite" values of the French officer corps—stress on the role of force and on nationalism, and preference for unity, self-sacrifice, hierarchy, and order over individualism and democratic politics—were still widely held among officers from 1945 to 1962. For example, there is a timeless quality to the comments of Major "G. F." (entitled "Military Ethic and Democracy") in *Message* of October, 1956:

> . . . The military ethic is founded on the recognition of the insufficiency of the individual, on the necessity of constraint, on the secondary value of human life in relation to other absolute values, on confidence in a hierarchy and a method, on the importance of force in human relations.[2]

Military values of discipline, respect, and self-sacrifice are so lacking in democratic society, he continues, that only the army is left to teach them.[3] Similarly, a high ranking French officer remarked in 1961:

> In reality, whether one wishes it or not, there is an incompatibility between liberal customs and habits as we practice them and the behavior of officers . . . who to be effective must be authoritarian in their acts and in their thoughts.[4]

The classic antagonism between French military values and those of liberal democracy became sharper and more dangerous in a post–World War II climate of political vacillation and military frustration. Cheated of victory by elusive revolutionary-guerrilla adversaries, on the one hand, and maddened by sniping politicians and journalists, on the other, the officer corps developed a smoldering hostility toward the timorous Fourth Republic and a widespread conviction that national salvation was now a military responsibility. The theme of military antipathy toward *le système* has been evoked often enough in earlier chapters to make its repetition here unnecessary.[5] Suffice it to say that colonial war cast the army in a position of power at the very moment when dominant civilian and military values were drawing further apart.[6]

Beyond victory in Algeria, stronger national unity (imposed, if necessary), and greater recognition for military men, French officers had no common conception of the nature of national salvation.[7] Antiparliamentarism among French military officers had no clearcut obverse side, for those who agreed on opposition to *le système* included reformist republicans, authoritarian traditionalists (on the early Vichy model), Bonapartists, and even a few fascists. The military values of unity, hierarchy, and discipline do not define a complete political regime. Historically, it might be argued, there was some affinity between military attitudes and the Bonapartist tradition, which was so closely tied to military glory. Among latter-day beneficiaries of the Napoleonic tradition, however, both Boulanger and De Gaulle derived their political strength primarily from civilian supporters. Boulanger was viewed as something of an upstart by senior officers, many of whom were of monarchist persuasion.[8] De Gaulle never enjoyed strong popularity in the army (except among those rare Gaullists of 1940).[9] He was pushed to the top in 1958 because he seemed to be the only man whom the country would accept peacefully. All in all, the persistence of the Napoleonic tradition into the Gaullist era owes more to civilians than to military officers.

Alongside the authoritarian, antiparliamentary strain of the traditional French military ethic, the nationalist strain also lived on into the post-1945 period. Mention has already been made of the army's tendency to consider itself a lonely defender of France against her enemies, both domestic and foreign.[10] Army nationalism also came occasionally to the surface when talk of European integration seemed to threaten French sovereignty. To be sure, French military leaders generally looked with favor on French ties to the Atlantic Alliance in the postwar years, despite considerable hostility among officers toward the United States and its anticolonial policy.[11] Yet when the integration of Western European military forces was proposed in the European Defense Community plan in the early 1950's, the only living marshal of France, Alphonse Juin, spoke out publicly against it in March, 1954—an action which led successively to his summons by the Premier, Juin's refusal to reply to that summons, his removal from all official French government posts, and finally, a rowdy veteran's demonstration at the Etoile in protest against these government sanctions.[12] Juin's opposition to E.D.C. was shared by *Message*, which led a campaign against what it held to be a threat to French national integrity.[13] Nationalism and patriotism, variously conceived, remained core values within the officer corps.

Among those traditional French military values stemming largely from the functional requisites of the military profession, political neutrality was the most serious casualty of the postwar years, especially within the *guerre révolutionnaire* school, where military effectiveness often was viewed as no longer compatible with unquestioning obedience.[14] With obedience to civil authority placed in the balance, in many an officer's mind, against the elemental demands of national defense, there was no obvious resolution to be found through reference to professional military values. If the role of the professional soldier generally required that he serve his civilian superiors loyally, it also required him to be a determined and effective warrior. The problem appeared simple, deceptively simple, to one contributor to *Message* who wrote in January, 1960, amid military fears of impending negotiations and self-determination. Picking up where his predecessors had left off in 1954, writing the epitaph to the battered French military tradition of unquestioning obedience, he asserted:

> When discipline—as a means—is no longer adapted to the goal—which is always to win—it can be rejected as dangerous and as no longer suited to its purpose. We see there the first clear and indisputable limit to discipline, in a fashion a "technical limitation."[15]

In his impatience, the officer had forgotten the teachings of Clausewitz: war is never an end in itself but a means to political ends.

The whole moral battle between obedience and victory (an elusive goal), however, was at base less a problem of conflicting functional-requisite values than one of discipline versus military honor. It will be pursued in that context shortly.

Before leaving the topic of functional-requisite values, the question must be posed, if not fully answered, whether military respect for discipline and hierarchy does not stem in part from personality factors present in officers before their entry into military service. It would seem reasonable to expect that a military career would attract men who respond favorably to order and hierarchy. The only precise evidence available on this point comes from a study of attitudes and motivation among all 1,250 candidates who applied to military academies in 1960. In that study the Centre d'Etudes et d'Instruction de l'Armée de l'Air found that the two most important reasons given by the candidates for preferring a military career were "patriotic ideal" and "liking for command." [16] While these findings are somewhat limited in value here because of the absence of data on a control group, control-group data was collected in the same study with regard to "militaristic" attitudes. Using four Guttman scales built on seven questions each, the air force researchers found roughly twice as many "militarists" among candidates as among a matched group of non-candidates in response to questions such as the following: "Do you believe that military personnel, in general, are more useful to their country than civilians?"; "Do you believe the army should allow itself to be criticized?" [17]

These findings, plus the rigid, hierarchical social system spontaneously adopted among students preparing for Saint-Cyr in at least one prep school, seem to indicate that some of the functional-requisite values of the military profession are strongly seconded by existing predispositions of men attracted to a military career.[18] Any systematic study of the French officer corps probably would find a wide variety of personality types. It would not be surprising, however, if officers (more often than civilians) were found to exhibit, like Marshal Pétain, that intolerance for ambiguity so characteristic of the authoritarian personality.[19]

Returning to the French professional military ethic, one must quickly add to attitudes and values deriving largely from professional requisites the further central value of military honor which, though used in a multitude of meanings to sanctify a variety of motives, retains some of its earlier power and meaning.[20] Among the consistent elements of military honor which have been passed from the feudal period to the twentieth-century officer corps via an aristocratic officer tradition and kept alive by the corporate interests of the officer corps are the following: (1) pursuit of glory through consistent willingness to fight and abhorrence of surrender; (2) Christian chivalry and fidelity; (3) personal loyalty to the commander; (4) cohesion of a self-regulating brotherhood.[21] Of these four aspects of military honor, chivalry suffered most from two world wars and sixteen years of revolutionary-guerrilla war.[22] Yet military honor still requires that an officer be true to his word. In all four of its major meanings military honor was often interpreted to be in conflict with discipline and political neutrality in the period from 1940–62. The significant role of military honor will be seen in the following discussions of important military attitudes which conflicted with discipline in those years after 1940.

The clash between discipline and honor in World War II need not be retold here.[23] Suffice it to say that De Gaulle's appeal of June, 1940, was based in part upon the dictum that the officer always fights: to surrender when there remain means for resistance is to dishonor oneself.[24] The lasting effect of that appeal and its aftermath on the tradition of military discipline is told by numerous military spokesmen, among them Colonel Argoud in the Barricades trial:

> Is not the path of duty all laid out: that of obedience without a murmur? In fact, that went without saying for Captain Alfred de Vigny, but since then many events have occurred which have completely modified the facts of the problem. First, on a certain day in June, 1940, officers of France were called upon to choose between the way of honor and that of discipline. Some chose honor; others, much more numerous, discipline. One cannot say precisely that all were rewarded for their decision.[25]

A similar thought was expressed by Vice Admiral Ploix, who was a defense witness in the Salan trial, despite his disapproval of the O.A.S.:

In order to respect this motto of 'Honor and Country' [the naval officer's motto], there are days, fortunately very rare, when it is necessary to take a decision, a capital decision, a grave decision, where—I have weighed my words carefully—it is necessary to choose between rebellion and perjury.

It is to the honor of General de Gaulle to have chosen the path he followed in June, 1940. Four years later, moreover, the people of France acclaimed him. Well, in my soul and conscience, I am convinced that it was the same path in the same dilemma which General Salan intended to follow.[26]

The lessons of World War II came to life when again honor and discipline appeared to part ways, even though this time the government of France was free from the chains of foreign occupation.

Perhaps no other factor was more significant in preparing a general climate of incipient revolt in the French Army than the bitter humiliation of successive defeats.[27] Spurred on by the pursuit of glory and the abhorrence of surrender (both of which found support in traditional military honor), French officers grew increasingly thirsty for victory after the defeat of 1940, the armistice in Indochina in 1954, withdrawal from Tunisia and Morocco in 1955, the Suez fiasco in 1956, and finally, threatened surrender in Algeria. This is a theme on which military testimony is abundant.

As he watched representatives of the victorious Vietminh cross the Hanoi bridge in 1954, one French colonel remarked, "Even so, it would be nice to be on the winning side from time to time." [28] A paratroop colonel was more emphatic when he looked back over his victoryless career in the early years of the Algerian war:

I have had enough of pulling down the flag. For fifteen years I have had that job. If it continues in Algeria, I will go over to the other side. I will become a communist.[29]

For many, humiliation brought with it a passionate desire for victory, a passion which reached full bloom in the *guerre révolutionnaire* school and which was already fully evident in a *Message* article of July, 1954:

We have had enough of defeats which are glorious, or so described by press accounts!!

Success is the only military rule.

The hope of one day being a victorious leader, honored, glorious, that is what is attractive for youth.

"Military servitude," that is the phrase of a sick poet. There is no more servitude. There is success and defeat. One does not teach oneself in order to serve. One teaches oneself in order to conquer. That is the only way of serving with honor![30]

Victory seemed within grasp at last during the Suez expedition in 1956, when French paratroopers moved into the Suez with almost no opposition. A brief euphoria gave way to deepened humiliation as the expeditionary corps was recalled. One air force officer, Major Raoul Bernard, who was with the *paras*, told of their reaction: "Nothing could describe the dejection of my paratroopers who, though victorious, had to leave Egypt, turning their backs on their victory. . . . "[31]

It was the long and frustrating Algerian war, however, which brought the desire to win to its greatest intensity. A few quotations will help re-create the mood:

A major in 1956: " . . . It [the Army] would not agree to liquidate Algeria the way it was forced to liquidate Indochina."[32]

A "Message" editorialist in early 1957: "The Army, faithful to its tradition, is above all thirsty for effectiveness and honor."[33]

Paratroop Colonel Marcel Bigeard, just a few days before the "treize mai": "That makes twenty years that we have been suffering defeat, and yet those defeats are not imputable to us. We are officers; we have chosen freely; we are dead men on deferment; but we have had enough of dying for a band of damn fools [cons]." [34]

A "Message" editorialist in April, 1958: "For the first time in eighteen years, the French Army feels that victory which would be solely of its own making is within grasp. And that revives a great hope.

"However, a doubt persists: instinctive, badly formulated perhaps, undoubtedly exaggerated. But why not say it clearly?

"Yes, the French Army is simply afraid of being cheated of its victory.

"And that victory is the last chance.

"Last chance for itself to begin with, for it is impossible to require of an army twenty years of successive reversals, captivities, humiliations. . . .

"Last chance for the country as a whole. . . . " [35]

An editorialist for Le Bled, a month later: "At the time when our soldiers in Algeria are accumulating success upon success, at the time when the enemy is physically crushed by our troops, it would be criminal and insane to cheat the French people and the Army of final victory. For having carried the heaviest weight of the struggle, neither would tolerate a moral capitulation and, without having suffered a single military reversal, end up with what M. Lacoste calls 'a diplomatic Dien-Bien-Phu.' "[36]

Rumors of impending negotiations with the F.L.N. renewed army fears of another humiliation, leading one regular army captain in Algeria to remark: "The Army will never accept negotiations. That would be to dishonor itself, to dishonor its comrades who died in Indochina and Algeria." [37] Again in April, 1961, the desire to win, to avoid a further humiliation, to prevent a decade and a half of war from having been in vain, was clearly a strong element in the motivations of men like Challe, Salan, and those who followed them.[38] Among those given prison sentences after the putsch was General André Petit, who in testimony affirmed his belief that defense of the entire national territory was the essential mission, "a transcedent truth" of the military profession. "No one," he argued, "has the power to divert the Army from its natural vocation, to make of it an army of abandonment." [39]

Military effectiveness, the quest for glory, and the abhorrence of surrender—all held unquestionable and legitimate places in the traditional French professional military value system. When swollen in importance by successive military frustrations, however, they tended to choke out the core value of professionalism—obedience to civil authority—without which the whole edifice would be opened to the danger of factionalism, schism, political strife, and a decline in technical proficiency.

Very closely linked with the widespread fear of further humiliation was a strong military attachment to the French Empire, an empire which had been largely conquered, pacified, and then administered by army leaders like Generals Bugeaud in Algeria, Gallieni in Madagascar and Indochina, and Lyautey in Algeria and Morocco.[40] The "abandonment" of Indochina, Morocco, Tunisia, and Algeria—all familiar lands to most officers—rather naturally appeared to be a direct affront to the army which had won and protected them, as well as a symbol of lost national glory. It was with great regret that French officers withdrew from these former colonies, where the uniform had long carried power and prestige, leaving behind colonists and native friends of France. In circumstances somewhat similar to those of the French Army in Algeria, even an army as steeped in civilian supremacy as that of Great Britain had experienced serious unrest in 1914 when called upon to implement the Liberal government's policy of Home Rule for the whole of Ireland against violent Protestant protest in Ulster.[41]

One must not conclude from the French Army's attachment to the empire and its defense of French Algeria that it shared the rigid conservatism of the *colons*. French Army traditionalism, so apparent at the time of the Dreyfus Affair, has (since 1900, at least) contained a certain paternalist, reformist element, as seen, for example, in the work of Lyautey and in the attitude of officers elected to the National Assembly before 1940.[42] Since World War II, probably aided by an influx of officers from rather modest social origins, that paternalist element has turned more clearly reformist. In Indochina a number of officers began to feel the injustice of privilege and wealth alongside dire poverty. One captain remembered the poignant parting words of a political commissar in his Vietminh prison camp: "You will soon be liberated and you will be able to go to North Africa to defend the property of the big colonial landowners ['gros colons']." [43] In Algeria the officer corps became a force for reform, strongly hostile to the privileges of the European settlers. General Massu and Colonel Godard both adopted Moslem orphans.[44] With few exceptions (though important ones) the officer corps learned to detest the *pieds noirs*, with their narrowly self-interested mentality and their racism, which fed the fire of Algerian nationalism. One captain, writing in a communist review (which might have been expected to lump together military and colonial "fascists") affirmed, " . . . Never have I heard around me a soldier come to the defense of a *pied-noir*. Never." [45] No theme is more recurrent in Claude Dufresnoy's interviews with officers in 1959–60.[46] Here is a sampling:

An unidentified officer (to Jules Roy, quoted in his *Introduction to "Des officiers parlent"*): "The day when we learn that they have expelled 500 Algerian Frenchmen who belong to the hundred families which remain opposed to all social progress and hold a great part of capital resources, champagne corks will pop in the mess halls. . . . In each village, there is a small or large potentate who must be destroyed. We are ready to do it, as we are ready to fix ourselves the vital minimum wage."[47]

A regular army lieutenant: "What is needed above all is to eliminate *'les colons.'* "[48]

Colonel de G., a regimental commander: " . . . There is one subject on which they [military personnel] are all agreed, from the private to the colonels, that would be to use all effective means against the *'colons'* and the 'little whites': means which would go as far as expropriation and expulsion from Algeria. The whole army, apart from a few generals and staff officers, would agree *en bloc* to participate in a purge of that order."[49]

Captain de R., an Indochina veteran: "Moreover, they are the first who play the game of communism with their racism, their sectarianism, and this [*pied noir*] 'Algerian nationalism.' . . . "[50]

Colonel A.: "Those people are bastards [*salauds*]; when I think of the fact that our boys are coming to get shot up for them and of the manner in which they receive us, ah, I assure you, I have a heavy heart."[51]

It is probably safe to say that the great majority of French officers in Algeria believed in the elimination of colonial privileges and saw in the social revolution that would follow the only hope for an enduring French Algeria.[52] There were, of course, some officers who were *pieds noirs* themselves. A number of these moved naturally into the camp of revolt in April, 1961.[53] A few other officers who joined the putsch, especially in the Tenth Paratroop Division, which was the idol of Algiers, were probably motivated partly by personal attachments in the *pied noir* community (often wives or mistresses).[54] In the main, however, the cause of French Algeria was viewed in quite different terms by officers and *colons.*

Throughout the trials of mutinous officers which followed the April putsch of 1961, the dominant theme of military apology was not so much defense of the empire or the humiliation of surrender (though these had their place) as the sacred pledges made by the army to stay and protect the Moslem friends of France.[55] The old concept of Christian chivalry was still alive in the minds of a few aristocratic officers like General Paris de Bollardière, but for most officers it had been badly battered by total war and revolutionary-guerrilla war. The close link between military honor and faithfulness to one's word, however, was as obvious to French officers after 1945 as it had been to Marshal Lyautey in 1904 when, after pushing his troops across the Moroccan border from Algeria, he asked to be replaced rather than obey a government order to withdraw—an order requiring the abandonment of a population which he had promised to protect.[56]

In 1954 many an officer carried with him out of Indochina a vivid memory of mountain people who had been recruited and then left to Vietminh vengeance,[57] of Catholic communities in the north which had been promised permanent protection, of those thousands of Vietnamese who had tried to climb on departing trucks or had attempted vainly to swim out to embarking French military ships in order to escape what they feared their fate would be in a communist Vietnam.[58] One of the many officers who lived through those years later testified, "When one has been mixed up in that tragedy he swears to himself never again to be an accomplice in such an affair." [59] Then, in Algeria the political character of the war against the F.L.N. forced thousands of French officers to promise native soldiers (the *harkis*) and villagers that France intended to stay in Algeria to protect those who chose the tricolor.[60] Without such assurances the number of Moslem *ralliés* would have been few indeed. Having given those assurances, officers like Challe, who greatly expanded *harki* forces, felt their honor at stake whenever French withdrawal from Algeria was rumored.

A host of government statements from 1954 to 1957 covered those military pledges in proclaiming the permanence of French Algeria. The firm commitment to French Algeria by Prime Minister Pierre Mendès-France and his government in November, 1954, has already been mentioned.[61] In late 1956 there had apparently been no change in official government policy: Prime Minister Guy Mollet assured the press, "France will never abandon

Algeria." [62] After May 13, 1958, the early statements of De Gaulle himself were taken as proof that pledges of French determination to stay in Algeria again had official government backing.[63] One has only to recall De Gaulle's pronouncements in Algiers on June 4, 1958 ("I have understood you. . . . There are only full Frenchmen"), and at Oran two days later ("France is here for good").[64] Yet as French officers were painfully aware, the De Gaulle Republic hesitated to commit itself fully to French Algeria, especially after the general's self-determination speech of September 16, 1959.[65] To be sure, Resident Minister Paul Delouvrier reassured his civilian and military subordinates in Algeria in November, 1959, with the words, "I say again with force: we are fighting for a *French Algeria*. . . ." [66] By the Week of the Barricades in January, 1960, few still believed that De Gaulle's commitment was so clear.

The events of 1958 and the activities of the Fifth Bureau further deepened the army's (if not the government's) commitment in Algeria. Soon after the fraternal demonstration of May 16, 1958, the Algiers Committee of Public Safety sent out a proclamation under General Massu's signature in which the Moslem population was assured of French protection: "Let them know that France will never abandon them. . . . All of us who have entered the fight in order to affirm the permanence of France in Algeria have given our solemn pledge of that permanence." [67] With the investiture of De Gaulle hundreds of officers were required to repeat that pledge in the course of the constitutional referendum of September 28, 1958, run by the army in Algeria.[68]

When Algerian independence and the renunciation of pledges again appeared imminent in the spring of 1961, Challe and his followers believed that military honor was at stake. An angry editorial in the March, 1961, issue of *Message* described the mood of those officers who were then on the brink of revolt. Recalling the *treize mai* as seen by the army, "that union of men for whom human sentiments are more than superstructures," the editorialist remarked:

It [the army] swore to all men of good will to protect their property, their families, their future. Would it suffer the shame tomorrow of breaking its pledge? Could it, without denying itself, abandon those

whom it has compromised, who risk death and torture for themselves and their families because they associated themselves with
our task?[69]

The answer came a month later with the April putsch. Among
the first public statements from putsch headquarters in Algiers
on April 22, 1961, was this radio announcement:

You have before you Generals Challe, Jouhaud, and Zeller. On May
13, the French Army gave a solemn pledge to keep Algeria under
French sovereignty. We come today to renew that pledge in the
name of the Army. . . . [70]

Challe later personally explained his fear of dishonor in the
concluding remarks of his court testimony:

Well then, we are told, "Obedience, Discipline, Duty." And we
reply, "Yes, obedience; yes, discipline; yes, duty; until death, and including death, but not including perjury repeated ten times, a hundred times. We are not domestic animals but human beings, and
there is no law in the world which can require a man to make
perjury his daily bread."[71]

Very similar testimony was given by one of Challe's faithful and
admiring subordinates, Major Denoix de Saint-Marc, who in April,
1961, had been interim commander of the First Foreign Paratroop
Regiment, the unit which provided shock troops for the putsch in
Algiers. Saint-Marc explained his attitude in these terms:

One can ask a great deal of a soldier. One cannot ask him to disavow
what he has said, to contradict himself, to lie, to cheat, to perjure
himself. Oh, I know, there is discipline. The drama of discipline was
familiar to our elders. We have also known it as young cadets. You
can believe that again it weighed painfully on our shoulders in face
of the destiny of Algeria about which our leaders have time and
again repeated that it was part of the national territory.[72]

Again and again in the testimony of those officers who followed
Challe—and of several who had no part in the putsch—the clash
between discipline and honor stands out.[73] While the putsch trials

were still in progress in June, 1961, General Valluy, who had no part in the affair, described honor as a core value for the French Army, one stressed at Saint-Cyr and throughout the army, and one which now was in open conflict with discipline.[74] General de Pouilly, who as commander of the Oran Army Corps in April, 1961, was one of those few commanders who took a firm and consistent stand against the Challists, came forward at the Salan trial in defense of the mutineers:

> I chose a direction completely different from that of General Salan;
> I chose discipline. But in choosing discipline I chose as well to share
> with my fellow citizens and the French Nation the shame of an
> abandonment. . . . History will tell perhaps that their crime is
> perhaps less serious than ours.[75]

Within the army officer corps it would appear that a strong majority (if not the "totality" claimed by Colonel Pierre Buchoud) was at least badly troubled by the dishonor of broken pledges.[76]

From the standpoint of General Challe and those officers who surrendered with him when the putsch failed (as opposed to Salan, Jouhaud, Argoud, Lacheroy, Gardes, Godard, and others, who fled to carry on the fight in the O.A.S.), the whole affair has much of the character of a *baroud d'honneur* (a fight for the defense of one's honor) intended, not so much to overthrow the Gaullist regime, as to cleanse a guilty conscience. One of Challe's aides in the putsch, General André Petit (an influential Gaullist in May, 1958), later testified, "To tell the truth, I never found that affair to be reasonable." [77] Challe, the very efficient military commander, gave remarkably little attention to such critical factors as the Algérian food supply.[78] Despite his claims to the contrary, Challe's plan to end the war in two to three months was decidedly utopian, given the French experience of the past six and a half years.[79] In his talks with a number of officers in Algeria and in his later court testimony, Challe claimed that he acted for strictly "military" goals, with no intent of carrying the battle to metropolitan France.[80] Challe and his defenders (including most of those officers who refused to join him in April, 1961) conveniently forgot two facts. The first was Challe's radio announcement of April 22 in which he declared:

> The High [Challist] Command reserves the right to extend its action to the *métropole* and reconstitute a constitutional and republican order which has been gravely compromised by a government whose illegality is obvious to the eyes of the nation.[81]

The second was the existence of an abortive military plot in Paris, of which Challe was certainly aware, led by General Jacques Faure.[82]

Even though Challe likely would have been pleased to have seen De Gaulle replaced, the putsch leader's primary goals were more limited, as evidenced by his reluctance to give over any real authority to civilian activists in Algiers,[83] by his lack of enthusiasm at the arrival in Algiers of General Salan, who was set upon a fight to the finish and was closely linked (through the O.A.S.) with civilian enemies of the Gaullist regime,[84] and by his decision to surrender, rather than call upon civilian-activist support or risk civil war.

From Challe's statements of mid-April, 1961, to the court testimony of imprisoned Challist officers after the collapse of the putsch, there runs a consistent thread: military honor can be safeguarded only through a desperate final attempt to save French Algeria. Several of these statements deserve to be quoted:

> *General Challe to Colonel Marcel Lennuyeux (who did not join him) on the eve of the putsch*: "If we fail, we will be shot, but we had our backs to the wall; we had to act. We will go all the way."[85]

> *Lieutenant Jacques Favreau of the First Foreign Paratroop Regiment in the Challe trial*: "I am convinced that we are all indebted to General Challe for being able to appear in court today with clean hands." [86]

> *General André Petit at his own trial*: "I am profoundly sad at what has happened, but I feel today relieved of all that weight of shame and guilt which has been building up inside me for two years. . . ."[87]

> *Captain Delacour in his own trial*: "I broke my career as officers formerly broke their swords rather than break their honor. But if

I had agreed to perjure myself, in my soul and conscience I would no longer have been worthy of my officer's ideal." [88]

Major Georges Robin at his own trial: " . . . When tomorrow, deprived of my rights as a citizen, dismissed from the officer corps of France, I present myself before my children, in the name of those who have given their lives in the past fifteen years so that the word of France might be respected, I will be able to leave them, in lieu of material security, the heritage of uncompromised honor." [89]

Clearly, the behavior of Challe and those forty-five other officers who surrendered and were convicted with him cannot be understood without reference to the concept of military honor, conceived primarily as fidelity to one's word and (a theme almost as recurrent) loyalty to the memory of all of those officers and men whose death could not be rendered vain.[90] The subsequent assassination and mistreatment of at least hundreds and probably thousands of Moslem *harkis* who fought with the French lend credence to the fears of men like Challe who recruited them.[91]

Fidelity to the pledged word was undoubtedly one important motivation for military revolt, though probably not so predominant a cause as the putsch trials might suggest. It must be borne in mind that officers on trial and those defending them were primarily concerned with justifying the mutinous behavior of the Challists. Their apologetics must not be taken at face value. Beneath the noble and romantic expressions of fidelity to military pledges often lay other powerful sentiments, particularly the frustrated desire to win, which would have sounded less generous in open court. Military honor, taken in the sense of fidelity to one's word and abhorrence of surrender, was closely intertwined with the defense of corporate military interests, notably military status and power, both of which seemed to many officers to require victory in Algeria and a continuing colonial role for the army.

We have examined so far the role of military honor conceived as abhorrence of surrender and fidelity to the pledged word. The last two aspects of military honor mentioned earlier—personal loyalty to the commander and the cohesion of a self-regulating brotherhood—were also sufficient motives for military revolt in some cases. One clear example was that of Major de Saint-Marc, the heavily decorated interim commander of the First Foreign Paratroop Regiment, for whom Challe was in April, 1962,

> . . . the great chief whom we admired and who, like de Lattre in Indochina, had given us hope of victory. He told me that it was necessary to complete that already acquired victory, that we should remain true to our promises to the troops, to the population, that we should save our honor. Well, *Monsieur le Président*, I followed General Challe. And today I am before you to answer for my actions and those of the officers of the first *R.É.P.* who acted on my orders.[92]

As in 1942, once the legitimacy of orders from Paris had been opened to question by a rival leader, officers like General Georges Héritier, joint chief of staff in Algiers, and General Léon Perrotat, commander of the central Oranais zone, looked for direction, not to governmental authority, but to their immediate commanders. Héritier refused to join the Challists, despite his apparent sympathy for them, because his superior, General Gambiez, joint commander in Algeria, had remained loyal to Paris. The case of Perrotat is even clearer. Confronted during the putsch by General Gardy, Challe's representative, Perrotat said: "I have no position. It is General de Pouilly alone who is my chief. It is up to him to take the positions and not up to me!"[93] Presumably, if De Pouilly had joined the revolt, Perrotat would himself have become a rebel.

As for the corporative spirit of the officer corps, it was largely that sentiment which discouraged loyalists from arresting Challist officers during the putsch and then, when he failed, brought them into the courtroom to testify in his defense.[94] It was that same sentiment which drew Marshal Juin and General Demetz, military governor of Paris, into Santé prison to visit the accused and which later allowed officer-deserters to plead the O.A.S. case among French units in Germany without fear of being denounced to French civil authorities. In March, 1962, for example, during a secret tour of French forces in Germany, Colonel Antoine Argoud of the O.A.S. was brought into the presence of General Vincent Moneglia, an infantry brigade commander who did not know whom he was to meet. According to the testimony of Lieutenant Colonel Piau, one of eight officers who were later tried for setting up an O.A.S. ring in Germany, Moneglia refused to support the O.A.S., though he decided to hush up the Argoud visit. In Piau's words, "He told me that he was afraid that if he denounced him [Argoud] the officers of the garrison would thereafter refuse to shake his hand." M. Dechezelles, the presiding magistrate, then added, "Ah yes! and that, you see, is the saddest and most lamentable aspect of this dossier." [95] Even though he had been condemned to death *in absentia* for his role in the April putsch, Argoud was protected by the fraternal feelings even of officers who opposed the O.A.S.

So far in the present chapter, discussion of French military attitudes has focused on threats to military discipline which arose out of the Indochina and Algerian wars. From one final and differing vantage point, one can see another supporting factor behind the weakening of military obedience in the French Army. One careful student of the American military establishment has concluded that there are tendencies among American officers toward (a) a shift from "authoritarian domination" to "manipulation," "persuasion," and "group consensus" as the typical style of military discipline, and toward (b) "civilianization" of the military establishment through the increasing importance of technical and managerial tasks.[96] The second of these tendencies was only beginning to become visible in the French Army during the period of revolutionary-guerrilla wars from 1945 to 1962. The first trend, however—a shift in the character of military discipline—was clearly observable in the French as well as in the American Army. As Morris Janowitz has hypothesized, in both cases it probably spurred on the military quest for a political answer to the question, "Why do we fight?"

In the early 1930's Charles de Gaulle was aware that the increasing importance of individual initiative in modern warfare and the weakening general respect for traditional authority which he saw in civilian society were already shifting the basis of military authority from rank alone to proved leadership ability.[97] More recently, with the political demands of revolutionary-guerrilla war to hasten the demise of blind obedience, a number of military writers have looked to social psychology for tools to bolster morale and cohesion within the French military establishment.[98] As the officer comes to feel he must win respect in order to command clear obedience from his troops, he is quite naturally drawn to explaining the goals which his orders are intended to serve. According to Captain André Souyris, for example, the old army attitude that "one must not seek to understand" is now outmoded in political and psychological warfare.[99] As chief of staff of national defense, General Paul Ely agreed but warned that, in the last analysis, spontaneous obedience is the touchstone of military effectiveness.[100] Indeed, the "understanding" provided by Fifth Bureau answers, we have already seen, intensified civil-military tensions when official war goals in Algeria were altered. Undoubtedly the political nature of revolutionary-guerrilla war was the primary reason for this new emphasis on understanding and commitment, as opposed to unquestioning obedience.[101] Even without the Indochinese and Algerian wars, however, the erosion of automatic obedience seen by De Gaulle probably would have continued.

As for the phenomenon of "civilianization" through technical modernization of the military establishment, the French Army before 1962 differed markedly from the American Army in that the primary French preoccupation was with antiguerrilla warfare which did not involve much ultramodern military hardware. The question of modernization, or rather military hostility to modernization, deserves attention, however, for it has been vested with great importance by at least two prominent French experts in military affairs. One of these is François Gromier, who views the modernization crisis, rather than the Algerian war, as the true root of the recent "uneasiness" (*malaise*) of the army.[102] There is no question but that the "military Poujadism" of which Gromier writes, i.e., the hostile reaction of threatened military branches to technical modernization, is a real phenomenon. I would argue, however, that without fifteen years of colonial wars, that problem could have been resolved without serious threat to civilian control. Let us examine the evidence.

In favor of the "military Poujadism" thesis, it must be said that military revolt has been fed mostly by the army, rather than by the more technical branches (the navy and the air force). And within the army, the largest number of angry men have been pro-

duced by the *paras*, the "knights of guerrilla war," who could expect
a serious loss of status in an army of missiles and technicians. Even
in the highest grades one hears warnings against jeopardizing the
officer's status and traditional values (honor, love of action, personal
responsibility) by transforming him into a technician or a manager.[103] Judging from the above-mentioned study of candidates to
French military schools, the army, as opposed to the navy, and
especially to the air force, tends to attract men whose attitudes are
characterized by a liking for combat, a clear preference for things
military over things civilian, and a distaste for technical specialization.[104] The same phenomenon is evident, in reverse, in the recent
aversion of graduates of the military engineering school, the Ecole
Polytechnique, for an army career.[105]

The fact of recent army hostility to technical modernization
appears less determining, however, when considered in historical
context. As suggested earlier, personal involvement in the commitments and frustrations of revolutionary-guerrilla war was more
important than branch affiliation in inclining officers toward the
camp of military revolt.[106] At least three of the four generals who
led the April putsch of 1961 were quite at home with technical
military questions. General Challe was an intelligent and highly
trained air force officer who had nothing to fear from modernization
of the military establishment.[107] General Jouhaud was also an air
force officer, and General Zeller spent most of his career, not as a
combat commander, but as a military manager and logistics specialist.[108] Zeller's protest resignation as chief of staff of the army in
1956 was not occasioned by modernization but, on the contrary, by
a government decision to break up modern French mechanized
units in Germany for service in Algeria. Among the colonels, the
most active and most powerful, Colonel Argoud, was a brilliant
graduate of the famed Ecole Polytechnique.[109]

As for the *guerre révolutionnaire* school generally, some of the
best and most original minds in the army were drawn into its circle.
They were attracted, in large measure, because the army's principal
and consuming assignment after 1946 was to stop colonial revolutions, a costly mission which required the temporary sacrifice of
technical modernization. Men like Hogard, Lacheroy, and Broizat

were no more defenders of military traditionalism than were those few strong military advocates of a French atomic bomb: they only conceived of the probable style of modern war in different terms. In the early years of the Algerian war *Message* spread the *guerre révolutionnaire* doctrine on the one hand and called for the development of a French atomic bomb on the other.[110] The Algerian war was the central concern of the *guerre révolutionnaire* school and the army officer corps in general, however, and when De Gaulle began dangling his atomic *force de frappe* as an alternative to victory in Algeria, most officers rejected the bait.[111]

In short, army opposition to technical modernization was real, especially among paratroop and Legion officers; in the main, however, it was of secondary importance in comparison with the Algerian question and the military pride, honor, and status which were invested therein. Without the Indochinese and Algerian wars, modernization and technical training would have spread gradually, thereby easing a transition which promised to be more difficult in the 1960's.

Discipline, the traditional capstone value in the French military ethic, came violently into conflict in the period from 1945–62 with military attitudes arising from three major sources: (a) the functional-requisite values of professional soldiers (from which discipline itself is derived), (b) military honor, and (c) the corporate interests of the military community. Out of the functional requisites of his profession, the officer derived his nationalism, his desire for military effectiveness, and indirectly, his distaste for parliamentary democracy. All of these attitudes helped to undermine civilian supremacy at a time when a divided nation and timid Fourth Republic governments seemed incapable either of defending the empire or of making peace with it. Weak and unstable governmental leadership before 1958 (when it was too late) left the army hamstrung in its essentially political battles against revolutionary-guerrilla movements. Out of the traditional concept of military honor came an abhorrence of surrender, a passionate desire to be faithful to innumerable army pledges to defend France's friends in the colonies, and a loyalty to fellow officers against attacks from the civilian world. From the corporate interests of the military community the officer derived a strong attachment to the empire built by his military forebears (though not to the social and economic status quo there) and a fear of further humiliation and permanent decline in military status and power should overseas France be lost. All of these sentiments came to focus on the defense of French Algeria and, with the army deeply committed to that cause by the late 1950's, on contempt for any government, weak or strong, which dared contemplate Algerian independence.

1. See Chapter 2 above.

2. "Ethique militaire et démocratie," *Message*, No. 16 (October, 1956), p. 9.

3. *Ibid.*, pp. 8–11. Similar military values are asserted by General Boucherie, "Protection du territoire et armée moderne," *RDN*, March, 1955, pp. 255–65; and by Colonel de Metz, "Du rôle national de l'officier," *RDN*, August–September, 1958, pp. 1320–38.

4. Quoted in *LM*, May 12, 1961.

5. See especially Chapters 4, 8, and 9.

6. Huntington has suggested that when dominant civilian values are strongly opposed to the professional military ethic, civilian control can be maintained only if (a) officers adapt to civilian values ("subjective civilian control"), or (b) if the army can be isolated from all access to political power (*The Soldier and the State*, chap. 4).

7. With regard to the variety of ideologies within the *guerre révolutionnaire* school, see Chapter 11 below.

8. See above, pp. 6, 17 nn. 14 and 15.

9. With regard to the roots of anti-Gaullism in the armistice army see Paxton, "Army Officers in Vichy France," pp. 230–53.

10. Chapter 4 above.

11. For strong statements of belief in NATO by key military leaders see Ely, *RDN*, February, 1959, pp. 213–18; and Valluy, *RDN*, July, 1959, pp. 1137–48. With respect to anti-Americanism, see Colonel de Crèvecoeur, "Raccourci de la Campagne de l'Indochine," p. 10; Navarre, *Agonie de l'Indochine*, pp. 27–28, 96–98, 136–38, 244–45, and 330–31; "La Situation en Algérie," *RMI*, No. 270 (April 10, 1956), p. 17; Colonel Schneider's proposal to the Assembly of the French Union in Azeau, *Révolte militaire*, p. 53; Alleg, *La Question*, p. 100; General Jean Marchand, "Perspectives africaines," *RDN*, November, 1959, pp. 1754–58; Marchand, "Les Puissances anti-colonialistes et l'Afrique noire française," *RDN*, May, 1961, pp. 568–80; and below, Chapter 11, note 36.

12. Juin stayed on as NATO commander of the east-central Europe zone (Juin, *Mémoires* [Paris: Fayard, 1960], II, 262–64; and *L'Année politique*, 1954, pp. 19–22). For another military voice raised in opposition to E.D.C., see Maxime Weygand, "Réflexions sur l'état militaire de la France," *Revue des*

deux mondes, October 15, 1952. The story of the E.D.C. is told in some detail in Furniss, *France, Troubled Ally,* pp. 60–109.

13. In *Message,* see especially "A nos lecteurs," No. 39 (October, 1952), p. 2; Evan le France, "Une Défaite militaire et politique," pp. 17–23 in the same issue; "Information à sens unique, à propos de l'Armée Européene du Général de Larminat," No. 40 (December, 1952), pp. 8–14; and "La Propagande dans l'armée en faveur de la C.E.D.," No. 3 (May, 1954), p. 17.

14. See Chapter 11 below.

15. "Réflexions sur la discipline," *Message,* No. 40 (January, 1960), p. 3.

16. Centre d'Etudes et d'Instruction Psychologique de l'Armée de l'Air, "Attitudes et motivation des candidats aux grandes écoles militaires," *Revue française de sociologie,* II, No. 2 (April–June, 1961), 133–51. The motives reported (in *ibid.,* p. 141) were as follows, in order of importance:

Important favorable factors: (1) Patriotic ideal and liking for command; (3) Desire to travel; (4) Liking for risk and combat; fraternity of arms.

Secondary favorable factors: (6) Glory of a military career; (7) Information on a military career; (8) Family tradition.

Factors having no influence on decisions: (9) Desire for technical specialization; (10) Search for professional stability; (11) Difficulty of civilian examinations; (12) Circumstances independent of your will; (13) Advice from teachers.

17. The two scales from which these items were taken produced respectively 86 per cent and 67 per cent classified as "militarists" among candidates and 41 per cent and 35 per cent "militarists" among non-candidates (*ibid.,* 142–43).

18. One student at the Lycée Saint-Louis in Paris told the writer that the Saint-Cyr prep students at that famous lycée assign each other military ranks, salute each other, and require new students to go through a lengthy hazing period (interview, February 22, 1962). A number of O.A.S. bombsetters were recruited from the ranks of students preparing for Saint-Cyr (*LM,* January 20, February 21 and 28, March 2, and April 14, 1962).

19. T. W. Adorno *et al., The Authoritarian Personality* (New York: Harper, 1950). Pétain's statement of August, 1940, condemning neutrality in all its forms is found above, p. 67.

20. An excellent example of the looseness of the term, which Alfred de Vigny described as "sovereign in the Army" but undefinable (*Servitude et grandeur militaire,* pp. 265–66), is to be found in *Le Métier des armes* by Colonel Jules Roy. Among the various meanings attached to military honor in Roy's book are: (1) facing up to battle to the end (pp. 73, 209–10); (2) action in accordance with the majority will of the nation (pp. 80–81); and (3) justice (pp. 150).

21. Janowitz, *The Professional Soldier,* pp. 215–17; and Kuntz, *L'Officier français dans la nation,* pp. 5–6.

22. There was an unreal, nostalgic quality to the confrontation, on June 22, 1940, between General Huntziger, head of the French armistice delegation, and the German General Keitel. Huntziger voiced his hope that he would not have to repent his act of surrender. Keitel replied, "It is honorable for a conqueror to honor the conquered," and then invited the French to rise with him to observe a minute of silence in honor of the dead on both sides (Aron, *Vichy,* p. 79).

23. See above, Chapter 3.

24. Pétain announced on June 25, 1940, that "du moins l'honneur est-il sauf," to which De Gaulle replied: "Ah, pour obtenir et pour accepter un

pareil acte d'asservissement, on n'avait pas besoin du vainqueur de Verdun: n'importe qui aurait suffi" (Aron, *Vichy*, p. 92).

25. *Sans commentaire*, p. 25.

26. May 21, 1962, in *Procès Salan*, p. 356. Ploix was one of those who tried to join De Gaulle in 1940, but he was caught, tried, and imprisoned by Vichy (*ibid.*, pp. 355–56). See also, on the same point, the testimony of General Salan (*ibid.*, p. 88); that of Madame de Lattre de Tassigny (*ibid.*, p. 159); *Procès du Putsch*, pp. 24, 224; Planchais, *Le Malaise de l'armée*, p. 19; Thierry Maulnier, "Du 13 mai au 28 septembre," *RDN*, November, 1958, p. 1160; and above, Chapter 3.

27. S. E. Finer has noted a similar sense of humiliation behind the political intervention of the Greek Army in 1909 and 1922 and of the Egyptian Army in 1952 (*The Man on Horseback*, pp. 64–67).

28. Quoted in Planchais, *Le Malaise de l'armée*, p. 23.

29. Quoted in Tournoux, *Secrets d'état*, pp. 103–4. In a similar vein a non-commissioned officer, Roger Holleindre, on trial for his participation in the O.A.S. "Maquis Bonaparte," testified that, "I left Indochina with the last paratroop battalions. That day we decided never again to pull down the flag" (*LM*, November 29, 1962).

30. "La Crise des vocations militaires," *Message*, No. 4 (July, 1954), p. 13. Regarding the *guerre révolutionnaire* school, see below, Chapter 11.

31. Liber, *Réalités*, p. 105. See also Tournoux, *Secrets d'état*, pp. 171, 178; and Lartéguy, *Les Centurions*, p. 359.

32. Major G., "Réflexions sur un cessez-le-feu," *Message*, No. 17 (November, 1956), p. 4.

33. Editorial, *Message*, No. 19 (February, 1957), p. 2.

34. To Euloge and Moulinier, *L'Envers des Barricades*, pp. 58–59. After his release from a Vietminh prison camp in 1954, Bigeard is reported to have told General Gogny, "Le système Viet est épouvantable, inhumain. Mais quel rendement à côté du système libéral" (Tournoux, *Secrets d'état*, p. 92).

35. "Pour des victoires acquises," *Message*, No. 29 (April, 1958), p. 3.

36. Editorial, *Le Bled*, May 7, 1958, p. 3. See also editorial, *Message*, No. 15 (August, 1956), before p. 1; Lacheroy, in *La Défense nationale*, p. 330; and Girardet, "Pouvoir civil et pouvoir militaire en France," pp. 11–12.

37. Captain N., in Dufresnoy, *Des officiers parlent*, p. 63. The captain continues: "Croyez-vous que je me suis battu pendant cinq ans en Indochine, que j'ai vu mes camarades, mes supérieures, mes subalternes, tomber autour de moi, pour accepter de capituler, pour être traité d'égal à égal avec les bandes du F.L.N., alors que nous sommes les plus forts, qu'il n'y a pas de défaite militaire possible de notre côté, qu'au contraire, la situation s'améliore d'une manière considérable?" See also *ibid.*, p. 154; editorial, *Message*, No. 38 (October, 1959), p. 1; editorial, *Message*, No. 43 (June, 1960), p. 2; and Buis, *La Grotte*, p. 80.

38. See Challe's testimony revealing his chagrin at being relieved of his command in Algeria in April, 1960, before being allowed to complete a French military victory, in *Procès Challe*, pp. 29–30. See also, in the same trial, the testimony of General Valluy, *ibid.*, p. 160. In *Procès Salan* see the testimony of General Valluy (p. 185), that of General Jacques Allard (p. 189), and that of Colonel Robert Thomazo (p. 375). Among subordinates a similar passion for victory is evident in the testimony of Captain Branca (*Procès du putsch*, pp. 106–7); and in the remarks of an anonymous officer to a radio

interviewer in Algiers on April 22, 1961, found in Azeau, *Révolte militaire*, p. 202.

39. *Procès du putsch*, p. 28.

40. In regard to the army's attachment to the empire and the agonies of decolonization, see: "X.X.X.," "L'Indépendance dans l'interdépendance," *RDN*, August–September, 1956, pp. 1055–59; editorial, *Message*, No. 40 (December, 1952), p. 3; "Milites," "L'Algérie, pierre de touche de la volonté française," *Message*, No. 13 (April, 1956), p. 12; "D'Algérie, une opinion sur le moral des officiers," *Message*, No. 20 (March, 1957), pp. 1–2 ("La quasi-totalité des officiers sent que la France joue en Algérie sa dernière carte . . . Un échec en Algérie, même déguisé sous des formes habiles, signifiera très probablement la révolte de l'armée" [*ibid.*, pp. 1–2]); Colonel Partiot in *Procès Salan*, pp. 330–32; Girardet *et al.*, *Crise militaire*, p. 196; Bernard Brown, *Journal of Politics*, May, 1961, p. 276; and Azeau, *Révolte militaire*, p. 7.

41. A. P. Ryan, *Mutiny at the Curragh* (London: Macmillan, 1956). The parallel between the attitude of the British Army in 1912–14 and the French Army in Algeria is noted (and somewhat exaggerated) by General Valluy, *Revue des deux mondes*, June 15, 1961, pp. 587–88; and by Colonel J. Nemo, "La Formation des cadres de défense nationale," *RDN*, March, 1958, p. 470. When Britain proceeded to loosen her hold on her colonies after 1945, the army accepted the retreat more graciously than in France. But lengthy and humiliating wars were avoided in the British case, and there was no large British population in the colonies comparable to the French population in Algeria to complicate matters.

42. Dogan, *Revue française de sociologie*, p. 97.

43. Captain Lamouliatte, quoted by Tournoux, *Secrets d'état*, p. 93. See also *ibid.*, pp. 22–23.

44. Paillat, *Dossier secret*, pp. 31–32; Azeau, *Révolte militaire*, p. 233.

45. "Journal de marche d'un capitaine en Kabylie," *La nouvelle critique*, XI, No. 107 (June, 1959), 9.

46. *Des officiers parlent*, pp. xv–xvii, xxi, 2, 10, 15, 16, 17, 19, 21, 22, 29, 38, 66, 67, 94–95, 176.

47. *Ibid.*, p. xviii.

48. *Ibid.*, p. 2.

49. *Ibid.*, p. 17.

50. *Ibid.*, p. 29.

51. *Ibid.*, p. 66.

52. See, for example, again in *ibid.*, pp. xv. 4, and 27; Aron, *L'Algérie et la république*, p. 98; Brombergers *et al.*, *Barricades et colonels*, p. 23–25; General Nemo, "La France et l'Afrique," *RDN*, December,1959, p. 1949; Max Lejeune, "La Mission de l'armée en Algérie," *RMI*, No. 278 (November, 1956), p. 87; Fauvet and Planchais, *La Fronde des généraux*, pp. 178–79 (regarding the reluctance of Challe and his entourage to ally with the *pieds noirs*, whom they blamed for the war); Barberot, *Malaventure en Algérie*, pp. 163–65, 169; Ferniot, *Les Ides de mai*, pp. 37–38 (Massu's dislike for the *ultras* who opposed the *loi cadre* and the single electoral college); Girardet, "Pouvoir civil et pouvoir militaire en France," pp. 38–41; Tournoux, *Secrets d'état*, pp. 208–9, 355; testimonies of Robert Lacoste and Colonel Robert Thomazo, *Procès Salan*, pp. 314, 373. With respect to attitudes of enlisted men, who were found to be more favorable to Moslems than to *pieds noirs*, see Grall, *La Génération du Djebel*, pp. 17–19, reporting on a questionnaire survey of 607 veterans.

53. Among them, General Jouhaud, Colonel Masselot, Majors Robin, Camelin, Botella, and Bonafos, and Captains Branca, Pompidou, and Patouraux (*Procès du putsch, passim*).

54. Lieutenant Colonel A. told me of one officer, now in prison, who became embroiled in the April putsch because of his *pied noir* mistress. Larténguy makes use of this theme in *Les Centurions*.

55. In *Procès Challe* see the testimonies of Challe (p. 45), Colonel de Boissieu, Challe's former chief of staff (pp. 143, 149), and Paul Delouvrier (p. 201). In *Procès du putsch* see the testimonies of Major Denoix de Saint-Marc (pp. 10–11), Colonel Guiraud (p. 16), Major Georges Robin (pp. 46–48), Colonel Masselot (p. 62), Captain Bonelli (p. 77), Captain Estoup (p. 81), General Vanuxem (pp. 114–15), Captain Georges Oudinot (pp. 131–33), Major Guy Perrier (pp. 137–38), Lieutenant de Vaisseau Pierre Guillaume (p. 147), Captain Delacour (p. 183), and Colonel Ogier de Baulny (pp. 190–91). In *Procès Salan* see the testimonies of Salan (pp. 76–85), Captain Bernard Moynet (pp. 167–68), General Pierre de Benouville (pp. 179–80), General Jacques Allard (p. 189), General de Pouilly (p. 224), Colonel Partiot (pp. 330–31), Captain Pierre de Boisanger (pp. 347–48), General Gracieux (p. 346), Vice-Admiral Ploix (p. 356), Colonel Georges-André Groussard (p. 361), and Colonel Robert Thomazo (pp. 371-72). See also the reports of testimony in the trial of Lieutenant Colonel Bastien-Thiry (*LM*, February, 16–21, 1963) and in that of Colonel Parisot and eight other officers (*LM*, December 19–20, 1962).

56. Lyautey's telegram to Paris, as quoted by André Maurois, *Lyautey* (Paris: Plon, 1932), p. 91, was read in the trial of Colonel Bastien-Thiry by defense attorney Maître Tizier-Vignancourt (*LM*, March 6, 1963). That brilliant attorney, who a year earlier had probably saved General Salan from a death sentence, failed to mention, however, that the government order to retreat was occasioned by Lyautey's unauthorized advances across the Moroccan border at a time when France was attempting to woo the Moroccan sultan into the French sphere of influence (Maurois, *Lyautey*, pp. 88–90).

57. In regard to the fate of some of those mountain people see Lancaster, *The Emancipation of French Indochina*, p. 361 n. 3.

58. Un Capitaine, "Le Mal Jaune," *Le Courrier de la nation*, p. 20; Tournoux, *Secrets d'état*, pp. 86–87; General Salan and Colonel Thomazo, in *Procès Salan*, pp. 76, 371–72; Commandant Denoix de Saint-Marc, in *Procès du putsch*, pp. 10–11; Commandant Georges Robin, *Procès du putsch*, p. 47; Captain Estoup, *Procès du putsch*, p. 81.

59. Captain Estoup, in *Procès du putsch*, p. 81.

60. See, for example, the testimony of General Jacques Faure in the Barricades trial, *Un Procès*, pp. 43–44; the testimony of Colonel Buchoud in *Procès Challe*, pp. 155–56; and the novel by Alquier, *Nous avons pacifié Tazalt*, especially pp. 270–71.

61. Chapter 8 n. 32 above.

62. This statement was headlined in *Le Bled* on January 12, 1957. See also this and other official statements in the following issues of *RMI*: No. 280 (January, 1957), pp. 78–82; No. 275 (August, 1956), pp. 4–5; and No. 290 (January, 1958), p. 4.

63. See Chapter 9 above.

64. These statements provided considerable headline material for the military press. See, for example, *Le Bled*, September 27, 1958; and *RMI*, No. 295 (June, 1958), p. 7.

65. See above, pp. 252, 262–63.

66. *Le Bled*, November 7, 1959.

67. In de Sérigny, *La Révolution du 13 mai*, p. 96.

68. An article by Jean Brune is particularly emphatic on this point ("L'Armée à la recherche d'une doctrine," *La Nation française*, No. 192 [June 11, 1959], pp. 6–7). See also Philippe Herreman in *LM*, September 28, 1958; *LM*, October 2, 1958; and Massu's testimony in *Un Procès*, p. 109.

69. *Message*, No. 48 (March, 1961), pp. 1–2. This was the last issue of *Message* to appear in 1961.

70. As quoted by Prosecutor General Besson, in *Procès Challe*, p. 235. See also Challe's address to the army in Fauvet and Planchais, *La Fronde des généraux*, p. 117.

71. *Procès Challe*, p. 45.

72. In *Procès du putsch*, p. 11.

73. See note 55 above.

74. *Revue des deux mondes*, June 15, 1961, pp. 582, 592.

75. *Procès Salan*, p. 224.

76. Buchoud's testimony is found in *Procès Challe*, p. 157. Six months after the putsch, Raoul Girardet, commenting upon De Gaulle's speech of November 23, 1961, wrote in *Combat* that no French officer could henceforth lead troops into battle with a clean conscience. "A group of officers" replied (*Combat*, December 11, 1961), minimizing the dishonor of broken pledges and emphasizing the sacredness of military discipline. In view of the behavior of officers in Algeria in April, 1961 (very few actually opposed Challe) and of testimony given in the trials of mutinous officers, it would appear that the "group of officers" represented only a minority opinion.

77. In his own trial, June 7, 1961 (*LM*, June 9, 1961). See also his testimony in *Procès Challe*, p. 29.

78. Zeller, in *ibid.*, pp. 59–60.

79. Challe's unconvincing denial of that charge is found in *ibid.*, p. 40.

80. In *Procès Challe* see the testimonies of Challe (pp. 40, 54–55), Paul Delouvrier (p. 201), General Georges Héritier, chief of the Etat-Major Interarmes d'Alger, who refused when requested to join the Challist movement (pp. 95–97), Colonel Marcel Lennuyeux (pp. 100–101), Colonel Pierre Julien Paul Goubard (pp. 106–10), General Francart (p. 134), and Lieutenant Jacques Favreau (p. 185).

81. As quoted in Fauvet and Planchais, *La Fronde des généraux*, p. 117. One Algiers newspaper, *La Dépêche quotidienne d'Alger*, attributed these words to Zeller, who later denied having spoken them. The voice was difficult to identify (*ibid.*, p. 117 n. 1).

82. *Ibid.*, pp. 149–56. Fauvet and Planchais claim that Faure was under the orders of Challe (*ibid.*, p. 151). However, the "soviet of colonels" probably had more of a hand in the plot, which called for a military takeover of the capital (*Procès Challe*, p. 228). It was broken up by the arrest of Faure and several other officers on the morning of April 22, 1961.

83. Colonel Goubard, in *Procès Challe*, p. 109; Fauvet and Planchais, *La Fronde des généraux*, p. 120.

84. In his trial Challe preferred not to answer the question of whether he was satisfied to see Salan arrive (*Procès Challe*, p. 64). Challe attempted to ease Lagaillarde into the army (and out of the way), (*ibid.*, p. 63; and Fauvet and Planchais, *La Fronde des généraux*, pp. 178-79).

85. *Procès Challe*, p. 101. See also the testimony of Colonel de Boissieu, in *ibid.*, p. 149; and J. Planchais, "L'Armée et la nation," *La Vie nouvelle*, No. 623 (March–April, 1962), p. 5.

86. *Procès Challe*, p. 185.

87. *Procès du putsch*, p. 28.

88. *Ibid.*, p. 154.

89. *Ibid.*, p. 48.

90. Of the forty-five convicted officers, thirty-five received suspended sentences. See the list in Fauvet and Planchais, *La Fronde des généraux*, pp. 259–60. With regard to the theme of loyalty to those who died in combat, see *Procès du putsch*, pp. 12, 16, 114, 131, 154. In *Procès Salan*, see pp. 168, 371. The *paras*, who bore the brunt of the fighting, lost 5,132 men from 1945 to 59, as opposed to 6,161 American paratroopers killed in action in World War II (Tournoux, *Secrets d'état*, p. 259 n).

91. According to French government figures, 61,500 North Africans had been recruited into regular military service with the French by June, 1960, in addition to some 85,500 native auxiliary troops and police (French Press and Information Service, New York, "Contribution des Français de souche nord-africaine à la pacification," as cited by Paret, *French Revolutionary Warfare*, pp. 40, 146). Most of these men were given the opportunity to go to France after the armistice, an offer taken up by *harkis* and their families, totaling 32,000 persons by November, 1962 (Defense Minister P. Messmer, as quoted in *LM*, November 17, 1962). Many of those who stayed (some press reports claimed 10,000) were killed, beaten, or otherwise mistreated by local F.L.N. and A.L.N. members, with no apparent obstruction from the new Algerian government. See *NYT*, November 17, 1962; Michel Legris, "Harkis et Moghaznis au Larzac," *LM*, July 10 and 12; General Weygand's remarks to the Centre d'Etudes Politiques et Civiques, excerpted in *LM*, June 16, 1962; and the testimonies of General Cazenave (who resigned his commission in protest, July 3, 1962), Captain Charie-Marsaine (a former S.A.S. officer), and others in *LM*, February 17–18, and 19, 1963.

92. *Procès du putsch*, p. 11. Regarding Challe's great prestige, see also *Procès Challe*, p. 243. The theme of personal loyalty is stressed (overstressed, in fact) by Planchais, *La Vie nouvelle*, p. 5.

93. Perrotat's testimony in *Procès Challe*, p. 126.

94. General Gambiez, who had been arrested by the Challists, was the only hostile military witness in the *Procès Challe*, pp. 76–86. Even Gambiez was indulgent toward Challist officers below the top ranks. See the summary of his testimony in the trial of officers from the First Foreign Paratroop Regiment (*LM*, July 9–10, 1961). See also *Procès du putsch*, pp. 37, 52; and Jean Planchais, "De l'unité de l'armée à la solidarité militaire," *LM*, July 5, 1961, p. 5.

95. In the trial of Colonel Parisot and eight other officers, as reported in *LM*, December 20, 1962. Moneglia had been relieved of his command in May, 1962, when word of the Argoud visit leaked out (*LM*, May 17, 1962).

96. Janowitz, *The Professional Soldier*, especially chaps. 1–3.

97. "Dans l'armée comme ailleurs, on dit que 'le respect s'en va.' Plutôt, il se déplace. L'homme qui commande, à quelque échelon qu'il soit placé, doit se fier pour être suivi moins à son élévation qu'à sa valeur. Il ne faut plus confondre la puissance et ses attributs" (*Le Fil de l'épée*, p. 75). See also *ibid.*, pp. 64–65, 74–76.

98. Bernard Brichaud, "La Conduite des hommes et ses techniques psychologiques," *RMI* No. 279 (December, 1956), pp. 40–60; Captain Boyer, 'De

l'aspect social de la profession militaire," *RMI*, No. 171 (April 10, 1951), pp. 26–27; Lieutenant Colonel Chandessais, "La Défense nationale face aux sciences humaines," *RDN*, October, 1954, pp. 276–85; Chandessais, "Le Morale et sa mesure," *RMI*, N. 327 (May, 1961), pp. 40-45; Lieutenant Colonel Jean Vial, "De la discipline," *RDN*, December, 1957, pp. 1890–1901; Vial, Introduction à la sociologie militaire," *RDN*, July, 1959, pp. 1225–35; Etienne, *RMI*, No. 319 (August–September, 1960), pp. 16–35; Souyris, *RMI*, No. 298 (October, 1958), pp. 44; and Lieutenant Colonel Livertout, "Relations humaines à l'Ecole Technique de l'Armée de l'Air," *RMI*, No. 327 (May, 1961), pp. 12–22.

99. *RMI*, No. 298, (October, 1958), p. 44.

100. "Jamais la réflexion ne doit devenir, plus ou moins consciemment, une critique systématique et jamais surtout la critique des chefs ne doit être un prétexte facile à éluder ses propres devoirs" (Ely, "Le Chef et l'évolution de la guerre," *RMI*, No. 284 [June, 1957], p. 16).

101. Chapter 7 above.

102. François Gromier (who also writes under the name Maurice Megret), "Une Conception archaïque," *Cahiers de la république*, No. 28 (November–December, 1960), pp. 15–30. See also Jean Planchais, "Crise de modernisme dans l'armée," *Revue française de sociologie*, II, No. 2 (April–June, 1961), pp. 118–23; Azeau, *Révolte militaire*, p. 83; and "In Search of Status," *Economist*, February 6, 1961, pp. 531–32.

103. " . . . On assiste actuellement à l'avènement dans l'armée d'un matérialisme à prétention scientifique qui vise à mettre la guerre en formules et à faire de l'officier un technicien, un contremaître de qualité, responsable d'une usine d'un genre particulier. Il ne semble pas que cette manière de concevoir le rôle de l'officier soit de nature à lui rendre la place à laquelle il a droit dans la nation" (Marshal Alphonse Juin, Preface to Kuntz, *L'Officier français dans la nation*, pp. ix–x). See also General Ely in *RMI*, June, 1960; and Planchais in the *Revue française de sociologie* article cited above.

104. Centre d'Etudes et d'Instruction Psychologique de l'Armée de l'Air, *Revue française de sociologie*, pp. 140–51. The most striking contrast was between air academy candidates, who were most interested in technical specialization, and the more militaristic and combat-minded Saint-Cyr candidates, who chose the "history" or "languages" entrance examination option rather than the "science" option (*ibid.*, pp. 148–49). From the same article: "Il est d'ailleurs intéressant de noter que l'acceptation d'une éventuelle orientation technique s'accompagne fréquemment, contrairement à la détermination de se battre, d'une aspiration à la stabilité professionnelle et à une certaine aisance matérielle" (*ibid.*, p. 147). "La constatation la plus importante est l'antinomie entre le militarisme et idéal patriotique d'une part, goût de la technique at aspiration à la stabilité professionnelle d'autre part" (*ibid.*, p. 149).

105. Chapter 5 above.

106. *Ibid.* See also Chapter 12 below.

107. Fauvet and Planchais, *La Fronde des généraux*, p. 46.

108. *Ibid.*, p. 58.

109. One of the few officers who was later executed for activities in the O.A.S., Lieutenant Colonel Bastien-Thiry, an air force officer, was also a Polytechnicien (*LM*, February 16–21, 1963.)

110. See, for example, by "un officier technicien," "Faut-il construire la bombe atomique?" *Message*, No. 5 (October, 1954), pp. 9–11; "Euratom: Nouvel obstacle à la création d'armements atomiques français," *Message*, No.

12 (February, 1956), pp. 19–24; "Echos et nouvelles," *Message*, No. 16 (October, 1956), pp. 27–28; and Major G., *Message*, No. 17 (November, 1956), pp. 1–4. In general, however, development of the bomb was of much less concern for army officers than was *la guerre révolutionnaire*. General Charles Ailleret, a specialist in atomic weaponry and later commander in chief of French forces in Algeria (after the April putsch), was one of the very few strong military campaigners for the bomb. He wrote numerous articles on the subject, one of which was "Energie nucléaire et problèmes de défense," *RMI*, No. 312 (January, 1960), pp. 98–108 (a special issue on atomic power).

111. "Reconversion de l'armée," *Message*, No. 43 (June, 1960), pp. 2–3; and "Insuffisances de la force de frappe," *Message*, No. 46 (November, 1960). For similar reasons, General Navarre had objected to the creation of modern French military units in Europe while the expeditionary corps in Indochina suffered from lack of men and planes (*Agonie de l'Indochine*, pp. 30, 102–3, 109).

Chapter 11

The French Military Doctrine of
"La Guerre Révolutionnaire"

In view of the wide range of religious and political beliefs within the professional officer corps, it is clearly inaccurate to speak of an all-inclusive French military ideology. Yet it is equally clear that the influential French military doctrine of *la guerre révolutionnaire* contained strong ideological elements. Moreover, that doctrine was sufficiently coherent and consistent to bear systematic analysis. Certain of its aspects have already received attention in connection with the discussions above of revolutionary-guerrilla war and French psychological action in Algeria. The threads of the doctrine must now be pulled together, with particular attention to its more ideological components.

The origins of the French military doctrine of *la guerre révolutionnaire* may be traced to two immediate roots in the latter years of the Indochinese war. With two books on Mao Tse-tung, General Lionel-Martin Chassin, former air commander in Indochina, attempted to draw military attention to Chinese Communist doctrine regarding revolutionary war; and with an article on the French Army's proper ideological role, he tried to show how the West must defend itself against communist subversion and revolution.[1] At that same time, from 1951–54, French officers in the field in Indochina learned about revolutionary war, not from library research, but from their enemy, the Vietminh. Colonel Charles Lacheroy was sent to Indochina with the warning from his superiors that there would be little to learn from the unmechanized war he would fight there. He and many other captains, majors, and colonels returned believing, on the contrary, that "no period of our military career was as formative. . . ."[2]

The *guerre révolutionnaire* school soon won over many of the most dynamic and intelligent younger officers in the army. After 1955 the military press was filled with articles on the subject and on the related topic of psychological action (the two terms were sometimes used almost interchangeably). *Guerre révolutionnaire* theorists like Major Hogard, Colonel Nemo, Colonel Lacheroy, and even Captain Souyris became familiar figures to readers of the *Revue militaire d'information* and the *Revue de défense nationale.*[3] Under General Lecomte the Ecole de Guerre helped to spread the *guerre révolutionnaire* doctrine.[4] By 1957 the *guerre révolutionnaire* school had won over General Jacques Massu, Chief of Staff of National Defense Paul Ely, Algerian Resident Minister Robert Lacoste, and Defense Minister Maurice Bourgès-Maunoury. Under their patronage it became the official military doctrine of the French Army.[5] The *guerre révolutionnaire* school never succeeded in winning over the entire officer corps; yet it is significant that almost all of the political colonels of 1958-62 were strongly committed theorists or practitioners of that doctrine. Among them, one finds Colonels Broizat, Argoud, Lacheroy, Gardes, and Godard—the master strategists of military revolt.

The basic elements of the French military doctrine of *la guerre révolutionnaire* may be summarized in the following propositions. First, since the early 1950's a nuclear stalemate between East and West has rendered nuclear war most unlikely. In fact, the most probable form of war which the West will be forced to fight (indeed, which it is already fighting) is subversive, revolutionary war. Second, the universal revolutionary war now in progress is unlike conventional war in that its primary object is not defeat of the enemy army but physical and moral conquest of the population. Third, that same revolutionary war is being conducted by international communism and may be characterized as *permanent* and *universal*. It uses anticolonial nationalism as a tactic to overwhelm the West by surrounding and weakening it. The battle for Algeria, like that for Indochina before it, is part of World War III; its outcome may well be decisive in the struggle between communism and Western civilization. Fourth, in order to defend itself against the communist foe, the West must do the following: it must adapt to its own purposes some of the techniques of the enemy, especially in regard to propaganda, indoctrination, and organization; and it must perfect a Western ideology with which and for which to fight.

The second proposition has already been discussed in Chapters VI and VII above. The other three propositions merit further exploration.

Revolutionary War as Modern War

Most military theorists and strategists in the West now probably would accept the argument made by General Chassin in December, 1954, at a time when the United States was adopting a defense policy of "massive retaliation":

> Thus the appearance of the atomic bomb [wrote General Chassin] and especially that of the fission bomb diminishes the probability and the risk of a generalized war. . . . But what we have said above shows as well that if the atomic bomb diminishes the risk of a world war, it increases the risk of localized jungle wars—and of wars which we will lose if we are not careful.[6]

Similar statements were made by a number of military spokesmen from 1954 to 1958,[7] among them Colonel Lacheroy, head of the Information and Psychological Action Service at the Ministry of National Defense, who told a group of reserve officers in July, 1958:

> There are many of us in the officer corps who think that perhaps we will not have an atomic war, perhaps we will not have a conventional war; but revolutionary wars—alas, we will have many of them. We have them already. That is all we do. Well then, we do not want it always to end at Geneva![8]

Clearly, if present and future wars were to be of the revolutionary-guerrilla variety, the armed forces, or at least important elements within them, should be trained in the political, as well as the military, requirements of that style of combat.

So far the argument is close to that voiced by American critics of the massive-retaliation policy in the 1950's—critics who prevailed after 1961, when the Kennedy administration gave increasing attention to both conventional war and unconventional (revolutionary-guerrilla) war. In the third proposition, however, the more dubious ideological elements of *la guerre révolutionnaire* begin to appear.

Permanent and Universal Revolution

French officers who had learned of revolutionary-guerrilla war against a communist enemy in Indochina were quick to raise the cry of "communism" when again they faced a similar style of war in Algeria. For those Indochina veterans who viewed the Algerian rebels as simply the "Viets" displaced from tropical rice paddies to the North African *bled,* it seemed that the similarity between F.L.N. and communist tactics was proof enough that the rebellion was under the direction of Moscow.[9]

For the French military propagandist and for many relatively unsophisticated combat officers, there seemed no reason to mince words in regard to communism in North Africa. Among those officers interviewed by Claude Dufresnoy in 1959–60, a number spoke of the communist menace, the following comments being particularly noteworthy:

Captain X (regular army, Fifth Bureau): "The F.L.N. is only a manifestation of communism." [10]

Major N. (Fifth Bureau): "If we leave, tomorrow Russia will be here in our place. . . . It is us or the Russians, and in the long term, the paralysis of Europe and its gradual slide into the communist orbit." [11]

Colonel B. (regimental commander on the Tunisian border): "The subversive war must never be forgotten; the communists are winning ground. Ethiopia is entirely in their hands *(sic).* Egypt, Tunisia,

Morocco have entered the soviet orbit. . . . Believe me, give up
Algeria and it is the end for the West." [12]

*Major M. (regular army, stationed in the hinterland), when asked
what he would think if the government proposed new talks with the
F.L.N.:* "That would be the defeat of France: the last bastion against
communism would crumble." [13]

It was more than incidental that among those officers whom
Dufresnoy interviewed the "F.L.N. equals communism" equation
was frequently suggested by psychological-action officers.[14] *Le Bled,*
the tool of the Fifth Bureau, moved from cautious identification
of the F.L.N. with communism in 1957 to much greater daring in
November, 1959, when there appeared an article entitled "The
F.L.N., Instrument of Communism." [15]

As was so often the case, the Fifth Bureau had the full support
of Resident Minister Robert Lacoste on this matter in 1957–58. In
fact, in his General Directive Number Four of April, 1957, he went
beyond them:

The whole of North Africa would normally be expected to follow the
Western pattern, and only our civilization is capable of preventing
it from falling into chaos. Only an Algeria profoundly united with
France can also prevent neighboring countries from falling into
disorder and then into the communism which now animates the
subversion in a quasi-official manner.[16]

By "the subversion" Lacoste could only have meant the F.L.N.

Most theorists of *la guerre révolutionnaire,* however, were more
subtle. Intelligent military writers eager to avoid the ridicule of
civilian as well as military critics could not ignore facts so blatant
as the early French Communist Party denunciations of the F.L.N.,
the insistence of the latter that no alliance be formed with the
Algerian Communist Party, and F.L.N. acceptance thereafter of
individual Communist participation only on subordinate levels.[17]
Most frequently, theorists of *la guerre révolutionnaire* found it
unnecessary to assert that F.L.N. leaders were *conscious* Communist
agents. Indeed, one leading theorist of that school, Major Jacques
Hogard, frequently remarked (usually in footnotes) that the Algerian nationalist movement was not essentially communist. It

was enough to state, as did Hogard, that the movement was the creation and the instrument of international communism for the destruction .of protective colonial ties.[18]

The basic premise of the *guerre révolutionnaire* doctrine, stated by Major Hogard, was that "the Revolutionary War is 'one' in space, in time, and in its methods. . . . The enemy is 'one' from Paris to Saigon, from Algiers to Brazzaville." [19] For Hogard and for the *guerre révolutionnaire* school generally, revolutionary war was, by definition, a communist phenomenon. Only after 1960 did military writers begin to distinguish between a general category of "subversive war" and a communist subcategory of "revolutionary war."[20] At about the same time that Hogard's statement appeared (in early 1957), a similar idea was stated more forcefully, as might be expected, by *Message:* "It must finally be clear even to the blindest eyes that for years now we have been engaged in the Third World War." The Algerian war, the writers continued, was only one "tactical phase of the permanent revolutionary war." [21]

Basing their analysis on the self-declared intent of the second congress of the Communist International in 1920 to use bourgeois nationalism as a weapon against imperialism,[22] the *guerre révolutionnaire* theorists concluded that anticolonial uprisings everywhere are communist controlled and, if successful, will open the way (in the words of Chief of Staff Paul Ely) to "an inexorable process: independence, neutralism, satellization. . . ." [23] For Colonel Broizat, for example, "Algerian nationalism was an artificial dialectical creation," designed solely to serve the purposes of international communism.[24] Similarly, a Fifth Bureau colonel declared in April, 1959, "There is no Moslem nationalism. There is communism which uses nationalism; that is different." [25] Taking up the same theme, General André Zeller and fifteen other retired generals declared in a pre-referendum statement of January 4, 1961: "The truth is that the rebellion, which has touched only an infinite fraction of Algerian youth, was fomented and is directed by international communism." [26] Other military spokesmen, among them Generals Navarre and Massu, tended to subsume Arab nationalism in its entirety under the category of communist subversion.[27] In that manner the Algerian war and the Suez campaign of 1956 could both be fitted into a global anticommunist crusade.

Frequently the writings of the *guerre révolutionnaire* school linked the notion of permanent and universal revolutionary war with a neat and complete bifurcation of the world into communist and anticommunist camps and a firm conviction that international communism must either conquer the world or disappear entirely.[28] Hogard, for example, seems to have expected the communist bloc to remain forever united and intransigent, even though as early as 1954 some French military writers had anticipated a Chinese-Soviet rift.[29]

A further recurrent theme in the *guerre révolutionnaire* literature was the notion that the French Army, almost singlehandedly, was defending Western civilization from what might well be a fatal blow in Algeria. Testifying at the Barricades trial, Colonel Jean Gardes first discussed the novel style of revolutionary-guerrilla war and added:

> And then, a second sentiment which still animates me, which perhaps animates me more than in December when I took charge of the Fifth Bureau: that is that over there we are waging, we are still waging today, our last battle as free men.[30]

Message had voiced the same cry of alarm as early as February, 1956, when "Milites" wrote:

> In brief, Algeria appears to be the keystone of the French Union. Its loss would produce definitively that of the French Union, probably that of our political institutions. In effect, it is the fate of the West and that of Christianity which is at stake at the present time in Algeria.[31]

Four years later, in January, 1960, the warning was repeated by Major Cogniet in a lecture at the Ecole Supérieure de Guerre. Referring to the army's state of mind in Algeria before May 13, 1958, he announced: "Then that war, that war which without doubt is the last battle, that war which is without the least doubt the Verdun of the revolutionary war, we decided not to lose it."[32] The same warning that liberty, Christianity, and all of Western civilization would probably be lost with Algeria came from the lips and pens of General Salan, Colonel Argoud, and many others.[33]

More cautious military theorists like Hogard and Souyris stopped short of resting the entire fate of the Western world upon that of Algeria; all were agreed, however, that the French Army in Algeria —alone, misunderstood, and maligned—was helping to hold the dike of Western civilization against the menacing communist floods. Time and time again military spokesmen cried out in anguish and anger that all but the army were blind to the mortal danger of communist-revolutionary war. "One can truthfully say," wrote Captain Souyris in October, 1958, "that the [French] Army is at present almost the only body of the Nation which understands that the Third World War has already begun." [34] Why was the French Communist Party left free to work its subversion, officers demanded, when the revolutionary war was *one*—in Indochina, in Algeria, in France itself? [35]

As for the international scene, where the French Army was again viewed as a rare beacon of light in the West, why did the nation's supposed allies come to her aid so late in Indochina and then, in fact, sabotage her defenses in Algeria and in the Suez expedition? Why was the United States so naïve as to feed the communist fires of anticolonialism, so blind as to ignore the universal character of communist-revolutionary war, so narrowly self-interested as to believe that she could continue to ease France out of her colonies and then replace her, as in Vietnam? [36]

Confident in the belief that by virtue of its experience and awareness the French Army was destined to play the leading role in the Counter-Revolution,[37] the *guerre révolutionnaire* school disregarded its domestic critics and set off to rally support in allied military headquarters. On November 15, 1957, General Jacques Allard, Commander of the Algiers Army Corps, presented in effect an introductory lecture on the French military doctrine of *la guerre révolutionnaire* to an interallied group assembled at SHAPE headquarters at Fontainbleau.[38] The basic elements were all there in his presentation: the communist nature of the underlying enemy in Algeria, the vital importance of that province for Western defense, the inevitable "communization and satellization" of an independent Algeria, and the political and ideological character of revolutionary-guerrilla war. NATO failed to embrace Algeria as Allard wished,[39] but his speech was a further indication that the *guerre révolutionnaire* doctrine had the stamp of official French military approval.[40]

Fire against Fire

Once the universal and virtually omnipotent communist enemy had been identified, theorists of *la guerre révolutionnaire* turned to the problem of defense against him. On the practitioner's level, where Colonel Lacheroy first studied revolutionary-guerrilla war, defense was often viewed simply as a matter of turning the rebel's organizational and psychological weapons back against him or, rather, against the population which both adversaries sought to "conquer." Here two basic difficulties emerged which were never quite resolved: Are parallel hierarchies, conditioning of the masses, and small-group indoctrination simply neutral techniques as Lacheroy suggested, or do they also foreclose certain kinds of value objectives?[41] And second, are techniques alone sufficient for the conquest of the population or is the choice of goals of equal importance?

Colonels Lacheroy, Trinquier, Godard, and Argoud were more concerned with winning than with safeguarding freedom of the individual conscience, especially in view of the coercion to which the Moslem population was already subjected by the F.L.N.[42] Trinquier provides the most complete description of the "organization of the population" in his book *La Guerre moderne,* wherein he argues that the totalitarian controlling apparatus must be in place in time to *prevent* a subversive attack.[43] Given a cold-war setting, where the threat of subversion may be felt to be permanent, it would appear that Trinquier's scheme would lead inevitably to permanent controls of a police-state nature, relatively clandestine in "peacetime," more overt in time of crisis. In fact, when the anticommunist paranoia of the *guerre révolutionnaire* school is combined with its deification of totalitarian techniques, some of the elements for a military neo-fascism are already assembled, as Maurice Duverger pointed out in 1958.[44] When pushed to the wall after the failure of the putsch in April, 1961, theorists and practitioners of *la guerre révolutionnaire,* now rebels themselves in the O.A.S., did not hesitate to use terrorism, threats, and all the techniques for "conquest of the population" against the French people themselves.[45]

Yet, lest Trinquier and the O.A.S. colonels be taken as typical spokesmen, it must be recalled that the theory of parallel hierarchies (or "organization of the population," to use Trinquier's phrase) was not universally espoused in the *guerre révolutionnaire* literature and was applied in only a few cases in Algeria.[46] Nor were brain-washing techniques used extensively, despite the curious impact they had made upon officer-veterans of Vietminh prison camps, where lasting conversions had been extremely rare.[47] In principle, French military psychological action within the context of *la guerre révolutionnaire* was intended to shun the "violent," "deforming," "lying" propaganda of the enemy, which appealed to base emotions and manipulation of the subconscious, in favor of the "honest" and "objective" exposition of the truth.[48] It hardly need be added that within the context of *la guerre révolutionnaire,* truth was invariably interpreted to coincide with the case against Algerian independence.[49] More often than not, the Fifth Bureau in Algeria told the truth, but rarely the whole truth.

> As it is a question of techniques and only of techniques, there is no reason why Franco-Vietnamese technicians cannot do as well as those of the Vietminh—and more rapidly since they benefit from the experience of the enemy.[50]

So wrote Colonel Lacheroy shortly before the Indochinese war ended in armistice and partition. The images which Lacheroy uses so well in his speeches and writings are indicative of his unconcern for goals as opposed to techniques: once a population is held in an organizational vice, like a flower vase in the hand, the holder may then put in it whatever he desires. When a man's coat is to be remade for a boy, it must not simply be shortened; it must be unsewn completely, laid flat, recut, and then reconstructed. So with human society, the colonel suggests.[51] The old attitudes must be compromised, placed in doubt, and then replaced through intensive propaganda within the tight physical and moral controls of parallel organizational hierarchies.

For Lacheroy and his fellow theorists, the world of revolutionary war was largely one in which skilful manipulators could turn the masses in any chosen direction—if only the manipulators' skills were great enough. French military specialists in "psychological action" owed their faith in mass manipulation through propaganda partly to careful study of Serge Chakotin's *The Rape of the Masses*, a book written in 1939, before World War II experiences such as that of occupied France had revealed the toughness of the psychological defenses of a hostile population.[52] Unlike some officers of the Tract and Loudspeaker Company set, Lacheroy, Trinquier, and Godard —particularly the last two—were aware of the limited power of propaganda unless supported by tight organizational controls over the population. The power which they denied to propaganda, however (and Trinquier and Godard were at odds with the Fifth Bureau on this point), they tended to attribute to coercion, organization, and police controls, minimizing the significance of popular aspirations and grievances.[53] Trinquier was convinced that threats, coercion, and terror were the only reasons for the F.L.N.'s successes.[54]

Critics of the *guerre révolutionnaire* school have pointed out, and rightly so, that in viewing colonial rebellion as "an artificial dialectical creation" (Broizat), this doctrine seriously neglected the political and sociological terrain which gave the rebels their decisive advantage in both Indochina and in Algeria.[55] Had French military officers viewed revolutionary-guerrilla war in less manipulative terms, had they given more attention to grievances actually felt, it is quite likely that they would have rallied earlier and more vigorously to the campaign against colonial privileges. But even when acting as agents of reform, as they often did, French officers were inescapably aliens working with an unassimilated native population. In any case, basic reform was a domain in which the government, not the army, should have been expected to provide leadership.

A *Creed to Defend*

Though it may at first appear paradoxical, the *guerre révolutionnaire* school, which placed such faith in techniques as opposed to ideas, was also vitally concerned with the construction of a Western ideology to throw against international communism. The paradox, though real in some cases, was most often only apparent, for ideology was viewed simply as another necessary tool for the "conquest" of the population. To be sure, as discussed earlier, the very nature of revolutionary-guerrilla war forced the defending French Army to ask why it was fighting; for some officers, the answers found undoubtedly had real and binding force. For many theorists of *la guerre révolutionnaire,* however, ideology took on a more instrumental role. The existence of a French military search for an ideology after 1954 is obvious in the military press.[56] The results of that search, however, were ambiguous and diverse. No single, all-encompassing ideology ever won over a majority of the officer corps, though three contrasting points of view are evident among the searchers.

One group, closest to the mainstream of French political thought, preferred to speak, not of ideology, but of refinement of national ideals such as freedom, respect for the individual, and faith in reason, justice, and progress.[57] These writers, with their democratic and vaguely Christian ideal, together with others who emphasized a renaissance of patriotism,[58] were most representative of the official French military attitude as taught in most military schools as a base for psychological action.[59]

Two opposing groups of military ideologists were more determined to produce a complete Weltanschauung on which to base the anticommunist crusade. Jean Planchais refers aptly to these two doctrines as "National-Catholicism" and "National-Communism.[60]

Ever since the French Revolution laid siege to the privileges of the Church as well as to those of the aristocracy, there have been

French Catholics who have rejected the principles of '89 and the republics which have been built upon them. Even after Rome came to terms with republicanism in 1893, Catholic conservatives and pseudo-Catholic reactionaries (particularly Charles Maurras and the Action Française) continued to figure prominently among the enemies of the republic. The Vichy experience discredited the anti-republican Catholic camp, prompting many French Catholics in the postwar period to align with liberal and even anticolonial forces. Cold-war and colonial-war tensions rapidly revived Catholicism of the extreme Right, however, as anticommunism definitively replaced anti-Semitism and anti-Masonry as the major focus of political action from this quarter. Several minority organizations sprang up on the fringes of the Church espousing an *intégriste* style of Catholicism which rejected liberal democracy and drew an authoritarian political philosophy directly from a dogmatic view of Catholic theology. The best known of these, founded in 1946, was the Cité Catholique, whose clandestine cellular organization was inspired by the communist enemy.[61]

The political doctrine of the Cité Catholique is laid out in detail in its official journal, *Verbe*.[62] Among the recurrent themes are these: legitimate power stems, not from the people, but from God; all civil authority is subordinate to the natural order and to natural law; above all, subversion and revolution must not be allowed to undermine the natural moral order of society. In the view of the editors of *Verbe* popular sovereignty and freedom of expression are guilty of enthroning Error alongside Truth. Liberalism is described as wrong in itself and, worse, as incapable of defending against a greater evil—communism.

In 1956-57 la Cité Catholique took advantage of the services of a modern-day counterrevolutionary, Captain Gérard de Cathelineau, who created some hundred small *intégriste* cells among military personnel in Algeria.[63] Later acclaimed as a saint of the anticommunist crusade,[64] De Cathelineau described his mission in the following terms in a report prepared for a Cité Catholique conference shortly before the captain's death on an Algerian battlefield on July 12, 1957:

Psychological action in the Army is the order of the day. It has at its disposal an official Service at the Ministry of Armed Forces and its essential objective is to oppose a national Faith to the Marxist faith. But it has become evident that there is no serious foundation for that national Faith except in an authentic patriotism rooted in the light of the doctrines of the Church. The Cité Catholique has no other goal than to spread that light.[65]

Henceforth until early 1959 *Verbe* took care to dovetail its efforts with the emerging military doctrine of *la guerre révolutionnaire* and psychological action.

Early in 1958 *Verbe* opened its pages to a "theologian in uniform," [66] writing under the nom de plume of Cornelius. Cornelius affirmed the ultimate anticommunist character of the French struggle in Algeria, defended the right of the military officer to disobey his government when its orders threaten to allow a subversion of the "natural order," and justified the use of torture (for the common good) against prisoners who are clearly guilty.[67] This article was reprinted under the cover of the Tenth Military Region headquarters in Algiers in the review *Contacts* and helped to calm military consciences after the battle of Algiers. Cornelius raised serious protests from Catholic clergymen with his argument that, when necessary for defense of the natural order, torture was more than justified: it could be an act of "true charity." [68] Yet he was not without kindred spirits. A year earlier, during the battle of Algiers, a military chaplain with the Tenth Paratroop Division, Father Louis Delarue, had pronounced a sermon in which he justified, in certain circumstances, "an effective interrogation, without sadism." [69] Like another clergyman, Abbé G. de Nantes, who wrote in September and October, 1957, for the review *l'Ordre français,* Delarue did not restrict the use of torture to prisoners known to be guilty, as did Cornelius, though he admitted "serious" interrogation only in search of information, not confession.[70] Following Delarue's sermon, General Massu addressed a secret memorandum to his officers, thanking the chaplain and inviting "all worried and disoriented souls to listen to him," for "the condition *sine qua non* of our action in Algeria is that these methods be accepted in our souls and consciences as necessary and morally valid." [71] Undoubtedly, Delarue was not the only military chaplain to calm guilty consciences. [72] There were others, however, who condemned the use of torture without reserve.

To return to the Cité Catholique, it would appear that numerous military supporters of that organization were found among instructors at the Ecole de Guerre and especially among psychological-action officers, some of whom accepted *intégriste* Catholicism as an official doctrine. [73] Among those in attendance at the Cité Catholique conferences of 1959 and/or 1960 were Marshal Juin, Generals Weygand, Chassin, Touzet du Vigier, and Frémiot, and Admirals Auphan, De Penfentenyo, and Moreau. [74] Chief of Staff Paul Ely sent a letter of encouragement to the 1960 conference. [75] Cité Catholique was not totally the creature of military activism, however. Beginning in February, 1959, *Verbe* became highly critical of military psychological action and its penchant for manipulative psychological techniques which appeal to the unconscious, rather than to reason. [76] In the final analysis, the directors of Cité Catholique were Catholics first and counterrevolutionaries second. [77]

Primary loyalty to the Church was not so clear in the founder of the *intégriste* Centre d'Etudes Supérieures de Psychologie Sociale, Georges Sauge. [78] Moulding *intégriste* Catholicism into a *guerre révolutionnaire* setting, Sauge was received eagerly in all the important French military schools. [79] His widely distributed lecture entitled "L'Armée face à la guerre psychologique" was delivered to an audience which included, among others, General Jouhaud, chief of staff of the air force, General Blanc, former army chief of staff, and the inevitable General L. M. Chassin. [80] He combined staunch patriotism, religious sanction, revolutionary-war tactics borrowed from the Communists, abiding faith in the army as a counterrevolutionary force, and hostility to civilian politicians in a doctrine well suited to catch the military' ear. Of all *intégriste* spokesmen Sauge was probably the most influential in military circles, especially with the Fifth Bureau.

In addition to the Cité Catholique and to Sauge's "civic committees," for which he claimed seven thousand active supporters, there was a scattering of other *intégriste* counterrevolutionary organizations; notably, Armée-Nation, the Centre d'Etudes Politiques et Civiques, and the Cherrière-Chassin organization mentioned earlier.[81] Probably under the auspices of Cherrière's Counter-revolutionary Organization, a manual was circulated among military officers entitled *Contre-révolution, stratégie et tactique.* Here, in a text written by the Belgian journalist Pierre Joly, one finds an exposition of the *guerre révolutionnaire* doctrine imbued with a strong religious tone.[82] The entire French population is aligned by Joly according to its "revolutionary" or "counterrevolutionary" character, with trade unions, the F.L.N., communists, *Progressistes,* state-school teachers, families opposed to religious education, all political parties of the "system," and even the French National Council of Manufacturers—all of these falling into the camp of evil. But the forces of good are said to be represented by the army, the French in Algeria, veterans, nationalist organizations, and most of the clergy and the faithful of the Church.[83]

The penetration among military officers of the doctrine of Cité Catholique, Sauge, Joly, and other *intégriste* counterrevolution-aries is difficult to determine with precision. Among the leaders of military revolt Colonel Broizat, Colonel Gardes, General Chassin, and General Zeller were clearly all in the *intégriste* camp. Colonels Argoud and Lacheroy may have made some instrumental use of the doctrine, as did a number of Fifth Bureau officers; but they likely were not themselves of that persuasion, nor were Colonel Trinquier, General Challe, or General Salan. Among Catholics generally within the officer corps the *intégriste* line undoubtedly strengthened and sharpened a commitment to French Algeria which had other primary origins.[84] The example of General Walker and his "pro-Blue" campaign within the American Army (though he is atypical) indicates that cold-war tensions have produced advocates of authoritarian politico-religious solutions elsewhere than in the French Army.[85] Sauge and Schwartz (head of the Christian Anti-Communist Crusade), moreover, have much in common, despite their contrasting Catholic and Protestant origins.

A third group of officer-ideologues deserves mention under Planchais' label of "National Communism," though here one finds neither a consistent doctrine nor a supporting organization. In this group belong Colonel Argoud, a very influential figure in military-activist circles, perhaps Colonel Trinquier, and certain elements within the O.A.S.[86] This current of thought is distinguishable from the *intégriste* school by reason of its secularism, as well as by its socialist, reformist bent, which would benefit the Moslem population, the French working class, and the small businessman at the expense of wealthy "capitalist" segments of society. Especially among younger officers, the traditional military conservation of the pre-World War II era was giving way to a closer identification with the social and economic underdog.

A second striking feature of the National Communism group was its dual hostility toward international communism, which would destroy French national independence, and toward what Trinquier prefers to call "Great International Capitalism." As seen by these officers, capitalism in France is guilty of blocking reforms needed to restore the loyalty both of the Moslem population in Algeria and the communist working class in the *métropole,* and of continuing to lend powerful support to De Gaulle after 1959. In the United States the same capitalist forces are said to be guilty of toying with anticolonialism and of attempting to root France out of her economic spheres of influence—first from Indochina, and then from her Algerian oil fields. The argument is clearly stated in the party platform of Colonel Trinquier's "People's Party," founded in 1961. On the one hand, France is menaced by the communist revolution, he writes, while

> at the other end of the world another menace has raised itself: GREAT INTERNATIONAL CAPITALISM materialized in America. Between these two blocs which seek to divide the world between them, our civilization and we ourselves are in danger of disappearing.[87]

As for the greater of the two evils, Colonel Trinquier told the writer in 1962 that "if ever I were forced to choose between communism and Great International Capitalism, I would choose communism." [88]

Adding nationalism to socialism, is not the product then national socialism, a revival of that totalitarian and revolutionary spirit of the radical Right, born in France with the fascist leagues of the

1930's? Certainly some of the elements are present: rejection of both communism and large-scale capitalism by young officers, many of them with origins in the lower middle class;[89] fascination with power (what else is the deification of totalitarian techniques of organization?) with little systematic interest in the purposes to which it will be put; and hostility toward the supposed flabbiness of political liberalism. If honest, Argoud would probably have to plead guilty to the charge of fascism, especially in his O.A.S. period.[90] So, indeed, would General Salan's O.A.S. adviser, Jean-Jacques Susini, though that organization was united on little else other than the defense of French Algeria and perhaps revenge on De Gaulle. Trinquier's case is a bit more ambiguous. Known for his weakness for totalitarian solutions in Algeria, he claims in his public statements to have some respect for individual liberties and popular sovereignty.[91] As for the review, *Patrie et progrès*, which appeared in 1959 and was often labeled fascist, its young editors combined socialism and French patriotism in a fashion more reminiscent of the liberal-democratic socialism of Jean Jaurès than of the national socialism of Marcel Déat or Jacques Doriot.[92]

It is simple enough to lay out the basic propositions of the *guerre révolutionnaire* doctrine and the ideological questions on which unity was not achieved. A more difficult task, but one which must be undertaken with full knowledge of the incompleteness of the evidence available regarding French military attitudes, is that of assessing the power of the *guerre révolutionnaire* doctrine in producing military indiscipline and revolt in favor of the Counter-Revolution. It is a matter of record that the colonels who were instrumental in the "cold" military revolt of January, 1960, and the "hot" revolt of April, 1961, were almost without exception enthusiasts and theorists of *la guerre révolutionnaire*. Moreover, General Challe announced twice during the April putsch that the army's purpose was to protect Algeria—and the *métropole*—from the communist threat.[93] Nevertheless, there are numerous indications that ideological factors were of only secondary importance.

Throughout the Algerian war there remained a sizable element within the officer corps which was unconvinced either of the effectiveness of psychological action or of the ultimate communist nature of the enemy. To be sure, the more articulate and dynamic younger officers were mostly in the *guerre révolutionnaire* camp. Yet writers on the subject of psychological action and *la guerre révolutionnaire* frequently complained of fellow officers who were skeptics and scoffers on this subject. The lead article in the special February–March, 1957, issue of the *Revue militaire d'information* on "La Guerre révolutionnaire," for example, begins with the statement, "Military opinion today has become allergic to the words themselves, *guerre révolutionnaire*." [94] Occasionally, but only occasionally, the skeptics spoke out publicly. There was the captain who wrote to *Message* in October, 1956, arguing that "As for psychological action . . . all of those people are not only useless (and they know that themselves, I believe) but even harmful. . . ."[95] Another of the rare public scoffers dared to raise his protest against "the war of brains" and "the assault of the loudspeaker companies" in the *Revue militaire d'information,* and that in October, 1959, when psychological action was still riding high.[96] Publicly dissenting voices were scattered and little noticed until late in 1961, when "a group of officers" wrote a letter to *Combat* stating: "If the Algerian War proved anything on the level of military doctrine, it was the inanity of wanting to lead the battle within the population and to conquer it with an army which is not drawn from the population itself. . . ."[97]

Among general officers, the *guerre révolutionnaire* school made proportionally fewer converts than among field-grade officers. Allard, Massu, and Salan were converted, as was Ely to a large degree; but Challe remained only partially convinced, and his two successors as French commanders in Algeria, Generals Gambiez and Ailleret, like many other generals, had little sympathy for Colonel Lacheroy *et cie.*[98] Challe's decision to take the lead of the April putsch probably was occasioned much more by a feeling that his honor and that of the army were at stake in Algeria than by a fear that Western civilization was in jeopardy.[99] Challe's invocation of the communist bogeyman during the putsch was at least in part a tactical move to attract domestic and American support.[100]

On the whole, the reasons for which French officers were willing to disobey and revolt were emotional, unreflective, and incapable of being formed into an ideology which might guide a military dictatorship. It is significant that the dominant theme of military testimony in the trials following the April putsch was not anti-communism but humiliation and dishonor. To be sure, there were officers—Colonel Broizat was certainly one of them—for whom the anticommunist Counter-Revolution was a vital and consuming crusade. In most cases, however, including initially even that of Colonel Gardes, ideology served more as a rationalization for primarily visceral reactions to frustrations and humiliation. The doctrine of *la guerre révolutionnaire* undoubtedly systematized and fortified those reactions, especially on the part of many of the leaders of military revolt. Even among the leaders, however, one must distinguish between those who followed Salan into the O.A.S. and those who surrendered with Challe in April, 1961. Argoud, Gardes, Lacheroy, Broizat, Salan himself—these are the officers who were most deeply politicized, who were intent, not only upon saving French Algeria, but also upon establishing a new political order more capable of pursuing the anticommunist Counter-Revolution (though they did not all agree on the nature of the new order). These men represented a small minority within the total officer corps. Even within that minority, moreover, and to a greater extent among the hesitant majority of the officer corps, one must seek the roots of praetorianism, not so much in ideology, as in less reflective emotional responses to a decade and a half of defeat, humiliation, and embitterment and to that prospective Algerian independence which seemed to threaten military honor, pride, and status.[101]

1. Chassin's writings include: *La Conquête de la Chine par Mao Tse-tung* (Paris: Payot, 1952); two articles by the same title, one in *RMI*, No. 169 (February 25, 1951), pp. 12–17, and the other in *RMI*, No. 170 (March 10–25, 1951), pp. 19–25; *L'Ascension de Mao Tse-tung* (Paris: Payot, 1953); and "Du rôle idéologique de l'armée," *RMI*, No. 239 (October 10, 1954), pp. 13–19.

2. Lacheroy, in *La Défense nationale*, p. 308. For Lacheroy's early writings on revolutionary-guerrilla war see above, Chapter 6, note 16. Other early French military students of revolutionary-guerrilla war included Colonel M. de Crèvecoeur and Captain André Souyris. See Crèvecoeur,, "Le Problème militaire français en Indochine," a lecture at the Ecole Supérieure de Guerre

in April, 1952, mimeographed by the Section de Documentation Militaire de l'Union Française (SDMUF); and Crèvecoeur, "Aperçus sur la stratégie du Viet-Minh," SDMUF, 1953. By Souyris see "L'Auto-défense des populations," *RDN*, June, 1956, pp. 686–99.

3. The French military literature on *la guerre révolutionnaire* is voluminous. Only some of the more important pieces will be listed here. The best-known general work on the subject was the special issue of *RMI* entitled "La Guerre révolutionnaire" (No. 281 [February–March, 1957]). See particularly the introductory article by "Ximenès" (a pseudonym) and the concluding article by Captain André Souyris. Perhaps the most careful writer of the *guerre révolutionnaire* group, and one of the most influential, was Commandant Jacques Hogard. His major articles are: "Guerre révolutionnaire ou révolution dans la guerre," *RDN*, December, 1956, pp. 1497–1513; "L'Armée Française devant la guerre révolutionnaire," *RDN*, January, 1957, pp. 77–89; "Guerre révolutionnaire et pacification," *RMI*, No. 280 (January, 1957), pp. 7–24; "Le Soldat dans la guerre révolutionnaire," *RDN*, February, 1957, pp. 211–26; "Tactique et stratégie dans la guerre révolutionnaire," *RMI*, No. 295 (June, 1958), pp. 23–35; and "Cette guerre de notre temps," *RDN*, August–September, 1958, pp. 1304–19. See also Colonel Charles Lacheroy, "La Guerre révolutionnaire," in Centre de Sciences Politiques de l'Institut d'Etudes Juridiques de Nice (ed.), *La Défense nationale*, pp. 307–30; Colonel Nemo, "La Guerre dans le milieu social," *RDN*, May, 1956, pp. 605–23, and Nemo, "La Guerre dans la foule," *RDN*, June, 1956, pp. 721–34; Claude Delmas, *La Guerre révolutionnaire* ("Que Sais-je" series [Paris: Presses Universitaires de France, 1959]); and, in English, George A. Kelly, "Revolutionary War and Psychological Action," *Military Review*, No. 11 (October, 1960), pp. 4–13; and Paret, *French Revolutionary Warfare*, especially chaps. 1–3.

4. René Delisle, "La Crise interne du corps des officiers," *La Nef*, No. 7 (July–September, 1961), pp. 44–45.

5. Ely, *RMI*, No. 297 (August–September, 1958), p. 9; and "Perspectives stratégiques d'avenir," *RDN*, November, 1958, pp. 1631–40. With respect to Lacoste and Bourgès–Maunoury, see above, Chapters 7 and 8.

6. "Réflexions stratégiques sur la guerre d'Indochine," *RDN*, December, 1954, p. 513.

7. Lieutenant Colonel Th. J. Delaye, "Cette guerre sans loi qui nous est imposée," *Message*, No. 7 (February, 1955) p. 23; Capitaine de Corvette X, "La 3ᵉ Guerre Mondiale n'aura pas lieu," *Message*, No. 11 (December, 1955), pp. 12–16; Marshal Alphonse Juin, "Que devons–nous penser de la sécurité française?" *RDN*, January, 1957, pp. 14–16; "Milites" (pseudonym), "L'Algérie, l'armée et la révolution," *Message*, February, 1957 (partially quoted in *RMI*, No. 283 [March, 1957], p. 103; and B. H. Liddel Hart (the famous British military writer), "Les Problèmes fondamentaux de la défense de l'Europe," *RDN*, January, 1959, pp. 19–34.

8. The lecture was originally given to reserve officers of the first military region at the Sorbonne, July 2, 1957. It was mimeographed by the Service d'Information et d'Action Psychologique and then reprinted in *La Défense nationale*. The quotation, in the last source, is on p. 330.

9. See Servan-Schreiber's description of Lieutenant Antoine ("Martin") in *Lieutenant en Algérie*, p. 19; and J.-J. Thieuloy, "L'Esprit 'para' décrit par un para," *L'Esprit*, July 10, 1958, p. 15. As intelligent an officer as Colonel Broizat argued in the Barricades trial that communist tactics were proof of communist intent. Presumably he would not draw similar conclusions

with regard to the French Army or the Secret Army Organization when they adopted some of the tactics of revolutionary war: propaganda, organization, and in the case of the O.A.S., terrorism. See *Un Procès*, p. 32.

10. Dufresnoy, *Des officiers parlent*, p. 8.

11. *Ibid.*, p. 49.

12. *Ibid.*, pp. 180–81.

13. *Ibid.*, p. 197. See also *ibid.*, pp. 25–26, 75.

14. Three of the six.

15. Nor, the writer adds, is it an unconscious instrument (November 7, 1959, p. 7). See also, "Le F.L.N. et le communisme," *Le Bled*, No. 45 (February 16, 1957), p. 4, wherein Nasser is described as sympathetic to the Soviets.

16. In Déon, *L'Armée d'Algérie*, Annex V, p. 236. Lacoste's earlier directives had warned against Arab dictatorship (No. 1, May 19, 1956), and against communist collaboration with the F.L.N. (No. 3, November 30, 1956). Only in April, 1957, however, did he speak of the "quasi-official" communist nature of the F.L.N. (*ibid.*, pp. 208, 224, 236).

17. See Chapter 7 n. 26 above. The policy of the F.L.N. after independence, notably the outlawing of the Algerian Communist Party, tended to verify the wisdom of distinguishing shades of gray between Western democracy and communism.

18. Hogard, "L'Armée Française devant la guerre révolutionnaire," *RDN*, January, 1957, p. 78 n.; and, by the same writer, "Cette guerre de notre temps," *RDN*, August–September, 1958, p. 1313 n. 14. See also Captain André Souyris, "Les Conditions de la parade et de la riposte à la guerre révolutionnaire," in the special issue of *RMI* entitled *La Guerre révolutionnaire*, No. 281 (February–March, 1957), pp. 93–95.

19. Hogard, *RDN*, January, 1957, pp. 78, 86. See also the above-mentioned article by the same writer in *RDN*, December, 1956, pp. 1508–9; Colonel de Villiers de l'Isle-Adam, "Cette guerre de notre siècle," *RDN*, July, 1956, p. 885; and Colonel Nemo, "Combat de mêlée et défense nationale," *RDN*, August–September, 1957, pp. 1289–1303.

20. It may well be that the high command and the military schools took to heart some of the criticisms leveled against the *guerre révolutionnaire* doctrine by, among others, Raoul Girardet, who was a part-time instructor at the Ecole Supérieure de Guerre for a time. See Girardet's "Réflexions critiques sur la doctrine militaire française de la guerre révolutionnaire," a paper presented to the Académie des Sciences Morales et Politiques, June 20, 1960 (mimeo.).

21. "Milites," *Message*, February, 1957, quoted in the review section of *RMI*, No. 283 (May, 1957), p. 103.

22. Lenin, "Preliminary Draft of the Theses on the National and Colonial Questions," and Lenin's introductory remarks to the second congress of the Communist International, in Lenin, *Selected Works* (New York: International Publishers, 1938), X, 231–38, 239–41.

23. Ely, *RMI*, No. 297 (August–September, 1958), p. 9. This same point made by Ely is also stressed, especially with regard to Algeria, by Chassin, "Vers un encerclement de l'Occident?" *RDN*, May, 1956, p. 551; Hogard, *RDN*, August–September, 1958, p. 1313 n. 14; Hogard, *RMI*, No. 295 (June, 1958), p. 33 n.; General Maurice Challe in *Procès Challe*, p. 38; and Jacques Soustelle in an interview given to the *National Review* in June, 1962, as

reported in *LM*, June 9, 1962. In regard to the linkage of anticolonialism with communism, see especially the articles by Captain André Souyris in *RMI*, No. 281 (February–March, 1957), pp. 93–94; and, also by Souyris, "Réalité et aspects de le guerre psychologique," *RMI*, No. 302 (February, 1959), p. 8.

24. Broizat, in the Barricades trial, as recorded in *Un Procès*, pp. 37–38. For a similar statement see Hogard in *RMI*, No. 295 (June, 1958), p. 23.

25. Colonel N. in Dufresnoy, *Des officiers parlent*, p. 25.

26. Quoted in Fauvet and Planchais, *La Fronde des généraux*, p. 42.

27. See Navarre's discussion of the Egyptian nationalization of the Suez Canal in *Agonie de l'Indochine*, pp. 327–28 ("Elle est dirigée de Moscou, dont les nationalistes arabes sont les instruments plus ou moins conscients"); and Massu's secret directive to his officers of the *Zone nord algérois* on March 19, 1957, in Vidal-Naquet, *Secrets d'état*, p. 110.

28. Hogard, in *RDN*, August–September, 1958, pp. 1308–9; and Broizat, letter to *LM*, January 20, 1961.

29. Hogard, *ibid.*, p. 1311. The most insistent French military prophet of a Sino-Soviet split was General L. M. Chassin. See, for example, his article, "Réflexions stratégiques sur la guerre d'Indochine," *RDN*, December, 1954, p. 512.

30. *Un Procès*, p. 56. An almost identical phrase was included in the message sent by Colonel Marcel Bigeard to the insurgents in Algiers during the Week of the Barricades. The presence of Colonel Gardes at Bigeard's side in Saïda explains the similarity of language (Brombergers *et al.*, *Barricades et colonels*, p. 378).

31. "Milites," *RMI*, No. 270 (April 10, 1956), p. 44, reprinted from *Message*, No. 12 (February, 1956). A month later, on March 14, 1956, Minister of Defense Bourgès-Maunoury adopted a similar attitude in regard to the French nation, if not with respect to Western civilization generally. In a message to all military officers, he stated: "I am profoundly convinced that the nation is each day growng more aware that the loss of Algeria—which would lead to the loss of all of overseas France—would represent its irremediable decadence" (*RMI*, No. 269 [March 25, 1956], opposite p. 1).

32. Cogniet, "Fondements idéologiques et principes d'emploi de l'action psychologiques," lecture at the Ecole Supérieure de Guerre, January 6, 1960, p. 51 (mimeo.).

33. In a statement made from Spain in the fall of 1959, Salan said, "L'Algérie doit rester française si nous voulons sauvegarder l'essence même de la liberté et de la religion" (Fauvet and Planchais, *La Fronde des généraux*, p. 33). Two and a half years later, at his own trial, Salan testified, "Je n'ai pas à me disculper d'avoir défendu, avec la France, située au sud de la Méditerranée, l'ensemble du monde libre, même dans l'indifférence de ce monde libre" (*Procès Salan*, p. 88). The same theme of defense of Western civilization was evoked by the following: Colonel Argoud (reading a declaration by Ortiz of which he approved), in *Sans commentaire*, p. 90; General Challe, in *Procès Challe*, pp. 37–38; Major François Raoul, in *Procès du putsch*, p. 182; "Milites," "Morale de la guerre et morale de l'armée," *Message*, No. 23 (April, 1957), p. 1; "Comprendre pour vouloir," *Message*, No. 29 (April, 1958), p. 5; General P. Ely, "Les Problèmes français et l'équilibre mondial," *RDN*, November, 1959, p. 1720; and P. Arrighi in *Procès Challe*, p. 252.

34. "L'Action psychologique dans les forces armées," *RMI*, No. 298 (October, 1958), p. 38. See also the article by an anonymous group of

officers entitled "L'Armée est-elle fasciste?" *Courrier de la nation,* No. 4 (August 7, 1958), pp. 9–12.

35. Hogard, *RDN,* January, 1957, p. 88; Navarre, *Agonie de l'Indochine,* p. 332; and "Liberté, Egalité, Fraternité," *Message,* No. 28 (March, 1958), p. 6.

36. For examples of the frequent anti-American strain in the writings of the *guerre révolutionnaire* school, see Chassin, *RDN,* May, 1956, pp. 531–53; General Jacques Allard, "L'OTAN et l'Afrique du Nord," *RDN,* June, 1958, pp. 907–11; Georges R. Manue, "La Leçon de Suez," *RDN,* October, 1956, pp. 1155–64; Ely, *RDN,* November, 1958, p. 1638; Ingénieur Général Combaux, "Nécessité d'une Eurafrique," *RDN,* December, 1957, pp. 1814–26; and editorial, *Message,* No. 28 (March, 1958) pp. 1–2. See also Chapter 10 n. 11 above.

37. "The French Army is the first army in the world which has agreed to fight on the ground of the human mind, on the ground chosen by the communist Revolution to destroy Western Civilization" ("Actualités d'Algérie," *Contacts,* March, 1958, pp. 13–14). On the same point see Nemo, *RDN,* May, 1956, p. 606; and Ely, *RDN,* November, 1958, p. 1640.

38. The text was printed in *RDN,* January, 1958, pp. 6–41, under the title, "Vérités sur l'affaire algérienne." See also Allard's later article in *RDN,* June, 1958, pp. 907–11.

39. At the time of the April putsch of 1961 the rumor circulated in Algiers and in Paris that the United States was behind General Challe. Kennedy rapidly demonstrated the falsity of the claim, but suspicions lingered of secret encouragement to Challe on the part of CIA agents or U.S. military officers in France. The story remains clouded in mystery, through it is quite possible that a few American officers in France bought the *guerre révolutionnaire* line and its political consequences (Fauvet and Planchais, *La Fronde des généraux,* pp. 265–67).

40. In an article of his own in November, 1958, General Ely adopted many of the themes of that doctrine, though in more guarded fashion than Allard (*RDN,* November, 1958, pp. 1631–40). See also Ely, "The Role of the French Army Today," *Réalités* (English edition), No. 125 (April, 1961), pp. 45–47.

41. Lacheroy, "La Campagne d'Indochine ou une leçon de guerre révolutionnaire," SDMUF, July, 1954, pp. 27–28.

42. *Ibid.,* p. 28; Argoud, in *Sans commentaire,* p. 29 (his "tryptique" of *protection, engagement, and contrôle*); and Trinquier, *La Guerre moderne,* pp. 18–19, 51–58, 188.

43. "Tout pays qui ne l'a pas mis en place risque en permanence d'être envahi" (p. 58).

44. See the chapter entitled "Un Fascisme d'un type nouveau?" in Duverger's book, *Demain la république,* pp. 127–36. See also Meisel, *The Fall of the Republic.*

45. See the excellent article by J. Planchais, "L'O.A.S. et la 'mise en condition,'" in *LM,* December 16, 1961.

46. See above, Chapter 7. Lacheroy, Trinquier, Godard, and Argoud were probably all favorable to the extension of the Algiers "organization of the population" to the entire population of Algeria, if not of France. Captain H. Martin took a similar position in "Guérilla, guerre en surface, guerre révolutionnaire," *RMI,* No. 286 (August, 1957), pp. 7–22; and *ibid.,* No. 288 (November, 1957), pp. 61–71. Like most other specialists, Captain André Souyris was less explicit than Trinquier, but nevertheless insistent on "une mobilisation

physique et morale de la population" (*RMI*, No. 281, [February–March, 1957], pp. 104–6). Major Hogard, however, while favoring the creation of a multiplicity of professional and self-defense organizations, shied from commitment to a more complete, totalitarian concept. See, for example, his rules of counter-revolutionary war in *RMI*, No. 295 (June, 1958), pp. 23–35.

47. De Braquilanges, "Cours de guerre subversive: Méthode psychologique utilisée pour forcer l'adhésion des esprits," Ecole d'Etat-Major, 1956–57, mimeo., and D'Esnon and Prestat, *Revue des forces terrestres*, pp. 31–46.

48. Souyris, *RMI*, No. 298 (October, 1958), pp. 40–45. Souyris' concluding remark is well taken but all too rare in the *guerre révolutionnaire* literature, and even in Souyris' own writings: "Renoncer, en effet, à un certain nombre de valeurs fondamentales de notre civilization, par souci d'efficacité, ce serait renoncer à la proie pour l'ombre, nous placer sur le même terrain que nos adversaires et nous condamner à une defaite psychologique qui annoncerait l'effondrement du monde que nous entendons défendre" (*ibid.*, p. 15). Similar warnings were made by Major Thillaud, "Vaincre sans trahir," *RDN*, April, 1958, pp. 643–53; and in "L'Action psychologique: Légitimité-limites," *Message*, No. 32 (November, 1958), pp. 1–6. See also Colonel Broizat's protest to a statement in *LM*, which suggested that he had adopted the methods of the enemy (*LM*, January 20, 1961). The original article "Un 'templier' des temps modernes," by J.-M. Théolleyre, appeared in *LM*, January 15–16, 1961.

49. See the article in *RDN* by a high ranking overseas administrator (J. Perrin, "L'Algérie et l'information," *RDN*, December, 1958, pp. 1935–44).

50. Lacheroy, "La Campagne d'Indochine," p. 27.

51. *Ibid.*, pp. 21–22; and in *La Défense nationale*, p. 317. Lacheroy used the coat analogy again in the speech found in *ibid.*, pp. 319–20, though here he seems to be describing only Vietminh brainwashing techniques and not, as in the earlier article, the general technique of mass conditioning which he hoped the French would use. The vase analogy was taken up by Captain Souyris in *RMI*, No. 281 (February–March, 1957), p. 99.

52. London, 1940 (originally printed as *Le Viol des foules*, [Paris, 1939]). In regard to French military attention to this work, see Megret, *L'Action psychologique*, p. 34.

53. Trinquier believed that psychological action was ineffective until after the rebel organization had been crushed. Because of his disagreement with the Fifth Bureau on this and a few other points, he never considered himself part of the *guerre révolutionnaire* school (interview, April 2, 1962).

54. Trinquier, *La Guerre moderne*, pp. 28, 40–44, 56–57, 175–76. See also Captain Amphioxus, "La Guerre en Algérie: Regards de l'autre côté," *RDN*, January, 1959, pp. 82–91.

55. Professor Georges Vedel, quoted by General Jean Valluy in "Armée Française, 1961: De quelques prolongements," *La Revue des deux mondes*, September, 1961, pp. 6–7; Girardet, "Réflexions critiques sur la doctrine militaire française de la guerre subversive," p. 8; and André Stil. "L'Idéologie de la dictature militaire," *La nouvelle revue internationale* (a communist review), No. 11 (July, 1959), pp. 116–27. For one of those rather rare articles in the *guerre révolutionnaire* literature which dealt extensively with social, economic, and political inequities in Algeria, see "Ximenès" (pseudonym), "Guerre révolutionnaire en Algérie," *RMI*, No. 297 (August–September, 1958), pp. 27–40.

56. See Chapter 7 n. 111 above; and "Enquête sur la crise de l'armée," *Message*, No. 18 (December, 1956), pp. 14–16; "Eléments pour une doctrine," *Message*, No. 26 (December, 1957), pp. 1–4; General Paul Ely (when chief

of staff of national defense), "Les véritables espérances de la France et de l'Occident," *RMI*, No. 298 (October, 1958), pp. 7–10; and, also by Ely, *Réalités*, April, 1961, pp. 45–47; Jean Brune, "L'Armée à la recherche d'une doctrine," *La Nation française*, No. 192 (June 10, 1959), pp. 6–7; and Girardet, "Pouvoir civil et pouvoir militaire en France," pp. 28–30.

57. Major J. Vial, "Pour un humanisme militaire," *RMI*, No. 245 (January, 1955), pp. 19–24; "Un idéal pour l'armée? Non, un idéal pour la nation," *Message*, No. 7 (February, 1955), pp. 7–11; Marcel Clément, "Les Valeurs que nous défendons," *RMI*, No. 313 (February, 1960), pp. 7–13; and Lieutenant Colonel Etienne, "L'Armée, la parade et la riposte psychologique" (Part II), *RMI*, No. 319 (August–September, 1960), pp. 16–21.

58. Captain X, "A la recherche d'un nouveau patriotisme," *Message*, No. 10 (October, 1955), pp. 3–7; "X . . . " "Réponse aux partisans d'une petite France," *RDN*, June, 1956, pp. 671–85; Colonel René de Metz, "Une idée force: Laquelle?" *RDN*, March, 1957, pp. 347–58; Ely, *RMI*, No. 298 (October, 1958), pp. 7–10; General J. Valluy, "Se défendre? Contre qui? Pourquoi? Comment?" *RDN*, November, 1960, pp. 1739–50; and Valluy's book by the same title (Paris: Plon, 1960).

59. Girardet, "Pouvoir civil et pouvoir militaire en France," pp. 28–29.

60. *LM*, April 3, 1959; *ibid.*, April 4, 1959.

61. The earliest beginnings of the Cité Catholique go back to 1938–39, though 1946 was the date when its immediate precursor, the Centre d'Etudes Critiques et de Synthèse, was formed. The Centre was renamed the Cité Catholique in 1949 (Jacques Maître, "Le Catholicisme d'extrême droite et la croisade anti-subversive," *Revue française de sociologie*, II, No. 2 [April–June, 1961], 106–17).

62. See especially the long series of articles entitled "Introduction à la politique," printed in 1960–61 (*Verbe*, Nos. 107–9, 111, 112, 114, 116–20).

63. De Cathelineau, "Le Rôle d'un animateur en unité opérationnelle," *Verbe*, August–September, 1957, pp. 120–23; and Michel Gasnier, O.P., *Un officier français: Le Capitaine Gérard de Cathelineau* (Paris: Nouvelles Editions Latines, 1960). The estimate of one hundred cells is from Fauvet and Planchais, *La Fronde des généraux*, pp. 68–69. According to de Cathelineau's report, these cells were made up primarily of half a dozen enlisted men per cell (*Verbe*, August–September, 1957, pp. 122–23). *Verbe* claimed in 1958 that military personnel made up only 3.5 per cent of the total number of its cell members, many of the civilians being drawn from professional circles, especially teachers and doctors (H. Fesquet, " 'Verbe,' revue de la Cité Catholique renie les principes de la révolution," *LM*, July 9, 1958).

64. See the Preface to Gasnier's biography, cited above, by General Arnoux de Maison Rouge, commandant of the Ecole Supérieure de Guerre, pp. 7–8.

65. De Cathelineau, *Verbe*, August–September, 1957, p. 122.

66. The description is from Fauvet and Planchais, *La Fronde des généraux*, p. 69.

67. "Cornelius" (pseudonym), "Morale et guerre révolutionnaire," *Verbe*, No. 90 (February, 1958), pp. 79–80; *ibid.*, No. 91 (March, 1958), pp. 68–71; and *ibid.*, No. 92 (April, 1958), pp. 55–75.

68. *Ibid.*, (No. 92), p. 68. For protests and Cornelius' rebuttal to them, see "Pour et contre Cornelius," *Verbe*, No. 101 (April, 1959), pp. 4–25.

69. This sermon was published in June, 1957, by *Alger université*, journal of the Algiers student association. It was picked up by *Témoignage chrétien*, June 21, 1957. See the background sketch of Delarue in *LM*, May 22, 1962.

See also Vidal-Naquet, *La Raison d'état,* pp. 108–9, from which the quotation is taken. Delarue made news again on November 14, 1960, when in a funeral ceremony for a member of the First Foreign Paratroop Regiment at Zeralda he said, "Vous êtes tombés à un moment où, si nous en croyons les discours, nous ne savons plus pour qui nous mourrons" (*LM,* May 22, 1962). He was then released from army service. In the Salan trial in May, 1962, he refused to condemn O.A.S. terrorism (*Procès Salan,* pp. 303–7).

70. *LM,* May 22, 1962; and De Nantes, "Morale et torture," *L'Ordre fran-çais,* September, 1957, pp. 52–64; *ibid.* (Part II), October, 1957, pp. 17–28; and *ibid.,* November, 1957, p. 56 (a rejoinder to a letter). Nantes found the immobile government of the Fourth Republic to be much more guilty than the army, for the latter was merely attempting to defend the *corps social.*

71. From the text of the memorandum, dated March 19, 1957, numbered 2616/2, as found in Vidal-Naquet, *La Raison d'état,* p. 110.

72. See Simon, *Portrait d'un officier,* pp. 133–41; and Father Ducatillon, "Le Sens chrétien de la vocation militaire," a sermon given in Saint Louis Chapel at the Ecole Militaire in Paris, May 26, 1957, printed in *L'Order français,* July–August, 1957, pp. 3–7.

73. Maître, *Revue française de sociologie,* p. 114; and Fauvet and Planchais, *La Fronde des généraux,* pp. 70–71.

74. Fauvet and Planchais, *La Fronde des généraux,* pp. 69–70 n. 2.

75. *Ibid.*

76. "Pour une doctrine catholique de l'action politique et sociale" (Part C), *Verbe,* No. 99 (February, 1959), pp. 1–22.

77. Cité catholique received papal greetings before its annual congresses (*Verbe,* August–September, 1957, p. 1). Yet Rome was concerned with Cité Catholique's tendency to define Catholic doctrine and its supposed political requirements. An unofficial warning against Cité Catholique was circulated at the Assembly of Cardinals and Archbishops in March, 1961 (Meisel, *Fall of the Republic,* p. 245, citing *LM,* November 10, 1961, p. 8) In comparison with other *intégriste* organizations, however, Cité was moderate in tone.

78. The "Centre" was founded in 1956. Sauge was later arrested briefly during the Week of the Barricades. He was not disturbed during the April putsch and the ensuing O.A.S. campaign, though he continued to campaign for French Algeria (Faucher, *Les Barricades d'Alger,* p. 294; *LM,* April 5, 1962).

79. Fauvet and Planchais, *La Fronde des généraux,* p. 66.

80. At the eighteenth "diner-débat" of the Centre d'Etudes Politiques et Civiques (C.E.P.E.C.), April 30, 1959, printed as Cahier No. 11, *Les Cahiers du C.E.P.E.C.* The lecture was also printed in *La Saint-Cyrienne* and in *Rhin-Danube,* a journal of a veterans' association.

81. In regard to "Armée-Nation," see Daniel, *L'Express,* March 3, 1960, pp. 10–11; and Fauvet and Planchais, *La Fronde des généraux,* p. 75.

82. According to Tournoux (*Secrets d'état,* p. 193), this manual dates originally from 1943. A Liège, Belgium, edition dates from the mid-1950's. The manual was then reprinted in Paris in 1958 by Berger-Levrault. Its contents are summarized in Azeau, *Révolte militaire,* pp. 37–43; and in Paret, *French Revolutionary Warfare,* pp. 115–19.

83. *Contre-révolution, stratégie et tactique* (Liège ed.), pp. 88–89, as cited by Azeau, *Révolte militaire,* pp. 41–42.

84. For examples of *intégriste* sentiments within the army during the Algerian war, see the following: Dufresnoy, *Des officiers parlent,* pp. 10, 52, 137;

"Le Sens chrétien de la vocation militaire," *Message,* No. 25 (November, 1957), pp. 1–4; L. L., "Du rôle politique de l'armée," *Message,* No. 31 (October, 1958), pp. 1–8; and the surprisingly eulogistic review of Oliveira Salazar, *Principes d'action,* in *Message,* No. 17 (November, 1956), p. 29. For an expression of a political philosophy very similar to that of *Verbe,* written by a leader of the Secret Army Organization after Algerian independence, see Colonel Pierre Chateau-Jobert, *Manifeste politique et social* (Meaux: Editions du Fuseau, 1964).

85. Significantly enough, the John Birch Society, with which Walker has been affiliated, warned in its July, 1963, bulletin against a communist-inspired Negro separationist movement in the U.S. after the pattern of the allegedly communist-directed nationalist movement in Algeria (*NYT,* western edition, August 16, 1963).

86. See the two biographical articles on Argoud in *LM,* February 28, 1963; Brune, *La Nation française,* No. 192 (June 10, 1959), pp. 6–7; and the O.A.S. "program" described in *L'Express,* June 15, 1961.

87. "Nécessité d'un parti du peuple," (Paris: Association pour l'Etude de la Réforme des Structures de l'Etat," n.d.), pages unnumbered. See also the summary of one current of thought within the O.A.S. in Azeau, *Révolte militaire,* pp. 251–53.

88. Interview, April, 1962. In his party platform Trinquier is somewhat milder, pledging his party to abide by Atlantic Alliance commitments.

89. See Chapter 5 above regarding the social origins of younger officers.

90. See the articles by Planchais and A. Jacobs in *LM,* February 28, 1963.

91. In a speech on *la guerre révolutionnaire* given to students at the Université d'Alger on June 7, 1958, he argued that the population must renounce (temporarily?) "un certain individualisme" in order to survive. He concluded, "Mais ce n'est pas un but, les militaires sont démocrates" (*LM,* July 10, 1958). See also the platform of the Parti du Peuple cited above.

92. See, for example, the editorials in the issues of November, 1959 (pp. 1–2), and December, 1959 (p. 1), and the article urging socialism on the army (p. 8 in the same December issue). See also, by one of the founders of *Patrie et progrès,* Jacques Gagliardi, *Les Hexagonaux* (Paris: Plon, 1962), especially chap. 10.

93. April 22, in a radio address: "Un gouvernement d'abandon s'apprête à livrer les départements d'Algérie à la rébellion. Voulez-vous que Mers-el-Kébir et Alger soient demain des bases soviétiques?"; and April 24, to a crowd in the Forum: "Les militaires ont pris le pouvoir pour que l'armée puisse sauvegarder la métropole du danger communiste qui la menace et établir une paix véritable en Algérie" (as quoted in Fauvet and Planchais, *La Fronde des généraux,* pp. 117 and 211).

94. "Ximenès," "Essai sur la guerre révolutionnaire," *RMI,* No. 281 (February–March, 1957), p. 1. He continues: "Certains nient qu'il existe d'autres formes de guerre que celles de la guerre classique, d'autres s'empêtrent dans un jargon nouveau, d'autres enfin dénoncent une sorte de fatalité inexorable" (*ibid.,* p. 9). See also Captain C., "Action psychologique en Algérie," *Message,* No. 16 (October, 1956), p. 19; and Delisle, *La Nef,* pp. 39–50. By 1958 the *guerre révolutionnaire* school had increased its number of converts. Even in its heyday, however, a large number of officers remained unconvinced.

95. Letter from an unnamed captain, *Message,* No. 16 (October, 1956), p. 24. The captain goes on to say that communism plays only a very secondary role in the Algerian war.

96. "Simplet" (pseudonym), "Guerre révolutionnaire, guerre psychologique, ou guerre 'tout court'?" *RMI*, No. 309, (October, 1959), pp. 97–102. A spokesman for the *guerre révolutionnaire* school hastened to reply (Un Chef de Corps en Algérie, "Non, Simplet, tout n'est pas si simple," *RMI*, No. 311 [December, 1959], pp. 101–2).

97. "A group of officers," writing in reply to an article by Raoul Girardet which criticized De Gaulle's speech before army troops in Strasbourg on November 23, 1961. The letter as quoted is found, reprinted from *Combat*, in *Message*, No. 49 (January, 1962). That group of officers very likely spoke for only a rather small minority in the officer corps when they argued that the cause of French Algeria was hopeless from the beginning. Their skeptical attitude toward psychological action was more representative. See Dufresnoy, *Des officiers parlent*, pp. 74, 118–19, and (Colonel) Buis, *La Grotte*, pp. 75, 88.

98. Challe's directives as military commander in Algeria (*Paillat, Dossier secret*, pp. 388–93) and his later testimony (*Procès Challe*, p. 38) reveal his acceptance of the "permanent war" doctrine; but his actions as French commander in Algeria from December, 1958, to April, 1960, demonstrate a primary reliance upon traditional military methods (*ibid.*, p. 26). In his testimony at the Barricades trial General Massu stated that revolutionary war was "peu connue aux échelons supérieurs . . ." (*Un Procès*, p. 80).

99. See Challe's testimony, *ibid.*, pp. 39–45; and Fauvet and Planchais, *La Fronde des généraux*, pp. 46–58, and especially p. 247.

100. *Ibid.*, p. 117. The O.A.S. continued to appeal to the U. S. on the same grounds. See the report of a "pirate broadcast" by the O.A.S. reported in *LM*, October 14, 1961.

101. On this point I must take issue with James Meisel, whose book *The Fall of the Republic* is in general a fine piece of work. Both within the French Army and in French politics generally, Meisel tends to exaggerate the initial and the continuing power of fascist ideology to the neglect of temporary situational factors. With regard to what he terms the "French crisis," he argues that "the Algerian trouble did much to precipitate that crisis but was merely its most blatant symptom" (*ibid.*, p. 241). The real threat of the "French counterrevolution," he argues, exists and will continue to exist, independent of the Algerian problem (*ibid.*, pp. 241-42). I would argue, on the contrary, that without the cancer of colonial wars (and especially the Algerian war) to eat away the limited base of French political consensus, the Fourth Republic, borne on by rising economic prosperity after the early 1950's, probably would have lived on for many years, as did the Third Republic. With the Algerian question settled the antirepublican Right, contrary to Professor Meisel's expectations, was virtually eliminated from the National Assembly in the elections of November, 1962.

Chapter 12

Cleavages within the Military Establishment

The major factors which produced a climate of indiscipline and incipient revolt in the officer corps by 1958 have now been laid out. A generation of officers emerged shaken from the schisms and purges of World War II to confront a decade and a half of defeat and dishonor in a highly political style of war, unsupported by the majority of the French civilian population at home and, at least until 1958, unguided by a chain of immobile governments which largely defaulted to the army in the definition of war goals. These experiences and the attitudes which grew out of them were common enough throughout the army, if not in the other branches, to produce solid officer support for the *treize mai* insurgency and, despite De Gaulle, to maintain general passive sympathy for the Challists in the April putsch of 1961. One critical task remains— that of delineating more carefully the distinctions between various groupings of officers with regard to political attitudes. What characteristics are to be found among the *leaders* of military revolt; and, below them, who were the officers who were still willing to *act,* to risk career and even freedom in order to prevent De Gaulle from granting Algerian independence? The answer is fourfold. They came primarily from the army (rather than from the navy or air force), usually from below the normal military elite, frequently from the *guerre révolutionnaire* school, and last, but most important of all, most often from the paratroopers. With the exception of the *guerre révolutionnaire* school, which has already been discussed in some detail, each of these points merits further attention.

Chief of Staff Paul Ely was quite correct in speaking of the unity of the armed forces during the death agony of the Fourth Republic. Civilian activists initiated the uprising, army officers in Algiers took over its leadership, and the majority of military officers in all branches were in obvious sympathy with them.[1] The naval commander in Algiers, Admiral Auboyneau, and the air commander, General Jouhaud, accompanied Salan at all local ceremonies after May 13.[2] Air officers were present on several committees of public safety.[3] Numerous air force planes flew back and forth across the Mediterranean despite official grounding of all flights.[4] A naval officer was the first Algiers appointee as military commander of Corsica;[5] and the maritime prefect in Toulon, Admiral Barjot, let the Algiers group know that the Mediterranean fleet would rally to its leadership if necessary.[6] No action was necessary, however, and the willingness of most naval and air force officers to act upon their sympathies was never tested. With De Gaulle at the helm, the air force, and especially the navy, remained loyal during the Week of the Barricades and the April putsch.

Naval officers were protected from the consequences of direct political activity by a fear of being burned as so many of their colleagues had been by political association with Vichy,[7] and by the relatively minor involvement of the navy in the Algerian war. Out of a total of seventy-three military officers who were tried and convicted for participation in the putsch of 1961 or the accompanying "Paris plot," only one was a naval officer.[8] The one exception, Naval Lieutenant Pierre Guillaume, had served for a time after 1957 as commander of a paratroop-commando unit in Algeria, a unit of which his brother had been commander until killed in combat.[9] After the failure of the putsch only a handful of naval officers were attracted into the O.A.S.[10]

The air force was more heavily represented, with fifteen of the seventy-three officers convicted, a ratio (20 per cent) fairly close to the proportional size of the air force and army officer corps. However, the figures are misleading. To be sure, the putsch claimed air force officers like General Challe, its leader, General Jean Louis Nicot, deputy chief of staff of the air force, General Pierre-Marie Bigot, commander of the fifth air force region (which covered Algeria), and General Edmond Jouhaud, former air force chief of staff. Despite this impressive array of air force brass, most air officers in Algeria followed the lead of General Clause, commander in the Constantine zone, and General Fourquet, air commander of the Constantine zone, both of whom remained loyal to the Paris government.[11] On two bases where Challists were in control, Blida and Maison-Blanche, a number of officers had to be arrested and paratroop detachments called in to prevent "loyalist" demonstrations.[12] Throughout the putsch, pilots on Challist-controlled bases had to be watched lest they attempt to fly off to "loyalist" territory.[13]

The rather sizable number of air force officers among the Challists is explicable largely in terms of three factors. At least three of the fifteen, including Jouhaud and Bigot, were *pieds noirs* and needed little other motive.[14] Another group, including General Challe himself, a former joint commander in Algeria, and three officers of an air force paratroop-commando unit, had been directly involved in revolutionary-guerrilla war to a degree rare among air force officers.[15] Those relatively few air force and naval officers who shared the experiences of army officers also frequently shared their political attitudes.[16] Lastly, the presence at the head of the insurgency movement of Jouhaud and especially Challe, both air force officers, undoubtedly drew into the revolt officers of their branch who otherwise would have remained loyal. General Nicot, for example, testified in his own defense that, though he rejected Jouhaud's appeals to join the movement, he could not think of "denouncing a friend" to his superiors.[17] It is significant that, once Challe had surrendered, only two air force officers fled to continue the fight with the O.A.S.[18] Thereafter, O.A.S. recruits within the air force corps were exceedingly rare.[19]

It was the army, then, which was the major source of military revolt, but not by any means the whole army officer corps. In the years following World War II, army officers developed strong attachment to the ideal of army unity, hoping at all costs to avoid a repetition of the internecine French Army battles of Dakar and Syria. Moreover, army unity was frequently held to be the irreplaceable guardian of national unity. Nonetheless, repetitious professions of army solidarity after 1945 contained as much myth as reality. After the postwar purges were over, the remaining officers of the armistice army mingled uneasily with colleagues drawn from the Free French forces and from the internal resistance.[20] These wounds gradually healed over, but new ones appeared in Indochina and Algeria as younger combat officers, especially in the Legion and in the paratroops, began to feel that they alone were bearing the brunt of the war. These new tensions in turn faded into the background during the *treize mai* crisis, when, in the words of General Paul Ely, the army's "obsession with unity and cohesion" was "one of the essential elements which prevented a split between Algeria and the *métropole*."[21] Yet internal cleavages reappeared stronger than ever when the defense of French Algeria came to mean a struggle against the popular and powerful President of the Fifth Republic. The army as a whole failed to follow the lead of psychological-action and paratroop colonels in the Week of the Barricades. Colonel Argoud, leader of the "soviet of colonels," testified in court that his fellow officers outside Algiers had failed to understand what was at stake, leaving him with no choice but to give in to De Gaulle in order to avoid a disastrous split in the army.[22]

With few exceptions[23] both military activists and disciplined officers continued to pay homage to the ideal of army unity until, in April, 1961, the putsch openly split the army into Challists, a few staunch loyalists, and a mass of hesitant officers between.[24] Army unity as fact and myth was shattered by the putsch as the joint commander in Algeria, General Gambiez, the Algiers Corps commander, General Vézinet, the commander of the Tenth Paratroop Division, General Saint-Hillier, and a number of lesser figures had to be arrested by the Challists. Challist officers like Colonel Charles de la Chapelle, commander of the First Foreign Cavalry Regiment, later argued that they had wanted only to preserve army unity and believed that this could be done only under Challe's leadership.[25] In fact, the unity ideal was no longer powerful enough (if, indeed, it had ever been) to justify disobedience in the face of a popular and determined government.

An emerging political consciousness among conscripts and reserve officers further deepened the schism within the army in Algeria.[26] Challe and his advisers were apparently taken completely by surprise when most conscripts chose to respond to the putsch as outraged citizens, rather than as blindly obedient soldiers.[27] As in the Russian Revolution of 1917 and in the German Revolution of 1918, numerous conscripted enlisted men broke with their officers when civilian attitudes and professional military attitudes clashed.[28]

In the aftermath of the putsch the army officer corps remained badly divided, though the beginnings of a renewed unity appeared by mid-1962, by which time the most embittered officers had deserted to join the O.A.S. and those remaining, of all political persuasions, shared a shocked reaction to O.A.S. terrorists attacks on military personnel.[29]

Those cleavages within the army and the army officer corps which appeared in April, 1961, were not so much created by the putsch as simply unmasked by it. One of the most persistent of divisions was that between older and younger generations of officers, between most generals and most of those who had been field commanders in Indochina and Algeria—the captains, majors, and colonels. After the *treize mai* crisis of 1958 one young officer told a journalist, with only slight exaggeration, "There must be no illusions. With us are 90% of all subordinate officers, 50% of field grade officers, and 5% of general officers." [30] Newspaper headlines often gave a misleading picture of the *treize mai* crisis and of the April putsch by focusing upon the role of the generals (like Massu, Salan, and Challe) to the neglect of the colonels behind the scenes who were the true instigators of military revolt. Massu, who as a paratroop commander was exceptionally close to the colonel mentality, unquestionably played an aggressive role in the *treize mai* crisis, but so did Colonels Thomazo, Vaudrey, Trinquier, Godard, Lacheroy, and Dufour, among others. And if four generals were recruited as platform leaders of the April putsch, the whole affair was in fact prepared by five colonels—Argoud, Gardes, Lacheroy, Godard, and Broizat.

There is nothing so very startling in the colonels', more than generals', being the driving force of French military revolt from the mid-1950's to 1962. So long as the status of generals at the top of the military-power pyramid is not badly threatened by the existing regime, so long as revolt involves a considerable risk, it is understandable that members of the military elite will be reluctant to gamble all they have achieved in an attempted putsch. Colonels, who have more to gain and less to lose, have figured heavily in the history of military revolt in both Western and non-Western countries.[31] Tension between conservative generals and their impatient subordinate officers was not new in the French Army,[32] though only after World War II did it become serious enough to pose a grave threat to internal military discipline. By the mid-1950's, according to an overwhelming number of reports, it was the common belief among field-grade, and especially company-grade, officers that most French generals were incompetent, self-interested, corrupted by political intrigue, imprisoned by *le système*, disinterested in the plight of field troops, unwilling or unable to understand revolutionary-guerrilla war, and lacking generally in initiative, courage, and character.[33] Jean-Jacques Servan-Schreiber returned in early 1957 from a tour of duty as a recalled reserve officer to report that "in the discussions of all the mess halls of Algeria the refrain is everywhere the same: 'The generals are damn fools [*cons*].' " [34]

This disrespect of subordinate officers for their generals is traceable to four major sources. First, as most officers were aware, the rapid collapse of the French Army in May and June of 1940 was largely attributable to incompetent and unimaginative military leaders who were, as the phrase goes, "a war behind" in their thinking.[35]

Second, high ranking officers emerged from World War II divided into clans according to their wartime patrons and affiliations (Free French, African army, internal resistance) and often maintained contact with the civilian politicians who had fought with them. Political contacts undoubtedly entered into high military appointments. In at least one case, the "Affair of the Generals" in 1949–50, career advancement became openly involved with political intrigue and unprincipled business interests.[36] In 1949 the chief of staff of national defense, General Georges Revers, visited Indochina and returned to report in a secret memorandum to the government that the war there was being grossly mismanaged. Within a month the Revers report had been leaked out, apparently from Revers to General Mast, an active candidate for Léon Pignon's job as French high commissioner in Indochina, then to one Roger Peyré, a political intriguer and profiteer, and finally, to a Vietnamese supporter of Bao Dai. A slightly different version of the report reached the hands of Vietminh agents, perhaps also via Peyré. Key Socialist and Radical cabinet ministers rapidly hushed up the affair—only to see it explode in the press in January, 1950. A parliamentary commission of inquiry was then created to investigate the scandal and discovered, among other things, that Revers, Mast, and Peyré (who was not above bribery) had been maneuvering with receptive Socialist and Radical politicians in an effort to oust Pignon, an M.R.P. appointee. Peyré, who managed to escape to Brazil before the public scandal broke, was revealed to be, not only a political confidant and mysterious influence peddler for Revers, but also a trafficker in the illegal piaster exchange in Indochina and a double agent attached to one of the rival French secret-police services. With the Communist Party drawing public attention to the scandal, prominent members of the government were accused of concealing evidence in an attempt to prevent a public unveiling of widespread corruption and partisan maneuvering in high governmental circles. In the end only Mast and Revers were sanctioned, both by being retired from active duty, leaving subordinate army officers with the twin example of political intrigue at high military levels and a penchant among politicians for blaming the army.[37]

Intrigue aside, General Grout de Beaufort described correctly the tendency at least of the Fourth Republic when in June, 1961, he stated: "Unfortunately . . . governments tend to appoint to top positions in the military hierarchy persons who accept too many things without protesting and leave their subordinates to manage for themselves." [38] Careerism and the tenacles of *le système* restrained the enthusiasm of the general staff in Paris for the gloryless Indochina war. Colonel Trinquier testified accurately in the Salan trial that, apart from Marshal de Lattre, full generals and lieutenant generals had avoided Indochina like the plague and devoted little attention to it, leaving colonels and subordinate officers to bear the brunt of military leadership. [39] One of those obscure generals who served as French commander in chief in Indochina, General Navarre, left his command feeling almost as venomous toward the general staff in Paris as toward politicians of the Fourth Republic.[40]

Naturally enough, in these circumstances it was the colonels and subordinate officers in the field, not the generals, who first studied and began to understand the radically new style of revolutionary-guerrilla war in which the French Army was engaged. With the single exception of General Chassin, all of the major leaders in the *guerre révolutionnaire* school were colonels, majors, or captains. The usual military elite proved itself, once again, too lethargic and unimaginative to understand changing modes of warfare.[41]

A last factor which contributed to dwindling respects for generals among company-grade and field-grade officers was the overabundance of officers in the highest grades which had developed by the mid-1950's.[42] War casualties were very largely in the lower officer grades and offered no promotion advantage to those numerous and unusually able majors, lieutenant colonels, and colonels who had entered the officer corps from 1936 to 1945. The lack of decisive large-scale battles, moreover, inhibited the normal rapid promotions and demotions of a wartime army seeking out its most capable leadership. Colonel Roger Barberot returned from a tour of temporary active duty in Algeria in 1956–57 with nothing but scorn for the rigidity and red tape of the high command:[43]

> In 1957, in the midst of war (the Algerian war is indeed a war), there would be no possibility that a Leclerc could be a general of the army at 45 years of age (he would be a colonel) that a Brosset,

who was a general and a division commander at the age of 42, would be anything more than a brilliant lieutenant colonel.[44]

And so it was that a whole generation of colonels, majors, and captains in the combat arms came to feel that they were led by slackards and incompetents who knew nothing of revolutionary-guerrilla war and who could not be trusted with the destiny of France's army. With the single notable exception of Argoud, who was never sent to Indochina, all of the political colonels—Lacheroy, Gardes, Trinquier, Godard, Vaudrey, Thomazo, Dufour, Broizat, and others—had in common a long personal experience on two continents in a highly political style of war. That experience set them apart—a long way apart—from the generals who supposedly led them.

Another, and a more important cleavage within the French Army, one which in part overlapped with the division by age, was that between "elite troops," especially the paratroopers, and the rest of the army. Two major factors were largely responsible for heavy French reliance on elite troops in Indochina and in Algeria. First, revolutionary-guerrilla war being essentially a war without fronts, the defending army is obliged to assign large numbers of troops to the immobilizing task of protecting the lives and property of the local population. Specialized, highly mobile units are then needed for the job of chasing rebel bands. In Indochina and particularly in Algeria the *paras* and the Foreign Legion made up the "general reserves," which did most of the chasing. Second, it must be borne in mind that in neither of these two colonial wars did the French Army receive much enthusiastic support from the French population at home. When conscripts were finally called upon in Algeria, they rarely exhibited that fighting spirit born of the belief that the homeland is in danger. With the Legion and the *paras* an extraordinary *esprit de corps* could substitute in part, but only in part, for the absence of a clear national cause.[45]

There developed the common practice of calling in the Legion and especially the *paras* whenever any serious fighting was to be done. Officers in non-elite units were often disturbed at the sight of their *para* colleagues monopolizing the little glory that was to be had in these wars,[46] and a few psychological-action officers regretted that the *paras* were more interested in glorious military victories than in the more fundamental task of wining over the population.[47] Nevertheless, all had to admit, as did Major Enrico in the novel by Colonel Georges Buis, that ". . . there are not thirty-six kinds of fighters. There are two. There is the infinitesimal minority who really attack and the others. The *paras* attack." [48] The *paras* and the Legion were given ample opportunity to attack. From reading newspaper accounts of the war in Algeria one would hardly have guessed that in 1959 the *paras* and the Legion made up only 3 per cent and 5 per cent, respectively, of all army troops in Algeria.[49]

Cast in a perpetual shock-troop role, paratroop officers and men came to symbolize the continuing battle for the defense of French Algeria. They were widely credited with all glory for French successes in Algeria and blamed for all atrocities. The *paras* generally, and the Tenth Paratroop Division in particular, became the object of idolization on the part of French colonists in Algeria. Even after the failure of the putsch in April, 1961, the camouflaged "leopardskin" combat uniform of the paratroopers continued to be a symbol of resistance to Algerian independence, even among those who had never been *paras* themselves. For example, Armond Belvisi, one of the instigators of the September, 1961, assassination attempt against De Gaulle, was located and trapped in his apartment by the police. Before surrendering he insisted on changing into the leopard-skin uniform, which had become a common garb for O.A.S. commandos.[50] For the Algerian rebels and their sympathizers, and for liberals in France who opposed the war, the *paras*, the "victors of Algiers," were equally symbolic of French Algeria. In June, 1957, in the midst of the battle of Algiers, an elementary school teacher in the Casbah of Algiers asked his Moslem pupils to write an essay on the subject, "What would you do if you were invisible?" [51] Almost all of the responses from his eleven- to thirteen-year-old charges mentioned vengeance on the *paras:*

"If I were invisible I would kill the soldiers and the paratroopers. . . . I would kill the *paras* who torture men. . . . I would kill all of Massu's Paras."—". . . I would kill all the *paras* because they are doing evil. . . ."—"I would attack Massu's *paras*, those *misérables*, those thieves, those imbeciles, those idiots, those cretins. Down with Massu's *paras*."—"If I were invisible, the first job I would do would be to go seek revenge on the *paras* who caused so much misery to my brothers. I would take a rope and I would strangle the last of the *paras* who patrol in the tunnel of our neighborhood and I would take his weapons, then I would run after the other *paras* and kill them. . . ." [52]

The *paras* were not entirely deserving of either all the credit or all the blame which they received. There was considerable truth to the legend however, not only with regard to the fighting effectiveness and the brutality of the *paras*, but also with respect to their key role in the army's attempts to prevent Algerian independence. The May 13, 1958, uprising could not have succeeded without the support of paratroop officers like General Massu and Colonels Trinquier, Thomazo, Godard, and Vaudrey.[53] The extension of that movement into Corsica and the reality of the military threat which it posed to Fourth Republic headquarters in Paris owed much to paratroop officers.[54] The Week of the Barricades, even more than *treize mai*, was largely the affair of paratroop officers, especially those of the Tenth Paratroop Division, without whose sympathy and support the civilian insurgents would have posed no serious threat to De Gaulle.[55] Whereas in May of 1958 *para* officers had been representative of army-officer attitudes generally, now, in face of De Gaulle, they could no longer count on the rest of the army to follow their daring lead. The clearest evidence of the important role of the *paras* in military activism and revolt is found in the April putsch of 1961. As mentioned above, the paratroop regiments formed the backbone of the Challist putsch. The trials of officers accused of supporting the putsch or of participating in the simultaneous "Paris plot" clearly revealed the extent of Challe's dependence on paratrooper support. Of a total of fifty-seven officers in the grade of colonel and below who were found guilty in those trials, thirty-six were paratroop officers.[56] Again, in the O.A.S. paratroop officers were fairly numerous, though not so predominant in numbers as in the putsch.[57]

Why, it must be asked, were paratroop officers so often in the spearhead of military indiscipline and revolt from 1958 to 1962, and why were their men so ready to follow? The shock-troop role of the *paras* was certainly one contributing factor, for it deepened their personal and group involvement in the cause of French Algeria. Out of that same shock-troop role came the *para* reputation for toughness and love of battle, which naturally attracted the most adventuresome officers and enlisted men into the paratroop regiments. Equally significant, however, was the *esprit para*—that constellation of attitudes, imposed and maintained by a vigorous *esprit de corps*, which set the paratrooper apart from his fellows in non-elite units. In order to understand the political role of French paratroop officers one must look at the spirit which permeated that arm and the unique relationship between paratroop officers and men: deprived of the solid and enthusiastic support of his men, the paratroop officer would have been no more fearsome a political threat than officers in other arms.

Careful studies of both the German and the American armies in World War II have indicated the importance of small-group solidarity in the maintenance of a fighting spirit in military units.[58] The *esprit para* owed a great deal to the extension of those same primary, face-to-face relationships from the squad level to the platoon, the company, and, on occasion, even so far as to the regiment. As Gilles Perrault, a former paratrooper, has perceptively remarked, the paratrooper officer generally rejected the traditional father-image role of the unit commander. Perrault writes:

> That Epinal-style imagery which showed the elite corps of former times going gaily into fire under the benevolent orders of the colonel, the "Father of the Regiment," is intolerable for paratroop officers. Bigeard wanted to be the elder brother of his men, their ringleader.[59]

The elder-brother role demanded a much more intimate social bond between officers and enlisted men than military tradition had normally allowed. Another former *para*, Jean Lartéguy, describes that bond in the making during the training period of recalled draftees.

Through the imaginary pen of one of the initially disgruntled draftees, we see this picture:

> We live mixed together, intermingled, officers, noncoms and privates; but it is Raspéguy's [read: Bigeard's] "wolves" who set the tone. They are seeking, it seems, to have themselves plebiscited by us, as if they expected us to name them to the grades and to the functions which they already occupy. Once chosen, no one will any longer be able to question the orders that they will give us.[60]

Nor did the elder-brother role cease once the unit entered into battle. Lartéguy describes the alarmed reaction of a fictional former commander in Tonkin who followed "Raspéguy" through a night of combat:

> I don't agree with Raspéguy's manner of commanding. It engages you too much. Because I send a soldier to die I don't believe myself obliged beforehand to invite him to coffee in my living room, nor listen to him tell me about his mother or his conception of the world. The units like the one commanded by your Raspéguy threaten to become one day a sort of sect which will no longer wage war for a country or an idea but for itself alone, like the monk gives himself up to his macerations in order to gain entry into his paradise.[61]

The general's fears were quite justified. The style of leadership which Bigeard symbolized and which, through his vigorous and prestigious example, permeated the whole paratroop arm with varying degrees of effectiveness, had as one of its strongest effects the creation of an unusually strong loyalty between enlisted men and officers. Even though some 70 per cent of all enlisted men in the paratroopers were draftees in 1961, officers like Lieutenant Colonel Lecomte, commander of the Fourteenth Paratroop Regiment (*Chasseurs*), and Colonel Masselot, commander of the Eighteenth Paratroop Regiment (*Chasseurs*), were able to rally to Challe and, in contradiction to clear orders from division headquarters, set their units off on a march which eventually led them across the breadth of Algeria in the service of the putsch.[62] Eventually, as the rest of the army in Algeria failed to rally to Challe, conscripts in the paratroopers became somewhat restless at the prospect of fighting fellow Frenchmen.[63] Paratroop units, however, were almost completely free from the conscript strikes and demonstrations which plagued Challist and uncommitted commanders in other arms. The sharp contrast between the behavior of conscripts in the *paras* and those in other units is explicable, in part, in terms of the attraction of that arm for men predisposed toward defense of French Algeria. Unquestionably, however, the unique *esprit de corps* of the *paras* also played an important part.[64] Tales of dramatic conversions of Left-leaning draftees and reserve officers are not uncommon.[65] Significantly enough, when the April putsch failed, the O.A.S. recruited a number of its cadre among former *paras*. One of these, Paul Stefani, was arrested for his role in an O.A.S. assassination and explained, "When one has been a *para*, one is always a *para*."[66]

If the unconventional *para* style of leadership was one factor in the development of that powerful *esprit de corps* which existed in most paratroop regiments, another factor was the sectlike character of the entire paratroop arm, a phenomenon which must be traced partly to the *paras'* being acknowledged as elite shock troops, and partly to the natural selectivity of jump training. The jump itself, first from the training tower and then from an airplane, took on many of the characteristics of a supreme test and an initiation into the sect. As Perrault puts it, "It is the whole man whom one pretends to judge at the jump door." [67] Another paratroop veteran, J.-J. Thieuloy, looks back on his own jump training and recalls the ridicule and abuse which were the lot of the *dégonflé*, the trainee who refused to jump. "Only bastards refuse to jump," Thieuloy's lieutenant told his group.[68] The former paratrooper continues:

The fifteen days of prison which are the lot of the *para* trainee who washes out are not degrading in themselves. More degrading are the insults of his superiors, under the eyes of his comrades who watch him crawl or run while shouting "I am a *dégonflé*, I am among the blessed [*un bien-heureux*], I am a *dégonflé*, I am among the blessed" around the practice tower from which he could not fling himself. Some training cadre were content to mark the letter "D" on the backs of failures, but I saw a Master Sergeant make two of the walk around the camp of the Base-School of Pau with signs on their backs saying, "*I am a dégonflé.*"

From the private to the colonel (grade is of little importance moreover in the airplane), the *para* knows that in jump school a *race* is formed.[69]

Like the U.S. Marine Corps, where the rigor of basic training also serves as a form of initiation into an elite fighting corps, the French paratroopers have come under public criticism for mistreatment of recruits.[70] In October, 1962, a corporal in the Fourteenth Paratroop Regiment (*Chasseurs*) in Toulouse was accused of slapping recruits in his charge and ordering them to carry out a number of humiliating acts of a fraternity-initiation variety.[71] His superiors were more amused than angered by his behavior, and the corporal himself claimed only to be doing what had been done to him in his own training period. In fact, the corporal had lacked discretion, even in the eyes of his superiors; yet humiliation and abuse apparently had a regular place in the initiation of paratroop recruits.

The *paras* prided themselves, as most elite troops do, on their unique dress, language, and manner.[72] Each item of apparel received minute attention, from the prized jump boots (or, better yet, American ranger boots) and colored beret to the Saint Michael medals (after the *paras*' patron saint), which most of them wore. *Paras* were allowed the privilege of wearing their bizarre leopard-skin combat uniform even when on pass. Following the April putsch of 1961, the Ministry of War ordered that the camouflage uniform be reserved strictly for combat, and that in summer the colored *para* beret be replaced by a new *képi*, or military peak cap, as part of the standard dress uniform of paratroop noncoms and officers.[73] These orders met angry resistance from the *paras*. First, regulation uniforms were said by the paratroop units to be "unavailable." [74] Then enlisted men proceeded to show their scorn for the khaki berets by ceremoniously stomping on them and burning them (in Nancy), posing the old crimson beret before the monument to the dead (in Bayonne), and demonstrating in mass against the new regulations (again in Nancy).[75]

The April putsch provided definitive proof that the famous *para esprit de corps* had become a serious threat to civilian control. The usual antagonism between in-group and out-group which is characteristic of tightly-knit social units had developed, in the case of the *paras,* into a scornful aloofness from the rest of the armed forces and a strong disgust for politicians and civilians generally. Colonel Marcel Bigeard set the tone with his frequent displays of disrespect and indiscipline toward the regular military hierarchy and toward other non-elite units.[76] Among the *paras,* who were well-trained, young, physically fit, and eager for combat, generals were frequently known as *"poireaux"* (leeks) and non-elite troops generally were referred to as "lead ass" (*cul-de-plomb*) units.

The paratrooper's typical attitude toward other army units appears almost generous in comparison with his disgust for civilians and especially for politicians.[77] Lartéguy's observant draftee again describes accurately the paratroop mold which was being imposed on him before the *treize mai:*

> Radio-Raspéguy [the regimental loudspeaker] insists on all that which can disgust the soldier about civilian life. The outside world is presented as vile, rotten, without grandeur, power being in the hands of a band of small-minded swindlers.

> My comrades already say "we" in opposition to everyone who does not wear the cap and the camouflaged uniform [Colonel Bigeard outfitted his regiment with a unique long-billed cap that became a proud symbol of his unit]. They are clean, sharp; they are becoming agile; they are pure, while in France, there reign corruption, cowardliness, baseness, "the world of sin" seen from our monasteries.[78]

Luxury, flabbiness, materialism, cowardliness, and treason—these were the evils frequently attributed to civilians and especially to politicians and intellectuals. Thieuloy, the paratroop veteran, suggests that the typical *para,* at least in 1958, tended to lump his outsider enemies together and to pick as their symbol the deputy:

> For the *para,* the deputy is the man-woman, the underman given to prattling and inaction.

The *para* has words, whose meaning no longer escape anyone, to describe the deputy. He calls him *tante* ["pansy"] or *pédale* ["homo"]. I heard our old captain, though more of a humorist than a fanatic, shout in speaking of the members of the Chamber, "We are going to give those prostitutes a thrashing." ["Ces filles de joie, nous irons les rosser!"][79]

When one looks beyond the famous *para esprit de corps* to the dominant mystique of the paratroop arm, this antagonism to French bourgeois society is more fully understandable. Most of those paratroop veterans who have written of their experiences agree on the central features of the *esprit para:* idealization of youth, of strength, of combat as the supreme test of self.[80] Join to these the romantic fascination with sacrifice and death, found especially in the writings of Bigeard, and one has a mystique which is fundamentally opposed to the values of an acquisitive and liberal French society. The "Paratroopers' Prayer," which was posted on many barracks walls, reveals that clash in values:

Give me, my God, that which you have left over. Give me that
for which you are never asked

I do not ask for wealth
Nor for success, nor even for health

You are asked so often, my God, for all that
That you must not have any left
Give me, my God, that which you have left over
Give me that which people refuse to take from you
I want insecurity and restlessness
I want torment and brawling

And that you should give them to me, my God,
Once and for all

Let me be sure to have them always
For I will not always have the courage
To ask you for them.[81]

The same love of battle and the same spirit of hardship and sacrifice are the predominant themes in the writings of Colonel Bigeard, especially in his captions to the collection of photographs entitled *Aucune Bête du Monde.* To take a few samples, on the subject of sacrifice and self-mastery he writes:

> It seemed to us then [in the desert] that in that privation and that solitude, in the thirst and in the hunger, we had found that enemy which we had been pursuing for so long: ourselves, our fear and that body which suddenly demanded of us juicy fruits, welcoming girls, deep beds, and a comfortable life.[82]

On love of battle:

> An immense sadness overtook us on the evening after the victory. . . .[83]

On death:

> At each turn of the road, behind each dune, each rock, we had a rendezvous, but it was with our death. . . .[84]

> [In his dedication of the book to a sergeant who was killed in combat]. Of us all he was the luckiest, for he made a success of his death after having led the tormented life which he had chosen.[85]

Nor was Bigeard alone in his romantic conception of war. In the instructions posted on the barracks doors in the Niel paratroop training center in Toulouse were the following words:

> *Paras,* you are the [*sic*] elite soldiers. You will seek out combat and you will train yourselves for the hardest tests. Battle will be for you the supreme test. . . . For you, either victory or death. There is no other alternative. It is a question of honor. . . .[86]

As Gilles Perrault has indicated at some length, there are unmistakable parallels between the *esprit para* and fascism, especially fascism of the German variety.[87] One finds in both a glorification of strength, sacrifice, and battle for its own sake (or, more precisely, for the sake of continual testing of one's strength and courage). In both, as well, there is a strong emphasis upon youth.[88]

In one sense the French paratroopers battled for the love of battle itself; yet one must not neglect, as does Perrault, the presence of ideologues of the *guerre révolutionnaire* school among paratroop officers. Men like Colonels Dufour and Broizat inevitably gave a political tone to the test of battle.[89] Even among those many paratroop officers who were not so dedicated to the Christian anticommunist crusade as were Dufour and Broizat, the prospect of termination of the Algerian war posed a serious threat to their status and style of life. Independence for Algeria, the last of the colonial battlegrounds, would mean the end of fighting, as well as an inevitable eclipse of the glorious *para* legend. In this sense, at the very least, the paratrooper was not completely indifferent to war goals.

Bound by a strong, sectlike *esprit de corps*, scornful of non-elite troops and officers who lacked its fighting spirit, resentful of civilians and especially politicians (who preferred abandonment to the sacrifices of battle), and inspired by a romantic fascination with war as a supreme test of strength and courage, the paratroop arm was indeed poorly equipped to carry out a policy aimed at Algerian independence.

Alongside the paratroopers in the general reserve was the Foreign Legion, which bore much of the heaviest fighting in Indochina and Algeria. The Legion enjoyed, as did the paratroopers, a strong *esprit de corps* and a tradition of unquestioning loyalty of men to their officers, most of whom were French. The Legion styles of leadership and discipline were more traditional than those of the paratroop regiments; yet unlike some *para* draftees, the Legionnaires, being foreigners, had no conflicting civil loyalties which might interfere with obedience to their officers. The power which that unquestioning obedience gave to Legion officers is particularly clear in the case of the Legion paratroop regiments.

Of all the regiments of the Legion, it was the paratroop regiments, and especially the First Foreign Paratroop Regiment (l⁺ʳ R.E.P.), which were most attracted to the Challist camp in the putsch of April, 1961. Despite the frantic Challist recruiting efforts of General Paul Gardy, a former inspector general of the Foreign

Legion, most Legion units remained loyal during the putsch, although there were intra-unit struggles for control in a few regiments, notably in the First Foreign Regiment, the Fifth Foreign Regiment (*Chasseurs*), and the Second Foreign Paratroop Regiment.[90] When General Gardy arrived at Legion headquarters at Sidi-Bel-Abbès, he was informed quite abruptly by Colonel Brothier, commander of the First Foreign Regiment, that the Legion, composed of foreigners, should be kept out of internal French political affairs.[91]

Out of a total of twenty-two French Legion officers who were convicted for insurgency against the government after the putsch had failed (out of a total of sixty-eight officers convicted), four were from the Second Foreign Paratroop Regiment (2ᵉ R.E.P.) and *fourteen* were from the First Foreign Paratroop Regiment.[92] Why were the Legion paratroop units so heavily represented among the insurgents? First, they were *paras*, as well as Legionnaires, and shared many *para* attitudes.[93] Second, a matter of circumstances, the First Foreign Paratroop Regiment was stationed near Algiers in April, 1961, making it a natural choice for the job of carrying out a palace revolution. Third, the First Regiment had suffered exceptionally heavy personnel losses both in Indochina and in Algeria. As the First Foreign Paratroop Battalion, it had twice been virtually annihilated in Indochina.[94] Reformed as the First Foreign Paratroop Regiment, it lost four hundred fifty men, including Regimental Commander Colonel Jeanpierre, in the battle of Guelma on the Tunisian border in 1957–58.[95] Out of long acquaintance with danger and sacrifice came an extraordinary unity within the First Regiment, a strengthening of that already famous loyalty of the Legionnaire to his officers and an attachment to the Algerian soil for which the unit had fought.[96] In view of a law (in force for one hundred and thirty years) forbidding the employment of the Foreign Legion in metropolitan France, there was considerable fear among Legionnaires that Algerian independence would mean the dissolution of their refuge-home.[97]

The collapse of the April putsch produced ample proof of the solidarity of the First Regiment (which was officially disbanded), as well as of its confirmed hostility to the Paris government. After blowing up much of the materiel left in their camp at Zeralda, enlisted men of the unit rode off to reassignment in Sidi-Bel-Abbès shouting "Algérie française" and throwing roses to the crowd, while the officers of the regiment rode into Algiers to face judgment singing, "Je ne regrette rien" and "Si tu doutes en ton destin, viens chez les paras!" [98] When twelve of the officers of the regiment were brought to trial, they snapped to attention upon the arrival in the courtroom of Major Saint-Marc, the interim commander of the regiment during the putsch, who had already been divested of rank and sentenced to ten years imprisonment.[99] One of the twelve, Lieutenant Ysquierdo, testified: "In refusing [to follow] Saint-Marc, I would have been a pitiful slob. I would have deserved to be in Fresnes [a prison] twice over." [100] As for those officers of the First Foreign Paratroop Regiment who were not brought to trial, at least seven of them demonstrated their solidarity with Saint-Marc by joining the O.A.S.[101] Enlisted men from the First Regiment, moreover, were exceptionally numerous among the killers and bomb-setters of the O.A.S.[102]

If some Legion officers, like Colonel Brothier, believed that foreign troops should be kept out of domestic political struggles, there were others, especially in the Legion paratroop regiments, who were closer to the *para* mentality and eager to avoid Algerian independence at any cost. Once a Legion commander like Saint-Marc had decided upon rebellion, he could count upon a habit of obedience and an extraordinary *esprit de corps* to unite his officers and men behind him.

Who were the officer-mutineers? For the most part, they were army officers from below the highest ranks, sometimes specialists in psychological action, but more often members of the elite corps, especially the paratroopers. They shared a high degree of personal and group involvement in the Algerian war. In the case of paratroop officers and, to a lesser degree, Legion officers, their French Algerian persuasion and their potential for action were frequently buttressed by a solid *esprit de corps*.

1. Looking back at the spring of 1958, Vice-Admiral Ploix declared in the Salan trial without too much exaggeration, "au point de vue militaire— je ne parle que des marins, il y avait tout ce qu'il fallait pour que n'importe quel sauveur se présentant soit acclamé" (*Procès Salan,* p. 354). See also Tournoux, *Secrets d'état,* pp. 372–73.

2. De Sérigny, *La Révolution du treize mai,* p. 140.

3. *Ibid.,* p. 141.

4. Tournoux, *Secrets d'état,* p. 372.

5. De Sérigny, *La Révolution du treize mai,* p. 122.

6. Brombergers, *13 Complots,* pp. 251–52.

7. See Admiral Nomy's statement to Defense Minister de Chévigny in May, 1958, as quoted by Tournoux, *Secrets d'état,* p. 325.

8. All but twenty-three sentences were suspended (*Procès du putsch, passim*); Fauvet and Planchais, *La Fronde des généraux,* pp. 259–60; and *LM,* May–December, 1961.

9. *Procès du putsch,* p. 145.

10. Among them were Guillaume, who received a suspended sentence after the putsch, Capitaine de Corvette Jacques Roy (*LM,* March 9, 1962; and, for a second offense, *LM,* April 4–5, 1963), Enseigne de Vaisseau Georges Buscia (*LM,* March 1, 1962), and Lieutenant de Corvette Jacques Piquet (*LM,* April 15–16, 1962).

11. Fauvet and Planchais, *La Fronde des généraux,* pp. 144, 220.

12. *Procès du putsch,* pp. 174, 176–77.

13. Planchais in *LM,* May 6, 1961; and *Procès du putsch,* pp. 176–77.

14. *Le Procès d'Edmond Jouhaud,* pp. 13–14; and *Procès du putsch,* pp. 20–21.

15. The three air-commando officers were Lieutenant Colonel M. Emery, Lieutenant Trouillas, and Lieutenant de Firmas de Péries.

16. In describing his experience as commander of air force commandos, Lieutenant Colonel Maurice Emery used terms very much like those one would expect from a similarly placed army commander: "Cela était impossible sans un idéal de lutte et une foi dans la victoire. Quand cette foi s'affaiblissait, les résultats étaient nuls et même négatifs" (in his own trial, July 27, 1961, as reported in *Procès du putsch;* p. 119).

17. In fact, Nicot facilitated Challe's escape to Algeria. The president of the Haut Tribunal Militaire asked him why he had not reported the conspiracy to his superiors, and he replied, "Cela revenait à dénoncer un camarade. Mon éducation familiale, religieuse, ce que j'ai appris à Saint-Cyr, me l'interdisait. C'aurait été un acte méprisable" (*Procès du putsch,* p. 37).

18. General Jouhaud and Major Roger Vailly, the latter being the de facto Challist Commander of the Blida Air Base during the putsch.

19. The one notable exception was a former Polytechnicien and military engineer, Lieutenant Colonel Jean-Marie Bastien-Thiry, who was condemned and shot for organizing an assassination attempt on De Gaulle at Petit-Clamart (near Paris) in August, 1962. (*LM,* February 3—March 12, 1963). Bastien-Thiry, however, had been assimilated into the air force officer corps from the separate and more civilian corps of military engineers only in January, 1962 (*LM,* March 12, 1963).

20. "Malaise dans l'armée," *Etudes,* No. 249 (April–June, 1946), pp. 77–85; and Lieutenant Colonel Th. J. Delaye in *Message,* No. 1 (December 7, 1953), p. 5.

21. Ely, *RMI, No.* 297 (August–September, 1958), pp. 7–8.

22. " . . . Dans les circonstances actuelles, nous estimions que l'armée était le suprême recours du pays. Cela est plus valable aujourd'hui que jamais. Il fallait donc que l'unité soit sauvegardée, que la hiérarchie soit maintenue, en particulier à la tête, expliquer au commandement l'état d'esprit de la population" (Argoud, *Sans commentaire,* p. 37). See also Argoud's comments to Claude Krief, "Portrait d'un 'colonel,' " *La Nef,* No. 7 (July–September, 1961), pp. 52–53.

23. One notable exception was a captain writing to *Message* in June, 1960: " . . . Je suis convaincu qu'il faut dénoncer impitoyablement ce mythe de l'unité de l'Armée et regrouper autour d'un même idéal les plus durs et les plus purs" (in "Courrier des lecteurs," *Message,* No. 43 (June, 1960), p. 1.

24. In February, 1960, when all intra-army publications were abolished and replaced by a single monthly, *L'Armée* (probably to allow tighter control from Paris), Army Chief of Staff André Demetz contributed a baptismal editorial in which he paid homage to army unity and denied military activists (Argoud *et cie.*) the right to speak as its defenders (editorial, *L'Armée,* No. 1 [February, 1960], pp. 7–8).

25. "On nous a dit que l'armée entière se ralliait à lui. Cette unité de l'armée c'était notre seul but" (De la Chapelle in his own trial, *Procès du putsch,* p. 56). See also *ibid.,* pp. 63 and 71; and Fauvet and Planchais, *La Fronde des généraux,* p. 111.

26. Chapter 9 above.

27. Azeau, *Révolte militaire,* pp. 171–74.

28. See, for example, Raphael R. Abramovitch, *The Soviet Revolution* (New York: International Universities Press, 1962), pp. 12–16; and Craig, *The Politics of the Prussian Army,* chap. 9. Mutiny in the enlisted ranks also helped to foil the German Kapp putsch in 1920, when a group of officers (parallel to the Challists) attempted to overthrow the young republic (*ibid.,* p. 378).

29. Among the targets of those attacks were the following: members of army anti-O.A.S. squads, like Major Post in October, 1961, and Lieutenant Colonel Rançon in December, 1961 (*LM,* October 29–30, 1961; December 19, 1961; December 29, 1961); officers who had helped to block the April putsch, like General Ginestat in June, 1962, and Major Kubaziack in June, 1962 (*LM,* June 26, 1962; March 7, 1963); high staff officers, like Lieutenant Colonel Wagner and Major Orsini (of Army Chief of Staff le Pulloch's staff) in March, 1962 (*LM,* March 7, 1962); and finally, army patrols in Algeria (*LM,* March 24, 1962).

30. Nicolas Pierre, "Qu'est-ce qui paralyse encore l'armée d'Algérie?", *La Nation française,* August 20, 1958, as quoted in Girardet *et al., Crise militaire,* p. 166 n. 18.

31. It will be recalled that Louis Napoleon was forced to "make some generals" in order to stage a coup in 1851, the most celebrated generals of the day being too content with the status quo (Ténot, *Paris in December, 1851,* p. 83, and above, Chapter 1). As for underdeveloped countries, numerous recent examples of political colonels include Colonel Perón in Argentina, Colonel Arbenz in Guatemala, and Colonel Nasser in Egypt. Generals have still been well represented among mutineers, however. Among them one finds, in France, Napoleon in 1799; in Germany, the leaders of the Kapp putsch in 1920 and the anti-Hitler putsch in 1944; and in underdeveloped countries, General Ne Win in Burma, General Ayub Khan in Pakistan,

General Chung Hi Pak in Korea, Marshal Sarit Thanarat in Thailand, Generals Minh and Kanh in South Vietnam, and General Gursel in Turkey.

32. Monteil, *Les Officiers*, p. 18; and Katzenbach, *Yale Review*, pp. 498–513.

33. As spokesman for younger officers, *Message* was especially critical of general officers. See particularly the following articles in *Message*: "La Crise des vocations militaires," No. 4 (July, 1954), p. 11; Capitaine B., "Pour une autocritique," No. 6 (December, 1954), pp. 9–11; Capitaine X, No. 12 (February, 1956), p. 6; the reports of two rather crude opinion surveys, one among *Message* readers, "Synthèse des résponses reçues à l'enquête de *Message* sur l'information dans l'armée," No. 13 (April, 1956), p. 26; and one among members of a Saint-Cyr graduating class of the World War II years, "Enquête sur la crise de l'armée," No. 18 (December, 1956), p. 14; editorial, No. 13 (April, 1956), pp. 1–2; "D'Algérie: Une opinion sur la morale des officiers," No. 20 (March, 1957), pp. 2–3; "Pour un effort de vérité," No. 32 (November, 1958), pp. 1–6. See also Barberot, *Malaventure en Algérie*, pp. 142–45, 147, 149–61; Planchais, *Revue française de Sociologie*, p. 122; Girardet *et al.*, *Crise militaire*, pp. 165–67; Brune, *La Nation française*, pp. 6–7; Tournoux, *Secrets d'état*, pp. 212, 338; Liber, *Réalités*, p. 39; Guy Mollet, *L'Armée et la nation* (Arras: Société d'Editions du Pas–de–Calais, 1960, pp. 28–29; Dufresnoy, *Des officiers parlent*, p. 177; and the testimony of Lieutenant Durand Ruell (who arrested General Gambiez in the April putsch), *LM*, July 8, 1961, p. 5.

34. *Lieutenant en Algérie*, p. 59. See also *ibid.*, pp. 60–63.

35. Even before the campaign of 1940 was over, young officers had begun to doubt the wisdom of their elders (Bloch, *L'étrange défaite*, p. 77).

36. Summaries of the "Affaire des Généraux" are found in Alexander Werth, *France, 1940–1958* (London: Robert Hale, 1956), pp. 459–67; Fauvet, *La IVᵉ République*, pp. 159–63; Lancaster, *The Emancipation of Indochina*, pp. 407–10; and (the most complete account) Georgette Elgey, *La République des illusions*, pp. 467–96.

37. Twelve years later the Conseil d'Etat annulled Revers' forced retirement, finding there had been technical errors of procedure (*LM*, March 24, 1962).

38. In the trial of Colonel de la Chapelle, June 27, 1961 (*Procès du Putsch*, p. 58). On the same theme a *Message* editorialist complained in April, 1956, that the high command was listened to by politicians only because it played the game of complacency: "C'est ainsi que nos chefs ont pris l'habitude, à de rares et inutiles exceptions près, d'être les instruments et les garants d'une politique à la petite semaine dont nous connaissons tous les effets" (editorial, No. 13 [April, 1956], p. 2).

39. " . . . Si on a parlé des colonels, eh bien! c'est parce qu'il y avait des colonels qui faisaient la guerre et que les autres ne la faisaient pas beaucoup" (Trinquier, in *Procès Salan*, pp. 408–9).

40. Navarre, *Agonie de l'Indochine*, pp. 318–19.

41. In his testimony in the Barricades trial General Massu associated himself with the *guerre révolutionnaire* camp and indirectly rebuked the "higher echelons" generally for failure to understand that doctrine: "Et si cette guerre [la guerre subversive] est peu connue aux échelons supérieurs, à celui du commandement des forces armées en Algérie du moins à celui-là était codifiée" (*Un Procès*, p. 80).

42. See above, p. 101.

43. *Malaventure en Algérie*, pp. 142–45, 147, 149–61.

44. *Ibid.*, p. 153.

45. In his book *Les Parachutistes*, (Paris: Editions du Seuil, 1961), pp. 27–41, former paratrooper Gilles Perrault describes the elite corps as being necessarily a symbol of national decadence, an admission that ordinary citizens are no longer willing to fight in defense of the nation. As Jean Planchais indicated in his review of the book (*LM*, February 16, 1962), Perrault errs in taking French popular disinterest in defense of the colonies as definitive proof of the unwillingness of Frenchmen to defend the homeland.

46. "Pourquoi nous avons 'perdu' la guerre d'Algérie," *La Nef*, No. 7 (July-September, 1961), (a special issue entitled *L'Armée Française*), pp. 30–31; Darboise *et al.*, *Officiers en Algérie*, pp. 12–13; the letter signed "Simplet," *RMI*, No. 309 (October, 1959), p. 102; and Barberot, *Malaventure en Algérie*, p. 36.

47. Colonel Charles Lacheroy was emphatic on this point: "Dans la guerre révolutionnaire, le condottière c'est un malheur, les croix de guerre aussi, parce que pour avoir une croix de guerre on fait le condottière. En réalité celui qui est le maître dans la guerre révolutionnaire c'est celui à qui on a donné un pré carré et qui considère ce pré carré comme sa chose" (*La Défense nationale*, p. 328). See also the remarks of an officer quoted by Jules Roy in his introduction to Dufresnoy, *Des officiers parlent*, p. xvi.

48. Buis, *La Grotte*, p. 50.

49. The largest army contingents were the regular infantry (46 per cent) and armor (10 per cent). Army personnel made up 88 per cent of the total French military forces in Algeria, while the air force contributed 6 per cent, the navy 3 per cent, and the Gendarmarie 3 per cent. Draftees made up two-thirds of the total (Colonel Montfort, "La Situation militaire en Algérie," *Revue militaire suisse* [February, 1960], p. 53).

50. *LM.*, June 1, 1962. See also the report of an O.A.S. "traffic control" operation near Paris carried out by men in *para* uniforms (*LM.*, June 8, 1962).

51. The essays were excerpted in a brochure, *Et ils pacifièrent Alger* (Brussels, 1959); in *Les Temps modernes*, No. 164 (October, 1959); and in Perrault, *Les Parachutistes*, p. 9. The quotations here are from excerpts found in P. Kessel and G. Pirelli, *Le Peuple algérien et la guerre: Lettres and témoignages, 1954–1962* (Paris: Maspero, 1962), pp. 109–11.

52. *Ibid.*, pp. 109–11.

53. See above, Chapter 9; Pierre Popie, *LM*, May 30, 1958; and Tournoux, *Secrets d'état*, p. 313 (for the role of *para* Captain Graziana, who was ready to arrest Salan for his failure to break with Paris).

54. The First Paratroop Shock Battalion under Captain Ignace-Jules Mantei was stationed in Corsica at the time and, after rallying to Algiers, met and "neutralized" gendarmes who had been sent from the *métropole* to halt the rebellion (De Sérigny, *La Révolution du treize mai*, pp. 118–19). As for metropolitan France, the commander of Massu's headquarters company, Major Vitasse, was in Paris after the *treize mai* and is said to have given clandestine orders to paratroop officers concerning Operation Resurrection, the plan for a military coup in the *métropole*. General Miquel, commander of that operation, planned to rely primarily on paratroop units stationed in southwest France (Tournoux, *Secrets d'état*, pp. 356, 377–78).

55. See above, Chapter 9; Brombergers *et al.*, *Barricades et colonels*, pp. 126–28, 182–85, 207, 375–79; and Argoud, in *Sans commentaire*, pp. 51–52.

56. Five of the seven who were given firm prison sentences were paratroopers, as were two of the six who were sentenced *in absentia* and twentynine of the forty-four who were given suspended sentences. See *Procès du putsch, passim*; and Fauvet and Planchais, *La Fronde des généraux*, pp. 259–60. Generals have been eliminated from the totals because they have no permanent arm of assignment.

57. Most paratroop officers stayed to face trial. Among those who deserted to joint the O.A.S., either in April, 1961, or later, were Colonels Broizat, Godard, Vaudrey, Dufour, and Chateau-Jobert. Enlisted *paras*, or former *paras*, were also numerous in the ranks of the O.A.S. To cite an example, all three of the men who attempted to burn down the Leftist Librairie Maspero were former *paras* and credited their political persuasion to that association (*LM*, February 21, 1962). See also the article by J.-M. Théollèyre in *LM*, July 12, 1962.

58. Shils and Janowitz, *Public Opinion Quarterly*, pp. 280–315; and Stouffer *et al.*, *The American Soldier*.

59. *Les Parachutistes*, p. 23.

60. *Les Centurions*, pp. 272–73.

61. *Ibid.*, p. 243.

62. The Twenty-fifth Division, of which these regiments were a part, was scheduled to launch a military operation against rebel bands in the Constantine area beginning April 22. Masselot and Lecomte headed toward Algiers with their units, rather than reporting for battle as ordered (Fauvet and Planchais, *La Fronde des généraux*, pp. 123–24).

63. J. Planchais, "Quelle est cette armée?" *La Nef*, No. 7 (July–September, 1961), p. 58.

64. Paratroop officers tended to attach considerable importance to the conversion of draftees. Colonel Trinquier believed they made better soldiers than enlistees (interview, April 2, 1962).

65. As mentioned above in Chapter 4, one former student at the Institut d'Etudes Politiques in Paris, an intellectual of the Left, did his military service in a paratroop unit and emerged, I was told, with nothing but enthusiasm for the *esprit para* and a considerable sympathy with the April putsch. I talked personally with another paratroop reserve lieutenant who had a similar experience. Apparently such "conversions" were quite common.

66. Quoted by J.M. Théollèyre in *LM*, July 12, 1962, p. 3.

67. *Les Parachutistes*, p. 131.

68. Thieuloy, "L'Esprit para décrit par un para," *L'Express*, July 10, 1958, p. 14. See also Perrault, *Les Parachutistes*, pp. 130–32.

69. *Ibid.* Perrault's description is very similar (*Les Parachutistes*, pp. 129–32).

70. When the need arose, draftees were sometimes assigned to paratroop units without volunteering. Normally, they went through basic training with the paratroopers but were kept in that arm only if they then volunteered for jump school, as many did. In one unit over 90 per cent volunteered (interview with Reserve Lieutenant F. L., who served in both the Tenth and the Twenty-fifth paratroop divisions). During the height of the Algerian war, when paratroopers rarely jumped, draftees without jump training were often assigned permanently to combat paratroop units.

71. See the reports of the court-martial of the accused, Corporal Lucien Tribut, in *LM*, January 16, 1963; and *ibid.*, January 17, 1963. He was sentenced to one year in prison.

72. Perrault, *Les Parachutistes*, pp. 47–48; Thieuloy, *L'Express*, July 10, 1958, p. 14; and Lartéguy, *Les Centurions*, p. 272.

73. *LM*, January 5, 1962; *ibid.*, June 19, 1962; Perrault, *Les Parachutistes*, p. 38.

74. Perrault, *Les Parachutistes*, p. 48.

75. *LM*, June 19, 1962.

76. A study of the "Bigeard Problem" supposedly done by another paratroop colonel, Chateau-Jobert, concluded: "Il n'y a pas de problème Bigeard, il y a un problème du commandement vis-à-vis de Bigeard. Bigeard sait faire naître immédiatement un complexe d'infériorité chez ceux qui n'ont pas ses titres de guerre. Des généraux ont peur de lui: il refuse d'en recevoir à l'hôpital. Il enfreint les ordres relatifs au maintien sur place des matériels de secteur et le commandement laisse faire. Des commandants de régiments dont Bigeard, sont convoqués par un général dans une tenue fixée par ce dernier. Bigeard arrive dans une autre tenue. Un commandant de régiment s'étonne: on lui répond que Bigeard a eu raison. . . . Devant le succès de Bigeard, la seule conclusion logique est qu'aujourd'hui tout officier doit pour réussir se moquer du commandement" (quoted in Paillat, *Dossier secret*, pp. 374–75). See also Lartéguy, *Les Centurions, passim*, for similar examples.

77. "We were taught to mistrust civilians," writes paratroop veteran J.-J. Thieuloy (*L'Express*, July 10, 1958, p. 14).

78. *Les Centurions*, p. 272. See also Perrault, *Les Parachutistes*, pp. 148–54, and Thieuloy, *L'Express*, July 10, 1958, pp. 14–15.

79. *L'Express*, July 10, 1958, p. 15.

80. *Ibid.*, pp. 14–15; Perrault, *Les Parachutistes*, pp. 157–66; Lartéguy, *Les Centurions*, pp. 229, 271–72. For a contrasting description of the paratroopers from the viewpoint of a disillusioned veteran who stresses the brutality and inanity of the Algerian war, see Leulliette, *Saint Michel et le dragon*.

81. From the text in Gilles Perrault, *Les Parachutistes*, p. 157.

82. Colonel Marcel Bigeard and Sergeant-Chef Marc Flament, *Aucune bête du monde* (Paris: Editions de la Pensée Moderne, 1959), pages unnumbered.

83. *Ibid.*

84. *Ibid.*

85. *Ibid.*

86. As quoted by Thieuloy, *L'Express*, July 10, 1958, pp. 14–15.

87. *Les Parachutistes*, especially pp. 157–63.

88. The *para* enlisted ranks were filled with very young men, most being eighteen to twenty years of age (Leulliette, *Saint Michel et le dragon*, p. 9; Perrault, *Les Parachutistes, passim*).

89. *Ibid.*, pp. 157–67, tends to ignore the key political role of the *paras* in Algeria, especially in the three major crises of May, 1958, January, 1960, and April, 1961.

90. Colonel Darmuzai, commander of the Second Foreign Paratroop Regiment, could not decide upon a course of action and saw his regiment snatched out from under him by the Challists. Colonels Pfirrmann of the Fifth Foreign Regiment and Brothier of the First, both absent from their units when the putsch broke out, returned to regain control of their regiments, which (under interim commanders) had been co-operating in part with the Challists. With regard to the behavior of the Legion during the putsch, see

Fauvet and Planchais, *La Fronde des généraux,* pp. 127, 132–36, 174–75; *Procès Challe,* pp. 116–19, 126–30; and *Procès du putsch,* pp. 104–8.

91. See the testimony of General Perrotat, who attended the meeting between Gardy and Brothier as commander of the Centre-Oranais zone, centered in Sidi-Bel-Abbès (*Procès Challe,* p. 126).

92. Fauvet and Planchais, *La Fronde des généraux,* pp. 259–60; and *Procès du Putsch, passim.*

93. According to Perrault, their Legion loyalties were stronger, however, as evidenced by their wearing the white Legion *képi* when off post, rather than the green beret which identified them as Legion paratroopers (*Les Parachutistes,* p. 47).

94. First at Cao Bang in 1950, when only three officers escaped capture or death, and again at Dien Bien Phu (Paillat, *Dossier secret,* pp. 44–45).

95. Testimony of Colonel Brothier in the trial of ex-Legionnaires Albert Dovecar, Claude Tenne, and Hubert Petri for the O.A.S. murder of Police Commissioner Gavoury (*LM,* March 30, 1962). See also Paillat, *Dossier secret,* p. 45.

96. Colonel Brothier, recalling the time when he took command of the First Foreign Paratroop Regiment in 1958, just after the battle of Guelma, gave this revealing testimony: "Je n'ai jamais compris autant le sens du mot unité qu'au temps du 1er R.E.P. Ce n'était pas une unité, c'était un bloc, mot officiers aux hommes. Les officiers avaient de l'estime pour leurs hommes. Les hommes de l'affection pour leurs officiers. Car, c'est une des characteristiques exceptionnelles de la légion que cette fidélité de chiens des hommes à leurs cadres. C'est auprès d'eux qu'ils trouvaient le squelette d'équilibre que la vie civile ne leur avait pas donné. Ainsi ils reportaient sur leurs officiers toute la somme d'attachement et d'affection dont ils sont capables. Car ils sont sans esprit critique. De leurs officiers ils admettent tout, même l'extravagant. C'est, je crois, ce qui les a menés ici . . . " (*LM,* March 30, 1962).

97. *Ibid.*; and Fauvet and Planchais, *La Fronde des généraux,* p. 134. In fact, the Legion was not dissolved with the advent of Algerian independence in 1962. Legion regiments were established in the Sahara, in Corsica, in Madagascar, in French Somaliland (Côte des Somalis), in French Guiana, and in southern France. See *LM,* May 13–14, 1962; May 31, 1962; June 16, 1962; and June 22, 1962.

98. See the personal report by W. Granger Blair in the *NYT,* April 28, 1961; and Perrault, *Les Parachutistes,* p. 167.

99. *Procès du putsch,* p. 84.

100. *LM,* July 8, 1961; and *Procès du putsch,* p. 78.

101. Captains Lesaur and Glasser, and Lieutenants Déguelde, Godot, Picot d'Aligny d'Assignies, de la Bigne, and Coatelem. In addition, at least one officer who was given a suspended sentence after the putsch, Captain Bonnel, made his way into the O.A.S., and another former officer of the First Foreign Paratroop Regiment from 1959 to 1960, Capitaine Sergent, became the O.A.S. chief in the *métropole.* See *LM,* March 15, 1962; June 16, 1962; April 11, 1962; January 8, 1962; February 28, 1962; and June 30, 1962 (Déguelde's death sentence).

102. For example, the Commando Delta, led by Lieutenant Déguelde, *LM,* March 30, 1962; and *ibid.,* June 30, 1962.

Conclusion

Those French civil-military tensions which erupted in May, 1958, may be viewed profitably from two points of view. On the one hand, military indiscipline and revolt in France were the result of a unique and impressive conjuncture of historical factors. A brief overview of the most important of those factors will serve to place them in perspective. From another point of view to be taken up following that brief survey—that of the student of comparative politics—the French experience casts new light on cross-national theories of civil-military relations.

The recent political adventures of the French Army are not explicable in terms of a long tradition of military intervention in politics. On the contrary, until World War II the army, with rare exceptions, was a disciplined servant of the government of the day, no matter what the political complexion of that government. When the army posed an open threat to civilian political institutions in France (in the years from 1958 to 1961), it acted under the impulse of a long series of grievances and frustrations, including a string of humiliating defeats which began in 1940. In the eyes of most army officers the Algerian war became the final, the decisive battleground on which military status, self-esteem, and honor had to be redeemed. Faced with a highly political style of war in Indochina and Algeria, on the one hand, and with a divided French nation which devoted little interest and gave even less support to wars for the defense of empire, on the other hand, the more dynamic elements within the French Army officer corps threw up an ideology to guide and justify their cause. They determined to save France despite herself. When the wars went badly, those officers, not entirely without cause, tended to blame their failures on treason in the *métropole* and weakness and immobility in government. A series of ephemeral governments of the Fourth Republic suffered from the shallowness of their authority, the flimsiness of the French political consensus, and a resulting general doubt as to the legitimacy of the whole structure of government. Unsupported by a strong public opinion, yet too weak to cut France free from her colonies, these governments defaulted in the definition of war goals and increasingly gave over the war, especially in Algeria, to psychological-action officers, military administrators, and aggressive elite troops.

With military honor, status, and self-esteem seemingly in the balance, officers naturally recalled the army experiences of World War II, when unquestioning obedience had been largely discredited. Those officers whose personal and group involvement in the Algerian war were deepest tended to take the lead in throwing the army behind the uprising of French settlers in Algeria on the *treize mai*. De Gaulle lent new authority to civil government; yet, though he was able finally to overcome military revolt, he was not able to prevent its occurrence. The symbolic importance which Algeria had assumed for the army, the extensive powers which military men had been given there, and the successful precedent of May 13—all conspired to encourage another military intervention into politics in April, 1961, again with the purpose of preventing Algerian independence.

Decolonization would have been a bitter pill for the army in any case. Coupled with the recent trauma of World War II, long and highly political wars in Indochina and Algeria, an unsympathetic public opinion at home, and a power vacuum in civilian government until 1958, it proved explosive.

Several of the key factors in this pattern deserve closer attention, particularly with respect to their implications for theories of civil-military relations. First, and most important, the French experience from 1945 to 1962 lends added weight to the theory that military intervention in politics is closely related to the degree of *legitimacy* of existing civilian political institutions, i.e., the strength and breadth of the national political consensus which supports them.[1] Had government leaders in Paris enjoyed solid authority and the backing of a more united nation, in all probability there never would have been a serious threat to civilian control in France. In fact, however, the authority of the Fourth Republic was challenged both on the Left, where the Communist Party commanded the votes of almost a quarter of the electorate, and—especially after the Poujadist gains of January, 1956—on the Right, where the army traditionally was viewed as a powerful potential ally.

Nor did the majority of Frenchmen between these political extremes feel much attachment to the existing regime. The apathy of the French population in May, 1958, when the Fourth Republic was fighting for its life, was a determining factor in the outcome of that crisis. The Pflimlin government and the National Assembly itself quickly discovered that very few Frenchmen indeed were willing to fight, or even to protest very loudly, in defense of *le système*. De Gaulle's trump card three years later in the April putsch was his command over public opinion. In April, 1961, army fears of "betrayal" and "abandonment" of French Algeria were more vivid and more soundly based than had been the case in 1958. Yet in 1961 the leaders of military revolt faced a hostile French public opinion which mobilized behind De Gaulle and which reached into the conscript ranks of the army itself. General Challe failed to attract the active support of the majority of officers, for these men saw that mutiny now meant civil war and a split within the army.

It may well be that the French citizenry in 1961 was no more deeply attached to the Fifth Republic as a pattern of institutions than it had been to its predecessor. Yet De Gaulle himself, as a charismatic leader, had succeeded in establishing the legitimacy of his own personal government to a degree unknown under the Fourth Republic. Aided by a widespread popular desire to have done with colonial wars (witness the referendum of January, 1961), De Gaulle could claim with good reason to represent the

French nation in throwing his enormous prestige behind the policy of self-determination for Algeria. However, based as it was on the unique historical and personal appeal of its leader, as well as his political acumen, De Gaulle's Republic benefited from a kind of legitimacy which would be unavailable for the defense of a successor government or for the protection of a constitutional transfer of power from one administration to another. Effective civilian leadership may compensate temporarily, but only temporarily, for the absence of a strong constitutional consensus.

The absence of a firm political consensus capable of lending legitimacy to political institutions may be a necessary condition for successful military revolt, as it was in postwar France; yet it is not sufficient in itself to produce a pattern of praetorianism, as French history in the nineteenth century reveals. Other compensating factors, to be reviewed shortly, were sufficient to maintain civilian control.

Two other factors which contributed to military indiscipline and revolt in France—military hostility to *le système* and delegation of power—are closely related to the weakness of governmental authority and to the political dissension which lay behind it. When a nation lacks the stable bonds of a strong political consensus and when, as a result, political authority is uncertain, the relation of the military establishment to politics may take one of two forms, or may partake of a mixture of the two. If dissension is chronic, the military establishment itself may suffer the same lack of authority and unity which characterizes the society around it. Such sometimes has been the case in Latin America, where military factions have opposed each other. On the other hand, if the military establishment is relatively cohesive (as a result, perhaps, of a professional military spirit and social isolation from civilian society), there is a tendency for officers to conceive of the military as an island of health, unity, and courage in a sea of corruption, conflict, and decay. Such was clearly the case in France, especially among younger officers in the field. From the 1930's onward the rise of the French Communist Party had loomed large in most military eyes as a vicious internal threat to national security. After 1945 the consistent attacks on the army by the French Communist Party and by other French anticolonialists, the government's reluctance to silence these critics, and the general absence of public support for colonial wars—all were taken by military men as evidence of advanced dry rot in the body politic.

When political authority wanes in a democracy, the latent conflict between military and civilian values is likely to come to the fore. By virtue of his primary responsibility for national defense, the military officer may be encouraged to believe that his devotion to country is stronger and purer than that of civilian politicians. Indeed, in some cases it may be so, though the belief is more important than the fact. The very distinction between nation and government which allowed French officers in the nineteenth century to serve a succession of governments had the reverse effect after 1945: it encouraged military resistance to governments viewed by many officers as antithetical to the interests of the nation. The tension between dominant civilian and military perspectives becomes particularly acute when, as in France, civilian politicians disagree among themselves as to the meaning and scope of national defense. For the military officer and for a decreasing proportion of French politicians, defense of the nation was taken to include defense of the colonies. Journalists, politicians, and then government ministers who rejected that interpretation were viewed as cowards at best, traitors at worst, deserving in any case of being silenced or ejected from their posts.

As is usually the case, in all probability, the French officers who sought to save France from her government—indeed, from herself—held a concept of national interest which meshed neatly with the defense of military interests. They protested bitterly against political attacks on the army and against the surrender of the colonies, which many saw as the locus of the army's last hope for the redemption of its prestige, glory, and honor. Like the doctrine of *la guerre révolutionnaire*, the military view of patriotism as nation above government served primarily to rationalize and to strengthen the defense of military interests, even by indiscipline and revolt, if necessary.

Suffering from lack of consensus with regard to war goals and from a generally doubtful authority, the Fourth Republic faced a dilemma in which delegation of power to the army was especially dangerous for civilian control, yet unavoidable if any action was to be taken. Civil administrators in the *métropole* protested at the very suggestion that they might be sent to Algeria. The government in Paris, hesitant to rely heavily upon conscripts in wars which were not strongly supported by the French public at home, fell back on the Legion and the paratroopers to carry the brunt of the fighting in Indochina and in Algeria. The psychological-action service, military administrators, and the paratroopers were all delegated extensive political powers. In the absence of national support for colonial wars, military power-wielders became increasingly angry, undisciplined, and, in some cases, mutinous. Within the *paras* the seeming weakness and cowardliness of civilian politicians turned a formidable *esprit de corps* into a mutinous force. Military *esprit de corps* in itself need not be a threat to civilian control: witness the disciplined U.S. Marine Corps. When civilian governmental authority is faltering, however, and when military interests clash with government policies, military *esprit de corps* (along with delegation of political power to the military) may have dangerous consequences for civilian control.

French experience in civil-military relations also lends some support, with important qualifications, to that theory, elaborated most completely by Samuel Huntington, which holds military professionalism to be the surest guarantee of civilian control in a democracy.[2] The progressive professionalization of the French Army in the nineteenth century was one important factor which helped to assure civilian control, despite the relative weakness of the French political consensus. In the course of the nineteenth century the army officers corps took on many of the characteristics of an order, drawing in men of diverse social origins and molding them into professional soldiers with similar values. Particularly during periods when commercial values and republican values dominated civilian society, the professional soldier's respect for authority, hierarchy, discipline, and service set him clearly apart. Disharmony between civilian and military values rarely led to open conflict, however, for the professional military code decreed that the officer must maintain strict political neutrality in his behavior, if not in his private attitudes. At least until World War II most officers believed that only military *apolitisme* could protect the honor, efficiency, and unity of the French Army.

The rather consistent loyalty of the French Army to civilian authority before 1939 cannot be explained entirely in terms of professional military restraints, however. Also of significance were the absence of long wars in the period from 1815–70, which might have strained civilian control, and the outlet furnished by colonial service for ambitious officers whose taste for power and glory could not be satisfied in the *métropole*. In the absence of serious threats to national security in the mid-nineteenth century, the military community could safely be left in relative social isolation, where it gradually developed an apolitical professional military code. After 1945, however, social isolation had the opposite effect—threatening, rather than deepening, the soldier's political neutrality—as revolutionary-guerrilla wars made the army dependent upon active popular and governmental support for victory.

In recent years it has become increasingly clear that professionalism alone is inadequate to assure civilian control, especially when the army is in the service of a liberal democracy: since professional military values may clash with dominant civilian values, the officer must also have a positive commitment to civil supremacy.[3] French experience clearly demonstrates the potential conflict between obedience and military honor, which is also a significant part of the professional officer's mental baggage, at least in the West. The bitter prospect of dishonoring themselves through surrender and through renunciation of military pledges overshadowed the sin of disobedience in the minds of a number of French officers.

If the notion of military professionalism is to attain its full utility, it also must be complemented with equal attention to the corporate interests of military men. For many French officers the colonies in general, and North Africa in particular, traditionally represented a coveted refuge in which they could escape the moral climate of the *métropole,* which was often bourgeois and antimilitary, and enjoy greater status, authority, and independence than were their lot at home. A decade and a half of humiliating defeat and retreat in the colonies built up in many French military minds the conviction that military status and self-esteem were inseparable from the cause of *Algérie Française.* French military indiscipline and revolt in Algeria are understandable, not so much in terms of a "breakdown of professionalism," as in terms of the impassioned defense of military power, status, and self-esteem.

Military professionalism, nevertheless, is still one of the most important supports to civilian control. Among the more difficult problems posed by revolutionary-guerrilla war is that of retaining professionalism while allowing professional military men to wage battle on the enemy's own (i.e., political) terms. The old solution of dividing defense neatly into political and military realms was always partly fiction; in revolutionary-guerrilla war it is altogether unfeasible.[4] Success in such a war requires, among other things, both a political program capable of inspiring popular support and a mobilization of the masses around that program through an extensive and intensive organizational effort. Organized popular support—not simply destruction of rebel guerrilla bands—is the key to success. The experience of the French in Indochina and in Algeria reveals the potential danger to civilian control (as well as to military effectiveness) inherent in governmental immobility in a revolutionary-war situation. Civil authorities must supply clear political directives, lest a defending army be either frustrated by defeat or tempted into the political vacuum to define its own war goals. The power of the French military doctrine of *la guerre révolutionnaire,* with all of its ideological overtones, was largely the result of governmental inaction and immobility in the definition of policy and war goals.

Political directives, no matter what their origin or intrinsic merit, will have very limited effect unless military officers and enlisted men in the field believe in them, for these are the men who will have the most direct contact with the population. The French experience suggests, as well, the difficulty of changing war goals once an army defending against a revolutionary-guerrilla enemy has come to believe in them. The effect of a policy change on army morale perhaps could be mitigated if government officials kept military leaders informed of the government's objectives, priorities, and alternative plans of action should the current policy fail. The problem is essentially that of finding a minimal political commitment which will allow the soldier to battle with conviction and with effect without, at the same time, throwing him into the domestic political struggle. The narrower the range of universally accepted political ideas and values in a society, the more difficult the problem.

After the stormy conclusion to the Algerian war, what can be said of the prospects for future civil-military relations in France? Civilianization, long delayed in the French Army, is now clearly underway. The officer-technician now being created will probably lack much of the militancy of the paratrooper and the theoretician of *la guerre révolutionnaire*, though he probably will develop skill as a political promoter of his new technical army. In view of the attitudes of recent army-officer recruits, the whole transformation from guerrilla fighter to technician will be a difficult one.

Under what circumstances might the army again threaten civilian control in France, despite the lesson of April, 1961? With colonial questions largely settled, the radical Right, which might encourage military intervention, has all but disappeared as an important political force. It is conceivable that the plight of uneconomical small farmers and businessmen might produce new Poujadist-style protest movements against the dominant, modern economic forces in the Gaullist camp. In the unlikely event of a serious economic depression, or perhaps in reaction to the excessive economic conservatism of a post-Gaullist government, it is possible that the Communist Party might burst out of its isolation and take the lead in a popular-front government. In such a circumstance it is possible that the army, which remains fiercely anticommunist, might again intervene, encouraged by the radical Right. Prosperity and the Common Market, however, should prevent such a development and strengthen the hand of political moderates. Nevertheless, civilian control in France continues to suffer from the absence of a clear and abiding public attachment to a stable constitutional framework. The emergence of a deeper constitutional consensus, which is not yet in sight, would greatly strengthen the hand of civilian authority, especially at such critical moments as the transfer of power from one government to the next.

1. Rapoport, "Praetorianism: Government without Consensus"; and Finer, *The Man on Horseback.*

2. Huntington, *The Soldier and the State.*

3. Finer, *The Man on Horseback*, chap. 4.

4. As Huntington himself is well aware (Huntington, *Changing Patterns of Military Politics*, p. 22).

Bibliography

Bibliography

Books

ALLEG, HENRI. *La Question.* Paris: Les Editions de Minuit, 1958.

ALQUIER, JEAN-YVES. *Nous avons pacifié Tazalt: Journal de marche d'un parachutiste rappelé en Algérie.* Paris: Lafont, 1957.

ANDREWS, WILLIAM G. *French Politics and Algeria: The Process of Policy Formation, 1954–1962.* New York: Appleton-Century-Crofts, 1962.

L'Année politique. Published annually by the Presses Universitaires de France, Paris.

ARGOUD, COLONEL ANTOINE. *Sans commentaire,* ed. Comité Audin. Paris: Editions de Minuit, 1961.

ARNAUD, GEORGES, and VERGÈS, JACQUES. *Pour Djamila Bouhired.* Paris: Les Editions de Minuit, 1957.

ARON, RAYMOND. *L'Algérie et la république.* Paris: Plon, 1958.

———. *La Tragédie algérienne.* Paris: Plon, 1957.

ARON, ROBERT. *Histoire de la Libération.* Paris: Fayard, 1959.

———. *Histoire de Vichy.* Paris: Fayard, 1954.

AVRIGNY, LUCIEN D'. *La Crise sociale et l'armée.* Paris: "Armée et Démocratie," 1911.

AZEAU, HENRI, *Révolte militaire: Alger, 22 avril 1961.* Paris: Plon, 1961.

BACLAGON, LIEUTENANT COLONEL ULDARICO S. *Lessons from the Huk Campaign in the Philippines.* Rizal, Philippines: Philippine Army Training Command, 1956; mimeo.

BANKWITZ, PHILIP. "Weygand: A Biographical Study." Unpublished Ph.D. dissertation, Harvard University, 1952.

BARALE, JEAN. *La IVeme République et la guerre*. Aix-en-Provence: La Pensée Universitaire, 1961; mimeo.

BARBEROT, ROGER. *Malaventure en Algérie avec le Général Paris de Bollardière*. Paris: Plon, 1957.

BASSOT, HUBERT. *Les Silencieux*. Paris: Berger-Levrault, 1958.

BEAUFRE, GENERAL ANDRÉ. *Le Drame de 1940*. Paris: Plon, 1965.

BEAUVOIR, SIMONE DE, and HALIM, GISÈLE. *Djamila Boupacha*. Paris: Gallimard, 1962. Translated by PETER GREEN. New York: Macmillan, 1962.

BIGEARD, COLONEL MARCEL, and FLAMENT, SERGENT-CHEF MARC. *Aucune bête au monde*. Paris: Editions de la Pensée Moderne, 1959.

BLET, HENRI. *Histoire de la colonisation française*. 3 vols. Grenoble and Paris: Arthaud, 1947 (Vol. II), 1950 (Vol. III).

BLOCH, MARC. *L'etrange défaite: Témoignage écrit en 1940*. Paris: Colin, 1947.

BONNEFOUS, EDOUARD. *Histoire politique de la Troisième République*. Paris: Presses Universitaires de France, 1962.

BONNET, COLONEL GABRIEL. *Les Guerres insurrectionnelles et révolutionnaires*. Paris: Payot, 1958.

BOUILLON, J. et al. *L'Armée de la Seconde République*. ("Bibliothèque de la Révolution de 1848," Vol. XVIII.) La Roche-sur-Yon: Imprimerie Centrale de l'Ouest, 1955.

BOURDIEU, PIERRE. *Sociologie de l'Algérie*. Paris: Presses Universitaires de France, 1958 (revised in 1961). Translated by ALAN C. M. ROSS as *The Algeriens*. Boston: Beacon Press, 1962.

BOURRET, GENERAL. *La Tragédie de l'Armée Française*. Paris: La Table Ronde, 1947.

BRACE, RICHARD, and BRACE, JOAN. *Ordeal in Algeria*. New York: Van Nostrand, 1960.

BROGAN, DENNIS W. *France under the Republic*. New York: Harper, 1940.

BROMBERGER, MERRY, and BROMBERGER, SERGE. *Les 13 complots du 13 mai*. Paris: Fayard, 1959.

BROMBERGER, MERRY; BROMBERGER, SERGE; ELGEY, GEORGETTE; and CHAUVEL, J.-F. *Barricades et colonels: 24 Janvier 1960*. Paris: Fayard, 1960.

BROMBERGER, SERGE. *Les Rebelles algériens*. Paris: Plon, 1958.

Buis, Georges. *La Grotte.* Paris: Julliard, 1961.

Carrias, Eugène. *La Pensée militaire française.* Paris: Presses Universitaires de France, 1960.

Castellane, Boniface de. *Journal du Maréchal de Castellane.* 4 vols. Paris: Plon, 1895–97.

Catroux, General Georges. *Deux actes du drame indochinois; Hanoi: Juin 1940; Dien-Bien-Phu: Mars-Mai 1954.* Paris: Plon, 1959.

Centre de Sciences Politiques de l'Institut d'Etudes Juridiques de Nice and Faculté de Droit et des Sciences Economiques d'Aix (eds.). *La Défense nationale.* Paris: Presses Universitaires de France. 1958.

Ceux d'Algérie. Lettres de rappelés. Paris: Plon, 1957.

Challener, Richard. *The French Theory of the Nation in Arms, 1866–1939.* New York: Columbia University Press, 1955.

Chalmin, Pierre. *L'Officier français de 1815 à 1870.* Paris: Rivière, 1957.

Chamine. *La Querelle des généraux.* Paris: Michel, 1952.

Chapman, Guy. *The Dreyfus Case: A Reassessment.* London: Rupert Hart-Davis, 1955.

Charnay, Jean-Paul. *Société militaire et suffrage politique en France depuis 1789.* Paris: S.E.V.P.E.N., 1964.

Chassin, General Lionel-Martin. *L'Ascension de Mao-tse-Tung.* Paris: Payot, 1953.

———. *La Conquête de la Chine par Mao-tse-Tung.* Paris: Payot, 1952.

Chateau-Jobert, Colonel Pierre. *Manifeste politique et social.* Meaux: Editions du Fuseau, 1964.

Clark, General Mark W. *Calculated Risk.* New York: Harper, 1950.

Clark, Michael K. *Algeria in Turmoil: A History of the Rebellion.* New York: Praeger, 1959.

Clausewitz, Karl von. *On War.* Translated by O. J. Matthijs Jolles. New York: Modern Library, 1943.

Cobban, Alfred. "Vichy France," in *Hitler's Europe,* ed. Arnold Toynbee and Veronica M. Toynbee ("Survey of International Affairs, 1939–1946"). London: Oxford University Press, 1954.

Coblentz, Paul. *The Silence of Sarrail.* London: Hutchinson, n.d.

Coles, Harry L. (ed.). *Total War and Cold War: Problems in Civilian Control of the Military.* Columbus: Ohio State University Press, 1962.

Comité Audin (ed.). *Sans Commentaire.* Paris: Editions de minuit, 1957.

COMMISSAIRE, SÉBASTIEN. *Mémoires et souvenirs*. Lyons: Meton, 1888.

COTTAZ, MAURICE. *Les Procès du putsch d'avril et du complot de Paris*. Paris: Nouvelles Editions Latines, 1962.

CRAIG, GORDON A. *The Politics of the Prussian Army, 1640–1945*. London: Oxford University Press, 1956.

CROZIER, BRIAN. *The Rebels*. Boston: Beacon Press, 1960.

DANSETTE, A. *Le Boulangisme*. Paris: Fayard, 1946.

DARBOISE, J.-M.; HEYNAUD, M.; and MARTEL, J. *Officiers en Algérie*. ("Cahiers libres," No. 11.) Paris: Maspero, 1960.

DEBENEY, GENERAL. *La Guerre et les hommes*. Paris: Plon, 1937.

DEBRÉ, MICHEL, *Ces Princes qui nous gouvernent*. Paris: Plon, 1957.

DELMAS, CLAUDE. *La Guerre révolutionnaire*. Paris: Presses Universitaires de France, 1959.

DÉON, MICHEL. *L'Armée d'Algérie et la pacification*. Paris: Plon, 1959.

DEVILLERS, PHILIPPE. *Histoire du Viet-Nam de 1940 à 1952*. Paris: Seuil, 1952.

DU BARAIL, GENERAL FRANÇOIS CHARLES. *Mes souvenirs*. 3 vols. Paris: Plon, 1897.

DUFRESNOY, CLAUDE. *Des officiers parlent*. Paris: Juilliard, 1961.

DUVERGER, MAURICE. *Demain la république*. Paris: Julliard, 1958.

EARLE, E. M. (ed.). *Makers of Modern Strategy*. Princeton: Princeton University Press, 1944.

ELGEY, GEORGETTE, *La République des illusions, 1945–1951: Ou la vie secrète de la IVᵉ République*. Paris: Fayard, 1965.

ELY, GENERAL PAUL. *l'Armée dans la nation*. Paris: Fayard, 1961.

EULOGE, ANDRÉ, and MOULINIER, ANTOINE. *l'Envers des Barricades: Vingt mois d'insurrection à Alger*. Paris: Plon, 1960.

FALL, BERNARD. *Street without Joy*. Harrisburg, Pa.: Stackpole, 1961.

FAUCHER, JEAN-ANDRÉ, *Les Barricades d'Alger*. Paris: Les Editions Atlantic, 1960.

FAUVET, JACQUES. *La IVᵉ République*. Paris: Fayard, 1959.

FAUVET, JACQUES, and PLANCHAIS, JEAN. *La Fronde des généraux*. Paris: Arthaud, 1961.

FAVROD, CHARLES-HENRI. *La Révolution algérienne*. Paris: Plon, 1959.

FERNIOT, JEAN. *Les Ides de mai*. Paris: Plon, 1958.

FINER, S. E. *The Man on Horseback: The Role of the Military in Politics*. New York: Praeger, 1962.

FLANDIN, PIERRE-ETIENNE. *Politique française, 1919–1940.* Paris: Les Editions Nouvelles, 1947.

FURNISS, EDGAR S., Jr. *France, Troubled Ally.* New York: Praeger, 1960.

———. *De Gaulle and the French Army.* New York: Twentieth Century Fund, 1964.

GAGLIARDI, JACQUES. *Les Hexagonaux.* Paris: Plon, 1962.

GAMELIN, GENERAL MAURICE. *Les Armées françaises de 1940.* (*Servir,* Vol. I.) Paris: Plon, 1946.

GASNIER, MICHEL. *Un Officier français: Le Capitaine Gérard de Cathelineau (1921–1957).* Paris: Nouvelles Editions Latines, 1960.

GAULLE, CHARLES DE. *The Army of the Future.* London: Hutchinson, 1940.

———. *Le Fil de l'épée.* Paris: Union Générale d'Editions, 1962.

———. *France and Her Army.* Translated by F. L. DASH. London: Hutchinson, 1945.

———. *Mémoires de guerre.* 3 vols. Paris: Plon, 1954.

GÉRIN, PAUL. *L'Algérie du 13 mai.* Paris: Gallimard, 1958.

GIAP, VO NGUYEN. *People's War, People's Army.* Hanoi: Foreign Languages Publishing House, 1961. Reprinted in facsimile edition. New York: Praeger, 1962.

GIRARDET, RAOUL. *La Société militaire dans la France contemporaine.* Paris, Plon, 1953.

GIRARDET, RAOUL; P.-M. BOUJU; and J.-P. THOMAS. *La Crise militaire française, 1945–1962.* ("Cahiers de la Fondation Nationale des Sciences Politique," No. 123.) Paris: Colin, 1964.

GOHIER, URBAIN. *L'Armée contre la nation.* Paris: Editions de la Revue Blanche, 1899.

GRALL, XAVIER. *La Génération du Djebel.* Paris: Editions du Cerf, 1962.

GREENE, LIEUTENANT COLONEL T. N. (ed.). *The Guerrilla—And How to Fight Him.* New York: Praeger, 1962.

GUEDALLA, PHILIP. *The Two Marshals: Bazaine, Pétain.* New York: Reynal and Hitchcock, 1943.

GUÉRARD, ALBERT. *Napoleon I.* New York: Knopf, 1959.

GUEVARRA, ERNESTO "CHE." *Guerrilla Warfare.* New York. Monthly Review Press, 1961.

GUILLEMIN, HENRI. *Le Coup du 2 décembre.* 8th ed.; Paris: Gallimard, 1951.

HANOTAUX, GABRIEL. *Histoire de la France contemporaine.* 4 vols. Paris: Société d'Editions Contemporaine, 1908.

HANOTAUX, GABRIEL; MANGIN, CHARLES; and FRANCHET D'ESPEREY, L.-F.-M. *Histoire militaire et navale.* (*Histoire de la nation française,* ed. GABRIEL HANOTAUX, Vol. VIII.) Paris: Plon, 1927.

HART, B. H. LIDDELL. *The Remaking of Modern Armies.* Boston: Little Brown, 1928.

HERVET, ROBERT. *Les Chantiers de la jeunesse.* Paris: Editions France-Empire, 1962.

HOFFMAN, STANLEY et al. *In Search of France.* Cambridge, Mass.: Harvard University Press, 1963.

The Hoover Institution of War, Revolution, and Peace, Stanford University. *France during the German Occupation, 1940–1944.* 3 vols. Stanford, Calif.: Stanford University Press, 1957.

HOWARD, MICHAEL (ed.). *Soldiers and Governments: Nine Studies in Civil-Military Relations.* London: Eyre and Spottiswoode, 1957.

HUNTINGTON, SAMUEL P. (ed.). *Changing Patterns of Military Politics.* New York: Free Press of Glencoe, 1962.

————. *The Soldier and the State: The Theory and Politics of Civil-Military Relations.* Cambridge, Mass.: Harvard University Press, 1957.

IUNG, GENERAL. *La République et l'armée.* Paris: Bibliothèque Charpentier, 1892.

JANOWITZ, MORRIS. *The Professional Soldier: A Social and Political Portrait.* Glencoe, Illinois: Free Press of Glencoe, 1960.

JAURÈS, JEAN. *L'Armée nouvelle.* (*Ouvres de Jean Jaurès,* Vol. IV.) Paris: Editions Reider, 1932.

JEANSON, François. *Notre Guerre.* Paris: Editions de Minuit, 1960.

JOFFRE, JOSEPH J. C. *Mémoires du Maréchal Joffre.* Paris, 1932.

JOHNSON, CHALMERS. *Peasant Nationalism and Communist Power.* Stanford, Calif.: Stanford University Press, 1962.

JOHNSON, JOHN J. (ed.). *The Role of the Military in Underdeveloped Countries.* Princeton, N.J.: Princeton University Press, 1962.

JUIN, MARSHAL ALPHONSE. *Mémoires.* 2 vols. Paris: Fayard, 1960.

KECSKEMETI, PAUL. *Strategic Surrender: The Politics of Victory and Defeat.* Stanford, Calif.: Stanford University Press, 1958.

KERAMANE, HAFID. *La Pacification: Livre noir de six années de guerre en Algérie.* Lausanne: La Cité Editeur, 1960.

KESSEL, PATRICK, and PIRELLI, GIOVANNI. *Le Peuple algérien et la guerre: Lettres et témoignages, 1954–1962.* Paris: Maspero, 1962.

KING, JERE C. *Foch v. Clemenceau.* Cambridge, Mass.: Harvard University Press, 1960.

————. *Generals and Politicians: Conflict between France's High Command, Parliament, and Government, 1914–1918.* Berkeley and Los Angeles: University of California Press, 1951.

KUNTZ, FRANÇOIS. *L'Officier français dans la nation.* Paris: Charles-Lavauzelle, 1960.

LA GORCE, PAUL-MARIE DE. *The French Army: A Military-Political History.* New York: Braziller, 1963.

LACOUTRE, JEAN, and DEVILLERS, PHILIPPE. *La Fin d'une guerre: Indochine 1954.* Paris: Seuil, 1960.

LAFON, MONIQUE (ed.). *La Lutte du Parti Communiste contre le colonialisme.* Paris: Editions Sociales, 1962.

LANCASTER, DONALD. *The Emancipation of French Indo-China.* London: Oxford University Press, 1961.

LARTÉGUY, JEAN. *Les Centurions.* Paris: Presses de la Cité, 1960. Translated by Xan Fielding as *The Centurions.* New York: Dutton, 1962.

————. *Les Prétoriens.* Paris: Presses de la Cité, 1961. Translated by Xan Fielding as *The Praetorians.* New York: Dutton, 1963.

LATTRE DE TASSIGNY, JEAN DE. *Histoire de la Première Armée Française.* Paris: Plon, 1949.

LAWRENCE, THOMAS E. *Oriental Assembly.* London: Williams and Norgate, 1939.

————. *Seven Pillars of Wisdom.* Garden City, N.Y.: Doubleday, 1935.

LE TOURNEAU, ROGER. *Evolution politique de l'Afrique du Nord Musulmane, 1920–1961.* Paris: Colin, 1962.

LEBRUN, ALBERT. *Témoignage.* Paris: Plon, 1945.

LEFÈBVRE, GEORGES. *Napoléon.* Paris, 1935.

LENIN, V. I. *Selected Works,* Vol. X. New York: International Publishers, 1938.

LÉONARD, EMILE, G. *L'Armée et ses problèmes au XVIIIᵉ siècle.* Paris: Plon, 1958.

LEROY, COLONEL JEAN. *Un Homme dans la rizière.* Paris: Editions de Paris, 1955.

LEULLIETTE, PIERRE. *Saint Michel et le dragon: Souvenirs d'un parachutiste.* Paris: Editions de Minuit, 1961.

LYAUTEY, LOUIS-HUBERT-GONZALVE. *Lettres du Tonkin et de Madagascar.* 2d ed.; Paris: Colin, 1921.

MANDOUZE, ANDRÉ (ed.). *La Révolution algérienne par les textes.* 3rd ed.; Paris: Maspero, 1962.

MAO TSE-TUNG. *Mao Tse-tung on Guerrilla Warfare.* ed. GENERAL SAMUEL B. GRIFFITH. New York: Praeger, 1961.

MAUPAS, CHARLEMAGNE EMILE DE. *The Story of the Coup d'Etat.* Trans. ALBERT D. VANDAM (original title: *Mémoire sur le Second Empire*). New York: Appleton, 1884.

MAUROIS, ANDRÉ. *Lyautey.* Paris: Plon, 1932.

MAYER, ARNO. *Political Origins of the New Diplomacy.* New Haven, Conn.: Yale University Press, 1959.

MEGRET, MAURICE. *L'Action psychologique.* Paris: Fayard, 1959.

MEISEL, JAMES. *The Fall of the Republic: Military Revolt in France.* Ann Arbor, Mich.: University of Michigan Press, 1962.

MENTION, LÉON. *L'Armée de l'Ancien Régime.* Paris, 1900.

MICAUD, CHARLES A. *The French Right and Nazi Germany, 1933–1939.* Durham, N.C.: Duke University Press, 1943.

MONTAGNON, COLONEL ANDRÉ. *Une guerre subversive: La Guerre de Vendée.* Paris: La Colombe, 1959.

MONTEIL, VINCENT. *Les Officiers.* Paris: Seuil, 1959.

MONTEILHET, JOSEPH. *Les Institutions militaires de la France (1814–1932).* Paris: Alcan, 1932.

MORDACQ, GENERAL H. *Faut-il changer le régime?* Paris: Michel, 1935.

MOSCA, GAETANO. *The Ruling Class.* New York: McGraw-Hill, 1939 (originally published in 1896 and revised in 1923).

NAEGELEN, MARCEL-EDMOND. *Mission en Algérie.* Paris: Flammarion, 1962.

NAVARRE, GENERAL HENRI. *Agonie de l'Indochine.* Paris: Plon, 1956.

ORNANO, ROLAND D'. *Gouvernement et haut-commandement en régime parlementaire français, 1814–1914.* Aix-en-Provence: La Pensée Universitaire, 1958.

OSANKA, FRANKLIN MARK (ed.). *Modern Guerrilla Warfare.* New York: Free Press, 1962.

PAILLAT, CLAUDE. *Dossier secret de l'Algérie, 13 mai 58/28 avril 1961.* Paris: Le Livre Contemporain, 1961.

PARET, PETER. *French Revolutionary Warfare from Indochina to Algeria:*

The Analysis of a Political and Military Doctrine. ("Princeton Studies in World Politics," No. 6.) New York: Praeger, 1964.

PARET, PETER, and SHY, JOHN W. *Guerrillas in the 1960's.* ("Princeton Studies in World Politics," No. 1) 2d ed.; New York: Praeger, 1962.

PAXTON, ROBERT O. "Army Officers in Vichy France." Unpublished Ph.D. dissertation, Harvard University, 1963.

PERRAULT, GILLES. *Les Parachutistes.* Paris: Seuil, 1961.

PICKLES, DOROTHY. *Algeria and France: From Colonialism to Cooperation.* New York: Praeger, 1963.

PISANI-FERRY, FRESNETTE. *Le Coup d'état manque de 16 mai 1877.* Paris: Laffont, 1965.

PLANCHAIS, JEAN. *Le Malaise de l'armée.* Paris: Plon, 1958.

———. *Où en est l'armée?* Paris: Editions Buchet/Chastel, 1959.

Le Procés de Raoul Salan, compte rendu sténographique. Paris: Albin Michel, 1962.

Le Procès d'Edmond Jouhaud, compte rendu sténographique. Paris: Albin Michel, 1962.

Le Procès des Généraux Challe et Zeller, texte intégral des débats. Paris: Nouvelles Editions Latines, 1961.

Le Procès du Maréchal Pétain, compte rendu sténographique. 2 vols. Paris: Albin Michel, 1945.

Provocation à la désobéissance: Le Procès d'un déserteur. Paris: Editions de Minuit, 1962.

PYE, LUCIEN W. *Guerrilla Communism in Malaya: Its Social and Political Meaning.* Princeton, N.J.: Princeton University Press, 1956.

RAHMANI, ABDELKADER. *L'Affaire des officiers algériens.* Paris: Seuil, 1959.

RAPOPORT, DAVID C. "Praetorianism: Government without Consensus." Ph.D. dissertation, University of California, 1960.

REINACH, JOSEPH. *Histoire de l'Affaire Dreyfus.* 7 vols. Paris: Fasquelle, 1901–8.

REY, BENOIST. *Les Egorgeurs.* Paris: Editions de Minuit, 1961.

REYNAUD, PAUL. *La France a sauvé l'Europe.* 2 vols. Paris: Flammarion, 1947.

———. *Le Problème militaire français.* Paris: Flammarion, 1937 and 1945.

————. *Au coeur de la melée.* Paris: Flammarion, 1951.

RIBET, MAURICE. *Le Procès de Riom.* Paris: Flammarion, 1945.

ROBERTS, STEPHEN H. *History of French Colonial Policy (1870–1925).* 2 vols. London: King, 1929.

ROLAND, PIERRE (pseudonym). *Contre-guérilla.* Paris: Editions Louvois, 1956.

ROY, JULES. *La Guerre d'Algérie.* Paris: Julliard, 1960.

————. *Le Métier des armes.* Paris: Julliard, 1948.

RYAN, A. P. *Mutiny at the Curragh.* London: Macmillan, 1956.

SACY, JACQUES SILVESTRE DE. *Le Maréchal de MacMahon.* Paris: Editions Internationales, 1960.

SALISBURY-JONES, GENERAL SIR GUY. *So Full a Glory.* New York: Praeger, 1955.

SAUGE, GEORGES. *L'Armée face à la guerre psychologique.* ('Les Cahiers du C.E.P.E.C.," No. 11.) Paris: Centre d'Etudes Politiques et Civiques, 1959.

SÉNÉCHAL, MICHEL. *Droits politiques et liberté d'expression des officiers des forces militaires.* Paris: Librairie Générale de Droit et de Jurisprudence, 1964.

SÉRIGNY, ALAIN DE (ed.). *Un Procès.* Paris: La Table Ronde, 1961.

————. *La Révolution du 13 mai.* Paris. Plon, 1958.

SERVAN-SCHREIBER, JEAN-JACQUES. *Lieutenant en Algérie.* Paris: Julliard, 1958.

SIMON, PIERRE-HENRI. *Contre la torture.* Paris: Seuil, 1957.

————. *Portrait d'un officier.* Paris: Seuil. 1958.

SOUBOUL, ALBERT. *L'Armée nationale sous la Révolution, 1789–1794.* Paris: Editions France d'Abord, 1945.

SOUCHON, CAPTAIN LUCIEN. *Feue lArmée Française.* Paris: Fayard, 1929.

SOUSTELLE, JACQUES. *Aimée et souffrante Algérie.* Paris. Fayard, 1929.

SPANIER, JOHN W. *The Truman-MacArthur Controversy and the Korean War.* Cambridge, Mass.: Harvard University Press, 1959.

SPEARS, MAJOR GENERAL SIR EDWARD. *Assignment to Catastrophe.* 2 vols. New York: Wyn, 1954 and 1955.

STOUFFER, SAMUEL A. *The American Soldier.* 2 vols. Princeton, N.J.: Princeton University Press, 1949.

SULZBERGER, C. L. *The Test: De Gaulle and Algeria.* New York: Harcourt, Brace, and World, 1962.

TÉNOT, EUGÈNE. *Paris in December, 1851.* Translated by S. W. ADAMS and A. H. BRANDON. New York: Hurd and Houghton, 1870.

TOCQUEVILLE, ALEXIS DE. *Democracy in America.* New York: Vintage, 1954. Vol. II.

———. *The Recollections of Alexis de Tocqueville.* New York: Macmillan, 1896.

TOURNOUX, J.-R. *L'Histoire secrète.* Paris: Plon, 1962.

———. *Secrets d'état.* Paris. Plon, 1960.

TRINQUIER, COLONEL ROGER. *Le Coup d'état du 13 mai.* Paris: L'Esprit Nouveau, 1962.

———. *La Guerre moderne.* Paris: La Table Ronde, 1961. Translated as *Modern Warfare* by DANIEL LEE. New York: Praeger, 1964.

TROCHU, GENERAL. *L'Armée Française en 1867.* 14th ed.; Paris: Amyot, 1867.

VAGTS, ALFRED. *A History of Militarism.* Rev. ed.; New York: Meridian, 1959.

VALLUY, GENERAL JEAN. *Se défendre? Contre qui? Pourquoi? Comment?* Paris: Plon, 1960.

VIDAL-NAQUET, PIERRE. *L'Affaire Audin.* Paris: Editions de Minuit, 1958.

———. *La Raison d'état.* Paris: Editions de Minuit, 1962.

———. *Torture: Cancer of Democracy.* Baltimore, Md.; Penguin, 1963.

VIGNY, ALFRED DE. *Servitude et grandeur militaires.* Edited, and with an Introduction by, A. BOUVET. Paris: Colin, 1960 (originally published in 1835).

WATT, RICHARD M. *Dare Call It Treason.* New York: Simon and Schuster, 1963.

WEBER, EUGENE. *Action Française.* Stanford, Calif.: Stanford University Press, 1962.

WERTH, ALEXANDER. *The De Gaulle Revolution.* London: Hale, 1960.

———. *The Twilight of France, 1933–1940.* New York and London: Harper, 1942.

———. *France, 1940–1955.* London: Hale, 1956.

WEYGAND, JACQUES. *Le Serment.* Paris: Flammarion, 1960.

WEYGAND, GENERAL MAXIME. *Mémoires.* 3 vols. Paris: Flammarion, 1950–57.

———. *Histoire de l'armée française.* Paris: Flammarion, 1938.

Articles

The following abbreviations are used throughout:

LM: *Le Monde*
RDN: *Revue de défense nationale*
RMI: *Revue militaire d'information*
Message: *Message des forces armées*

"A la recherche d'un nouveau patriotisme," (by "Capitaine X."), *Message*, No. 10 (October, 1955), pp. 3–7.

"A propos du rôle idéologique de l'armée," *RMI*, No. 242 (November 25, 1954), pp. 19–21.

ABRAMS, PHILIP. "Democracy, Technology, and the Retired British Officer," in S. P. HUNTINGTON (ed.), *Changing Patterns of Military Politics*. New York: Free Press, 1962, pp. 150–89.

ACHARD-JAMES, COLONEL. "Possibilités et volonté, *RDN*, November, 1957, pp. 1684–91.

"L'Action psychologique: Légitimité-Limites," *Message*, No. 32 (November, 1958). (Note: Starting with No. 19 [February, 1957] each article is separate in pagination.)

"Action psychologique en Algérie" (by "Capitaine C."), *Message*, No. 16 (October, 1956), p. 19.

"L'Action psychologique plaide non coupable," *Contacts*, No. 7 (1959), pp. 9–23.

"L'Affaire des fuites," *Message*, No. 14 (June, 1956), pp. 20–24.

AILLERET, COLONEL (then General) CHARLES. "L'Arme atomique: Arme à bon marché," *RDN*, October, 1954, pp. 315–24.

————. "L'Arme atomique, facteur de paix," *RDN*, January 1955, pp. 34–41.

————. L'Arme atomique, *ultima ratio* des peuples," *RDN*, December, 1954, pp. 553–663.

————. "Energie nucléaire et problèmes de défense," *RMI*, No. 312 (January, 1960), pp. 98–108.

————. "De l'Euratom au programme atomique national," *RDN*, November, 1956, pp. 1319–27.

————. Illusion ou réalité de l'arme absolue," *RDN*, July, 1957, pp. 1067–81.

ALBORD, TONY. "La Pensée militaire française," *RDN*, October, 1960, pp. 1578–87.

ALEXINSKY, GRÉGOIRE. "Genèse de la doctrine de guerre révolutionnaire," *RMI*, No. 303 (March, 1959), pp. 41–58, and No. 307 (July, 1959), pp. 41–59.

"L'Algérie et la volonté de vaincre," *Message*, No. 42 (April, 1960).

ALLARD, GENERAL JACQUES. "L'OTAN et l'Afrique du Nord," *RDN*, June, 1958, pp. 907–11.

————. "Vérités sur l'affaire algérienne," *RDN*, January, 1958, pp. 6–41.

AMPHIOXUS, CAPTAIN. "La Guerre en Algérie: Regards de l'autre côté," *RDN*, January, 1957, pp. 82–91.

ARBONNEAU, CAPTAIN D'. "Réflexions sur les formes non spécifiquement militaires de la guerre," *RMI*, No. 328 (June, 1961), pp. 6–17.

ARGOUD, CAPTAIN ANTOINE. "La guerre psychologique," *RDN*, March, 1948, pp. 291–300, and April, 1948, pp. 460–71.

"L'Armée de l'armistice" (by "XXX"), *Revue des deux mondes*, February 1, 1941.

"L'Armée est-elle fasciste?", *Le Courrier de la nation*, August 7, 1958, p. 9–12.

"L'Armée et les attaques de presse," *L'Armée*, No. 1 (February, 1960), pp. 95–96.

L'Armée Française, a special issue of *La Nef*, No. 7 (July–September, 1961).

"Armées et université," *RMI*, No. 307 (July, 1959), pp. 75–77.

"L'Atlantique," *RMI*, No. 321 (November, 1960).

"Avant qu'il ne soit trop tard," *Message*, No. 42 (April, 1960).

BAILLIF, GENERAL. "Les Forces armées dans la nation," *RDN*, February, 1960, pp. 217–23.

————. "Forces armées et psychologie," *RDN*, May, 1960, pp. 819–29.

BANKWITZ, PHILIP C. F. "Maxime Weygand and the Fall of France: A Study in Civil-Military Relations," *Journal of Modern History*, XXXI, No. 3 (September, 1959), pp. 215–42.

BÉDARIDA, FRANÇOIS. "L'Armée et la république: Les Opinions politiques des officiers français en 1876–1878," *Revue historique*, No. 232 (July–September, 1964), pp. 119–164.

BERGER, GASTON. "Hommes politiques et chefs militaires (Etude psycho-sociologique)," in Centre de Sciences Politiques de l'Institut d'Etudes Juridiques de Nice (ed.), *La Défense nationale*. Paris: Presses Universitaires de France, 1958, pp. 15–29.

BERNARD, JACQUELINE. "L'Origine sociale des officiers," *LM*, December 28–29, 1960.

BILLOTTE, GENERAL P. "La Discipline militaire et la torture," *LM*, October 6–7, 1957 (reprinted from a letter to *Preuves*).

BLOCH-MICHEL, JEAN, and BLOCH-MICHEL, J. C. "La Discipline des généraux; Les Lois de la guerre et la torture," *Preuves*, No. 83 (January, 1958), pp. 50–56.

BONNET, COLONEL GABRIEL. "Culture et humanisme militaire," *RDN*, June, 1955, pp. 668–84.

———. "L'Importance du facteur 'moral' dans le complexe 'armée-nation,'" *RDN*, November, 1955, pp. 435–41.

———. "Mao tse-Toung et la stratégie révolutionnaire," *RDN*, January, 1955, pp. 22–33.

BOUCHERIE, GENERAL MARCEL. "Les Bureaux arabes: Leur rôle dans la conquête de l'Algérie," *RDN*, July, 1957, pp. 1052–66.

———. "Les Causes politiques et morales d'un désastre: 1940," *RDN*, March, 1958, pp. 409–16.

BOUPACHA, DJAMILA. "Deux lettres de Djamila Boupacha et de son père," *Les Temps modernes*, XV, No. 171 (June, 1960), 1828–32.

BOURGEOIS, CHEF DE BATAILLON M. "L'Officier français peut-il faire la guerre révolutionnaire?" Thesis, Ecole Supérieure de Guerre, 73d Promotion, 1960; mimeo.

BOURGÈS-MAUNOURY, MAURICE. "Nous voulons continuer à écrire notre histoire," *RMI*, No. 275 (November 10, 1955), pp. 10–11.

BOUTHOUL, GASTON. "Une nouvelle branche des sciences sociales: La Polémologie," *RMI*, No. 300 (December, 1958), pp. 7–10.

BOYER, CAPTAIN. "De l'aspect social de la profession militaire," *RMI*, No. 171 (April 10, 1951), pp. 26–27.

BRAQUILANGES, CAPTAIN DE. "Cours de guerre subversive, méthode psychologique utilisée pour forcer l'adhésion des esprits." Lecture to Ecole d'Etat-Major-Armée 1956–57, XVIIIᵉ Promotion, n.d.; mimeo.

BRAUCHAMP, MARC. "Le Progressisme," *RMI*, No. 323 (January, 1961), pp. 16–24.

BRICHAUD, BERNARD. "La Conduite des hommes et ses techniques psychologiques," *RMI*, No. 279 (December, 1956), pp. 40–60.

BROIZAT, COLONEL. Letter in *LM*, January 20, 1961.

BROWN, BERNARD E. "The Army and Politics in France," *Journal of Politics*, XXIII, No. 2 (May, 1961), pp. 262–78.

BRUNE, JEAN. "L'Armée à la recherche d'une doctrine," *La Nation française*, No. 192 (June 10, 1959), pp. 6–7.

BRUNO, R. B. "Soldat en Algérie," *Les Temps modernes*, XV, No. 171 (June, 1960), pp. 1833–36.

CABANNE, CLAUDE. "Formes et problèmes de la décolonisation," *RMI*, No. 328 (June, 1961), pp. 18–32.

CAIRNS, JOHN C., "Along the Road Back to France 1940," *American Historical Review*, LXIV, No. 3 (April, 1959), 583–603.

CANTONI, ROBERT. "Réflexions sur le métier militaire," *RMI*, No. 335 (February, 1962), pp. 23–25.

CARRERE D'ENCAUSSE, H. "La 'Persuasion' des consciences: Méthodes de propagande soviétique," *RMI*, No. 282 (April, 1957), pp. 43–52.

CATHELINEAU, CAPTAIN GÉRARD DE. "Le Rôle d'un animateur en unité opérationnelle," *Verbe*, August-September 1957, pp. 120–23.

Centre d'Etudes et d'Instruction Psychologiques de l'Armée de l'Air, "Attitudes et motivation des candidats aux grandes écoles militaires," *Revue française de sociologie*, II, No. 2 (April–June, 1961), 133–51.

"Ceux qui forment notre jeunesse," *Message*, No. 43 (June, 1960).

CHALLENER, RICHARD C. "The Third Republic and the Generals: The Gravediggers Revisited," in H. L. Coles (ed.), *Total War and Cold War*. Columbus, Ohio: Ohio State University Press, 1962, pp. 91–107.

CHALMIN, PIERRE. "La Crise morale de l'armée française," in J. BOUILLON *et al.*, *L'Armée de la Seconde République*. ("Bibliothèque de la Révolution de 1848," Vol. XVIII.) La Roche-sur-Yon: Imprimerie Centrale de l'Ouest, 1955.

CHANDESSAIS, COLONEL. "Le Morale et sa mesure," *RMI*, No. 327 (May, 1961), pp. 40–45.

———. "Observations sur un symposium de psychologie de la défense," *Revue française de sociologie*, II, No. 2 (April–June, 1961), 124–32.

CHAPMAN, GUY. "France: The French Army and Politics," in M. HOWARD, (ed.), *Soldiers and Governments*. London: Eyre and Spottiswoode, 1957.

CHARRASSE, PIERRE. "L'Algérie et l'Europe," *RDN*, May, 1960, pp. 853–62.

————. "L'Armée et l'Algérie de demain," *RDN*, March, 1959, pp. 420–32.

CHASSIN, GENERAL LIONEL-MARTIN. *"La Conquête de la Chine par Mao Tse–Toung,"* *RMI*, No. 169 (February 25, 1951), pp. 12–17, and No. 170 (March 10–25, 1951), pp. 19–25.

————. "Du rôle historique de l'armée," *RDN*, October, 1956, pp. 1182–99.

————. "Du rôle idéologique de l'armée," *RMI*, No. 239 (October 10, 1954), pp. 13–19.

————. "Insuffisance de la stratégie nucléaire," *RDN*, July, 1960, pp. 1200–12.

————. "Réflexions stratégiques sur la guerre d'Indochine," *RDN*, December, 1954, pp. 507–22.

————. "Technique de l'insurrection," *RDN*, May, 1957, pp. 696–713.

————. "Vers un encerclement de l'Occident," *RDN*, May, 1956, pp. 531–53.

CHERRIÈRE, GENERAL C. R. "Les Débuts: de l'insurrection algérienne," *RDN*, December, 1956, pp. 1450–62.

"Les 50,000 officiers français—qui sont-ils, comment vivent-ils?" *Enterprise*, December 27, 1958, pp. 47–49.

CLÉMENT, MARCEL. "Les Valeurs que nous défendons," *RMI*, No. 313 (February, 1960), pp. 7–13.

CLIFFORD-VAUGHAN, M., "Changing Attitudes to the Army's Role in French Society," *British Journal of Sociology*, XV, No. 4 (December, 1964), 338–49.

COGNIET, COMMANDANT. "Fondements idéologiques et principes d'emploi de l'action psychologique." Lecture to the Ecole Supérieure de Guerre, January 6, 1960, mimeo.

COLES, HARRY L. Introduction to Harry L. Coles (ed.), *Total War and Cold War*. Columbus, Ohio: Ohio State University Press, 1962, pp. 3–23.

COMBAUX, INGÉNIEUR GÉNÉRAL. "Armes atomiques et non atomiques dans la défense de l'Eurafrique," *RDN*, January, 1958, pp. 59–71.

————. "Au-delà de Clausewitz," *RDN*, April, 1957, pp. 518–32.

————. "Nécessité d'une Eurafrique," *RDN*, December, 1957, pp. 1814–26.

"Comprendre pour vouloir," *Message*, No. 29 (April, 1958).

"La Condition militaire," *RMI*, No. 234 (June, 1954), pp. 7–10.

"CORNELIUS" (pseudonym). "Morale et guerre révolutionnaire," *Verbe*, Nos. 90 (February, 1958), 91 (March, 1958), and 92 (April, 1958).

CREVÈCOEUR, COLONEL M. DE. "Aperçus sur la stratégie du Viet Minh." Paris: Section de Documentation Militaire de l'Union Française, 1953; mimeo.

————. "Le Problème militaire française en Indochine," Paris: Section de Documentation Militaire de l'Union Française, 1952; mimeo.

————. "Raccourci de la campagne d'Indochine," Paris: Section de Documentation Militaire de l'Union Française, 1950; mimeo.

"La Crise des vocations militaires," *Message*, No. 4 (July, 1954), p. 13.

"La Crise morale du corps des officiers," *Message*, No. 12 (February, 1956).

DAALDER, H. "The Role of the Military in the Emerging Countries," The Hague: Mouton, 1962.

"D'Algérie, une opinion sur le morale des officiers," *Message*, No. 20 (March, 1957).

DANIEL, JEAN. "Le Dossier numéro un," *L'Express*, March 3, 1960, pp. 10–11.

DELAYE, LIEUTENANT COLONEL TH.J. "Cette guerre sans loi qui nous est imposé," *Message*, No. 7 (February, 1955).

DELMAS, CLAUDE. "La 'Force de Frappe' nationale: Les Données du problème," *RDN*, October, 1960, pp. 1549–65.

————. "La France et sa défense nationale," *RDN*, October, 1957, pp. 1434–48.

————. "Notes sur les fondements d'une doctrine de défense nationale," *RDN*, June, 1958, pp. 912–24.

————. "La Rébellion algérienne après l'arrestation des chefs du F.L.N.," *RDN*, December, 1956, pp. 1463–74.

DEMETZ, GENERAL. "Editorial," *L'Armée*, No. 1 (February, 1960), pp. 7–8.

DENOYER, PIERRE. "L'Armée et la presse," *RMI*, No. 287 (September–October, 1957), pp. 103–7.

————. "L'Armée et la presse," *RDN*, April, 1957, pp. 533–44.

DINFREVILLE, JACQUES. "La Victoire de l'Armée Grecque sur la guérilla communiste," *RDN*, October, 1955, pp. 323–33, and November, 1955, pp. 442–53.

DOGAN, MATTEI. "Les Officiers dans la carrière politique: Du Maréchal Mac-Mahon au Général de Gaulle, *Revue française de sociologie*, II, No. 2 (April–June, 1961), pp. 88–99.

Doumic, R. "L'Armée et la formation de l'opinion publique," *RMI*, No. 274 (July, 1956), pp. 14–16.

Dours, J., and Duroc, J. "La nouvelle organisation générale de la défense," *RDN*, February, 1959, pp. 219–26.

"Du rôle politique de l'armée" (by "M. L. L."), *Message*, No. 31 (October, 1958).

Ducatillon, Père. "Le Sens chrétien de la vocation militaire," *L'Ordre française*, July–August, 1957, pp. 3–7.

"Eléments pour une doctrine," *Message*, No. 26 (December, 1957).

Ely, General Paul. "L'Armée dans la nation," *RMI*, No. 297 (August–September, 1958), pp. 7–14.

———. Le Chef et l'évolution de la guerre," *RMI*, No. 284 (June, 1957), pp. 13–17.

———. "Notre politique militaire," *RDN*, July, 1957, pp. 1033–51.

———. "Perspectives stratégiques d'avenir," *RDN*, November, 1958, pp. 1631–40.

———. "Les Problèmes français et l'équilibre mondial," *RDN*, November, 1959, pp. 1709–25.

———. "The Role of the French Army Today," *Réalités* (English edition), April, 1961, pp. 45–47.

———. "Les véritables espérances de la France et de l'Occident," *RMI*, No. 298 (October, 1958), pp. 7–10.

———. "Vers une évolution possible de l'Occident," *RDN*, February, 1959, pp. 213–18.

"Enquête sur la crise de l'armée," *Message*, No. 18 (December, 1956), pp. 14–16.

"Essai sur la structure sociale de l'Armée Française" (by "Capitaines T. and A."), *La Nouvelle Critique*, No. 107 (June, 1959), pp. 43–84.

"Ethique militaire et démocratie," *Message*, No. 16 (October, 1956).

Etienne, Lieutenant Colonel. "L'Armée, la parade et la riposte psychologique," *RMI*, No. 317 (June, 1960), pp. 20–35, and No. 319 (August–September, 1960), pp. 16–35.

———. "Problèmes humains," *RMI*, No. 326 (April, 1961), pp. 48–66.

"Le F.L.N. et le communisme," *Le Bled*, February 16, 1957, p. 4.

Feld, Maury. "A Typology of Military Organization," *Public Policy*, No. 8, (1958), pp. 3–40.

Féral, Commandant. "L'Armée devant la presse," *RDN*, December, 1957, pp. 1864–71.

Fesquet, Henri. " 'Verbe,' revue de la Cité Catholique renie les principes de la révolution," *LM*, July 9, 1958.

"La Fin et les moyens," *Message*, No. 26 (December, 1957).

Fox, WILLIAM T. R. "Representativeness and Efficiency: Dual Problem of Civil-Military Relations," *Political Science Quarterly*, LXXVI, No. 3 (September, 1961), 354–66.

La France, puissance atomique, special issue of *RMI*, No. 312 (January, 1960).

La France devant l'échéance atomique, special issue of *RDN*, January, 1956.

GARAND, A. "A. M. Pierre-Henri Simon," *Contacts*, No. 7 (1959), pp. 25–39.

GEFFEN, R. VAN. "La Pacification, tâche primordiale," *Message*, No. 11 (December, 1955).

GENEVEY, CONTRÔLEUR GÉNÉRAL. "Le Service national," *RDN*, March, 1959, pp. 395–401.

GÉRARDOT, GENERAL PAUL. "L'Art de préparer la guerre," *RDN*, November, 1958, pp. 1664–82.

GERBET, PIERRE. "Les Rapports entre pouvoir civil et pouvoir militaire en France dans l'élaboration de la politique de défense." Paper presented to the civil-military relations sessions, Fifth Congress, International Political Science Association, Paris, 1961; mimeo.

GIBBS, NORMAN. "Winston Churchill and the British War Cabinet," in HARRY COLES (ed.), *Total War and Cold War*. Columbus, Ohio: Ohio State University Press, 1962, pp. 27–41.

GIGNOUX, C.-J. "Armée Française 1961: De quelques réponses," *Revue des deux mondes*, August 1, 1961, pp. 353–60.

GIRARDET, RAOUL, "Algérie 1960: Victoires et servitudes des capitaines," Paris: *Combat*, n.d. [1960].

―――. "Pouvoir civil et pouvoir militaire dans la France contemporaine," *Revue française de science politique*, No. 10 (March, 1960), pp. 5–38. Translated and printed as "Civil and Military Power in the Fourth Republic" in S. P. HUNTINGTON (ed.), *Changing Patterns of Military Politics*. New York: Free Press of Glencoe, 1962, pp. 121–49.

―――. "Pouvoir civil et pouvoir militaire en France sous la Quatrième République." Paper presented to the seventh roundtable, International Political Science Association, Opatija, Yugoslavia, 1959; mimeo.

―――. "Réflexions critiques sur la doctrine militaire française de la guerre subversive." Paper presented to the Académie des Sciences Morales et Politiques, June 20, 1960.

GLORIES, JEAN. "Quelques observations sur la révolution algérienne et le communisme," *l'Afrique et l'Asie*, No. 41 (1958), pp. 16–44.

GOUTARD, COLONEL. "Ménace atomique et défense nationale," *RDN*, November–December, 1948, pp. 459–68, 615–27.

GRAND D'ESNON, COMMANDANT, and PRESTAT, CAPTAIN. "L'Endoctrinement des prisonniers de guerre dans les camps du Vietminh," *Revue des forces terrestres*, No. 6 (October, 1956), pp. 31–46.

GROMIER, FRANÇOIS. "Une conception archaïque," *Cahiers de la republique*, No. 28 (November–December, 1960), pp. 15–30.

————. "Le 'Trouble' de l'armée," *La Nef*, No. 7 (July–September, 1961), pp. 5–18.

GROS, ANDRÉ, and GUÉRON, GEORGES. "Quelques réflexions sur l'officier français," *RDN*, November, 1960, pp. 1763–70.

Guerre, Armée, Société, special issue of *Revue française de sociologie*, II, No. 2 (April–June, 1961).

"La Guerre du Viet-Minh," (by "un groupe d'officiers"), *RMI*, No. 281 (February–March, 1957), pp. 23–39.

La Guerre révolutionnaire, a special issue of *RMI*, No. 281 (February–March, 1957).

"La Guerre subversive à la lumière des expériences d'Algérie," *Message*, No. 27 (February, 1958).

GUILLARD, JEAN-LOUIS. "Les Soldats perdus," *La Nef*, No. 19 (October, 1962–January, 1963), pp. 116–24.

HALIMI, GISÈLE, "D'Henri Alleg à Djamila Boupacha," *Les Temps modernes*, XV, No. 171 (June, 1960), 1822–27.

HARRISON, MARTIN. "The French Experience of Exceptional Powers: 1961," *Journal of Politics*, XXV, No. 1 (February, 1963), 139–58.

————. "Government and Press in France during the Algerian War," *American Political Science Review*, LVIII, No. 2 (June, 1964), 273–84.

HART, B. H. LIDDELL. "Les Problèmes fondamentaux de la défense de l'Europe," *RDN*, January, 1959, pp. 19–34.

HERVOUËT, CAPTAIN YVES. "Enseignements militaires à tirer de la guerre d'Indochine," *RMI*, No. 203 (November 10, 1952), pp. 21–24.

————. "Essai sur la propagande et la mission politique des officiers," *RMI*, No. 184 ((December 10, 1951), pp. 10–15.

Histoire de la guerre d'Algérie suivie d'une histoire de l'O.A.S., special issue of *La Nef*, Nos. 12–13, combined in one issue (October, 1962–January, 1963).

HOGARD, COMMANDANT JACQUES. "L'Armée Française devant la guerre révolutionnaire," *RDN*, January, 1957, pp. 77–89.

————. "Cette guerre de notre temps," *RDN*, August–September, 1958, pp. 1304–19.

————. "Guerre révolutionnaire et pacification," *RMI*, No. 280 (January, 1957), pp. 7–24.

————. "Guerre révolutionnaire ou révolution dans l'art de la guerre," *RDN*, December, 1956, pp. 1497–1513.

————. "Le Soldat dans la guerre révolutionnaire," *RDN*, February, 1957, pp. 211–26.

————. "Tactique et stratégie dans la guerre révolutionnaire," *RMI*, No. 295 (June, 1958), pp. 23–35.

HUNTINGTON, SAMUEL P. "Civilian Control of the Military: A Theoretical Statement," in H. EULAU (ed.), *Political Behavior*. Glencoe, Ill.: Free Press of Glencoe, 1956, pp. 380–85.

————. "Patterns of Violence in World Politics," in S. P. HUNTINGTON (ed.), *Changing Patterns of Military Politics*. New York: Free Press of Glencoe, 1962, pp. 17–50.

"Un idéal pour l'armée? Non, un idéal pour la nation," *Message*, No. 7 (February, 1955), pp. 7–11.

"In Search of Status," *Economist*, February 6, 1961, pp. 531–32.

"Introduction à la politique," *Verbe*, Nos. 107–9, 111–12, 114, 116–20 (1960–61).

JOHNSON, CHALMERS. "Civilian Loyalties and Guerrilla Conflict," *World Politics*, XVI, No. 4 (July, 1962), 646–61.

JOLLY, COMMANDANT. "Demain, l'Amérique du Sud," *RDN*, December, 1956, pp. 1523–36, and January, 1957, pp. 110–22.

JOUANNET, G.-P. "Le Maréchal de Lattre: Formateur de la jeunesse," *RMI*, No. 290 (January, 1958), pp. 93–99.

————. "Un témoin de la conscience française," *RMI*, No. 285 (July, 1957), pp. 47–56.

"Journal de marche d'un capitaine en Kabylie," *La Nouvelle Critique*, No. 107 (June, 1959), pp. 1–41.

JUIN, MARÉCHAL ALPHONSE. "Que devons-nous penser de la sécurité française?" *RDN*, January, 1957, pp. 5–16.

KATZENBACH, EDWARD L., JR. "The French Army," *Yale Review*, XLV, No. 4 (June, 1956), 498–513.

————. "Political Parties and the French Army since Liberation," in E. M. EARLE (ed.), *Modern France*. Princeton, N.J.: Princeton University Press, 1951. pp. 432–46.

KELLY, GEORGE A. "Algeria, the Army, and the Fifth Republic (1959–1961): A Scenario of Civil-Military Conflict," *Political Science Quarterly*, LXXIX, No. 3 (September, 1964).

————. "The French Army Re-enters Politics, 1940-1955," *Political Science Quarterly*, LXXXVI, No. 3 (September, 1961), 367–92.

————. "Revolutionary War and Psychological Action," *Military Review*, XL, No. 7 (October, 1960), 4–13.

KERR, WALTER. "The French Army in Trouble," *Foreign Affairs*, XL, No. 1 (October, 1961), 86–94.

KRIEF, CLAUDE. "Portrait d'un 'colonel,'" *La Nef*, No. 7 (July–September, 1961), pp. 51–56.

LA CHAPELLE, GENERAL DE. "Les Aspects particuliers de la guerre possible," *RDN*, February, 1956, pp. 133–57.

LA TOUSCHE, COMMANDANT R. DE. "Déterminisme et détermination," *RMI*, No. 311 (December, 1959), pp. 32–38.

LABIGNETTE, CAPTAIN. "Insurrection communiste en Grèce (1946–1949)," *RMI*, No. 281 (February–March, 1957), pp. 41–49.

LACHEROY, COLONEL CHARLES. "Action viet-minh et communiste en Indochine ou une leçon de 'guerre révolutionnaire.'" Paris: Section de Documentation Militaire de l'Outre-Mer, n.d. [about 1955]; mimeo.

————. "Une arme du Viet-Minh: Hiérarchies parallèles." Paris: Section de Documentation Militaire de l'Union Française, 1954; mimeo.

————. "La Campagne d'Indochine ou une leçon de guerre révolutionnaire." Paris: Section de Documentation Militaire de l'Union Française, 1954; mimeo.

————. "La Guerre révolutionnaire," in Centre de Sciences Politiques de l'Institut d'Etudes Juridiques de Nice (ed.), *La Défense nationale*. Paris: Presses Universitaires de France, 1958, pp. 307–30.

————. "Scénario-type de guerre révolutionnaire." Paris: Section de Documentation Militaire de l'Outre-Mer, 1955; mimeo.

LANG, KURT. "Tradition, Skill, and Politics in the German Army." Unpublished manuscript.

LEJEUNE, MAX. "La Mission de l'armée en Algérie," *RMI*, No. 278 (November, 1956), pp. 85–87.

LÉON-DUFOUR, COLONEL. "Fiche sur les théories du Père Teilhard de Chardin et conclusions personnelles sur une idéologie possible comme base de l'action psychologique," *Contacts*, No. 7 (1959), pp. 133–41.

LEPOTIER, REAR ADMIRAL R. "Pourquoi la 'force de frappe'?", *RDN*, March, 1960, pp. 413–29.

LEVY, ROGER. "La plus grande Chine: L'Armée", *RDN*, June, 1956, pp. 735–44.

LIBER, NADINE. "La grande frustration du jeune officier supérieur," *Réalités*, May, 1957, pp. 36–41.

"Liberté, Egalité, Fraternité," *Message*, No. 28 (March, 1958).

"L'Indépendance dans l'interdépendance" (by "X.X.X."), *RDN*, August–September, 1956, pp. 1055–59.

LIVERTOUT, LIEUTENANT COLONEL. "Relations humaines à l'Ecole Technique de l'armée de l'air," *RMI*, No. 327 (May, 1961), pp. 12–22.

LOMBARD, J. M. "La grande démission," *Message*, No. 39 (October, 1959), pp. 29–32.

LOMBARD, M. "Le Logement des cadres," *Message*, No. 40 (December, 1952), pp. 31–34.

LUCHAIRE, FRANÇOIS. "L'Union française et l'Islam," *RDN*, July, 1956, pp. 828–46.

LYAUTEY, L.-H.-G. "Du rôle social de l'officier," *Revue des deux mondes*, March 15, 1891, pp. 433–59.

MACCARTHY, LIEUTENANT COLONEL. "L'Armée Française et la politique," *L'Armée*, No. 1 (February, 1960), pp. 30–40, and No. 2 (March, 1960), pp. 38–48.

"Le Magneto et le bazooka ou la complicité du mépris," *Les Temps modernes*, XV, No. 171 (June, 1960), 1837–43.

MAÎTRE, JACQUES. "Le Catholicisme d'extrême droite et la croisade anti-subversive," *Revue française de sociologie*, II No. 2 (April–June, 1961), 106–117.

"Le Mal Jaune," (by "un capitaine"), *Le Courrier de la nation*, August 7, 1958, p. 20.

MALGRÉ, GENERAL JEAN. "Recrutement des officiers et structure sociale: La Crise de Saint-Cyr et ses remèdes," *Revue politique et parlementaire*, No. 657 (April, 1956), pp. 21–29.

MANUE, GEORGES R. "La Guerre psychologique," *RMI*, No. 275 (August, 1956), pp. 86–87.

———. "La Leçon de Suez," *RDN*, October, 1956, pp. 1155–64.

MARCHAND, GENERAL JEAN. "Perspectives africaines," *RDN*, November, 1959, pp. 1749–58.

———. "Les Puissances anticolonialistes et l'Afrique noire française," *RDN*, May, 1961, pp. 568–80.

MARCHAT, LIEUTENANT PHILIPPE. "Rappelé en Algérie," *RDN*, December, 1957, pp. 1827–52.

MARTIN, CAPTAIN H. "Guérilla, guerre en surface, guerre révolutionnaire," *RMI*, No. 286 (August, 1957), pp. 7–22.

MARTIN, JEAN-MAURICE. "Soldats et citoyens," *RMI*, No. 320 (October, 1960), pp. 39–51.

MAULNIER, THIERRY. "Du 13 mai au 28 septembre," *RDN*, November, 1958, pp. 1655–63.

MAZAUD, B. "Signification politique de l'Armée Soviétique," *RMI*, No. 302 (February, 1959), pp. 29–44.

MEGRET, MAURICE. "Armée et université: A la recherche d'un langage commun," *RDN*, December, 1958, pp. 1860–68.

———. "L'Officier de réserve, la défense de la nation," *LM*, June 25 and June 27, 1959.

MÉRIC, CAPTAIN A. "Jugurtha et Rome," *RMI*, No. 267 (February 25, 1956), pp. 21–23.

"Le Message de Jeanne," *Le Bled*, May 14, 1958, p. 3.

METZ, COLONEL RENÉ DE. "Du rôle national de l'officier," *RDN*, August–September, 1958, pp. 1320–38.

———. "Une idée force: Laquelle?", *RDN*, March, 1957, pp. 347–58.

———. "La Notion traditionnelle de l'ordre public est-elle sur le point d'évoluer?" *RDN*, August–September, 1959, pp. 1451–59.

———. "Propos sur la défense intérieure du territoire," *RDN*, October, 1957, pp. 1482–95.

MEURISSE, ROBERT. "Psychologie civile et psychologie militaire," *RMI*, No. 305 (May 1956), pp. 66–68.

MEYNAUD, JEAN. "Les Militaires et le pouvoir," *Revue française de sociologie*, II, No. 2 (April–June, 1961), 75–87.

MEYRE, JEAN. "L'Algérie après les élections," *RDN*, April, 1959, pp. 588–603.

———. "Considérations militaires sur la guerre d'Algérie," *RDN*, May, 1959, pp. 807–21.

MIKSCHE, F. L. "Politique, stratégie et technique," *RDN*, May, 1959, pp. 791–806.

"MILITES" (pseudonym). "L'Algérie, l'armée et la révolution," *Message*, February, 1957. Partially reprinted in *RMI*, No. 283 (March, 1958), p. 103.

————. "L'Algérie, pierre de touche de la volonté française," *Message,* No. 13 (April, 1956), p. 12.

————. "L'Algérie n'est pas l'Indochine," *Message,* No. 12 (February, 1956). Reprinted in *RMI,* No. 270 (April 10, 1956), pp. 40–44.

————. "Morale de la guerre et morale de l'armée," *Message,* No. 21 (April, 1957).

MOLLET, GUY. "L'Armée et la nation." Arras: Société d'Editions du Pas-de-Calais, 1960.

MONGRILLON, HENRI. "L'Attitude de la presse à propos de Dien-Bien-Phu," *Message,* No. 3 (May, 1954), pp. 16–17.

MONNEROT, J. "L'Action psychologique dans la guerre." Paris: Ecole Supérieure de Guerre, 1954; mimeo.

MONTFORD, COLONEL-DIVISIONNAIRE. "La Situation militaire en Algérie," *Revue militaire suisse,* No. 2 (February, 1962), pp. 49–57.

MOREAU, CLAUDE-ALBERT. "Sens et portée d'une réforme," *RMI,* No. 327 (May, 1961), pp. 5–11.

MOREAU, CAPTAIN RENÉ. "La Recherche opérationnelle," *RMI,* Nos. 293 (April, 1958), 295 (June, 1958), and 297 (August-September, 1958).

MURRAY, COLONEL J. C. "The Anti-Bandit War," *Marine Corps Gazette,* XXXVIII, Nos. 1–5 (January–May, 1954). Reprinted in LIEUTENANT COLONEL T. N. GREENE (ed.), *The Guerrilla—And How to Fight Him.* New York: Praeger, 1962, pp. 65–111.

NANTES, ABBÉ G. DE. "Morale et torture," *L'Ordre française,* No. 14 (September, 1957), pp. 52–64, and No. 15 (October, 1957), pp. 17–28.

NAVARRE, GENERAL HENRI. "Les Données de la défense de l'Indochine," *RDN,* March, 1956, pp. 271–79.

NEMO, COLONEL J. "Combat de mêlée et défense nationale," *RDN,* August–September, 1957, pp. 1289–1303.

————. "La Formation des cadres de défense nationale," *RDN,* March, 1958, pp. 471–86.

————. "La France et l'Afrique," *RDN,* December, 1959, pp. 1939–49.

————. "La Guerre dans la foule," *RDN,* June, 1956, pp. 721–34.

————. "La Guerre dans le milieu social," *RDN,* May, 1956, pp. 605–23.

————. "L'Organisation territoriale tactique de défense nationale," *RDN* July, 1958, pp. 1143–60.

————. "Réflexions sur la guerre limitée," *RDN,* March, 1959, pp. 447–57.

NEY, VIRGIL. "Guerrilla War and Modern Strategy," *Orbis*, II, No. 1 (Spring, 1958), pp. 66–82.

NOGUES, CHEF DE BATAILLON J., and GALZY, CHEF DE BATAILLON G. "A propos des enseignements de la guerre d'Indochine," *RDN*, April, 1956, pp. 427–35.

"Non, Simplet, tout n'est pas si simple" (by "un chef de corps en Algérie"), *RMI*, No. 311 (December, 1959), pp. 101–2.

"Les Nouveau collaborateurs," *Message*, No. 43 (June, 1960).

"Les Officiers," *La Nouvelle Critique*, No. 107 (June, 1959).

"Les Officiers itinérants," *Message*, No. 25 (November, 1957), pp. 1–7.

OGER, CAPTAIN DE CORVETTE JACQUES. "Les 'public relations' et la défense nationale," *RMI*, No. 172 (April 25, 1951), pp. 19–22.

ORTOLA, ADMIRAL. "Le Général de Gaulle: Soldat—écrivain—homme d'état," *RDN*, April, 1959, pp. 565–87.

PAPAGOS, FIELD MARSHAL ALEXANDER. "Guerrilla Warfare," *Foreign Affairs*, No. 30 (January, 1952), pp. 215–30.

PEROL, RAOUL. "De l'armée de métier à l'armée groupe économico-social," *RMI*, No. 298 (October, 1958), pp. 66–68.

PERRIN, J. "L'Algérie et l'information," *RDN*, December, 1958, pp. 1935–44.

———. "L'Impuissance à choisir," *RDN*, February, 1958, pp. 265–76.

PESQUIDOUX, RENAUD-JOSEPH DE. "Guerre révolutionnaire et lutte anti-religieuse," *RMI*, No. 301 (January, 1959), pp. 23–40.

PISANI, EDGARD. "L'Organisation de la défense nationale," *RDN*, February, 1956, pp. 158–68.

PLANCHAIS, JEAN. "L'Action psychologique hier et aujourd'hui," *LM*, April 3–4, 1959.

———. "L'Armée et la nation," *La Vie nouvelle*, No. 623 (March–April, 1962), pp. 3–5.

———. "L'Armée et la nation: Trois années de rencontre," *LM*, May 17, 1961.

———. "Crise de modernisme dans l'armée," *Revue française de sociologie*, II, No. 2 (April–June, 1961), 118–23.

———. "L'O.A.S. et la 'mise en condition,'" *LM*, December 16, 1961.

———. "Petite histoire de l'action psychologique," *Signes du temps*, No. 1 (January, 1959), pp. 10–14.

———. "Quelle est cette armée?", *La Nef*, No. 7 (July–September, 1961), pp. 57–63.

Pogue, Forrest C. "Political Problems of a Coalition Government," in Harry L. Coles (ed.), *Total War and Cold War*, Columbus, Ohio: Ohio State University Press, 1962, p. 108–28.

"Le Poignard dans le dos," *Message*, No. 44 (July–August, 1960).

Poirier, Commandant Lucien. "Thomas Edward Lawrence," *RMI*, No. 318 (July, 1960), pp. 26–44, and No. 320 (October, 1960), pp. 52–70.

————. "Un instrument de guerre révolutionnaire; Le F.L.N.," *RMI*, No. 289 (December, 1957), pp. 7–34, and No. 290 (January, 1958), pp. 69–92.

Pophillat, Captain F. "Pour une psychologie sociale dans l'armée," *RMI*, No. 293 (April, 1958), pp. 61–72.

Popie, Pierre. "Comment fut préparé la journée du 13 mai à Alger," *LM*, May 30, 1958.

"Pour comprendre l'armée," *Message*, No. 30 (July, 1958).

"Pour et contre Cornelius," *Verbe*, No. 101 (April, 1959), pp. 4–25.

"Pourquoi nous avons 'perdu' la guerre d'Algérie" (by "Lieutenant X."), *La Nef*, No. 7 (July–September, 1961), pp. 19–38.

"Pour un effort de vérité," *Message*, No. 32 (November, 1958).

"Pour une autocritique," *Message*, No. 6 (December, 1954), pp. 9–11.

"Pour une doctrine catholique de l'action politique et sociale: Enseignement de *La Cité Catholique*," *Verbe*, No. 99 (February, 1959), pp. 1–22.

"Pour une politique du logement dans l'armée," *Message*, No. 2 (February, 1954), pp. 7–8.

Prause, François-Marie. "L'Armée et la politique au Pakistan," *RDN*, July, 1960, pp. 1280–88.

La Presse, a special issue of *RMI*, No. 287 (September–October, 1957).

Prost, Commandant Jean. "Le Recrutement des officiers." Thesis, Ecole Supérieure de Guerre, Commission de Sociologie, 72ᵉ Promotion, 1962; mimeo.

"Un programme de 30,000 logements," *RMI*, No. 282 (April, 1957), pp. 35–52.

"Quelques réflexions sur les pouvoirs civils et militaires en Algérie," *Message*, No. 34 (February, 1959).

Rapoport, David C. "A Comparative Theory of Military and Political Types," in S. P. Huntington (ed.), *Changing Patterns of Military Politics*. New York: Free Press of Glencoe, 1962.

REBOUL, LIEUTENANT COLONEL. "Le Malaise de l'armée," *Revue des deux mondes*, March 15, 1925, pp. 378–97.

"Réflexions sur un cessez-le-feu," *Message*, No. 17 (November, 1956), p. 4.

"Réflexions sur la discipline," *Message*, No. 40 (January, 1960).

RÉMOND RENÉ. "Les Anciens combattants et la politique," *Revue française de science politique*, V, No. 2 (April–June, 1955), 267–90.

"Réponse aux partisans d'une Petite France" (by "X . . . "), *RDN*, June, 1956, pp. 671–85.

ROCOLLE, COLONEL. "Les Constantes de la guerre subversive," *RDN*, February, 1958, pp. 245–64.

ROCQUIGNY, COLONEL DE. "Le Terrorisme urbain," *RMI*, No. 291 (February, 1958), pp. 77–83.

ROUSSET, LIEUTENANT COLONEL J. "A propos de subversion et d'insurrection," *RDN*, March, 1960, pp. 498–506.

RUBY, EDMOND. "L'Armée en péril," *Ecrits de Paris*, September, 1961, pp. 67–72.

———. "La Crise de recrutement des cadres de l'armée, *Ecrits de Paris*, November, 1957, pp. 65–73.

RUFFRAY, PATRICK DE. "Le Procès du centurion," *RMI*, No. 305 (May, 1959), pp. 7–18.

"Salus Populi supreme Lex esto," *Message*, No. 44 (July–August, 1960).

SARRAILH, RECTEUR JEAN. "Education nationale et civisme," *RMI*, No. 304 (April, 1959), pp. 11–16.

SCHNEIDER, COLONEL F. "La Stratégie révolutionnaire de Mao Tse-Toung," *RDN*, October, 1960, pp. 1633–50.

SCHUMANN, MAURICE. "De la continuité du Gaullisme," *RDN*, February, 1960, pp. 201–16.

SCHWARTZ, LAURENT. "Le Problème de la torture dans la France d'aujourd'hui," *Cahiers de la république*, VI, No. 38 (November, 1961), 17–31.

SHILS, EDWARD A., and JANOWITZ, MORRIS. "Cohesion and Disintegration in the Wehrmacht in World War II," *Public Opinion Quarterly*, Summer, 1948, pp. 280–315.

"SIMPLET" (pseudonym). "Guerre révolutionnaire, guerre psychologique ou guerre 'tout court'?" *RMI*, No. 309 (October, 1959), pp. 97–102.

SOUSTELLE, JACQUES, "La Révolution algérienne dans le cadre du panarabisme," *RDN*, July, 1956, pp. 823–27.

SOUYRIS, CAPTAIN ANDRÉ. "L'Action psychologique dans les forces armées," *RMI*, No. 298 (October, 1958), pp. 34–45.

———. "Les Cadres de l'armée dans la société française," *Cahiers français*, No. 23 (November, 1957), pp. 2–8.

———. "Les Conditions de la parade et de la riposte à la guerre révolutionnaire," *RMI*, No. 281 (February–March, 1957), pp. 91–109.

———. "Le Mécanisme de la révolution tunisien (1934–1954)," *RDN*, October, 1956, pp. 1216–29.

———. "Un procédé de contre-guérilla: L'Auto-défense des populations," *RDN*, June, 1956, pp. 686–99.

———. "Réalités et aspects de la guerre psychologique," *RMI*, No. 302 (February, 1959), pp. 7–28.

———. "Le Révolution tunisienne," *RMI*, No. 281 (February-March, 1957), pp. 63–74.

STIL, A. "L'Idéologie de la dictature militaire en France," *Nouvelle revue internationale*, II, No. 11 (July, 1959), 116–27.

"Synthèse des réponses reçues à l'enquête de *Message* sur l'information dans l'armée," *Message*, No. 13 (April, 1956), p. 26.

THEIBAUT, FERNAND. "Par-delà les normes de la guerre conventionnelle . . . les leçons de l'histoire," *RDN*, February, 1960, pp. 296–317.

THÉOLLÈYRE, J.-M. "Un 'templier' des temps modernes," *LM*, January 15–16, 1961.

THIEULOY, J.-J. "L'Esprit 'para' décrit par un para," *L'Express*, July 10, 1958, pp. 14–15.

THILLAUD, CHEF DE BATAILLON. "Vaincre sans trahir," *RDN*, April, 1958, pp. 643–53.

TOURNOUX, J.-R. "A Proletarian Army," *The Reporter*, February 18, 1960, pp. 19–21.

"La troisième guerre mondiale n'aura pas lieu," *Message*, No. 11 (December, 1955), pp. 12–16.

VALLUY, GENERAL JEAN E. "Armée Française 1961," *Revue des deux mondes*, June 15, 1961, pp. 577–94.

———. "Armée Française 1961; De quelques prolongements," *Revue des deux mondes*, September 1, 1961, pp. 3–15.

———. "L'OTAN à l'ère atomique," *RDN*, July, 1959, pp. 1137–48.

———. "Se défendre? Contre qui? Pourquoi? Comment?", *RDN*, November, 1960, pp. 1739–50.

VIAL, LIEUTENANT COLONEL JEAN. "A propos de relations sociales," *RMI*, No. 309 (October, 1959), pp. 62–68.

————. "De la discipline," *RDN*, December, 1957, pp. 1890–1901.

————. "Introduction à la sociologie militaire," *RDN*, July, 1959, pp. 1225–35.

————. "Le Pédagogue et le soldat," *RMI*, No. 327 (May, 1961), pp. 23–30.

————. "Pour un humanisme militaire," *RMI*, No. 245 (January, 1955), pp. 19–24.

————. "Problèmes sociaux et impératifs militaires," *RDN*, August–September, 1960, pp. 1432–43.

VILLARS, FRANCE. "Un para m'a confié," *Le Bled*, No. 53 (April 13, 1957), pp. 6–7.

VILLIERS DE L'ISLE-ADAM, COLONEL G. DE. "Bourguibisme et matérialisme dialectique," *RMI*, No. 305 (May, 1959), pp. 51–59.

————. "Cette guerre de notre siècle," *RDN*, July, 1956, pp. 874–93.

WEYGAND, GENERAL MAXIME, "Des chefs?" *RDN*, December, 1956, pp. 1447–49.

————. "Réflexions sur l'état militaire de la France," *Revue des deux mondes*, October 15, 1952.

WEYGAND, JACQUES. "L'Officier des Affaires Indigènes," *RMI*, No. 269 (March 25, 1956), pp. 63–66.

WILLIAMS, PHILIP. "The French Army, or The Collapse of Soldierly Ideals," *Encounter*, XVIII, No. 6 (December, 1961), 30–37.

"XIMENÈS" (pseudonym). "Essai sur la guerre révolutionnaire," *RMI*, No. 281 (February–March, 1957), pp. 7–20.

————. "Guerre révolutionnaire en Algérie," *RMI*, No. 297 (August–September, 1958), pp. 27–40.

ZELLER, GENERAL ANDRÉ. "L'Armée de terre liée à la nation," *RDN*, June, 1959, pp. 957–66.

————. Armée et politique," *RDN*, April, 1957, pp. 499–517.

————. "Le Prix de la défense," *RDN*, August–September, 1957, pp. 1235–49.

ZINK, HAROLD. "American Civil-Military Relations in the Occupation of Germany," in HARRY L. COLES (ed.), *Total War and Cold War*. Columbus: Ohio State University Press, 1962, pp. 211–37.

Index

Index